Philip Brown

Harston, Cambridge

July 1992

THE WISDEN PAPERS

1888 – 1946

THE WISDEN PAPERS

1888 – 1946

EDITED BY BENNY GREEN

Stanley Paul

LONDON SYDNEY AUCKLAND
JOHANNESBURG

To E. W. Swanton

Stanley Paul & Co. Ltd

An imprint of Century Hutchinson Ltd
62-65 Chandos Place, London WC2N 4NW

Century Hutchinson Australia (Pty) Ltd
89-91 Albion Street, Surry Hills, NSW 2010

Century Hutchinson New Zealand Limited
PO Box 40-086, Glenfield, Auckland 10

Century Hutchinson South Africa (Pty) Ltd
PO Box 337, Bergvlei 2012, South Africa

First published 1989

Set in Times

Printed and bound in Great Britain by
Mackays of Chatham PLC, Chatham, Kent

British Library Cataloguing in Publication Data
Green, Benny, *1927*
The Wisden Papers 1895–1940
1. England. Cricket to 1977
I. Title
796.35'8'0942

ISBN 0 09 173825 3

CONTENTS

	Introduction *by Benny Green*	1

PART ONE

1888	Formation of a County Cricket Council *Anon.*	7
1889	A Few Jottings *by R. Thoms*	17
1890	The Reforms of 1889 *by C.F. Pardon*	19
1890	Some Questions of the Day *by C.F. Pardon*	24
1890	In Memoriam: Charles F. Pardon *by John Wisden and Co.*	33
1891	Cambridge Memories *by A.G. Steel*	33
1892	The Development of Cricket *by Hon. R.H. Lyttelton*	39
1893	Hints from the Press Box *by C.S. Caine*	45
1894	The 'Follow On' *edited by S.H. Pardon*	50
1895	Cricketers – Past and Present *by an Old Cambridge Captain*	57
1896	Personal Recollections of W.G. Grace *by Lord Harris and by A.G. Steel*	65
1897	Mr. W.G. Grace and the Surrey Club *by the Surrey County Cricket Club Committee*	73
1897	Some Current Topics *by S.H. Pardon*	74
1901	Fielding in 1900 *by D.L.A. Jephson*	77
1905	On the Preparation of Wickets *by A.C. MacLaren*	82
1908	South African Bowling *by R.E. Foster*	86

PART TWO

1915	Notes by the Editor *by S.H. Pardon*	95
1919	A Tribute to Gregor MacGregor *by D.L.A. Jephson*	99
1924	The Googly *by B.J.T. Bosanquet*	103
1925	Sydney Pardon *by C.S. Caine and others*	109

1926	Jack Hobbs *Anon.*	112
1927	Recollections of Mr. F.R. Spofforth *by Lord Harris, by the Earl of Darnley, and by Mr. C.I. Thornton*	114
1928	Oxford Memories *by Lord Harris*	119
1929	My Years at Cambridge *by G.H. Longman*	122
1930	Australian Tours and their Management *by Sir Frederick Toone*	127
1931	Lord's and the M.C.C. *by Sir Francis Lacey*	130
1932	Fifty Years of Yorkshire County *by Lord Hawke*	136
1933	The Umpire's Point of View *by F. Chester*	146
1934	The Bowling Controversy *by C.S. Caine*	150
1935	The Hobbs Era *by J. Hobbs*	161
1935	Australian Cricket *by the Hon. Mr. Justice H.V. Evatt*	168
1936	Trials of a County Secretary *by R.V. Ryder*	172
1936	Success of the L.B.W. Experiment *by W.H. Brookes*	177
1936	Miscellany *by W.H. Brookes*	181
1937	Recollections of Oxford Cricket *by H.D.G. Leveson-Gower*	183
1938	Spin Bowling *by A.P. Freeman*	190
1938	Reflections *by E. (Patsy) Hendren*	196
1938	A Case for More Natural Wickets *by G.O. Allen*	201
1938	Centenary of Trent Bridge *by A.W. Shelton*	206
1939	Cricket at the Cross Roads *by D.G. Bradman*	209
1939	My Happy Cricket Life *by F.E. Woolley*	213
1939	Cricket Conundrums *by A.E.R. Gilligan*	218

PART THREE

1940	Notes on the 1939 Season *by R.C. Robertson-Glasgow*	227
1940	Cricket in War-Time *by Major H.S. Altham*	239
1941	W.R. Hammond in First Class Cricket *by R.C. Robertson-Glasgow*	245
1941	County Championship Reviewed *by H. Preston*	251
1942	Notes *by R.C. Robertson-Glasgow*	259

1943	Notes on Season 1942 *by R.C. Robertson-Glasgow*	269
1944	The Best Fast Bowler *by Sir Stanley Jackson*	279
1945	Views and Values *by R.C. Robertson-Glasgow*	283
1945	Australian Survey *by Lieut. Col. A.G. Moyes*	286
1946	Edward Paynter *by R.C. Robertson-Glasgow*	290
1946	Cricket under the Japs *by Major E.W. Swanton, R A.*	294
1946	Hundred Years of Surrey Cricket *by H.D.G. Leveson-Gower*	298
1946	Notes by the Editor *by H. Preston*	307

ACKNOWLEDGEMENT

The publishers would like to thank Roger Mann for making his photographic collection available to them.

INTRODUCTION

The evolution of Wisden's Cricketers' Almanack from its chaotic beginnings to the magisterial publication of later years constitutes a remarkable pageant of ineptitude giving way first to competence and finally to eloquence. When John Wisden first conceived the idea of an annual publication registering the history of the game season by season, he had virtually no idea what he was about, even though a perfectly good model already existed in the pioneer work of his friend Lillywhite. The inaugural Wisden edition of 1864, had it been followed by no successive attempts to repair the damage, would be long-forgotten today, a fossilised exhibit on a library shelf, and a terrible warning to would be archivists and annalists. But the first fiasco, padded with comically extraneous material, was soon redeemed by commonsensical amendments, as it began to dawn on the editor-owner that it might be just as well if a cricket almanack confined itself to cricketing affairs. Evidently perceiving the extent of his gaffe, John Wisden bravely began to play himself in. Within two years all the incongruities of 1864 had been dropped, and the space allocated to full scores of the previous season's fixtures. In 1867 there first appeared 'Births and Deaths of Cricketers', and also the very earliest advertisements. In 1870 each score-card was prefaced by a brief account of the match, and two years later the convention was established of an introductory essay to the records of each county. The work went on after Wisden's death in 1884. Three years later readers were offered a comprehensive list of batting and bowling statistics for the previous season and a fixture list for the coming one.

But it was not until 1888 that it occurred to anyone that an almanack, in addition to being referred to, might also be read. In that edition there appeared the first piece of prose narrative, a discursive report of a discussion concerning 'The Formation of a Cricket Council'. The report ran to more than 3,000 words, and its effect was to bring readers of the Almanack into the very room where the debate had taken place. Reading matter, as distinct from statistical detail, was followed in 1889 by the first photographs and the inclusion of a Cricket Records section. In 1892 came the first comprehensive obituary notices, and from 1895 the practice was established of including amateurs and professionals together in the first-class averages. By 1899 these averages were being computed in the modern style, to two places of decimals. By 1900 the Almanack, which on its début had consisted of 112 pages, had grown to over 500.

The minds behind this impressive transition belonged to the brothers Pardon C.F, S.H. and E.S. who in 1880 had joined forces with one or two other journalistic enthusiasts to form the Cricket Reporting Agency, whose work instantly became an intrinsic part of the Almanack. It was only natural that when the 1886 edition collapsed in chaos and appeared in the shops a year late, the proprietors should turn to the Pardons in search of salvation. By 1887 Charles Pardon was installed as editor with his brothers in support, and it was this regime which published the first sizeable piece of reading matter in the 1888 edition. Pardon might well have become one of the great editors of the age had not premature death passed that distinction on to his younger brother Sydney, who assumed editorship in 1891 and remained in control until his death in 1925. Sydney was born for the job and the job was made for Sydney. His first edition encompassed the known cricketing world in 420 pages, his penultimate one in 1,010. He inherited a 'Births and Deaths' section incorporating 753 names; by the time his own death was incorporated into that list it had grown to over 6,000 items. Many of the essays in this volume were commissioned by him, and there is no question that he remains the most gifted and influential editor in cricket history.

Neville Cardus describes Pardon as: 'a typical English gentlemen, late Victorian and ripe Edwardian, aristocratic of countenance, with a curving moustache, heavily lidded eyes, delicate fingers and a voice which he seldom, if ever, raised'. The photographic portrait in the centenary edition of 1963 tells a rather different story, of a far less imposing and romantic man, plebeian rather than aristocratic, a friendly sort of chap with a stubborn mouth, a gaze tinctured with the hint of whimsy, and a skull bisected with geometric exactitude by the fashionable centre-parting of the period. Sydney was an examplar of the type who poses the rhetorical question: 'What do they know of cricket who only cricket know?'. In the context of the sport reporting of the period, Sydney was a man of considerable urbanity, whose outside interests not only embraced other sports like billiards, racing, athletics, rowing and boxing, but also extended into the fine arts, where his judgement in matters operatic and dramatic was considered subtle enough to be published in 'The Times'. He witnessed his first first-class match in 1863, the year of John Wisden's retirement, and wrote his first match report nine years later. Cardus remembers that 'he watched the game from the Lord's Press Box through small ivory-ornamented opera glasses through which, the evening of the same day, he would look at Jean de Reszke or Destinn at Covent Garden'.

A connoisseur with a conservative view of technique and breeding, Pardon was one of those sticklers for good form who would have preferred defeat to any avoidance of it through heretical methods. One day at Lord's he left the Press box to go to the Pavilion to learn who had won the Derby. According to the poetic truth of Cardus, 'After inspecting the tape he bit his fingernails. "Dear me", he murmured, "won by an outsider, a non-thoroughbred. I'm deeply thankful I didn't accidentally back it" '. This same tendency to trust in tradition was reflected in his editorial postures. Any alteration to the laws of the game met with deep suspicion from Sydney. When in 1907 there was a campaign for shorter boundaries, he wrote: 'Nothing could be worse for the game. To my mind it is essential that boundaries should be as deep as possible so that hits may be worth the runs given for them. Short boundaries, by decreasing the opportunities for good fielding, rob cricket of half its charm'. He also opposed the covering of the whole wicket, the introduction of the Triangular Tournament, the reduction of first-class matches to two days' duration, and, most revealingly in the context of a later age, the importing of overseas players by the counties:

> Clubs with money to spend should encourage native talent and not buy cricketers of established reputation. Partly for the reason that it would open the door to financial dealings I was glad that the registration scheme, drawn up at the request of the counties by Lord Harris, was rejected by the Advisory Committee . . . Even at the risk of being described, as I have been before now, as a hide-bound Tory, I must affirm my belief that the two-years residential qualification is a great safeguard in preserving the true spirit of county cricket.

He was outspoken against the method of England team selection in 1909; against the sluggishness and inefficiency of the England side at Lord's in 1921; and above all against any suspicion of an illegal action by a bowler. His remarks concerning the detection of throwing are still worth remembering: 'I wonder what my old friend Bob Thoms would say if anyone told him he could not tell a throw from a fairly-bowled ball. A throw may be difficult to define in words, but to the eye of a practical and unbiased cricketer it is, I think, very obvious'.

After Pardon's death the editorship of Wisden passed on to his old associate, C. Stewart Caine, who left undisturbed Pardon's general policy. Caine died in 1933, and there followed, for the first time in half a century, some rapid changes in editorship which only underlined the good fortune enjoyed by the proprietors in the long Pardon years. In 1934 the well-known club cricketer S. J. Southerton took over, but after only two editions he died, to be followed by W. H. Brookes who began a large-scale reorganisation of the Almanack before resigning in 1939. The 1940 edition was edited, in the days of the Phoney War, by the Almanack's publisher, Haddon Whitaker. Some of these editors were more partial than others to the attractions of the occasional prose item, but although the frequency of the Wisden essay fluctuated over the years, it was always regarded as an acceptable and often indispensable part of the Almanack once the Pardons had shown the way. Very often these essays were contributed either by men not generally known as writers, or by men not generally known as cricket fanciers; very often what these men wrote was both entertaining and revealing. For both these reasons, it is a highly pleasurable as well as a highly educational experience bringing them back into the light of day, endowing them with a life independent of the Almanack for the first time in history.

BENNY GREEN

PART ONE

1888 – 1914

FORMATION OF A COUNTY CRICKET COUNCIL [1888]

The first meeting at Lord's

The first indication that the compilers of the Almanack were beginning to consider the proposition that readers might welcome the occasional relief from mere statistics came with the edition for 1888. There, among the advertisements for Ransome's Horse-Power Lawn Mowers, Carter's Grass Seeds for Cricket Grounds, and the ubiquitous Dr. J. Collis-Browne's Chlorodyne, claiming as usual to cure cholera, dysentry, hysteria, cancer and toothache, appeared an item comprising more than 3,000 words of reading matter under the banner: 'The Formation of a County Cricket Council'. The report of the debate on this theme which followed can hardly be defined as a literary creation, rather more a sort of Hansard parliamentary account of opinions inside the world of cricket. The result was a half-way house between reportage and the formal essay, but quite apart from the novelty of its inclusion, and the frisson *which readers must have felt on being invited to eavesdrop on the ramblings of some of the most prestigious figures in the game, the appearance of 'Formation of a County Cricket Council' was a broad hint that amendments to the editorial policy of the Almanack were in the wind, amendments which seemed likely to add considerably to the appeal of the publication.*

ON TUESDAY morning, July 12th, 1887, a meeting of county delegates was held at the Lord's Cricket Ground to receive the report of the sub-committee appointed at the county secretaries' meeting in the previous December to consider the advisability of forming a County Cricket Council. In their report, while suggesting the advisability of forming such a Council, the sub-committee recommended that the Council should have no power to deal with the laws of cricket or the rules of county qualification, but that the M.C.C. should remain as heretofore the arbiter in such matters. Thirteen counties were represented at the meeting, viz.:—Nottingham, Mr. W. H. C. Oates and Captain Holden; Yorkshire, Mr. M. J. Ellison and Mr. J. B. Wostinholm; Lancashire, Mr. S. H. Swire and Mr. J. M'Laren; Surrey, Mr. C. W. Alcock; Middlesex, Mr. A. J. Webbe; Sussex, Mr. Montagu Turner; Kent, Mr. George Marsham and Lord Harris; Cheshire, Mr. J. Horner; Hampshire, Mr. R. Bencraft; Warwickshire, Mr. W. Ansell; Leicestershire, Mr. T. Burdett; Northamptonshire, Mr. T. H. Vials; and Somersetshire, Mr. H. Murray-Anderdon.

Of the more important counties it will be noticed that Gloucestershire and Derbyshire were absentees, but Mr. W. G. Grace, who usually represents the Western shire, was engaged in the match, Gentlemen v. Players, which was proceeding while the meeting was sitting.

Lord HARRIS, having been voted to the chair, remarked that what the meeting had to do was to decide whether a County Cricket Council should be formed, and in order to raise that question he moved that the report of the sub-committee be received.

Captain HOLDEN seconded the motion, which, after a brief discussion, was carried unanimously.

Mr. ELLISON then moved, and Mr. ALCOCK seconded, the following motion: 'That a County Cricket Council be formed.'

Captain HOLDEN asked whether it would not be well to first of all know what the duties of this Council would be. If it was going to interfere with the powers of the Marylebone Club, then he should object to it.

Mr. ELLISON pointed out that the report distinctly recommended that the Council should not interfere with the Marylebone Club.

The CHAIRMAN also observed that the report clearly laid down that the duties of the Council should not extend to any interference with the laws of cricket. But what the Council could do would be to discuss suggested alterations in the law, and to make such recommendations as were deemed advisable to the M.C.C.

Mr. ANSELL said that his impression as regards the laws of the game was that the M.C.C. were the best judges, and in cases of dispute on the subject of county qualification the M.C.C. would be the best arbiters.

Captain HOLDEN observed that the laws of county cricket were made by the counties, and the M.C.C. adopted the rules of county qualification laid down by them.

Mr. ALCOCK said it seemed to him that as the counties made the rules of county qualification it was quite competent for them to suggest alterations.

The CHAIRMAN: Leaving it to the Marylebone Club to be the arbiter.

Mr. ALCOCK: Distinctly.

Captain HOLDEN said it would be within the recollection of those present that this question was discussed at the general meeting, when the Chairman (Lord Harris) proposed some alteration, which was negatived by a large majority.

The CHAIRMAN said there was no question of alteration, but whether the Council should have the power to make any alteration. He suggested that the simplest course would be to put Mr. Ellison's motion, and if it were adopted it would then be open for the meeting to limit its own powers. It was important that the meeting should proceed formally and gradually, and that the powers of the Council should be clearly defined.

Captain HOLDEN was opposed to the idea of forming a Council in which the smaller counties would be on an equality with those that supplied half the players of England. If such a Council were formed, the county qualification would soon be done away with, and they might have a case, as he once remembered, of a gentleman playing for three counties in one year.

Mr. WEBBE thought it ought to be left to the first-class counties to frame the county qualification.

Mr. BURDETT said Leicestershire did not consider itself below some of the first-class counties.

Mr. WEBBE suggested that the matter might be left to the counties who originally framed the rules.

Mr. ANSELL was opposed to such a suggestion, as circumstances had altered. When the rules were framed the first-class counties were the only counties; but things had changed, and it would be absurd to shut out the more recently formed county clubs.

The CHAIRMAN said he would now take the liberty of making an appeal to them on behalf of the game, whether it was worth while for them to extend a difference of opinion which undoubtedly had arisen between what were called first-class and second-class counties. Was it worth while to extend that difference at a moment when it was possible to establish what he believed would be a most valuable Council—one which would have the power of improving cricket in several ways, and putting it within the power of second-class counties—if they would allow him to use the misnomer—of getting up into the first rank? At present there was a great difficulty in the way of their so doing, but he thought that difficulty might be settled by the Council. Mr. Ellison had moved that this Council should be formed, and if they went into the question of first and second-class counties there would be such a difference of opinion that it would very likely be impossible to carry the motion. He should regret that, for the sub-committee took a great deal of trouble over the question, and were unanimous that the Council should be formed; and they further pointed out that, once formed, then would be the time to raise the question of county status. He thought the raising of the question of what were first and what were second-class counties before they came to the motion upon the formation of the Council might result in those old feelings being revived, and that the first-class counties would vote that the rules of county qualification should only be altered by them, while the second-class counties would vote the other way, and there would be a great danger of the whole scheme falling to the ground. He appealed to them first to carry Mr. Ellison's motion and then leave it to the Council to deal with the vexed question of county qualification. If they carried Mr. Ellison's motion they would have no reason to regret it.

Mr. ALCOCK pointed out that two years ago he proposed there should be no difference in the status of the counties. That motion was carried, and it seemed rather strange to introduce the question again.

Captain HOLDEN said that if a Cricket Council were formed for all the counties, he felt perfectly certain there would be an attempt to alter the county qualification, and that he strongly objected to. That qualification had been settled and carried on for years, and he was opposed to a council interfering with it.

Mr. BURDETT observed that, so far as Leicestershire was concerned, Captain Holden was quite in error. That county was in favour of the term for residential qualification being extended from two years to three.

Mr. ANSELL objected to the conclusion that those counties who in 1870 were so fortunate as to possess a county club, should be deemed to constitute the cricket wisdom of England for the rest of time. County clubs were springing up all over the country, and it would be absurd to shut them out now.

Mr. Ellison's motion was then put and carried *nem. con.*, all the counties voting except Middlesex.

The CHAIRMAN then moved, and Mr. ANSELL seconded, the following resolution:—'That as regards the laws of cricket, the Council shall have no executive powers.'

The motion was carried unanimously.

Captain HOLDEN then raised the question as to whether the Council should have power to deal with the subject of county qualification, and a long discussion took place upon the point.

The CHAIRMAN observed that it was an open question whether at some future time the counties which considered themselves the chief counties might not alter the rules if they pleased. He would beg to point out that the question was never raised when he made his motion last autumn at the meeting of county secretaries, proposing an alteration of the county qualification. The question as to whether that secretaries' meeting had the power to alter the rules never arose, it being seemingly assumed that it could do so, and had there been sufficient in agreement with him (Lord Harris) his motion would have come into force immediately. That being so, he was inclined to think that, the Council having been formed, it would have the power to make alterations.

Mr. ALCOCK suggested that the Council should have control over all matters connected with county cricket, but more over the laws of the game itself. He thought it was absurd that the counties should have no power over their own affairs.

Mr. WEBBE asked whether the Council would decide the vexed question of the qualification.

The CHAIRMAN thought it would be in the power of the Council. The counties should lay down what the rules were, leaving the M.C.C. to be arbiters.

Mr. OATES objected to any alteration as regarded the M.C.C. being arbiters, and moved, 'That upon all questions raised under the rules of County Cricket Qualification the Committee of the M.C.C. shall adjudicate.'

Mr. Swire seconded the motion, which, after some little discussion, was carried unanimously.

Mr. Alcock proposed, 'That it shall be competent for the Council to alter or amend the rules of County Cricket Qualification.'

Mr. Horner seconded the motion, which was also carried *nem. con.*, Notts being the only county which did not vote.

The Chairman said the next business of the meeting would be to consider the composition of the Council. He was anxious to afford equal justice to the so-called second-class counties, but they must be careful themselves that no county should be admitted that could not be looked upon as playing real county matches. His own impression as to the definition of what constituted a cricketing county was that it should have an established club and should play matches extending over three days. It might be very difficult to come to a decision upon this point, as he understood that in some cases of second-class counties playing first-class counties the latter had refused to play three-day matches. He submitted it would be possible to lay down the definition, and he first suggested that no county should be qualified to send a representative to the Council that did not possess a county cricket club.

Some little discussion took place on the subject, and eventually, on the proposition of Mr. Marsham, seconded by Mr. Ellison, the following motion was unanimously agreed to:—'That the Council consist of one representative each from those counties assembled at the meeting held at Lord's in December, 1886.' It may be mentioned that the counties represented at that meeting were:—Notts, Yorkshire, Surrey, Kent, Lancashire, Sussex, Gloucestershire, Middlesex, Derbyshire, Essex, Warwickshire, Norfolk, Leicestershire, Staffordshire, Somersetshire, Northamptonshire, Hampshire, Durham, Hertfordshire, and Cheshire.

Some little difficulty was then experienced in selecting a sub-committee to frame by-laws, and to decide upon subscriptions, time and place of meeting, and other details, but the meeting at length agreed to the following motion, proposed by Mr. Oates, and seconded by Mr. Vials:—'That a committee of five representatives from the counties of Middlesex, Kent, Surrey, Sussex, and Gloucestershire be appointed to frame by-laws, and to report to the Council before the end of the year.' This motion, it may be stated, practically amounted to the reappointment of the sub-committee, whose report had formed the subject of the day's discussion.

A vote of thanks was then proposed to Lord Harris for presiding, and the proceedings came to a close.

The second meeting at Lord's

On Monday, Dec. 5th, the County Cricket Council, which was formed in the previous July, held its first meeting in the Pavilion at Lord's Ground, and the following is a list of the delegates of the eighteen counties represented who attended:—

Surrey, Messrs. C. W. Alcock and J. Shuter; Lancashire, Messrs. S. H. Swire and A. Appleby; Middlesex, Messrs. P. M. Thornton and A. J. Webbe; Yorkshire, Messrs. M. J. Ellison and J. B. Wostinholm; Notts, Messrs. W. H. C. Oates and E. Browne; Kent, Lord Harris and Mr. George Marsham; Gloucestershire, Mr. W. G. Grace; Sussex, Messrs. C. H. Smith and M. Turner; Derbyshire, Hon. W. M. Jervis; Essex, Messrs. M. P. Betts and H. Fowler; Leicestershire, Messrs. J. Bonner and T. Burdett; Staffordshire, Mr. A. H. Heath; Cheshire, Mr. J. Horner; Warwickshire, Mr. W. Ansell; Somersetshire, Mr. H. Murray-Anderdon; Hampshire, Dr. Russell Bencraft; Herts, Mr. C. Pigg; and Durham, Mr. R. H. Mallett. Of the counties that are affiliated to the council only Norfolk and Northampton were not represented. Mr. H. Perkins, secretary of the Marylebone Club, was also present, at the request of Lord Harris, on behalf of that body.

Lord Harris having been voted to the chair, the meeting at once proceeded to discuss the bye-laws which had been drafted by the sub-committee. These, with a few trifling alterations, were adopted after little or no discussion, and below we give them in a complete form:—

1. This association shall be styled the County Cricket Council, and shall consist of one delegate from each affiliated county cricket club.

2. The original county cricket clubs affiliated are as follow:—Notts, Yorkshire, Surrey, Kent, Lancashire, Sussex, Gloucestershire, Middlesex, Derbyshire, Essex, Warwickshire, Norfolk, Leicestershire, Staffordshire, Somersetshire, Northamptonshire, Hampshire, Durham, Hertfordshire, and Cheshire. Any county cricket club other than the above-mentioned desirous of affiliation subsequent to December 5, 1887, must be elected at the annual meeting, held in December, and must be duly proposed and seconded, after notice given in accordance with Rule 10.

3. The officers of the council shall be a chairman, a treasurer, and secretary.

4. The chairman shall be elected at the meeting in December, and shall hold his office for one year, or until his successor is appointed, and shall be eligible for re-election.

5. The treasurer and secretary shall be appointed for such time, and the secretary at such salary as the council see fit to determine, and shall be removable by the council at any time.

6. Meetings of the council shall be held twice in every year at least.

7. The annual meeting, at which the election of officers and the affiliation of county cricket clubs shall take place, shall be held on the day preceding the meeting of the county secretaries in London.

8. Special meetings of the council shall be summoned by the secretary, on the written request of the chairman or of not less than five members of the council, but not less than fourteen days' notice shall be given to the delegates or secretaries of such special meeting, and no business shall be

transacted at any such meeting except that for which the council has been specially summoned.

9. The Secretary shall send to all the secretaries of affiliated county clubs a notice, with agenda paper, of the date of the council meetings, not less than twenty-eight days before such meetings.

10. Not less than thirty days' notice shall be given of all motions, and such notice shall be sent to the secretary of the council in writing and signed by the mover.

11. The order of business at each meeting shall be:

(1) Minutes to be read.
(2) Reports of any sub-committees to be considered.
(3) Letters.
(4) Motions.

And at each annual meeting the following in addition:

(5) Election of officers.
(6) Election of counties.

12. No decision shall be come to on any subject not on the agenda paper, but other matters may be discussed by permission of the chair.

13. In the absence of the chairman, a chairman for the meeting shall be appointed by those present.

14. At all meetings of the council five shall form a quorum, and the chairman of meeting shall have a casting vote in addition to his own, in the event of the voting being equal.

15. Each affiliated county club shall contribute annually out of its funds such a sum as the council may from time to time fix.

16. The treasurer shall have charge of the funds of the council, and shall keep its accounts in proper books to be provided for the purpose; and at the annual meetings in December he shall present an audited account up to October 1 of all pecuniary transactions during the year past.

17. All orders for the payment of money shall be signed by the chairman or his deputy, and countersigned by the secretary.

18. There shall be two auditors, who shall be appointed at the annual meeting in December, and they shall hold office for one year only, but shall be eligible for re-appointment.

Mr. P. M. THORNTON proposed, and Mr. J. BONNER seconded, 'That the subscription to this Association be £1, payable on the 1st of May'; and the motion was adopted.

Mr. M. J. ELLISON moved, and Mr. W. H. C. OATES seconded, that Lord Harris be appointed chairman of the council; and the motion was carried unanimously.

Lord HARRIS, in acknowledging the compliment, remarked that there was every opportunity for the council to do good work, and he thought that, taking all things into consideration, it had come into existence at an opportune time. At the present moment there were questions current amongst cricketers with regard to the working of the rules of cricket, which would lead one to suppose there was room for improvement. If, by wise counsel, they could induce cricketers in the county to place confidence in them, without endeavouring to push their way in front of the authority of the Marylebone Club, they should be able to do a considerable amount of good for the cricket world.

A little discussion ensued as to the appointment of secretary and treasurer, and eventually Mr. A. J. Webbe consented to undertake the duties of both offices in an honorary capacity.

The formal business having been disposed of, Lord HARRIS rose to call attention to a subject of which he had given notice, viz., the abnormally long scoring of last season. He remarked that as the council was in a rather embryo state he should not conclude with a motion, his intention being merely to raise a discussion, so that the delegates would be prepared to consider at a subsequent meeting a definite proposal to recommend to the Marylebone Club any alteration in the laws of cricket. In view of the long scores of the past season, he thought they might consider whether the time had not arrived when the bowler, in the interest of cricket, should be placed on more equal terms with the batsman. He was unable to place before the meeting any statistics of the heavy scoring, but he should be surprised if anyone would not acknowledge that in several cases last season the scores were very abnormal. Certainly, in his own recollection of cricket he could not call to mind any season in which there were so many long scores, both by individuals and by sides. And there was a very strong feeling that these scores had been very much the effect of a style of play that had become noticeable within the last three or four years; and from the letters he had received he had no hesitation in saying that gentlemen of the older cricket world were decidedly of opinion that some alteration was required in the law of leg before wicket. Perhaps cricketers as a body were inclined to undervalue the opinion of men of an old time—and he would not exempt himself from the category—but at the same time there was always some value to be placed upon their opinion. Last year he was doubtful himself whether the bowler would not be given a better chance against the batsman if some alteration was made in the height or width of the wicket. But he now felt it would scarcely be possible to arrive at any really valuable decision on that point without practical experience, and it would be difficult to arrange and carry out a series of matches with wickets of different heights and widths. He had therefore abandoned any idea of changing the size of the wicket, and was inclined to think that an alteration of the leg-before-wicket rule would be valuable and of importance. The first question was: 'Is it necessary to give the bowler a better chance or not?' and he thought that the scores of last year were a justification for thinking it was necessary. He thought the style of play which had become—he would not say notorious, but—noticeable during the last two or three years, was one that had given the bowler as few chances as possible, and had allowed the batsman far more chance than he was ever intended to have against the bowler. On the question of altering the law, he had received a valuable suggestion from Mr. R. A. H. Mitchell, who had written stating he was of opinion that a man should be out whose leg was between wicket and wicket and was hit by a ball that would take the wicket. Another old cricketer, Mr. V. E. Walker, had also written expressing himself in favour of an extension of the law, so that a man who wilfully put his leg in front of the wicket and was hit by a ball, which in the umpire's opinion would take the wicket, should be out; while Lord Bessborough was also in favour of an alteration in the law. There were other questions which they might consider, including the hours for commencing a three days' match, and he suggested that a special meeting should be held, when the delegates, being instructed by their various committees, could make a definite recommendation to the Marylebone Club.

Mr. M. J. Ellison submitted for consideration the following resolution, which had been adopted by the Yorkshire County Club: —'That the striker is out if with any part of his person he stop a ball which, in the opinion of the umpire at the bowler's end, would have hit the wicket, such part of the striker's person when hit being in a straight line between wicket and wicket.'

Mr. A. J. Webbe thought such a rule would give too much latitude to the umpire, and would be too favourable to leg-twisters like Cooper or Nepean. He thought the rule should be altered so as to prevent batsmen wilfully crossing the wicket to stop balls on the off side with their legs.

Lord Harris read a portion of Lord Bessborough's letter, in which the writer suggested a return to the old law of fifty years ago. This course, Lord Bessborough thought, would have the result of lessening the leg-before-wicket nuisance, and would teach men to play more with the bat and less with the legs.

Mr. P. M. Thornton read an extract from a letter from H. H. Stephenson, who stated that it was quite painful to see the way in which men used their pads and not the bat to play the ball. Stephenson thought the law was a difficult thing to meddle with, and more power than at present should not be placed in the umpires. To give them more power would answer very well in first-class matches, but would fail in second-class.

Mr. J. B. Wostinholm said the Yorkshire Committee felt strongly on the subject. The attendances of the public were becoming smaller year by year, and if the practice which was now in vogue continued, the interest in cricket, so far as the North of England was concerned, would materially diminish. It was important to alter the rule as soon as possible.

A good deal of general discussion followed, and eventually Mr. Ellison gave notice that, 'At a special meeting of the council, to be held in February, he would move a resolution "to call the attention of the Marylebone Club to the unsatisfactory effect of Law 24, and to recommend that it should be so altered as to secure that a batsman shall be out if with any part of his person, being in a straight line between wicket and wicket, he stop the ball, which in the opinion of the umpire would have hit the wicket." '

The necessary requisition for a special meeting was then made in the following manner:—

'We, the undersigned, request the chairman should summon a special meeting of the council in February.

(Signed) 'M. J. ELLISON, Yorkshire.
'W. M. JERVIS, Derbyshire.
'W. H. C. OATES, Nottinghamshire.
'JOHN SHUTER, Surrey.
'A. J. WEBBE, Middlesex.'

Mr. A. H. HEATH thought something might be done in the interest of cricket by enclosing the grounds with a board two feet high, and causing boundary hits to be run out. A cricket match now was a rather tame thing to watch, as in every three hours the ball was dead at least twenty-five minutes. If they could make the game more interesting to the spectators they would be doing a service.

Lord HARRIS thought Mr. Heath's suggestion worthy of consideration, and hoped the delegates would bring it before their county committees.

Mr. ELLISON drew attention to the question of drawing stumps on the concluding day of a match, and suggested that it should be left to the discretion of umpires to prolong play so that a game might be finished, provided not more than twenty runs were required, or not more than two wickets to fall.

Lord HARRIS observed that this suggestion was open to two objections, first of placing more responsibility on the umpires, and secondly whether umpires were men on whom more responsibility should be placed. He thought Yorkshire was beginning at the wrong end—and it was better to commence early in the morning.

Mr. ELLISON said the Yorkshire Committee were quite willing to begin early.

Mr. W. G. GRACE agreed with Lord Harris. He thought every county match should begin on the first day at twelve o'clock, and on the second and third days at eleven, though he was afraid Gloucestershire were very slack in that matter at home.

Mr. H. PERKINS said the practice of beginning early had been adopted with such success at Lord's that a drawn game was rare. He found from reading the newspapers that matches did not begin until after the announced time, and the time wasted was generally more than sufficient to have allowed the match to be finished. He did not think the plan of giving the umpires discretionary power would answer, and it might lead to disturbances.

The meeting shortly afterwards terminated with a vote of thanks to Lord Harris for presiding.

A FEW JOTTINGS [1889]

BY ROBERT THOMS

In the following year of 1889, the Pardon brothers took a further step along the road to reading matter by inviting a prominent figure in the English cricket world to offer his reflections on a lifetime in the game. In selecting Robert Thoms as the first authentic Wisden essayist the Pardons were choosing shrewdly, for there could have been few men, Dr. Grace included, whose experience was more extensive. Thoms (1825–1903) was born virtually in the shadow of Thomas Lord's ground, at Lisson Grove; the connection was cemented by the close friendship between his father, a baker, and James Henry Dark, the proprietor of Lord's ground. From the age of 15 Thoms was a cricketer to the exclusion of all else. His Lord's début came in 1844, and by 1850 he had received an invitation from William Clarke to join the All-England eleven. By the end of the 1860s he was umpiring, and continued to do so until his retirement in 1900.

Thoms' recollection of great players stretched back to the days of his youth, when he had batted against the proprietor of the Almanack and reached the conclusion that John Wisden was one of the finest bowlers of his era. In those distant days, young Thoms was a talented athlete reputed to have run the hundred yards in 10.5 seconds. This feat sounds comically incongruous in the staid and stolid context of the man as posterity is inclined to see him, as the magisterial figure of the photographic portraits of later years, billycocked and waistcoated, clearly a man to be reckoned with from his piercing gaze to his sensible black boots. Just as Turgenev might say of his hero that he was 'a man of the 1840s' and tell us all we need to know, so Wisden placed Thoms 'in dress, manner and appearance a man of the 1860s' and tells us just as much. Admiration for his umpiring was universal, ranging from W. G.'s 'one of the very best umpires the world has seen', to the sesquipedalian Albert Knight's: 'The impression left upon you by the man was so beautiful, you felt the game was something of a passion to him, an affaire du coeur*'. What Thoms would have made of Knight's effusions remains unknown, but Knight would certainly have placed Thoms' literary style firmly in the school of the Crimson Rambler; in recalling an innings by his hero, W. G. Grace, Thoms said: 'The Champion, upsetting all the arrangements of the Northern bowlers, spanked the leather about most unmercifully to all points of the weathercock and won the match off the reel for the Southerners'. It is curious as well as revealing that Thoms, a stickler for the rule of law, and an implacable enemy of illegal bowling actions, was never happy calling those bowlers suspected of throwing. He felt it was a problem for the Amateurs to deal with in their own way; his contribution was both quaint and risible. Instead of hounding a suspected thrower out of the first-class game, Thoms would* *procure for him what the editors of the Almanack described as 'alternative employment'.*

THIS time last year, when I seized the pen, by request, to do something for my old friend 'Wisden's,' the air was full of the sound of cricket revolution because a few of the leading batsmen had gone out of their way and transgressed by palpably using their legs—instead of their bats—to play the ball with. And here let me again remark, as I oft have done, that it was only the great batsmen, and they can do without it, that knew how to put on the scientific legging according to the pitch of the ball, and even they at times legged themselves out by misjudgment. Anyhow, I think cricketers will admit that this temporary blemish has almost died out without any law being called forth to run the perpetrators in, and in the few instances in which it has occurred wherein batsmen forgot themselves, their very looks seemed to say, I wish I had not done it. Therefore, I fancy, and hope, that the unsightly legging, like the dodo and the tinder box, may be booked as extinct, and gone from our gaze. The past season has undoubtedly been a bowler's one, for the grounds on many occasions were so treacherous through rain that most of the leading bowlers could do a nice little bit of conjuring with the batsmen. Cricket, like other events of life, alters according to its surroundings, and the goodness of the wickets during the last twenty years has brought forth not only more forcing batting, but also deep out-fielding, with bowling that partakes more of the art of trying to get the batsman caught than, as of yore, going for the sticks. Times were—even at Lord's, as many can well recollect—when Mynn, Wisden, Jackson, Willsher, Tarrant, Fellowes, and others, did indeed want nerve and pluck to look at, much more play, for with balls bounding frequently from the pitch over the batsman's head into the long-stop's hands, it can well be imagined what a punishing game it then was; the more so when 'tis still further brought to mind that in those days batsmen were not treated with much of the Southerton, or cock-a-doodle, style of slow bowling, but had to put up with the 'I'll warm you' fast bowlers. But this dissertation leads me on to recount that it is improvement in the grounds that has to a great extent made the fast bowler more harmless; and batsmen in due course came along, of whom the marvellous little Doctor (E. M. Grace) was the pioneer, who upset all the stereotyped fast-footed play by going to the ball, when the pitch suited, and cracking it all over the shop. Not that I for a moment put less value on the fast bowler in these days of good wickets, for I well know he is still the most effective; but length and pace, without spin, break-back, or rearing-up qualities, don't count for much on modern wickets. Length is certainly one of the most essential points for a bowler, but 'tis not rigid length that has now placed a Southern player in the foremost rank as the best bowler in England. The great secret of his success is variation of pace, with the tricky flights and the spin he puts on to the ball—*à la* Spofforth. Our Australian friends certainly woke us up with their displays of bowling and fielding; and from what we have seen in the way of samples since

1878—Spofforth, Allan, Palmer, Tommy Garratt, one of the best perpetual peggers at the 'off-stump;' Harry Boyle, the reliable; George Giffen, the all-rounder; Evans, a sparkler, whom I should like to have seen in his best day; Trott, the skimmer; Ferris, the every-day trundler; and Turner, the rearer-up and destructive—taking the lot altogether, I think we can fairly designate Australia a land of bowlers. But withal, memory will bring back the doughty deeds of Jackson, Tarrant, Freeman, Tom Emmett, Jem Shaw, Allan Hill, Jem Grundy, George Wootton, Atkinson, Howitt, Willsher, Stephenson, Hinkley, Wisden, and many more, as specimens of first-class pace bowlers, and if I had to decide, with a casting vote, which of these professionals I had looked upon as the very best, I should plump for—but there, hold hard, 'Over;' and thus I finish with best wishes to all cricketers and with the hope that succeeding issues of 'Wisden's Almanack' will in the future happily record from time to time, the doings of yet unborn champions of England and Australia—after the style of a Grace and a Murdoch.

THE REFORMS OF 1889 [1890]

BY C. F. PARDON

In preparing the 1890 edition, Charles Pardon concerned himself among other things with two extremely important amendments to the rules of the game, the legalisation of the five-ball over, and the limiting of declarations by the batting side to the third day in a three-day match. Pardon addressed himself also to the editorial overview, contributing an essay on various issues of the day. It ran to 3,000 words, and was the last gesture that Charles Pardon was to make. Before the next year's issue was ready, he was dead and his position taken by his younger brother Sydney.

At their meeting last May the Marylebone Club adopted some changes in the laws of cricket, and the game was everywhere played last summer under the new conditions. The Authorised Laws as they now stand, and a report of the meeting at which the reforms were carried, will be found elsewhere in this Almanack. What was done was, briefly, to make the Over consist of five balls instead of four, to permit a bowler to change ends as often as he pleased, and to empower the captain of the batting side to declare the innings at an end whenever he chose to do so. There were, of course, some qualifications. Thus, although a bowler is now allowed to change ends as often as he likes—which practically means as often as the captain of his side likes—he may not bowl two overs in succession. Again, although what has been generally called the closure can be applied at any time in a one-day match, it can only be put into force on the last day of a match arranged for more than one day. Naturally these changes caused a good deal of discussion. The closure was only, I think applied about half-a-dozen times in important matches, but the other alterations affected every match except the comparatively few games where the bowlers put out the opposing sides in the fashion that Turner and Ferris accustomed us to in the May of 1888. Amateurs and professionals alike expressed their views pretty freely on the alterations that had been carried out, and, except on the part of those good, worthy people who never can see good in any change, the opinions were for the most part strongly favourable. Still there was evidently a good deal of opposition, and I thought it might interest the readers of WISDEN'S ALMANACK if I could obtain from captains of great elevens and from famous cricketers generally their ideas on how the new laws had worked and were likely to work. I accordingly asked the following questions:—

1. Do you think the change to five balls per over has worked well?
2. If not, will you state your objection?
3. Do you think the change has worked well which prevents a man bowling two overs in succession, and, therefore, does not allow bowlers to change ends without someone else bowling an odd over? Would it not suffice, at any rate in matches extending over more than one day, if the restriction were upon his bowling more than two overs in succession?
4. Do you think the closure rule likely to work well?

Very courteous and frank answers were received from nearly all the gentlemen and players written to, and as it is far better that they should speak for themselves than that I should attempt to classify their views, I have published below this most interesting collection of expert opinion on cricket subjects. I ought, perhaps, to say that the reasons why the questions were framed as they appear were: (1) because some people said the bowlers would be overtired by bowling five balls in succession instead of four; (2) because some few persons had told me that the proper and ideal over consisted of six balls; (3) because, when you wanted your present bowlers to change ends, I considered it very awkward to have to call upon another man to bowl an odd over, and because I thought that in matches extending over more than one day there would be little risk in allowing two successive overs to one man; and (4) because the closure seemed likely to diminish the number of drawn matches and to give victory to the stronger and better team; but further, because there seemed a want of knowledge among public cricketers of the fact that in some one-day matches the law had been abused. Instances were brought to my knowledge in which captains had closed their innings when their score was less than that of the other side, and had done other things I do not think were contemplated by the framers of the law. There were other questions that I asked of the experts, but, as they do not relate to the reforms of the year, I have dealt with them, and with the answers to them, in another article. My esteemed friend, Bob Thoms, has with the wilfulness of youth, mixed all the ingredients together, but still, I think, his jottings will be found interesting in what he has characteristically said as well as in what he has judiciously left unsaid. Without further preface I publish the answers I received:—

Mr. I. D. WALKER thinks well of the change to five balls per over and of the closure rule, while as to bowlers changing ends, he says, 'The objection to a man bowling two overs in succession with unlimited change of ends is, that it would be possible for a man to bowl eight overs out of eleven, which is too large a proportion.'

Mr. W. H. PATTERSON expresses his approval of five balls per over and of the closure rule, but does not see much practical good in the suggestion as to changing ends.

C. K. PULLIN approves of the increase of the over to five balls, as it saves time; and he points out that a man might bowl four overs out of five if the suggestion were adopted that he might bowl two overs in succession and change ends as often as he liked. This experienced umpire does not think the closure rule ought to apply to one-day matches.

JOHN BEAUMONT is opposed to the increase of the over from four balls to five, as it gives fast bowlers too much work. He, however, approves of the other new laws, as to changing ends and declaring an innings over.

Mr. J. A. DIXON believes the extra ball to the over saved a lot of time and made very little difference, even to fast bowlers. He therefore supports the new law, and so he does the closure rule. As to changing ends, Mr. Dixon thinks the new regulation acted fairly well, although the odd over was a difficulty sometimes. The suggestion to allow two overs in succession would be open to abuse, and he prefers the rule as it is.

Mr. C. PIGG is in favour of all the new laws—the increase to five balls, the changing of ends, and the closure.

TOM HEARNE, the veteran chief of the ground staff at Lord's, also says emphatically 'yes' to these three questions.

The Hon. IVO BLIGH, in his individual capacity, of course, and not as secretary to the County Council, also gives an unqualified assent to the new laws of 1889.

Mr. W. G. GRACE supports the increase to five balls per over; and, on the subject of changing ends, says, 'Certainly; if a bowler can change ends as often as he likes you must restrict him not to bowl two overs in succession, or he could bowl four overs out of five.' Asked, however, if the closure rule is likely to work well, the Champion says, 'Certainly not, as it may lead to disagreement.'

W. ATTEWELL favours the increase in the length of the over, believes in the closure, and thinks a bowler ought to be allowed to bowl two overs in succession.

Mr. S. M. J. WOODS says the new law as to bowlers changing ends has done no harm, and he approves of the longer over and the legal closing of an innings.

Mr. A. G. STEEL thinks the change to five balls an over is a great improvement. As to changing ends he makes the following suggestion, which in my judgement is well worth consideration as a way of avoiding the present awkwardness and yet preventing any abuse of the law:—'I think the best rule would be to allow a bowler to change ends as often as he likes, so long as he does not bowl two overs in succession more than once in an innings; three overs consecutively never to be allowed.' Then, as to whether the closure rule is likely to work well, Mr. Steel says, 'Yes, in three-day matches. In one-day matches I, for one, would hesitate to use it. The good bats gets an innings and not the others. Lawn-tennis is already in many places a formidable rival to cricket; we cricketers should not help it.'

LOUIS HALL likes the increase of the over to five balls, and is in favour of the changing-ends rule as it is at present. He thinks the closure rule will work well, as it will cause more excitement in trying to finish matches, which is what the public enjoy.

H. H. STEPHENSON thinks the change to five balls per over a good one, and likely to work well. As to the closure, he likes what he has seen of it, but does not care to say much on the subject until another cricket season. Stephenson expresses no opinion on the question of bowlers changing ends, and in a letter to me says he is not enough connected with county cricket now to answer all my questions. On the subject of the approaching Australian visit, however, the Surrey veteran is enthusiastic. He says, 'The Australians have done much good to cricket in this country. They have taught us several valuable lessons, and they have 'mettled' our cricketers up, and put great life into the game. I am sure they will be well supported by the cricket public of the country.' It is refreshing to read this from the man who was captain of the first English cricket team that went to Australia, in 1861; the man who was in his prime, a great batsman, a most difficult bowler, and an accomplished wicket-keeper, when I as a boy, used to be taken to see cricket at the Oval; and I have been scribbling about the game now for nearly twenty years!

ROBERT PEEL considers the increase of the over to five balls is an advantage; he believes in the closure, and would 'advocate a bowler being allowed to bowl two successive overs, one at each end.'

Mr. HARRY THORNBER, of Cheshire, thinks well of the closure and the longer over; and, as to changing ends, 'would prefer that a bowler be allowed to bowl two overs in succession so long as he did not do it more than twice in one innings.' [This is a variant of Mr. Steel's suggestion.—C. F. P]

Lord HARRIS has not noticed any disadvantage from the increased length of the over. He thinks the closure rule is likely to work well; and regards it as inconvenient that bowlers are not allowed to bowl two consecutive overs.

Mr. A. H. HEATH favours the over of five balls, can see no objection to the new law about bowlers changing ends, and approves of the closure, 'as the captain can always use his discretion, while if he applied of the rule without due consideration for his side he would be supplanted.'

R. G. BARLOW thinks well of the closure and the increase in the length of over but believes the old rule is preferable which allowed a man to bowl two overs in succession, but only permitted him to change ends twice.

Mr. H. W. BAINBRIDGE says the change to five balls per over seems to him a success, the additional strain on the bowlers not being very apparent. He likes the closure, but thinks the rule as to changing ends is not satisfactory as it stands. He remarks, 'A bowler should be prevented bowling more than two consecutive overs. I do not think any further restriction is necessary.'

Mr. F. E. LACEY regards the increase of the over to five balls as an advantageous change, and believes the closure rule will work well. As to the bowling question the Hampshire batsman says:—'This is a change that is especially felt in country cricket, where victory often depends on the local professional. In the interests of cricket generally I think the change is a good one, and that it tends to reduce the power of the one good bowler.'

W. CHATTERTON quite agrees with the present rule as to the changing ends, believes in the longer over, and thinks 'the closure will work well.'

Mr. C. I. THORNTON thinks well of the bowling of five balls instead of four every over, because it saves time. As to changing ends, he 'would put the restriction at two overs instead of one;' and on the closure question says, 'I think it hard to put a side in the position that they cannot win and may lose.'

Mr. R. A. H. MITCHELL approves the increase of the over to five balls, and says he has long wished it. He also thinks well of the closure rule: while on the question of bowlers changing ends, the famous Old Oxonian says, 'I tried to get this change introduced twenty years ago, and approve of it. I approve of the rule as it now stands without further alteration.'

G. A. LOHMANN believes the change to five balls per over has certainly worked well, from the spectators' point of view. He favours the other new laws as to closing an innings and changing ends.

G. G. HEARNE likes the increase of the over from four balls to five, and also the power to legally close an innings. He would not allow a bowler to bowl more than two overs in succession.

In sending me his answers, Mr. I. D. Walker said he thought that, on some points at any rate, there would be much difference of opinion among my correspondents. He has proved quite correct in that surmise, but the experiment was worth trying, if only for the general favour expressed for the longer over, the dangers shown to exist of the closure rule being abused in one-day matches, and the suggestion of Mr. A. G. Steel as to how bowlers should be restricted as to changing ends.

SOME QUESTIONS OF THE DAY [1890]

BY C. F. PARDON

ALTHOUGH there is no burning question now vexing the minds of the cricket public, yet several matters have been earnestly debated during the past summer, and especially since the close of the county season; and while I was asking for the opinions of leading experts on the reformed laws, I thought I would also obtain views on the system of umpiring, the plan of tossing for choice of innings, and the county championship. Many gentlemen and players, and some committees, sent answers, and it is with pleasure that I acknowledge the courtesy that has been extended to me. As there are three distinct subjects, I have kept them separate, and dealt with them rather differently from the 'Reforms'.

TOSSING FOR CHOICE OF INNINGS

I think I am stating the general opinion when I say that in the great majority of matches it is best to toss for choice of innings. Captains and secretaries of hundreds of weak clubs would find the difficulties of getting the eleven to the ground with punctuality to be vastly increased if the team knew beforehand that 'the other fellows' were going to bat first. And on occasions when those other fellows were known to be the stronger side, or when the best bowler had sprained his ankle, the difficulties might be too serious to be overcome. It is not a great task to imagine scores of excuses that selfish or indolent players might make to avoid the 'fag' of fielding. We may take it for granted, then, in one-day and half-day matches tossing for choice is the right thing to do. It is, however, possible that in some of the great contests set for three days practical unfairness is not an unknown thing. I mean, of course, those matches of which two are played in the same season – out and home. Complaints have often been made of the condition of certain well known grounds, and men have said that playing on them was simply tossing for the match. For my part I think there are difficulties in the way of any pre-arrangement, but we will let the experts speak for themselves.

The questions I put were –

Would you retain the present plan of tossing for choice of innings in all matches?

If not, would you support – in home and home matches only – either of the suggested plans – (*a*) that the visitors should have choice of innings; (*b*) that the side which lost the toss in the first match should have choice in the return?

Mr. W. G. GRACE says 'yes' to the first question, and thinks the suggested methods would not be any improvement on tossing.

The Hon. Ivo Bligh answers the opening question in the negative, and says he thinks plan *b* is the best. He further makes the remark that where three matches are played in one season – as England v. Australia – he would apply the principle to the first two matches and toss in the third.

R. G. Barlow says:- 'No; the visiting team in all cases of home and home matches should have choice of innings.'

Mr. H. W. Bainbridge is of opinion that the present is a good working rule, and that if there were a previous knowledge as to which side would probably bat first, an opportunity might occur to dishonest people of preparing wickets improperly.

Mr. F. E. Lacey would only retain the present system in matches where no return is played; and, 'as reducing the element of luck,' he thinks the visitors should have choice of innings.

Mr. R. A. H. Mitchell supports the system of tossing, saying 'I think there are objections to any other plan.'

John Beaumont thinks that in county cricket the visitors should have choice of innings.

G. G. Hearne would prefer either of the suggested plans to the present system, and would only retain tossing in one-day matches, when no return was played.

Mr. A. G. Steel answers the first question, 'Certainly I would.'

Louis Hall, on the other hand, is in favour of an alternate choice – that is, plan *a*, giving the visitors choice of innings.

R. Peel says 'certainly' to the first question, and would not support either of the suggested changes.

Lord Harris would like to see a change, and would prefer that the side which lost the toss in the first match should have choice in the second.

Mr. J. A. Dixon says: 'I do not think it would work well to know beforehand which side would have choice of innings, uncertainty being one of the attractions of the game.'

Tom Hearne, Mr. C. Pigg, W. Attewell, Mr. A. H. Heath, Mr. H. Thornber. H. H. Stephenson, Mr. S. M. J. Woods, Mr. I. D. Walker, W. Chatterton, C. K. Pullin, Mr. W. H. Patterson, G. A. Lohmann, and Mr. C. I. Thornton all say 'yes' to the first question.

THE SYSTEM OF APPOINTING UMPIRES

Here we approach a more simple question, and one upon which there is comparatively little difference of opinion. We can all remember when the counties did as clubs generally do now – appointed their own umpires in all matches. I do not think there was much downright dishonesty under the old plan. There was some, no doubt, but the real objections were that the county umpire got to regard himself as a member of the team – and a pretty useful twelfth man he sometimes was – and, further, that no man could forget he had to look for his living to the county that employed him. The plan was emphatically open to suspicion, and I suppose no one would wish to go back to it. The reformed system is that in all county matches the Marylebone Club appoints the umpires from a list of men previously nominated by the counties themselves, the provision to insure neutrality being that no man shall stand umpire in a match in which his own county is engaged.

It was with the view of ascertaining what was thought of the working of this system that I asked –

Are you in favour of the present method of appointing umpires in county matches?

If so, do you think the plan could be better worked?

I naturally expected a great majority of favourable answers, but I also hoped that many suggestions would be thrown out as to the manner in which we might be better served than we are. The counties and the M.C.C. admitted the need of reform when they declared that the umpires in county matches should have no pecuniary connection with, or sentiment of allegiance towards, the contending elevens. They therefore set on foot the new plan, which is excellent in theory, and which, in practice, though it works faultily, is of course a long way better than what it replaced. My object in asking these questions was to see if I could not obtain from the experts some notions as to certificates of efficiency and competence, and some expressions of opinion that the best men should do the best work. I think a professional has every right to look forward to a period of employment as umpire when he is past active play; and by reason of their experience and knowledge of the game I would give veteran players the preference over other men. But it is not every old player who is qualified to act as umpire; and if, as it should be, the remuneration were more liberal, there might be men apply for nomination who could pass the suggested physical and technical examinations, and who might make valuable recruits to a very small army. I must confess that I am disappointed in the quality of the replies I obtained – so much so that where, as in the great majority of cases, my correspondents have merely expressed contentment with the present plan, I have passed them by. The opinions quoted below are therefore only of those experts who have apparently thought out the whole subject. I should add that here, as upon the Championship question, I invited the views of county committees as well as of individuals.

H. H. Stephenson answers the first question in the affirmative, but says:- 'I think great care should be taken in choosing men who thoroughly understand the game, whose hearing and eyesight are perfect, and who have good nerves.'

The Norfolk County Committee are unfavourable to the present plan, and say:- 'The Cricket Council should, we think, exercise some authority in the arrangement and management of all county matches. The appointment of umpire, if carefully considered by them, might, we think, be improved upon.'

Mr. A. G. Steel, while 'most decidedly' in favour of the present method, says:- 'I think it would be as well to lay down a rule that if one of the nominated umpires has ever played for one or more county or counties he is debarred from umpiring in a match in which either of those counties takes part.'

The Warwickshire County Committee think that the list of umpires from which the M.C.C. selects should be annually revised by the Cricket Council.

Mr. I. D. Walker's idea is that so long as counties are divided into first and second class, umpires nominated by first-class counties should be appointed for those matches only, and, of course, *vice versa*.

C. K. Pullin says: 'I have not heard any good reason given for any alteration.'

R. G. Barlow writes: 'I am firmly of opinion that there are a few umpires who are not competent, and others who, unfortunately, are too aged to act in a competent manner; and I think that all county committees should be consulted as to the merits of the umpires at present engaged (told off for matches?) by the M.C.C. An umpire should essentially have a sound judgment on the game, be quick with eye and ear, and of decisive action.'

THE COUNTY CHAMPIONSHIP

It may be as well to say here that I had no more to do with inventing the phrase 'County Championship' that I had with creating the competition itself. Some good-natured, old-fashioned friends of mine are pleased to say that the championship is a myth, and the competition itself exists only in my imagination, that a game at cricket is just a game at cricket – enjoyable for itself, delightful both as an exercise and a spectacle – and no more. All I can say is that in 1870 Yorkshire was the Champion County, and was so regarded, and this was not only long before my pen had acquired any influence in the cricket world but before I had commenced to write on the game at all. What I have done is simply to record and comment upon this competition as it developed season after season, and to chronicle the self-evident fact that the county programme became more and more systematic and regular until in the last year or two it only wanted a home-and-home fixture between Sussex and Middlesex to make it complete – that is, every one of eight great counties would play every other one twice, a total of fifty-six first-class matches. Two points became prominent as time went on. First, we had to 'classify' the counties, and rigidly exclude those below leading rank; and next we had to settle upon a method of computing results. I need not now defend my views on the classification question, as the counties themselves have accepted and adopted them entirely. We will, therefore, proceed to discuss the system of calculation. I must explain for those readers who do not follow the subject closely that the old way was to regard as champion the county team who had lost fewest county matches during the season. This plan was understandable enough, but it took no account of proportion, and would give preference, say, to a side that had won six matches, drawn seven, and lost but one game, over a team that had won twelve matches, but had been twice beaten. So the time came when the cricketers and the public complained of the system. Several very elaborate schemes were proposed, and the lovers of decimals had a good innings. I think even logarithms were introduced by one malicious joker! In the end, as the old plan had few friends, a system was accepted the basis of which was to divide the drawn games between the wins and losses, counting half a point to each. Thus, if a county played twelve matches, winning four, losing four, and drawing four, they would be counted as having scored six points – that is, six-twelfths of their entire matches, or one-half. This was generally adopted by the newspapers and the public, and, indeed, by the vast majority of cricketers. It was upon this plan that Kent and Yorkshire were bracketed second to Surrey in 1888; and, without a doubt or a dissentient voice, the county season of 1889 was played through on an understanding that this method of calculation would decide the positions of the counties. The issue, as everyone knows, was that after Nottinghamshire had held the lead all the summer, they lost their last match with Kent, and three counties were bracketed equal for first place. I declined to go behind the record. Notts partisans urged that their form was the best until they were just beaten on a wretched wicket at the end of the season, and that even then they had lost fewer matches than anyone else. Lancashire supporters pointed with confidence to the double victory over the then champions, Surrey; while the friends of the county last named said they were champions before, and their record was still as good as that of anyone else. Surrey further declared that if the championship were represented by a Trophy – which the dread Fates forfend – instead of being an informal and honorary title, they would certainly retain that title. To these arguments, and to many others not so reasonable, but consisting chiefly of sentiment and partisan feeling, I was obdurate. The position I took up was that the competition had been commenced, continued, and concluded under the accepted rule that a win would count one point and a draw half a point, and that it was absurd to attempt to alter the rule now that the competition was over. Further, that it was by no means a bad thing for the game, but rather the reverse, that three counties should tie for first place. Still, I knew that I was in the position of defending, or at any rate supporting, an unpopular contention. I did not see how, fairly and logically, anything else could be said, but I was aware that, when party feeling ran high, logic was often drowned in a flood of words. The discussion was carried on with moderation and good temper, however, and I think a good many people, even if they don't like it, admit that Surrey, Notts, and Lancashire were equal on last season's record. Then various suggestions were made as to what ought to be done in future, and it was said that either drawn games should be adjudicated upon or else ignored altogether. In a word, counting half a point for a draw was as friendless a system as the old one had been of counting by the 'fewest defeats.' I was not by any means wedded to the existing plan, except to enforce it for what had already happened, and I heartily accept the County Secretaries' decision to ignore drawn games in the Championship competition for the future. Premising that the ignoring of drawn games was not seriously considered when the recent system was adopted, I append the questions that were submitted for consideration:-

1. Are you in favour of counting a draw as half a win, and, therefore, half a loss?
2. If not, can you suggest an improvement?
3. Do you favour either of the suggested plans – (*a*) ignoring drawn games altogether; (*b*) having drawn games adjudicated upon by a committee of sporting journalists representing *The Field, Land and Water, Sporting Life, Sportsman*, and *Sporting Chronicle*, the basis of adjudication being to count a draw half to each side, or three-quarters to one side and a quarter to the other, according to the opinion of the Committee on the position of the game?

Below is an epitome of the principal answers, received, of course, before the Counties took action in the matter:-

Mr. E. M. GRACE, speaking for himself and not for his committee, says drawn games should not count, but be ignored altogether.

TOM HEARNE would also ignore drawn games.

The LANCASHIRE COUNTY COMMITTEE are unanimously of opinion that these matters should be referred to and settled by the County Council only.

Mr. C. I. THORNTON would give one point for a win and one for a loss, and ignore draws.

Mr. R. A. H. MITCHELL says: 'If a satisfactory committee could be formed for the purpose, I would let them adjudicate on all drawn matches, cut out matches altogether where the result was an open question, and, where the match would clearly have been won by one side, count it as a victory for that side. I would never submit any cricket question to anyone but a committee of cricketers elected by cricketers.'

G. A. LOHMANN thinks that the Marylebone Club might with advantage move in the matter.

The NORFOLK COUNTY COMMITTEE answer questions 1 and 2, 'No,' and, regarding the alternative suggestions, say 'No, leave the drawn games to stand on their merits.'

Mr. W. H. C. OATES, writing personally and not on behalf of the Nottinghamshire Committee, declares against adjudication, and says should score, 'Wins one, draws half; deduct one for each loss.'

Mr. A. G. STEEL says:– 'I think draws should be ignored altogether. It is impossible in a game like cricket to score for head county by points. It must, except in exceptional years, always be a matter of opinion as to which is the best county.' Further, Mr. Steel remarks, 'Why sporting journalists should adjudicate upon drawn games I am at a loss to understand. I think, first, they don't want adjudicating upon; and, secondly, if they do, that the M.C.C. Committee are quite competent to decide any cricket point without troubling anyone else.'

The WARWICKSHIRE COUNTY COMMITTEE think the plan of counting draws works very well, as a side with the game well in hand ought now, with the new rule, generally to finish the game. After declaring decidedly against the ignoring of drawn games, Warwickshire go on to say:– 'The three-quarters and a quarter or half and half seems a fair basis for adjudication, providing all surrounding circumstances are known by the adjudicating committee. The Cricket Council ought to settle such things.'

R. PEEL is in favour of going on as before.

The KENT COUNTY COMMITTEE say they are indifferent to the system of marking which the Press make use of, but object strongly to a committee of representatives of the sporting papers deciding whether a drawn match is to be reckoned as a win or not. [This was never suggested. – C. F. P.]

W. ATTEWELL would ignore drawn games altogether, and count only wins and losses.

The DERBYSHIRE COUNTY COMMITTEE are of opinion that drawn games should not be counted at all.

JOHN BEAUMONT is not in favour of the existing plan, but thinks drawn games would be done away with if the visitors had choice of innings.

Mr. I. D. WALKER is opposed to counting half for a draw. 'Witness,' he says, 'the cases of Gloucester v. Kent and Gloucester v. Surrey in 1889.' Mr. Walker's suggestion is: 'I should not count drawn matches; in the event of two counties being equal in wins and losses, cricketers can form their own opinion as to their relative merits from the state of the drawn matches.'

G. G. HEARNE is against the present plan, and favours the adjudication suggestion.

Mr. W. H. PATTERSON says the existing system might not infrequently work injustice, *vide* Kent v. Gloucestershire, 1889. He thinks some well-considered basis of adjudication would be an improvement.

C. K. PULLIN would keep the present plan until he saw something better. He thinks 'When the stumps are drawn the match should be finished in every way. Cricket varies so much that no committee could say what would be a fair division of points.'

Dr. RUSSELL BENCRAFT was unable to get the Hampshire Committee to express their views on the subjects submitted. [I should say that some other committees declined to commit themselves to a formal opinion, as indeed did some few individual gentlemen. Other committees had held their meetings before my questions reached the secretaries, and were not going to meet again until after the 1890 programme was fixed. – C. F. P.]

Mr. S. M. J. WOODS is against the present plan, and thinks adjudication a very good idea.

The Hon. IVO BLIGH favours the ignoring of drawn games, as under the new system they will be less frequent.

R. G. BARLOW would give the umpires power to extend the time to complete a match, light and weather being favourable. The umpires should be the sole judges of these points, and in the case of their not agreeing the game to count half a win and half a loss to each side.

The YORKSHIRE COUNTY COMMITTEE see no necessity to enter into these questions, as they do not recognise any arbitrary distinctions between counties.

I hope I have made it quite clear that these questions were asked and that the answers were sent to me before the meetings of the Cricket Council and of the County Secretaries, at which the Classification was officially adopted, and the determination arrived at to ignore drawn games in calculating the season's results in the Championship competition, and in the encounters of the second-class counties. I was tempted to cancel all the portion of this article relating to the Championship, although it was already in type. Perhaps it would have been better to do so, but as the resolution on drawn games was not unanimous, but a majority vote, and as, moreover, it is liable to revision by the same body that adopted it, I thought I would allow the matter to stand, as an interesting permanent record of opinion.

My personal position on the classification question may be thus defined:

I do not hold and never did hold that, for purposes of cricket reform or on questions touching qualification or the general good of the game, there is or should be any difference between counties. Notts and Northumberland are equal there. But the leading fact about modern cricket is that the great counties play every year a regular series of matches among themselves – matches which furnish the best cricket of the season, which fan the spirit of emulation among the players, and arouse enthusiasm among the spectators on many a county ground. I believe this feeling of rivalry is the best thing about the game. It excites and keeps alive interest in an honest and honourable competition, where the prize is, and I hope always will be, an empty title. The local interest, the county feeling, brings in not only gate-money but subscriptions, and so clubs rise and flourish. It is surely better that responsible clubs should receive this money and spend it for the advancement of the county than that we should go back to the plan of touring with speculating teams. This regular programme among the great counties necessitated the preparation of separate averages; and so, 'for the purposes of statistical comparison,' we did what the County Council's sub-committee are about to do officially – we divided counties into first-class and second-class. We drew a hard and fast line between the two; it would be unworkable to attempt to muddle up all the results together. In doing this I claim that we were not injuring but actually assisting the second-class counties in the most direct and practical way. If Surrey were to have counted against them a defeat by Essex or Leicestershire, they would probably not play those counties, and so the weaker teams would not get matches which are invaluable to them for the experience gained against great players, and the attraction of the appearance of famous teams on their grounds. Again, the stronger side – the first-class county – would lose the opportunity they now embrace of trying new men of promise, and of giving men who are out of form the chance of a good hit. It was the same all over the country, and if the Yorkshire Committee did not until now recognise arbitrary distinction, all

I can say is that their programme for 1889 was a curious result of chance. The article on Yorkshire elsewhere in this Almanack will explain what I mean; but I may say here that I regarded as intentional the fixing of dates which provided that, until nearly the end of June, no match should be played that would count for the championship. I thought it a wise attempt to get an unlucky team into a form before the real work of the season began, and I felt sorry the experiment met with so little success.

As to other matters raised, chiefly by Lancashire, Warwickshire, Mr. R. A. H. Mitchell, and Mr. A.G. Steel, I had written expressing my hope that the County Council would take action, when unexpected but very welcome activity was shown by that body. They are the proper and responsible people to settle difficulties and lay down rules, and I am glad indeed that the public will now have official decisions to guide them. I hope the Council will not regard it as beneath them to periodically examine and discuss the list of nominated umpires, and will consider whether there is anything in the ideas of those persons who are discontented with the practice – in home and home matches – of tossing for choice of innings. Further, there are the subjects of Mr. Steel's acute amendment to the changing-ends rules, the abuse of the closure in one-day matches, and the excessive licence allowed bowlers in having trial balls, and so learning the pace of the ground, and finding a length while supposed to be 'loosening their arms.'

One word in conclusion. I quite believe in counties making fair and legitimate use of the residential qualification and importing unemployed players, but I can see no excuse whatever for attempting to entice players away from counties for which they are regularly engaged.

And now we will be silent for another year, until time fulfils its fated task of bringing fresh subjects before the lovers of our famous game – subjects that I hope will always be freely and good-humouredly discussed in the pages of WISDEN'S ALMANACK.

IN MEMORIAM
[1890]

Charles F. Pardon

BY JOHN WISDEN AND CO.

It would scarcely be fitting to allow the twenty eighth issue of Wisden to appear without some tribute to the memory of the gentleman who for four years filled the post of editor with so much zeal and ability. When Mr. Pardon first became associated with it, the Almanack had reached a critical stage of its existence, an unfortunate delay in the production of the volume for 1886 – a delay for which we were in no way responsible – having to some extent injured its influence. However, Mr. Pardon set to work with characteristic energy to make up the lost ground, and the best proof of his success was found in the largely increased favour extended to the Almanack by the public during the years of his editorship. His untimely death terminated a friendship to which we shall always look back with keen pleasure.

CAMBRIDGE MEMORIES

BY A. G. STEEL

It was more than fortunate for John Wisden and Company, for the Almanack and for the general good health of the game that when Charles Pardon died there were other Pardons to call upon. Sydney took over with a clear idea of what the Almanack should comprise and very decided views on how to achieve his ends. Among the features which blossomed under his touch was the essay, which until now had been very much a peripheral feature, inching its way uncertainly into the list of contents. In his first year as editor, Sydney commissioned a much broader and much more personalised contribution than had ever appeared in Wisden before. If the report of the controversy surrounding the formation of a County Cricket Council was the first piece of prose in Wisden and Bob Thoms' recollections the first statement by a distinguished veteran, A. G. Steel's 'Cambridge Memories', running to more than 2,500 words, was the first true essay, in that its mood was expansive, its approach idiosyncratic and its style aspiring vaguely to literature as distinct from the recording of fact. This is clear from the wonderfully archetypal opening, which reads dangerously like parody:

> I was sitting in the smoking-room of a country house one night last autumn, thoroughly tired out after a long day's shooting. I felt perfectly comfortable in my armchair watching the smoke slowly ascend from my 'briar'.

In those few words the writer is letting us know that he moves in exalted circles, has no need to work for a living, and is, in the peculiar terminology of the period, a sportsman. Many of the Almanack's readers, obliged to run families on less than young men like Steel spent on tobacco and horses, must have thrilled at the essayist's affable assumption that he and his readers were as one, socially speaking.

The truth was that Alan Gibson Steel (1858–1914) was at one with nobody, being a prodigy, a schoolboy genius, a virtuoso. Of the seven Steel boys, six became associated with cricket, but none of the others remotely approached A. G. either in skill or in strength of personality. A star of the Marlborough College side for four years, a Test player who represented England thirteen times and scored two centuries against Australia, and one of the finest all-round cricketers ever to represent Lancashire, Steel's true greatness was as a slow right-arm bowler. Even as a schoolboy he was able to reduce the world's greatest batsmen to impotence, and as the craft of bowling slow right-arm spin to right-handed batsmen is one which usually takes several years to master, his virtuosity becomes doubly freakish. A solicitor by profession, Steel may have been making his literary début when he contributed this entertaining essay to Sydney Pardon's first Wisden. It was certainly not his last piece of published writing. In 1904 he and R. H. Lyttelton jointly edited the 'Badminton Book of Cricket', in which Steel wrote exhaustive chapters on Bowling, Captaincy and Umpiring. The chapter on bowling, defined many years later by H. S. Altham as a masterpiece, remains one of the finest expositions on the subject ever written, but it is in the 'Captaincy' chapter that there may be found a remark which best conveys the true spirit of the man: 'A captain is born, not made, and very seldom born too'. In composing this essay, Steel was drawing on memories of the great Cambridge elevens of 1877–81, in all of which he appeared against Oxford, and the third of which he captained.

I WAS sitting in the smoking-room of a country house one night last autumn, thoroughly tired out after a long day's shooting. I felt perfectly comfortable in my large armchair watching the smoke slowly ascend from my 'briar.' My companions, of whom there were several, were all lazily inclined, and beyond an occasional remark about some shooting incident of the day none seemed inclined to do much talking. I was dreamily thinking of some old Cambridge friends now scattered over various quarters of the globe, and as their names flashed through my mind each one brought happy recollections of well-fought matches at Fenner's, Lord's, and the Oval. I was far away, oblivious almost to the presence of others, and my thoughts in their hazy wanderings had fixed on one particular hit – never by me to be forgotten. Charley Bannerman was the striker, P. H. Morton the bowler, and the match Cambridge v. Australians at Lord's 1878. Half-asleep I seemed to see again that sturdy striker raise his massive shoulders and hit the ball a warrior's knock; the ball flew low, over the bowler's head, struck the iron-bound ground twenty yards in front of the outfield, and bounded right over the awning of Lord Londesborough's drag and struck the wall behind. Truly a mighty hit. I could almost hear the cheers and shouts that greeted it.

Alas! too soon was my pleasant reverie ended. A low voice sitting at my elbow recalled me to the smoking-room and its surroundings. The speaker was a young Cambridge under-graduate, and the words he was uttering were these: 'I am not much of a cricketer myself, but the general opinion is that our eleven this year is the best we have had for twenty years at Cambridge.' 'What about 1878?' said I, quietly. '1878,' said my young friend contemptuously. 'That year had a good bat or two – A. P. Lucas, Alfred and Edward Lyttelton were not bad players – but what bowlers had it? There was none to be compared to Woods, the present captain.

It is hardly necessary to say that a long discussion followed and afterwards it occurred to me that a few remarks in WISDEN on Cambridge cricketers of the last dozen years or so by one who has played with most, if not all of them, might be interesting to University men and, perhaps, others.

As I was one of the unvanquished 1878 team I am naturally open to the charge of prejudice; I shall risk that, however, and say that in my opinion that was the best side that Cambridge has turned out in my recollection. It played eight matches, and *won* every one, including a defeat of Gregory's Australian team by an innings and 72 runs. As a batting side it was exceptionally strong. Alfred and Edward Lyttelton were then at their very best; in fact, the latter's success that one season was phenomenal. Always a good batsman, the office of captain had no sooner become his than he played as he never did before, or since. He went to the very top of the tree, and the close of the season's record showed his to be the highest amateur average – viz., 29.25, the champion running a very close second. Alfred Lyttelton was then, as always, a really great batsman. No *first-class* cricketer ever possessed the elegance of style that was his; no flourish, but the maximum of power with the minimum of exertion.

These two, with that perfect master of stylish defence, A. P. Lucas, made a really sound nucleus for the batting strength of the side. The last-named batsman, when the bowling was very accurate, was a slow scorer, *but* always a treat to watch. If the present generation of stone-wall cricketers, such as Scotton, Hall, Barlow, A. Bannerman, nay, even Shrewsbury, possessed such beautiful ease of style the tens of thousands that used to frequent the beautiful Australian grounds would still flock there, instead of the hundred or two patient gazers on feasts of Job-like patience that now attend them. There were several lesser lights of the team who were far from useless with the bat – Ivo Bligh, Whitfeld, L. K. Jarvis, and A. G. Steel – as will be seen from the fact that the average of the whole eleven came to 219 runs per innings, and that in one of the very wettest seasons on record.

The bowling of the team was strong, though looking at it now, after a dozen years, one cannot help wondering at its success. P. H. Morton was during that season a really good fast bowler; not as good as Woods of to-day, certainly not; but at times he was very deadly. The 'divilment' in his bowling was the great pace the ball left the pitch. Tallish, but of spare physique, he scarcely looked the stamp of man to bowl really fast, but he had most powerful muscles at the back of his shoulders, and it was to these that he owed his success. I owed my great success of taking seventy-five wickets for the University at a cost of 7.32 runs apiece to the novelty of my bowling. At that time no bowler in first-rate cricket broke from the leg-side, and for a short period many a first-class batsman made but sorry attempts to play the 'curly' ones. A. F. J. Ford and A. P. Lucas were the only changes. With a good fielding side and a superb wicket-keeper the team was one that in 1878 would have taken a very high-class side to beat.

Alfred Lyttelton's year as captain, 1879, saw the Cambridge eleven again undefeated. This was a good side, but lacking Edward Lyttelton and A. P. Lucas it could not be considered equal to the preceding one. G. B. Studd first made his appearance, getting the last place by the mere skin of his teeth. It is a strange fact that two such fine cricketers as Ivo Bligh and G. B. Studd just managed to scrape as eleventh men into the team in their respective years. The rival of each for the last place was the same man, O. P. Lancashire – hard lines indeed just to miss his blue so narrowly two consecutive years. This year saw the last of the Lytteltons – doughty champions indeed for Cambridge cricket. During the five years, 1874 to 1879, the ranks of Cambridge cricket were being continually recruited by some of the very best boy players – D. Q. Steel, W. S. Patterson, A. P. Lucas, Edward and Alfred Lyttelton, A. G. Steel, Ivo Bligh, P. H. Morton, and G. B. Studd were amongst the most prominent. It was hardly to be expected that the public schools could go on supplying such good men; but in 1880 Eton sent up C. T. Studd, who, in a very short time, took his place in quite the first flight of cricketers. He had a fine, upright, commanding style as a batsman, and was a very useful slow bowler, quick from the pitch, and on a hard ground getting up to an inconvenient height. In 1881 Cambridge suffered their first defeat by Oxford since the great collapse in 1877. The eleven was strong in batting, but sadly weak in bowling, especially on the hard fast ground on which the University match was played. A. H. Evans at last had his revenge; as hard working a cricketer as ever played for either University, his bowling for Oxford in the three preceding 'Varsity matches had been magnificent, and that against strong batting sides. Supported by very weak batting all his efforts had been unavailing till 1881, and then his bowling, backed up by a beautiful innings of over a hundred by that finished player, W. H.

Patterson, and a seventy (ever memorable for a strange stroll to the pavilion at its beginning) by C. F. H. Leslie, secured a well-earned and long-desired victory for Oxford.

The Australians fared but badly in their first three contests with the representatives of Cambridge. In 1878 the Australian management had found it impossible to give a date for a Cambridge fixture until after the University match at Lord's. I believe that this is the first occasion on which a University team has played as a University after the meeting at Lord's. However, keen for the fray, full of confidence after a most successful season, we reunited on July 22nd to try conclusions with the eleven which early in the year had inflicted such a terrible defeat upon a good team of the M.C.C. It was glorious weather, and a perfect wicket. We won the toss, and despite the unavoidable absence of A. P. Lucas ran up a total of 285. The most noticeable feature of the innings was the woeful lack of judgment the Australians showed in placing their field. In the first two hours their bowling was collared, and away went the majority of the field to the boundary. I recollect well batting to Spofforth that day without any cover-point or third man. We have learnt a lot from the Australians in bowling; they have learnt a lot from us in batting and general knowledge of the game.

The Australians' two innings were 111 and 102. These small scores were entirely owing to P. H. Morton, whose bowling on that day was about the best fast bowling on a true wicket I ever saw. He got twelve wickets for 90 runs, and clean bowled nine, most of them with really fast breakbacks.

The next match between Cambridge and the Australians was in 1882 at Fenner's. Their team this year was undoubtedly the best they ever brought over, before or since, and Cambridge did a great performance in beating them by six wickets. The wicket was a fine one and the weather splendid, and the Australians won the toss. C. T. Studd and R. C. Ramsay bowled them out for 139. Cambridge retaliated with 266, the chief feature being a grand 118 by C. T. Studd. His off-driving of Spofforth and Palmer was perfection. The Australians making 291 in their second innings left the 'Varsity a big task – 165 to win on a well-used wicket. The weather, however, kept fine, the wicket played well, and the runs were got for four wickets. J. E. K. Studd played a fine innings of 66, and G. P. Studd 48. It will be a long time before I forget the face of the old President (Rev. A. Ward) when Cambridge had won. 'Mr. Steel,' he said, 'I never yet got a new hat, except for the University match: I shall order one tomorrow in honour of this victory.'

The next match was at Portsmouth the same year, and was Australians v. Past and Present Cambridge. This was a magnificent game, and the finish never to be forgotten by those who witnessed it. Cambridge won by 20 runs after many exciting incidents. The University went in first, and made 196. C. I. Thornton and A. P. Lucas, 45 and 42 respectively, were the highest scorers. The Australians made 141. Then Cambridge ran up 152, Alfred Lyttelton's 60 being the highest score, and left the Australians 208 to win. They began their task well – too well it seemed to the numerous partisans of the University. I have no record of how the wickets fell in this innings, but unless my memory plays me false I think that the Australians at the fall of the second wicket – Bonnor's – were about 90 to 100. This was not pleasant. Bonnor had made 66 in just half-an-hour. His hitting of C. T. Studd's bowling was appalling. The wicket seemed good and played well; but late in the innings I noticed that several balls that pitched on the middle and off stumps got up very uncomfortably for the batsmen. I happened to be bowling, and keeping the ball as well as I could on that spot, innocent of all break, and almost medium pace, I met with great success. The finish was exciting when the Australians wanted about 25 runs to win and two wickets to get them; horror of horrors, two catches were missed, one a very very easy one – imagine our feelings. However, all was well eventually, and amidst the very wildest excitement amongst the blue jackets we won. One of the Australians said to me afterwards: 'After this third defeat, you've only to hold up a light-blue coat and we'll run.' However, since 1882 the Australians have amply avenged themselves both against the University and Cambridge Past and Present.

Since 1882 many fairly good batsmen have appeared in the ranks of the Cambridge teams, and a few moderate bowlers, but the decade has been one remarkably deficient in any brilliant talent. We look in vain for any names that have taken such a high place as the old ones. Not one Cambridge batsman during this period has earned the distinction of representing England; and it was not till 1888 that two such first-class men in their respective spheres as Woods and M'Gregor appeared. Lord Hawke, C. W. Wright (for a short period), F. Marchant, F. Thomas, Mordaunt, Foley, G. Kemp, Hon. J. W. Mansfield, C. D. Buxton, and F. G. J. Ford are amongst the best batsmen. There have been fewer good bowlers than batsmen. Rock was a very steady, slow bowler; Toppin at one time showed considerable promise, but never realised expectations. The young Australian, S. M. J. Woods, the present captain, is far away the finest fast bowler Cambridge has had for many years. Very fast, straight, with a good command over the ball both as regards pitch and change of pace, he is the *beau ideal* of a fine amateur bowler. He is a dangerous batsman too, one of those plucky, dashing players who appear to greater advantage the more things are going wrong for their side. What a pity we cannot keep this fine young cricketer at home; we could do very well with him in Gentlemen v. Players matches for the next five or six years. We are told that Ferris has taken a house or cottage of some sort near Bristol in order to secure some so-called qualification for Gloucestershire, though from all accounts he himself is at present in Australia. I should like to hear Woods had done the same thing in any English city he pleased.

Wicket-keeping has been of late above the average. Orford, the predecessor of M'Gregor, was as good as any University team wants, and very much better than the ordinary run, but M'Gregor, another pupil of that best of old cricketers H. H. Stephenson, has now reached the very top of the tree, as this last season he was deservedly chosen to keep wicket for England in preference to any of the professionals. He is a great wicket-keeper, and though I have not seen quite as much of him as I have of some other of the past stumpers, my own opinion is that he is the best amateur I ever saw. Firm and steady as a rock, without a whisper of a flourish, he takes the ball close to the stumps. Alfred Lyttelton was a great wicket-keeper; as a *catcher* at the wicket he was unsurpassed, for the very reason that made him a slow stumper, viz., he allowed the ball to pass the line of stumps a considerable distance before taking it. M'Gregor is a quick stumper and a fine catcher, too, and his quiet and sure style reminds me of that prince of wicket-keepers Richard Pilling.

With Woods and M'Gregor up again next season, and with the two promising youngsters, Streatfeild and Douglas, Cambridge should hold her own again at Lord's next year.

To old Cantabs the University pavilion is hardly the same now that our late President, 'old' (as we used to call him) Ward, has passed away. Who that ever played at Cambridge in days gone by can forget his portly figure, his round and ruddy face? His jokes, some, alas, so oft-told yet always new to him, his laughter, his kindly genial sympathy as he greeted the discomfited batsman in the pavilion, will ever live in the memory of those who knew him. A cricketer's visit to Cambridge in the old President's days was never complete without an attack of the presidential 'Bollinger,' which according to its owner could only cheer but not inebriate – an idle tale as many a thirsty soul could prove.

THE DEVELOPMENT OF CRICKET [1892]

BY HON R. H. LYTTELTON

The Hon. Robert Henry Lyttelton (1854–1939), a dedicated student of the game, and co-editor of 'The Badminton Book of Cricket' was among the lesser cricketers of his family but ranked among their most knowledgeable writers on the game. The sixth son of the fourth Lord Lyttelton, and one of eight brothers, seven of whom played for Eton between 1857 and 1872, he failed to get his Blue at Cambridge but always excelled as a student and critic of cricket. His great bête noire *was the use by a batsman of his pads to protect his wicket. To the end of his life he regarded pad-play as a breach of sporting etiquette, and strove for half his life to bring about amendments to the law which would penalise any batsman who resorted to such distasteful tactics. Lyttelton was widely recognised as a writer on the game, and his appearance in the 1892 edition surprised nobody. When, in the 'Badminton Book', he wrote an account of the famous University match of 1870 in which F. C. Cobden took the last three Oxford wickets in three balls to snatch a sensational Cambridge victory by two runs, Lyttelton was moved to such dithyrambic passion that his description was included in 'The Oxford Book of English Prose'. While scaling no such literary heights in his Wisden début, Lyttelton gives a lucid and readable account of the game's development.*

SOME old-fashioned critics, every cricketer knows them well, will say on reading the heading of this article that cricket has developed only in the sense of becoming worse, that, leaving W. G. Grace out of the question, Shrewsbury is no better than Joe Guy, nor Gunn than Fuller Pilch, that the bowling altogether is not so good, and the fielding distinctly much inferior. Why are the old fogies at all games apt to become a little tiresome, or what ill-natured people would call bores? We venture to assert that it is partly owing to a lack of proportion; they do not recognise that in their youthful days everything they saw was seen when the mind was enthusiastic and unable, from its simple joyousness, to notice the ugly and bad side of anything. The bowling might not have been so straight, but if it was well hit, the youth remembered the hit, but forgot the crooked ball.

The grounds were rougher than they are now, and fine gallery bits of wicket-keeping were perhaps commoner; but how does our venerable friend account for the fact that, even with a long-stop, extras were far more numerous than they are in these days with only a wicket-keeper? Boys will always be impressed by the one fine stroke; the man weighs and balances, and sees a very trifling inaccuracy; in other words, he becomes the critic, while the boy is only the charmed spectator; he does not yet know enough to be critical, though his faculty of enjoyment is intense. Hence it is that an accurate and attentive perusal of scores is apt to irritate the veteran; it recalls facts that should be forgotten; he is bewildered, he cannot remember such things, and the reason is obvious – he remembers what is good and forgets what is amiss, and who can blame him?

Of all inventions that ever worked a revolution in cricket, nothing had more effect than the heavy roller and the mowing machine. The old scythe, however deftly wielded, left a tuft of grass here and there; you can see it rather exaggerated in your newly-mown meadow. But watch the mowing machine – it shaves to a perfectly uniform length or shortness, the wicket becomes a billiard table, while, if the weather is dry, only a ponderous modern roller can have any effect on a clay soil; so in former days, in addition to the tufts of grass you had little lumps of clay. With such a wicket as this you wanted a fast bowler, who would keep short in the sense that he never would bowl half-volleys, and the ground would do the rest. Of course, in circumstances like these, there were any amount of bowlers who could get wickets at small cost, and speaking of the years from 1858 to 1868, one cannot fail to be struck with the fact that the number of fast or fastish bowlers was enormous, while the real slow round-arm bowler was very rarely found.

You may take the representative matches at random, and you will find that the leading bowlers were men who kept a fairish length, and were straight and fast, and in cricket, as in all other things in life, the predominant style is predominant because it answers its purpose – in other words, because it succeeds. Modern opinion, in judging of the merits of strictly fast and slow head-bowling, judges that on hard true wickets the straight fast bowler is easy as compared to slow bowlers, or bowlers who, at any rate, are more slow than fast, and if we look at the years 1861 to 1864 inclusive, we can find some corroboration of this. There were in those days two grounds almost, if not quite, as easy and as true as the modern grounds. There were very likely more, but these two – Kennington Oval and the University Ground at Cambridge – are taken as samples. A comparison of the scores of the period just mentioned and the present day will not show an average excess of runs now as compared to the former time.

The four Gentlemen and Players' matches, 1861 to 1864, show the average number of runs per wicket to be 24. The same matches for the four years ending 1891 show an average of 21. In the famous Surrey *v.* Cambridgeshire match at the Oval in 1861, the average number of runs per wicket was 27, and there were three individual innings of over 100. In the corresponding match at Cambridge on Fenner's, only 21 wickets were lowered, Caffyn and Tom Hayward each got 100, and the average number of runs per wicket was 31. Even in the years when W. G. Grace was in his prime – when, on going in first, he so demoralized the bowling and fielding that his side, at any rate, nearly always made a big score – we shall find the same story. W. G.'s average for the four years, 1871, 1872, 1873, and 1874 was 78, 57, 71, and 53. And let us look at Gentlemen and Players' matches at the Oval during these years. The average number of runs per wicket for these years amounts to 22 against 24 from 1861 to 1864.

Our object in quoting these figures is to show that on the same level wickets there is not much difference in the number of runs scored thirty years ago and now, but that, in consequence of the far more numerous good grounds that now exist, owing to the invention of the mowing-machine and the greater expenditure of time and money on their making and preservation, there are more good bats now than then, and the runs have not increased, because the bowling is better.

We can see our venerable friend's face as this opinion is stated, and three of his white hairs drop off. Lohmann, Briggs, Attewell and Mold better than Willsher, Wootton, Jackson, and Caffyn; the idea is preposterous! We are talking of English bowlers only. We do not say anything of Spofforth, Palmer, Giffen, and Turner; that marvellous batch of bowlers, whose deeds and feats, considering whom they opposed, have never been equalled.

Wherein does the greater merit of the modern bowlers lie? Simply in the fact that, in these days of greater batting science and perfect wickets, the mere accuracy and pace are of no avail – you must use your head. The excellence of grounds and the consequent facilities afforded to batsmen have worked the revolution. Bowlers have found out that it is no good pounding away on good wickets, for you will only tire yourself out. You must bowl every variety of good length. You must even, on purpose, bowl one or two balls to be hit for four, to raise the batsman's hopes and tempt him to hit at the next ball – a little shorter and a tiny bit slower – with the prospect of seeing him mistime it and send it up.

On Lord's Ground thirty years ago Jackson, Willsher, and Tarrant had merely to bowl their fastest and straightest, and the batsman might any ball expect either a dead shooter or a body blow. No wonder, under these circumstances, that it did not pay to bowl anything except fast and straight. Who can deny that the higher form of art is that of the modern bowler, where accuracy has to be assisted by craft, cuteness, and artifice of every description? What the rougher wickets in old days did to get batsmen out has to be done now by generalship in bowlers, indifference to being hit and longheadedness. To see Lohmann bowl on an Oval wicket is an intellectual delight. 'To a right-hand batsman he bowls on or just outside the off-stump, and breaks back very quickly, but now and then he puts in a very fast one with a break from leg. Should a left-hand batsman follow, especially if he can hit well on the leg side, he pitches everything on the wicket or off-stump, varying it with a faster one, breaking slightly from the off-to leg. But the ball he has been as successful with as any is a simple, straight, good length one, without any break. The batsman expects something exceptional from him every ball, and never thinks that he will treat him with such an easy one; and so, while he is looking for the break, his wicket is bowled down.' So writes W. G. Grace of Lohmann, and this description shows what a vast amount of head and skill is required to become a successful bowler on modern wickets.

The improvement of grounds is, perhaps, the chief cause of the development of bowling, but the batting of W. G. Grace and the bowling of the Australians of 1878, 1880, and 1882, are two other factors to be considered, W. G. Grace began his first-class cricket on the old-fashioned wickets to the old-fashioned bowling. As the wickets gradually improved, all fast bowling became to him child's play. Cricketers of that time will tell you that if you wanted to get him out on a good wicket, you stood a better chance of doing so with two inferior slow bowlers than with Freeman and Martin McIntyre. Slow bowling, largely owing to this cause, came in, and about 1877 there were a host of slow bowlers – Shaw, Lockwood, Barratt, Watson, Southerton, Midwinter, Strachan, Grace, W. S. Patterson, F. M. Buckland, A. P. Lucas, and many others – playing in first-class cricket. They were not all good; some were almost bad, but, bad as they were, they succeeded better than good fast bowlers did, and at this time English bowling was at a low ebb.

In the following year, 1878, the Australians first came to England, and Spofforth and Boyle began a new and glorious era. Spectators rubbed their eyes at what they saw. They saw two bowlers of consummate skill adopting a quite new method. On the hard dry wickets at Sydney and Melbourne, these bowlers had found out what English bowlers had not yet discovered, that to get batsmen out on modern wickets it was no good trusting to any assistance from the ground, but to your own head. They bowled differently, and they placed the field differently. They dispensed altogether with a long-stop, they bowled many balls off the wicket, and no two consecutive balls were bowled with similar paces. The famous M.C.C. match, when Spofforth and Boyle got rid of a strong M.C.C. eleven for 33 and 19, may well be taken as a starting point in the new era of cricket.

From this time, slowly, perhaps, but surely, the English learnt from the Colonists, and now they have beaten them on their own ground. From 1860 to 1870 bowling was mainly fast; from 1870 to 1878 it became mainly slow; from 1878 to 1891 it cannot be accurately classified under either of these heads. Lohmann, Peel, and Attewell, are not slow or fast. They never bowl a raking fast ball, but a mistake of the wicket-keep to Attewell or Peel on Woolwich Common would mean five byes. The bowling of the present day is of infinite variety of pace, length, and direction, and the change is owing to the improvement of grounds, which made fast bowling easy. W. G. Grace's skill first brought this fact powerfully to the cricketer's mind, and the example of Spofforth, Boyle, and Palmer, who inaugurated the new order of bowlers, completed the tale.

What we have said hitherto refers chiefly to the development of bowling, which so largely influences batting that the two act and re-act on each other. It is quite as difficult to judge of the respective merits of the batting giants of twenty-five or thirty years ago as compared with those of to-day, as it is in the case of bowlers. As difficult wickets make batsmen weak and bowlers strong, so easy wickets make batsmen strong and bowlers weak. It is quite safe to assume that Hayward, Carpenter, Parr, Mitchell, and Daft, for instance, would have been great bats in any age and under any circumstances, as Shrewsbury, Gunn, O'Brien, and Steel would. The great bats of any particular time would be great under any conditions. In one sense, however, we admit that the batsmen of twenty-five years ago excelled those of to-day, and we say, judging from a purely aesthetic standard, the play of first-class bats now is infinitely less graceful than it used to be. We are not prepared to admit that this fact is owing to the fault of the batsmen themselves; on the contrary, we think it is the fault of the bowlers for the following reason.

There can be no question that bowling is far more accurate now than formerly, for fast bowling must, of necessity, afford greater facilities to the hitter than the slow and medium. The bowling is now so accurate, and the field so carefully placed, that the batsman, in order to get runs, must resort to what our venerable friend would call unorthodox hitting. If Attewell is bowling nine out of ten balls on the off-stump, or outside the off-stump, of a beautiful length, and with eight fields on the off-side, what are you to do to score? You must obviously hit where fields do not stand, and this is only on the on-side; in other words, you must pull, and if the pull comes off, you score four runs. Now a pull is ugly, brutal, and effective, and is a product of modern accuracy in attack, and if you want to see it in full development, go to the Oval and watch W. W. Read and K. J. Key.

Take another hit that modern bowling has completely wiped out of first-class cricket – the leg hit. Look at the accounts of the players of thirty years ago, and you will find So-and-so described as a fine leg hitter. Who can be so described now, and how can anyone be, when there are no leg balls bowled to hit? You will see more leg hitting in one public school match to-day than you will in any four first-class matches you may choose. A striking testimony, no doubt, to the splendid science of the modern bowler: but, shade of Parr, we should like to see Parr at one end and R. A. H. Mitchell at the other for an hour, and each get a leg ball every four overs. To hit a leg ball square over the ropes at Lord's is the greatest and most supreme delight that can fall to the lot of a batsman, and next, perhaps, to the perfect cut, there is nothing in cricket more enjoyable to watch, from the spectators' point of view. We heard an old cricketer remark, at this year's Eton and Harrow match, when Brewis made a fine hit to square leg, 'That is the first genuine leg hit I have seen this year.'

So many modern bowlers bowl for catchers – that is, they place the fields and bowl accordingly – that the batsmen, knowing and understanding the tactics, hesitate to hit, and that is another reason why play is less graceful – it has to be more careful. Broadly speaking, we assert that if hitting has declined in form and style, accurate defence has developed in a wonderful degree, but defence, however good, cannot be so fascinating as graceful and vigorous hitting.

Fielding is easier now than it used to be, for the grounds are smoother, but it ought to be better than it is, and the same remark, we suspect, would have applied thirty years ago. There is not much fault to be found with the ground fielding, but far too many catches are dropped, breaking the hearts of bowlers and creating unspeakable feelings in the minds of partisans. Why so many catches are dropped, it is difficult to understand. We are not discussing catches that are not easy, but the feasible two-hand catches that go straight into the hands and promptly drop out again; and it is a shocking sight to see young cricketers, amateur and professional, equally blameable as the veteran.

There is one development of fielding that is the outcome of the smooth grounds and accurate bowling, and that is the astonishing precision of the wicket-keeping. There is nothing so awe-inspiring in cricket at the present day as to see Woods bowling on a hard wicket, and McGregor calmly standing up to the wicket with no long-stop. This state of things never existed in the wildest imagination of anybody thirty years ago, and from it we learn the facts, that even the fast amateur bowlers practically never bowl a leg ball, and that the modern wickets are so good that the old-fashioned shooter is nearly as extinct as the dodo. It was Blackham, the great Australian, who first set this fashion, and we cannot close this article in any more graceful way than by rendering our tribute to the Australians, that, while they taught us little, or perhaps nothing, in batting, to Blackham we owe the dispensing with a long-stop, and that in

Spofforth, Boyle, Palmer, Giffen, and Turner, we have glorious examples of the infinite resource, intelligence, and accuracy that, together blended, make the great bowlers of this year of grace, 1891.

HINTS FROM THE PRESS BOX [1893]

BY C. S. C.

It was perfectly natural that men like the Pardons and their assistants should feel particularly strongly about conditions offered to them by the various county committees. Facilities in the Press boxes of the period were often so primitive that the very term was no more than a euphemism for no facilities at all, and Pardon campaigned against this neglect for most his tenure at the Almanack, particularly with reference to the M.C.C. Not until 1867 had the Marylebone Club bothered with the Press at all; before then, any reporters had to take their chances in the crowd. One of Wisden's men, W. H. Knight, was obliged to compose his fulsome orotundities from the sanctuary of the shrubberies on either side of the pavilion, taking care also to compile his own score-book in the absence of match-cards. In 1893 Pardon was moved to complain in his annual editorial notes:

> At Lord's the arrangements for Press men are far from adequate, and, I imagine, it is only the uniform courtesy which one experiences from everyone connected with the Headquarters of cricket that has prevented strong representations being made to the M.C.C. The accommodation is far too tough and limited, and, indeed, quite unworthy of Lord's Cricket Ground.

By 1900 the scandal of the Press facilities at Lord's had spilled over into the correspondence columns of 'The Times', where a small group of choleric gentlemen raved and ranted about assorted inadequacies on the Ground. In 1901 the M.C.C. opened a new improved Press box, which disappeared during a severe storm in 1906. For the next fifty-two years the Press was housed in an extension of the pavilion, before being moved to the Warner Stand in 1958, from which they could watch the game from the peculiar perspective of long leg. These conditions, while not quite ideal, were at least an improvement on the facilities suggested with bitter irony by the 'Punch' cartoonist Harry Furniss, well-known for his determination to be vituperative about something at all times. Furniss, in a splendid burst of Wodehousean lunacy, accused the M.C.C. of behaving so badly that 'the Press is turned out of the stand and relegated to the tool-shed, or, perhaps, to the roller horse's stable'. In the following year Pardon, in registering the sober truth, was obliged to go very nearly as far as Furniss's irony when he complained that:

> I cannot pass over without comment the treatment of the Press representatives at Lord's on the occasion of the Oxford and Cambridge, and Eton and Harrow matches. It was an ungracious and uncalled-for act to shift them from the grandstand to the roof of the ground bowler's house in the corner of the ground.

The truth was that representatives of the Press, even of Wisden and 'The Times', were looked down on by more than one county committee as no more than beggars at the feast, necessary evils which were part of the price to be paid for the ever-rising public interest in the game. In his 1893 edition, not only did Pardon publish his own list of grievances, but he also printed a pseudonymous essay on life in the Press box by a certain C. S. C. whose identity is not very difficult to deduce.

Charles Stewart Caine (1861–1933), Portsmouth-born, lived all his life in the purlieus of Fleet Street, even being educated at Stationers' School, located in Bolt Court. After leaving school he began reporting cricket matches, and was one of a group of young men who joined the Pardon brothers in the Cricket Reporting Agency. A modest man renowned for his powers of discretion, Caine was eventually to succeed to the editorship, in which post he strove mightily to contain the Almanack within manageable proportions. He always believed that the Almanack was 'essentially a book of reference, and as such should not be allowed to become unwieldy'. This sounds like an enemy of the discursive essay, but Caine, when at last he did succeed to the editorial chair, was wise enough to maintain the policy of the Pardons. His 'Hints from the Press Box' is a perfect example of journalistic sobriety.

MANY men I have met have said to me, 'What a jolly life is yours, watching cricket matches all through the summer!' Yes, the life of a cricket reporter is in many respects a jolly one, seeing that his duty takes him where many thousands of his countrymen assemble for their pleasure. Given fine weather and a good wicket, I know no greater enjoyment than watching the varying fortunes of a game between two well-matched sides, and there are very few phases of journalistic life for which I would care to exchange that of a cricket reporter. One's duties, however, are not confined to looking on at a game at cricket and then sending off an account of what has taken place, as appears to be the idea of the general public. In the first place, looking on at a cricket match as a casual spectator and as a reporter are two very different things. The ordinary onlooker watches the play perhaps quite as keenly as he who has to record the many incidents of the game for the newspapers, but his attention is close or slack according as the play is exciting or not, whereas the man whose duty it is to give a faithful record of what takes place must not let his attention wander for a moment. From the time the first ball is bowled until the drawing of stumps, a matter often of more than seven hours, he has to keep his attention closely fixed upon the game and note every incident. This duty of itself would be a very slight one, but unfortunately for the reporter the exigencies of modern newspaper work necessitate the despatch of telegrams at frequent intervals from within a few minutes of the start of play until the call of time. Now were absolute accuracy not an essential, there would be no great strain in all this, but as that must be the first consideration, with promptitude of despatch next, the cricket writer who aims furthermore to bring out the salient features of the day's cricket (and in this respect the writers on the game to-day have, on Lord Harris's testimony, improved upon their predecessors) has no easy task before him. If he makes a slip in adding up a score, or fails to exercise the utmost promptitude in handing in a message at the telegraph office, he is speedily brought to book: whilst if in writing for morning papers he omits to notice any remarkable incident or prominent feature in the day's play, he is disgusted with himself.

That the cricket reporter does strive his utmost to furnish an accurate and intelligent account of what has taken place I can state as the result of many years' experience; indeed, I know no body of Press men who are keener about their work. Therefore it is that I claim they should be enabled to pursue their avocation under the most advantageous conditions. Three things are absolutely necessary in order that a cricket reporter may follow his calling with advantage to the public and with comfort to himself. First of all a good view of the game is required; next, a convenient place in which to write; and, beyond these necessities, he should be placed in close proximity to the scorers. At many grounds in days gone by, and at some enclosures at the present time, the last consideration was the placing of the Press tent or box in a position whence anything like a fair idea of the game was obtainable. Some corner at long-leg or deep in the slips was apparently the most suitable spot, according to the ideas of a county committee, and if the ground fell off in any direction, there, at the bottom of the slope, were the reporters placed. How, seated as they were, anyone but a committeeman could expect them to obtain an accurate idea of what was taking place passed comprehension, and yet, apart from the players, who, especially the young ones, never care what is said in the papers, there were no people more ready to complain of a real or imagined inaccuracy than the members of a county executive. A tent, usually facing the wind, was considered the most desirable covering for men during eight hours of the day, and even when a Press box was provided, the structure was generally a bare wooden erection in which little protection was afforded from sun, wind, or rain. Again, the Press men were placed at one end of the ground, and their very good friends, the official scorers, at the other; whilst when, owing largely to the representations of newspaper men, the telegraph wires were extended to the ground, no effort was made to place the Press box and the telegraph office in proximity.

In many respects matters have, I am glad to think, changed for the better within the last fifteen years, and the managers of cricket grounds are beginning to realise that cricket reporters are not so much necessary evils as men whose efforts do much to popularise the game. While much has been improved of late years, however, only at a few grounds is the necessity of affording immediate and accurate information as to the prospects of play, for instance, adequately recognised. At one ground, too, admission to the pavilion is barred to newspaper men in quest of information concerning a match, but only in a district where it is considered desirable to separate by iron fences the members of a county club from the ordinary visitors to a cricket match. It may not be out of place if I briefly run through the chief cricket grounds of England, and point out where they might easily be improved. In many respects Kennington Oval affords an excellent example to other grounds, for the Press box is lofty and spacious, near the scorers, and in connection by lift with the telegraph office, whilst lavatory accommodation – no slight comfort on a hot August day – is also provided. The desks, however, are ill-adapted for hard work, and better seats – dare I say cushioned seats? – might also be provided.

At Lord's the arrangements for Press men are far from adequate, and, I imagine, it is only the uniform courtesy which one experiences from everyone connected with the headquarters of cricket that has prevented strong representations being made to the M.C.C. The accommodation is far too rough and limited, and indeed quite unworthy of Lord's Cricket Ground. Up in Yorkshire a good view is, as a rule, obtainable, but the managers of grounds have an abominable habit of placing the scorers about a hundred yards away from the reporters' box, and thus quite fail to realise the necessity for placing reporters, scorers, and telegraph clerks close to one another. At Sheffield, too, the place reserved for reporters is absurdly small, and should at least be doubled in extent. There is a wooden shanty in a bad position which does duty for a Press box at Trent Bridge, Nottingham, but except that it is shared by the telegraph clerks, anything more inadequate as a place for newspaper men to do their work in, it would not be easy to imagine. The view obtainable there from is a long-leg one; the box is raised only two or three feet from the ground, and, furthermore, attention is distracted by people passing in front all day long. Nottingham is a delightful town, but Trent Bridge can boast, I think, of the least desirable Press box in England.

After troublous times with the officials at Old Trafford, and journeying from the corner of a covered stand to a wretched box which let in wind, rain, and dust (whichever was the most prominent nuisance of the day), the Manchester Press men have at length obtained a suitable structure in which to do their work. A capital view is obtainable, and the telegraph office is below, but, with that perversity which is the curse of county committees, the scorers are still placed a hundred yards or so distant. Old Trafford, however, is probably the most difficult cricket ground in England at which to obtain information; and whereas everywhere else a Press man can after rain make inquiries in the pavilion whether play is to be continued or the game to be abandoned, I have known the first news of a decision to be conveyed by the sight of the players carrying away their bags to the gates of the Manchester ground. Inasmuch as the executive have built a very good Press box, and thereby shown some consideration for those who, in the pursuit of their calling, have brought heaps of money to the Lancashire County Club, I trust they will take further steps in the path of courtesy, and remove from the Manchester ground the reputation it possesses amongst Press men of being the most disagreeable place in England at which to have to do work. Liverpool, owing to the lack of consideration shown by the telegraph authorities, would have no big cricket matches if reporters had their way; but the arrangements at the ground are fairly good, and one may venture into the pavilion without risk of suffering an indignity. At Derby, Press men are fairly well off, except for the distance from the scorers; but at Leicester, of late, the arrangements are far from good, whilst at Birmingham the defects have, I am glad to know, been remedied, with the important exception of a telegraph office on the ground. Down in Kent reporters at cricket matches generally have to sit in tents, and if these were placed with better judgment they would be by no means disagreeable in fine weather; but at the great Canterbury festival I have noticed a gradual tendency to diminish the extent of the Press tent, until it is nowadays by no means large enough to enable those whose duties take them to the St. Lawrence ground to conduct their business in comfort. One of the first of Press boxes was that at Brighton, and though it is now a little old-fashioned, the scorers are at hand and the telegraph office is at no great distance. When, however, the Sussex County Club have money to spare, they would do well to erect a structure at one end of the ground, with the telegraph office below and room for both scorers and reporters above.

In the West, again, or rather I should say in Gloucestershire, badly-placed tents are still in vogue, but they are preferable to the small and unsatisfactory box at the Bristol ground, whence only two or three can properly view the game. Down at Taunton everything naturally is on a smaller scale than at the more famous cricket centres, but I take this opportunity of tendering to the Somerset County Club, on behalf of my fellow-Press men, the assurance of our appreciation of the efforts made for the convenience of reporters. With the scorers on our left and the telegraph-office below, the Taunton Press box is one which, with some increase in dimensions, might serve as a pattern all over the country.

Another help to reporters I should like to see extended to all grounds would be the erection of scoring boards, upon which each one is registered as it is made, such are in use at Lord's, Kennington Oval, and Nottingham, and the practice at Lord's, the Oval, and Brighton of granting newspaper men unlimited printed slips of the score during the day is also a great convenience. A Press box should be placed as nearly as possible in a line with the two wickets, so that an end-on view is obtained therefrom, and it should be raised a considerable height from the ground, with the scorers close at hand, and the telegraph clerks below. These requirements are absolutely necessary for the due fulfilment of a cricket reporter's duties, and considering the importance which is now attached to the game of cricket, and the space which is devoted to it in the newspapers, I think that they are no more than county cricket clubs may be reasonably asked to concede.

THE 'FOLLOW-ON' [1894]

BY S. H. PARDON

Ever on the alert for controversial topics, Pardon in his 1894 edition pounced on the issues raised by the sensational Varsity match of the previous season, in which the two captains became so obsessed with outmanoeuvring each other that they turned Lord's into a bear-garden. In those days, any side batting second and failing to come within 80 runs of its opponent's total was obliged to follow on. With the Oxford score at 98 for 9, with 5 runs still required to avoid the follow-on, the last Oxford pair were seen conversing in the centre of the pitch, at which point it became clear to some of the shrewder observers that the Oxford tactic was to throw away the last wicket and bat again, thus obliging Cambridge to bat last on what seemed certain to be a crumbling wicket. But the Cambridge star bowler C. M. Wells, deducing the situation, decided to frustrate one piece of deviousness with another. When the two batsmen were ready to resume play, Wells bowled a no-ball wide to the boundary, and then attempted, unsuccessfully as it happened, to bowl a wide all along the ground. He then sent a round-arm wide to the ropes, thus giving away 8 runs and swelling Oxford's score to beyond the mark at which they would have to follow on.
The uproar which followed obliged the M.C.C. to consider altering the rules, and in July 1984 it was decreed that the margin of deficit should be 100 runs instead of 80. Unwisely, the legislators resisted demands that in order to avoid further fiascos, the follow-on should not be compulsory. In 1896 with Oxford in the identical position of being 9 wickets down and a handful of runs short of the required amount, the Cambridge captain instructed his bowler to deliver three no-balls to the boundary, thus giving his opponents 12 runs and enabling Cambridge to bat again. In his history of Lord's, Pelham Warner writes that 'on returning to the pavilion the Cambridge eleven were hooted at by members of the M.C.C., and in the pavilion itself there were angry scenes, many members losing all control over themselves'. Pardon's view was that 'this display of passion was altogether uncalled for'. It is surprising that it was not until the annual general meeting of the M.C.C.

in May 1900 that the law was again amended, this time to read: 'The side which leads by 150 runs in a three-day match shall have the option *of calling on the other side to follow its innings'. But surely more remarkable than any of this was the revelation appearing in the Almanack for 1894, where, in the symposium on 'The Follow On', featuring the views of such distinguished figures as E. M. Grace, Richard Daft, Ivo Bligh, F. S. Jackson and Johnny Briggs, it was stated that 'neither W. G. Grace, Andrew Stoddart or William Gunn preferred to express any opinion on the point'.*
The 1894 Almanack is also remembered as the one in which the youthful C. B. Fry, reviewing Public School cricket, made an inspired stab at prophecy by writing that 'J. R. Mason of Winchester is a performer of phenomenal merit'. Mason went on to become captain of Kent, an England player and one of the outstanding all-rounders of the Edwardian era.

THE much-discussed incident in the Oxford and Cambridge match last season brought into sudden prominence the question of the advisability of some alteration being made in the present law which governs the follow on. Up till within a comparatively recent period it was generally regarded as a distinct advantage to gain a lead of 80 or more runs on the first innings, and so compel the opposing side to go in for the second time; but there has gradually come about a marked change of opinion on this point, captains having found that on the carefully-prepared wickets to which we are accustomed at the present day there is considerable risk in having to bowl and field through two innings in succession. So far as I am aware, the desirability of some change in the law was first broached in Australia, where the big matches are played through to a finish, irrespective of the number of days they may occupy, and where, moreover, the dryness of the grounds made the question more pressing than up to last season it had been with us. Indeed, little attention had been given to the matter in England until the occasion of the Oxford and Cambridge match in July, when Oxford's attempt to secure a follow on and Mr. C. M. Wells's successful endeavours to frustrate their intention set all cricketing England talking upon the subject. Thinking that a free discussion on the point would be of interest to the readers of WISDEN'S ALMANACK, I communicated with a large number of prominent players and other first-rate authorities, whose various views may be found in the following pages. As might have been expected, I found considerable diversity of opinion existing.—S. H. P.

MR. E. M. GRACE says:—'The rule about the "follow on" was no doubt made with the idea that the apparently winning side should still have an advantage, and the same thing follows about declaring the innings over. I think it would be a good alteration in the rule if the leading side should have the option of doing which they thought best. This would prevent both the bowlers from bowling wides and the batsman from trying to get out. And in one-day matches it would prevent such a case as this. Say A. is playing B. A. makes 121 runs, and when B. has made 60 he has one, two, or three wickets to fall, as the case might be B.'s captain says,

"Our innings is over," and, as the law now is, B.'s side go on batting, instead of, perhaps, having to field the rest of the day.'

MR. R. A. H. MITCHELL writes:—'I think the best solution of the difficulty is to abolish the "follow on" altogether, and to allow the closure to be applied at any time, instead of restricting it to the last day of the match. Gate-money considerations may cause some objection to be raised to this, but they ought not to outweigh the interests of sport. When the present rule was made, there was not power, as now, to close the innings. In one-day matches I would let the rule stand as it is now for many obvious reasons. Some have proposed that the side which is 80 or more runs ahead at the close of the first innings shall have the option of putting the other side in, or going in again themselves. This, I think, would be very unfair. The side that has the advantage has already won the toss, and possibly gained this advantage thereby. The option would again give them the choice of going in first or second, as their interests decided. In this way you would increase the value of winning the toss. Now, most people think that the advantage is already unduly great. You might, of course, raise the number from 80 to 100, 120, or 150, or fix a percentage to decide whether a side is to follow on, but I do not think this would be so satisfactory.'

MR. RICHARD DAFT says:—'I think the "follow on" rule should be done away with now that the declaring rule has come in.'

MR. A. P. LUCAS writes:—'With regard to the "follow on" rule, I do not see how it can be altered. I do not think the number of runs a side is behind ought to be increased so that they must follow on, as it would be putting them to a greater disadvantage than they are now. Generally the side winning the toss has a great advantage, and therefore I think the other side ought to have some advantage if possible. It sometimes happens that the side going in first have a good hard wicket to bat on, and then there is some rain, so that the side which lost the toss have a wet wicket to bat on, and so have to follow on. By the time their second innings is finished the wicket is fast again, and the other side have a great advantage. In a case like this I do not think the side winning the toss ought to have so great an advantage. The only way to avoid this would be to do away with the "follow on" altogether, and this I should like to see done. Now that the closure rule is in force I do not think the following on rule is needed. I cannot help thinking that the closure might be applied on the second day of a match instead of the third.'

MR. JOHN SHUTER, one of the very few cricketers who are in favour of letting the matter stand exactly as it does, writes:—'I am very strongly of opinion that the present law in connection with the "follow on" needs no alteration. I think I am correct in stating that in the very large majority of cases the side which follows on loses the match. For this reason alone the present law must be a good one. Any change in the law in the direction of abolishing the compulsory part of the "follow on" would, in all probability, tend to an increase in the number of drawn matches—a result which is most undesirable.'

The Hon. Ivo Bligh says:—'I hold the opinion strongly that the rule *re* "following on" should be altered, making it optional for the side who have the lead whether they make the others follow on or not.'

Mr. J. A. Dixon is of the same opinion as Mr. Bligh. He writes:—'I am in favour of an alteration in the present rule to the effect that the "follow on" shall be at the option of the side batting first and scoring 80 runs more than their opponents.'

Mr. H. T. Hewett says:—'I should like to see the "follow on" entirely abolished and Law 54 amended so as to empower a side to close their innings at any period of the match, and, should occasion arise, to waive their claim to a second innings.'

Mr. F. S. Jackson, who was captain of the Cambridge team in 1893, had necessarily a strong personal interest in the matter. He says:—'The present rule, "80 runs behind, follow on," is out of date, and that for two reasons—(1) a new rule has been introduced enabling the captains to declare an innings on the last day of a match at an end; (2) the grounds are too good, and give too much advantage, in my opinion, to the side 80 runs behind on the first innings. This is my proposal: To make the number of runs behind 90, and make it optional for the captain of the side with 90 runs advantage either to go in himself—having in view, of course, the declaring of his innings at an end—or put the other side in again, which, of course, he would do if he saw any advantage. You would thus do away with such a forced fiasco as a 4 no-ball, a 4 wide, &c., as in the 'Varsity match of 1893. I very much want to hear other views on the subject.'

The veteran Robert Carpenter is another of the supporters of the "optional" theory. He writes:—'In my opinion the granting to that side who have placed their opponents 80 runs behind on the first innings the option of going in themselves or making the others follow on would do good, it being a harmless alteration of the law. It would be difficult to frame a law to keep cricketers from playing as suited them best, according to how the match stood, but this giving choice would do away with certain loose play connected with the "follow on." '

Robert Thoms, the most experienced of umpires, and an old and valued correspondent of Wisden, is also in favour of letting the "follow on" be at the option of the side which has gained a lead of 80 or more on the first innings, his view, though expressed at greater length being identical with that of Carpenter. He says:—'Like the closure, which latterly was added to the laws, I am inclined to think it would be beneficial if our cricket legislators—the Marylebone Club—were to modify Law 53 as to the "follow on," by giving the option of choice to the side holding the lead of whether they will put their opponents in the minority of 80 on the first innings in again, or whether they would go in for their second innings themselves instead. Having on many occasions seen false play arise—attached to this "follow on" business—wherein bowlers and fieldsmen don't try to get the batsmen out, but rather to let them get runs, and *vice versa*—batsmen wilfully getting themselves out—leads me to believe that if the law were qualified—to render it optional—as above stated, it would, like the "closure," do away with a loophole that tends at times to bring forth unseemly play in the cricket ground. Not that, if even this alteration be granted, it will stop other "subterfuges" from occasionally cropping up. For in cricket, as in every other game, *finesse* will be resorted to in the hope of averting defeat. But that I need not dwell on, for the grand old game is played with the greatest keenness and integrity, and this matter of alteration—to be or not to be—will be decided by the M.C.C., who are ever watchful for the best interests of our national game.'

MR. W. NEWHAM says:—'My opinion is that the side holding the advantage of the 80 runs lead should have the option of either going in themselves or sending their opponents in the second time. My reason for taking such a view as this is that, under ordinary circumstances, this advantage would not be gained until some time on the second day of the match, so that the side having this lead could bat for the remainder of the day, and then, taking advantage of the closure rule, would be able to send in their opponents as soon as they wished on the third day.'

MR. M. C. KEMP writes:—'I am in favour of any change in the law with regard to the "follow on" which will be likely to reduce the number of drawn games, and not give the side which follows on an advantage to which its failure to avert the follow on does not entitle it. I am in favour of raising the number of runs considerably—up to 120 if necessary. If the present number, 80, be retained, the question of the "follow on" should, in my opinion, be left to the decision of the captain of the side which has the lead of 80 runs. I should also have no objection to seeing a captain empowered to declare his innings over on the second day if his side have, in his opinion, made a sufficient number of runs. This, I fancy, would diminish the number of drawn games due to one side making a phenomenal score, and not leaving themselves time to get their opponents out.'

MR. C. W. WRIGHT shares Mr. Shuter's opinion that the law should remain unchanged. He says:—'Of course there are distinctly two sides to the question of the "follow on." In the first place I don't think the question would have arisen if the past had not been an exceptional season for hard wickets and batsmen, and the unfortunate incident had not occurred in the 'Varsity match. We all know that after getting a big score—say, 380—when the opposite side goes in and makes 290, it seems very hard to have to go on bowling and fielding when tired out, but then that depends solely on the toss. If you alter the rule, and say the fielding side shall have the choice whether they bat or make the other side follow on, you give a distinct advantage to the stronger side over the weaker, which isn't fair. For instance, in our ordinary English summer this may happen at any time:—Notts v. Yorkshire, Monday, July 1st. Notts win the toss; go in on a good, slow wicket (weather threatening); make 160; all out at 4.30. Yorkshire go in; make 20 for two wickets, when down comes the rain. It also rains early Tuesday morning. At ten o'clock out comes a blazing sun; Yorkshire have a piece of birdlime to bat on at first;

never recover themselves, though the wicket improves, and are all out for 70 (90 behind). The wicket rolls out plumb. It is a monstrous thing that Notts should have the option of going in to bat on a plumb wicket after Yorkshire have had all the bad luck of losing the toss and in the matter of weather. To go on: Notts go in again; make 260 for six wickets at lunch on Wednesday; declare; put Yorkshire in, with 350 to win. Notts cannot lose, and have ample time to get Yorkshire out fourth innings on the worn wicket. Yorkshire in this case may be a better side than Notts, and yet are robbed of the match through the weather and not being allowed to follow on. My illustration is, of course, rather far-fetched, but still you will see the gist of my argument, and on the whole, I think, the law ought to remain as it is.'

The HON. EDWARD LYTTELTON writes:—'In my opinion the 60 and 80 runs should be 100 and 150 to constitute the difference between two totals necessary for a "follow on," in a one day's and two (three) days' match respectively. I should reserve the option to the side which lost the toss, both of following on and of making the enemy follow on. The result would be that it would not often occur; but with the rule of closing the innings it would not often be required.'

MR. GEORGE MARSHAM, of the Kent County Club, writes:— 'I am of opinion that the closure should be allowed at any time on the second or third day of a county match. I think this matter is closely connected with the "follow on," which I should do away with altogether, unless the number of runs be altered to some percentage to be agreed upon after due consideration.'

MR. C. M. WELLS, whose action in the University match—so unjustly blamed in some quarters—brought the question into prominence, writes: —'I feel very strongly that some change should be made in the rule for "following on." Surely it is not right that the side following on should thereby gain a distinct advantage, as happens not infrequently; for example, in the Australian match against Cambridge University, when the former, being about 90 runs behind on the first innings, followed on and battled against tired bowling on a perfect wicket, with the result that they piled up a large score and made the 'Varsity take fourth innings on a crumbled wicket. I think that the simplest alteration would be as follows:—If one side A is 80 runs behind another side B on the first innings, then the captain of B shall have the power to decide whether A shall follow on or his own side take their second innings.'

JAMES LILLYWHITE says:—'With regard to the "following on" law when a side is 80 runs behind, my opinion is that the side 80 runs to the good should have the choice of again sending their opponents to the wickets or batting again themselves, whichever in their judgment was thought best, so that the advantage gained, probably by superior play under even conditions, should not be so often lost by having to bat last on a worn wicket, or, perhaps worse, a sticky one, after a wet night. By the leading team having the option of doing this the farce that we sometimes see of one side trying to get out, and the other trying to allow them to get a few more runs, will be stopped, and the difficulty, I think, surmounted. I think 80 runs a fair margin.'

WILLIAM ATTEWELL says:—'My opinion on the "follow on" is that it ought to be at the option of the side which has gained the lead, and I would keep the number of runs at 80 as at present.'

JOHN BRIGGS:—'As regards the "follow on" at cricket, my opinion is that it ought to be altered. Suppose Notts are playing against Lancashire, and Lancashire make, say, over 300 runs. Notts go in on a good wicket, and make the runs, less 83; they would, as the rule stands, follow on to their advantage, bowlers being tired. Notts then make a very good score against loose bowling, and as a matter of fact have the best of the game. I think in this case Lancashire should have the choice to bat or send Notts in again. I do not know if anyone else will fall in with my views, but I should like the change to come into force.'

MAURICE READ writes:—'As regards the "follow on," I think that if there is anything that can be done to further the interest of the game, it should be done, and there is no doubt there will be a great deal said about "following on," as I see the question is to be brought up at Lord's. I think in the event of a side failing to save the follow on, the opposing captain should be allowed to go in or send his opponents in, because I have often known it happen that it has been much better for a side not to save the follow on after having lost their best bats, and with the wicket still good, and the consequence is that only wanting a few runs to save the follow, and the last man going in, he, as is so often the case, has orders to get out. Perhaps it might be altered to advantage by making the number higher—instead of 80 runs make it more.'

The HON. R. H. LYTTELTON, discussing the question more fully than any of my other correspondents, and also taking an entirely independent view, writes as follows:—'The number of runs a side have to be behind in order to follow their innings is 80. This rule holds good in Australia, where there is comparatively an equable climate and the wickets are generally easy, and in England, where the wickets are sometimes in favour of batsmen and sometimes in favour of bowlers, seldom equally divided between the two. Twenty-five years ago a side that won the toss on a good wicket were happy when they got 180 runs, and got their opponents out for 100 in their first innings. But if on following their innings their opponents secured 150, they would have put the first side in for 70 runs to win, and in those days that was a sufficient number to keep up the interest of the match. Now in a year like 1893 the first innings of the side that wins the toss realises 300, the other side gets 220, and follows on and gets 230. The wicket, even on Lord's or Fenner's, has now begun to show some signs of wear and tear, the side that won the toss have fielded out for 450 runs, and the odds are about even that they will not get 150 runs to win the match. But suppose the side that went in second saved the follow by one run, the first side with a light heart would go in again with a majority of 79, and would very likely knock up 200 runs and stand to win the match. There can be no doubt that if 80 runs was a fair number twenty-five years ago, it is too few now on hard wickets favouring the batsmen. But on soft, tricky wickets, favouring the bowlers, it is too many, for if ever a bet is safe at cricket it is, on such wickets, to back the side that is 50 or even 40 runs ahead at the end of the first innings. On such wickets 50 runs behind would be fairer than 80 to follow on. What, if any, is the remedy for these inconsistencies? It is rumoured that the law is to be altered whereby the side that is 80 runs ahead on the first innings is to have the option of making the other side follow on or go in themselves. One great objection there is to this amended rule, and that is that it adds another to the already formidable number of advantages gained by winning the toss. But speaking with a measure of reserve, I think it would be worth while to try the experiment of amending the rule in this way; if it did not answer it could be repealed. But I also think there must be a limit each way. On hard, easy wickets perhaps 120 runs behind would be a fairer number than 80; on soft, difficult wickets 50 would be enough. But it seems ridiculous to have one fixed number for all countries, climates, and wickets, and though I am by no means sure that the change would, in the long run, be beneficial, I think it might be tried, for at any rate it would abolish the fixed quantity absurdity.'

MR. W. G. GRACE, MR. A. E. STODDART, and WILLIAM GUNN preferred not to express any opinion on the point.

MR. V. E. WALKER writes:—'Being on the committee of the M.C.C., who are now discussing the "follow on" rule, I do not wish my private opinion to appear, but I shall read with interest the opinions you propose to publish in WISDEN.'

MR. HENRY PERKINS, the secretary of the M.C.C., expressed no personal opinion on the matter, but stated that the committee of the M.C.C. have already taken the opinion of leading cricketers as to the desirability of amending Law 53, and will bring the question before the general meeting of the club on May 2, 1894.

CRICKETERS – PAST AND PRESENT [1895]

BY AN OLD CAMBRIDGE CAPTAIN

In 1895 the Almanack inadvertently set a puzzle to be solved, perhaps by the investigators of a later age. For reasons which can only be guessed at, the ex-Cambridge University captain who expressed his view of 'Cricketers, Past and Present' preferred to remain cloaked by the pseudonymous device which confounded readers. As by this time there had been dozens of old

Cambridge captains, and as any one of them would have been happy to respond to an invitation from the cricketer's bible, it becomes a hopeless task trying to narrow down the likely culprits. Whoever he was, this old leader must have been ranging in age between, say 22—he could have captained his varsity in the previous season—and at least 90. We know also that he was no iconoclast, because the sentiments with which he ends his review are as beautifully conventional as the most fanatical traditionalist could wish. If today a writer on cricket were to take his leave with 'in all religious, political, and secular affairs of life, as well as in every match, may the best side win', he would be greeted with derision, for reasons which might not stand too much scrutiny. At any rate, the writer of this essay represents one of the many minor unsolved mysteries of cricket history. Many of the documents pertaining to the history of the Almanack were destroyed in the Second World War, with the result that the trail seems now to be as dead as the old Cambridge captain himself.

VERY few persons will agree about the relative merits of past and present cricketers. Wherein do they differ? Were the batsmen of half a century ago equal to those of to-day? Was the bowling as straight and as difficult then as it is now? These are questions which are not very easy to answer. I do not wish to take the position of a dogmatic umpire upon them, as some of my friends do. 'What,' they exclaim, 'is the good of discussing the subject? Look at the gigantic scores. Look at the batting averages. Look at the bowling feats. Look at the brilliant fielding. Look at the truly magnificent wicket-keeping. The past will not bear comparison with the present in any department of the game.' But I venture to think that there is a little, at any rate, to be said on the other side. The cricketers of a bygone age are not to be robbed of their glory without some calm considerations. Are the environments similar? Were the general purposes of the old batsmen the same as those of the modern school? In what respect is the bowling of to-day superior to that of the best bowlers, say, of the day when W. G. Grace first began to play?

I notice that most of the writers upon cricket make gods of their own contemporary heroes; and this is very natural, for their special style and exploits get indelibly fixed in the mind and necessarily affect the judgment. But it is a little irritating to be told that such a boat was the finest that ever rowed on the Thames; or such an eleven the best that ever left any University; or some particular batsman the best (W. G. being, of course condescendingly barred) that ever handled the willow. Superlatives are dangerous weapons and require very cautious handling. And equally annoying is the modest, if not half-hearted, patronage of athletes of the first rank, because they happen not to be contemporaries. If some of the cricketers of the past had given themselves up to cricket, not for one season but for several seasons, as many cricketers of to-day do, a long list of new names would have been added to the roll of cricket heroes. Public opinion has changed about our national game. An absentee from the Oxford and Cambridge cricket match, even under parental authority, would create a commotion all over the country. Parsons are not now supposed to have deserted their cloth by appearing upon the tented field. Assumed names in matches are things of the past. Partly because of prejudices, partly because of business, partly because of the clerical or legal profession, partly because of emigration, some of the most skilful of players have been lost to cricket in early life. Yardley, the best batsman I ever bowled to on the leg side; Alfred Lubbock, a very correct and finished player; F. Penn, with his cool judgment and straight bat; Mitchell, with his long reach, hard drives, and leg hitting; C. T. Studd, with his masterly defence—had only comparatively short cricket careers. It would be very hard to say what these men might have accomplished had they been able to play as much as some distinguished men do now. For myself, I never had the privilege of playing even through a single season, so that I never could really measure myself with others. Yet, I may add, lest my readers should think I have little right to address them about cricket, that, when I could play, I was admitted to all the best matches and made my century, while my bowling average for such season as I could obtain, stood at the top with about nine runs per wicket.

In weighing the difference between past and present players much is said about the improved state of the grounds. While this is quite true, still such grounds as Fenner's at Cambridge, the Canterbury ground, the Oval, etc., etc., were both true and good. They had not, indeed, the advantage of the mowing machine, but they were well kept and sheep-eaten, and the ball travelled truly. What the other-hand balls would have done on those wickets I cannot say. On Lord's they would probably have broken our heads! Then (as now) Lord's was the finest ground in the world for scoring runs upon. There is something in the soil that makes the ball travel very fast. I have seen a four made from a middle-stump shooter. It is a fact that men who could score at the Oval could not distinguish themselves at Lord's. It really required some courage to face Jackson or Willsher when the wicket happened to be 'a bit bumpy.' The batsmen got hit on the legs and fingers a little more frequently then than on our present easy grounds. But it stands to reason that the men who could skilfully score on wickets where the ball twisted and bumped and shot, could surely score to a far greater extent on wickets that were smooth. If George Parr then made his fifty, would not the fifty have become a hundred under the present easier conditions? As regards batting itself, I do not allow that the playing of to-day is more skilful or scientific than it was thirty or forty years ago. It has to a great extent altered its style. There is far more cricket in the whole country, and as a natural consequence there is a greater number of really first-class players. That is obvious to every one. And the driving is more general and far harder than it was formerly. You may watch a player have a long innings and note that nearly all his runs, as far as hits are concerned, are made by drives or hard forward play. His position at the wickets suggests these forward strokes. He is not afraid of shooters because he has no experience of them, and they hardly ever come. He never sets himself to hit a ball to leg because balls on the leg side are so rare. He is afraid of cutting because there are so many fields on the off-side, and he may be caught. And so he waits, sometimes with amazing patience, for the one ball off which he can score safely. As an all-round player he is inferior to a Parr, a Hayward, or a Carpenter. The old players had to play every species of ball, including shooters and poppers, and to hit all round the wicket; and they did so with wonderful success. One thing I think I can say positively—they were never yorked out as they are too frequently nowadays. A yorker is very apt to capture a hitter, but why it should get a player out is to me very strange. I never saw W. G. Grace puzzled with one. It is possible that the very high delivery may be deceptive, but to be out to an over-tossed ball is rather a disgrace to a batsman with anything like a decent reputation.

There is no stroke in which there is greater variety than the cut. George Parr and W. G. Grace made the cut safe by hitting it on to the ground—by chopping it; but that is quite a different stroke from the old-fashioned cut. Felix, Julius Caesar, C. G. Lyttleton, Carpenter, and many others hit with the bat parallel to the ground with a power that no chop can ever give to the ball. But with all the fielders on the off-side, men are afraid of making this stroke lest they should be caught; and they either leave the ball alone altogether or gently tap it. A literal 'tip' in the slips, not because the ball has beaten the batsman, but of set purpose, is considered scientific play by too many spectators at a match! The practice of leaving balls to the off alone is downright bad cricket. If the ball is off the wicket it ought to be hit somehow or other. Shrewsbury, Gunn, Brockwell, and others may think it an evidence of skill and science, but it is nothing of the kind. It is a proof that there is a ball they do not know how to hit correctly. Either the off ball ought to be driven, or hit with a mowing kind of stroke in front of cover-point, or cut with tremendous force towards point's left side. I have seen ball after ball, of beautiful length for hitting and just about the height of the wickets, allowed to pass without any attempt to score off it! 'But the field!' The batsman's first business is to hit the ball correctly, no matter where the fieldsmen are; and if he loses his chance of doing so, he shows himself to be a defective player.

In modern cricket the leg hit has almost disappeared, partly because there are few balls given on the leg side, and partly because few men know how to make it correctly. When Spofforth was at his best he often placed Boyle close up on the leg side, not behind but in front of the batsman, who secured many a catch off him. I do not think I am wrong in saying that George Parr or Mitchell instead of poking Spofforth's deliveries into Boyle's hands would have sent them into the ring, if not out of the ground to leg. How seldom one sees a hit out of Lord's now; but Parr, Adams, Fitzgerald, and others used to give us this treat. It should be remembered that those half drive and half square leg hits which are sometimes made in our matchs would have been *bona fide* leg hits by Parr.

There is a fashion in cricket as in everything else; and in my time, and particularly before my time, it was not considered good form to go to the wicket with the idea of sticking there all day, and working to obtain a high average. After getting thirty or forty runs it was considered quite proper to go in for a little free hitting. Exception of course was made in some of the grander matches. I am bound to give it as my opinion that if there had been that settled determination to make run-getting a serious business, the averages of some of the old batsmen would have been much higher. In a scientific point of view men like Pilch, Guy, Parr, Carpenter, Ponsonby, Haygarth, and Hankey were most correct. They played the game, the whole game, and nothing but the game—forward play, back play, and always with straight bats, and they hit at all loose balls. There was of old far too much tame blocking, and the forward play, was not strong enough. The batsmen scarcely ever took a liberty with straight balls. I doubt, however, whether our modern bowlers would have found it very easy to capture their wickets. One of the Australian eleven, when he first met Gunn, said: 'If he played forward more, we would never get him out.' He has improved in this respect of late years, and with great advantage. On hard, fast, dry wickets the excellent reach and forward play of the old batsmen, with their perfectly straight bats, would master some of the best of our modern fast bowlers. Fuller Pilch, Guy, and Tom Hayward, with their tremendous reach, on fast and smooth wickets, might have given a lesson to some players of great reputation. Nor should it be forgotten, when a question of averages is raised, that it is one thing to get fours by a hit into the ring and another to have to run them out. Many fine players and grand hitters have lost their wickets through the exhaustion caused by rapid scoring. Their behaviour at the wickets savoured more of modesty than of conceited actions. They were not given to making a fuss over a hard blow on fingers, legs or body. They did not pat the ground, when patting was not of the slightest service. Nor did they take a long time in recovering their wind after a mild tap for three! Nor did the bowlers waste time, at every change, by bowling four, five, or six balls to 'get the arm in.' The penalty of greater crowds is the exhibition of a few little weaknesses.

Turning now to another department of the game, I must confess myself surprised to find that Grace and R. H. Lyttelton both think that the bowling of to-day is straighter than it was some years ago. W. G. ought certainly to know, for he has had marvellous experience both of round-arm and 'over-hand' deliveries. I grant that there are more straight bowlers than there used to be, and that probably the high delivery is conducive to accuracy. A year or two ago Carpenter asked me what I thought of the bowling as compared with my own day. After I had expressed my opinion he said:—'Well, sir, I have been umpiring now for a long time. I have had opportunities of watching all the best bowlers in the country, and I have come to the conclusion that they are neither as straight nor do they keep as good a length as they did when I myself played.' Was Carpenter right? I say nothing about what the over-hand bowlers might do if they really tried; but, as a matter of fact they are not careful about being particularly straight. Almost to a man they bowl over the wicket, and as nearly every fielder they possess is on the off-side, they purposely send many a ball a little wide of the outside stump. No doubt this often pays, but it takes away from the straightness of the bowling. Nor would it probably be so frequently repeated if the batsmen had the ability to punish crooked balls to the off. There is a terrible sameness in over-the-wicket break-back bowling, and it should be remembered that some batsmen are seldom puzzled by off balls, for they can see them more easily than those on the leg side. The breaking-back off bowler never gives the really difficult leg-stump ball, for when it is pitched straight on that stump it misses the wicket on account of the break, and very often it escapes the wicket keeper's vigilance and runs away in byes. There was far greater variety in the bowlers of a past day, and straightness and a good length distinguished the most celebrated of them. If old Clarke could hit the same spot on the ground nine times out of ten with his under-hand balls, so could Wisden with his round-arm. I have seen Grundy bowl nine or ten maiden overs in succession, and every ball on the wicket. Alfred Shaw was famous for his accuracy. Willsher was marvellously straight, even when his arm was lowered. Once, in a tent at Canterbury, we discussed his ability as a bowler both before and after he was no-balled. As he happened to pass, I asked him, 'Are you as difficult as you were before you lowered your arm?' He answered, 'No. The difference is to me like the difference between light and darkness.' He never got back the old 'spin' that took so many wickets, yet what a wonderful bowler he was up to the end of his career! I often speculate as to how modern batsmen would fare with Bickley, Jackson, Buttress, Hillyer, Wisden, and others, who bowled round the wicket and 'came in a bit' from leg. I hold strongly that the most difficult ball to play is that on, or just inside of, the leg stump; and yet it is a ball that the players of to-day seldom have to face. There is no really good bowler who can make the ball, at any decent pace, turn in from leg when delivering from round the wicket. I agree with A. G. Steel, that it is much easier to break back than to twist in. Great pains and trouble have to be expended in learning the latter art. Some, like Jackson of Nottingham, turn in naturally, but then only to a limited extent, and because of a spin. Buttress could do more with the ball than any man I ever saw, and on any ground he could get wickets. He possessed long, thin fingers which went all round the ball, and his twist in from leg was done by his third finger. He could make the ball leave his hand just as a top spins. Like Spofforth, he could deceive the batsman by a scarcely perceptible alteration of pace. After a tremendous spinner, he would give what appeared like the same ball, but it was found not to have an atom of the devil in it—perfectly plain and commonplace. The great difference was the great danger. There have been remarkable feats performed by modern bowlers, but mostly on 'bowlers' wickets.' A reference to old scores will show that Bickley, Buttress, and Jackson have got crack elevens out, even on 'batsmen's wickets,' for very small totals. The bowling averages compare very favourably with those of modern times.

One reason why so few bowlers bowl round the wicket now is because they cannot do so safely without a long stop. I may be wrong, but my opinion is that the ball which beats the batsman inside the leg stump will very often beat the wicket-keeper too, especially if it shoots. Bowlers don't like the balls to go for byes. Aiming at the leg stump, some balls must go crookedly and outside the legs of the batsman, and these the very best of wicket-keepers cannot always secure. Nor is it always a bad thing to send a twisting leg ball, for a catch at square leg or long leg or short leg or long stop is not at all an unlikely result. Lyttelton seems to think that George Parr would have made short work of bowlers of the Martingell type, but Buttress, who was famous for curly ones from leg, used to get Parr's wicket. Of this I am perfectly certain—that the cricket world of to-day needs a tip-top bowler round the wicket, who would hammer away at the leg stump; and, from a conversation I had some time ago with Earl Bessborough and W. G. Grace, they both think he would be successful. I believe he would 'skiddadle' some of our swell players one after the other; but the labour of learning to bowl this way is very great, and all fingers are not suitable for it. Besides, it requires courage to run the risk of byes and to alter the field to the old-fashioned style. I do not think that very high bowling is suitable for the telling balls I once more desire to see. I am quite confident that if Buttress had been able to go just a bit above the shoulder now and then he would have captured by catches more wickets. It may be granted that high bowling gives some special powers; but old round arm is not without its advantages. Were I a bowler of to-day I should use both styles, but never be too high or too low. It is said that the excellent condition of the ground prevents shooters; but I am sure that such is the case. I never saw a match on the very best grounds in my time in which some wickets were not taken by shooters. With spinning round-arm bowling some shooters are bound to come. A 'screw' will, every now and then, go differently to what was intended. I have pitched such a ball on the off stump and hit the leg bail! not because there was anything in the ground, but because in the air the ball got some change and fell differently to what was intended, and with all its spin upon it, it was bound to do something irregularly. For the same reason shooters are bowled—the spin as well as the ground makes them.

I would put in a plea also for a really good lob bowler of the old school. Clarke stood alone as a slow bowler. He was not, strictly speaking, a lob bowler, nor is it right to say that he had a tremendous twist. He was an underhand bowler with his hand higher than his hips and close to his side while his elbow was well out; and though he could twist he only liked the ball to have what he called 'the bias'—about the breadth of the ball. He did not 'lob' so much as bowl, and his success lay in his accuracy and in his judgment. Bowling with him was a well-studied art. After a season in which Felix bothered him by running half down the pitch to hit him, Clarke during the winter practised in his back yard, so that he might be able to pitch a ball right on top of the stumps, and what was the result? As soon as he met Felix again he tempted him off his ground to hit him, but a ball or two after Felix was down the pitch and found himself bowled. Before I went to Cambridge I met Clarke in a match. According to his custom he went to the practice wickets with a ball in his hand. 'Might I bowl you a ball or two?' he asked, and I was quite flattered by the request and said, 'Certainly.' He gave me about a dozen, made an observation or two on my play, and passed on to another wicket. Now what happened? He saw that I was a player and a hard hitter, but no 'slogger.' As soon as I came in he tossed me up one to hit, and I hit hard along the ground and got a couple of runs. Before he gave the next ball he brought Anderson up from the long field and put him about thirty yards behind him on his left side. He then pitched a ball in the same place as before, but a trifle slower, and I drove it hard and low straight into Anderson's hands, and I had to retire. He not only carefully watched men's play, but he had the rare faculty of remembering them when they came to the wickets, though they were strangers to him. There have been only four or five good lob bowlers that I can remember, the Walkers, Money, Rose, Ridley, and E. T. Drake. In my opinion V. E. Walker was out and out the best, and his fielding to his own bowling was most brilliant. Money was very successful in the University and Gentlemen and Players' matches. Wood of Oxford is too fast for a *bona fide* lob bowler, and by no means accurate, but how badly the Cambridge men played him! It was quite evident that, with one or two exceptions, there was no real knowledge as to how such bowling ought to be dealt with. I think it not at all improbable that V. E. Walker would have sent the best of the Australian elevens to the right about, for what a mess they made of very second-rate lobs! It is absurd to suppose that 'anyone can bowl a few lobs,' and that some stale old cricketers are the right men to 'have a try' at them in a match. No department of bowling requires greater care, study, accuracy, judgment, or more continuous practice. It is just this latter point that is the weakness of our gentlemen bowlers—they will not give themselves sufficient time and trouble really to learn the art. I like to see a man of the Matt Kempson type bowling by the half hour at a single stump, with perhaps one or more bits of paper on the ground as marks for a good pitch. I like to note that he holds the ball in a variety of ways, seamwise, across the seam, not touching the seam, in a full band or with two or three fingers, and closely watching what each ball does. I like to observe that he does his best to make the ball get up quickly, or in a commonplace way, at will. Random bowling is irritating, and accidental wickets are not satisfactory; but nothing is more delightful than to watch a good, true, painstaking bowler, with accuracy, a good length and judgment, working to gain his end. His success is an exhibition of real art.

As regards fielding, the difference between ancient and modern players is not very great. The latter, I think, are more skilful in their returns, and certainly more accurate in having a shot at the wickets; but none of them have eclipsed Broughton, Royds, Hornby, and Bell at cover point, Absolom and Kempson at short slip, I. D. Walker at mid-off, Bob Fitzgerald and Smith at long leg, E. M. Grace at point, and Teddy Drake and V. E. Walker to their own bowling and in almost any place in the field. Nicholson and Lockyer had indomitable pluck as well as skill at the wickets, and under the altered conditions of the grounds would be inferior to no one in the present day.

As time passes it is to me a matter of joy that the game of cricket has become so universal and that it retains its purity and its freedom from those evils which surround some other of our pastimes. No whisper of matches being sold for money is ever heard. No charge of cheating is brought against players. No system of gambling is attached to the greatest of English games. Cliquism, with its silly exclusiveness in too many country mansions and social gatherings, has not destroyed the unanimity which works with the common goal of victory in view, and makes a match both agreeable and intensely interesting. 'The gravity with which Englishmen disport themselves,' as a Frenchman said, is an element of success; and it goes a long way to develop those distinctive features of endurance, patience, and fair play which form noble and chivalrous characters. If differences of opinion exist about the merits and advantages of old and present cricketers, there is one sentiment which sways every true player and every good man, and it is this—that in all the religious, political, and secular affairs of life, as well as in every match, may the best side win.

PERSONAL RECOLLECTIONS OF W. G. GRACE [1896]

BY LORD HARRIS AND BY A. G. STEEL

In 1895 Dr. William Gilbert Grace (1848–1915) had enjoyed the most astonishing successes ever of his career. By now the youthful giant of the 1870s had blossomed into the heaviest man in first-class cricket, his weight approaching 20 stone, his figurative bulk larger still. He was already at a stage in his life when normal men retire from the rigours of the game, but Grace, whose whole essence was of course that he bore no resemblance to a normal man, launched into his thirty-first season with enthusiasm if not the frame of a stripling. He began with the stupefying flourish of 1,000 runs in May, including two double centuries. One of these doubles, scored against Somerset at Bristol, marked his one hundredth first-class hundred. The nation sensed that at the age of 48 Grace was enjoying some sort of apotheosis, and flocked to watch and be part of the process. He was entertained at banquets in London and at Bristol, and 'The Daily Telegraph' organised a National Testimonial, by inviting readers to send in one shilling contributions. Among those who sent in their shilling were

Sir Compton Mackenzie (see Wisden for 1973), and Sir Max Beerbohm whose contribution was accompanied by a note explaining that his response was due not to any love of cricket but as an expression of his detestation of golf. The newspaper raised £5,000 by this method, and a contribution from M.C.C. of £2,377.2s.0d less expenses of £21.8s.10d, boosted the fund to what was by standards of the period a huge sum. 'The Sportsman' and the Gloucestershire County Club also contributed to the grand total of £9,073.6s.5d. The best-known of the contributors, although not quite as eminent as the beneficiary, was the Prime Minister Lord Salisbury who, in sending £5, wrote:

> I beg to enclose a centenary of shillings to use the current phrase. I have not touched a cricket ball for more than fifty years, so I am afraid that I can only claim a *locus standi* as owner of a village cricket ground. You are kind to refer to the cricket of my sons. I regret to say that it is wholly despicable.

Wisden's contribution was to publish twin tributes to this apparently indestructible man by two of his greatest admirers. W. G. was now at the very apex of his fame. The euphoria was to endure for exactly one season.

THE editor of this ANNUAL has asked me to write a short account of Dr. W. G. Grace as I have found him during my cricket career. I fear I have but little that is new to add to all that has been already written about W. G., and I also find that five years' absence from first-class cricket, about a quarter of a man's first class cricketing life, has made sad breaches in my memory.

I well remember the first time I saw the old man—as all cricketers love to call him; it must have been about '67 or '68 that a few of the Eton eleven were taken up to Lord's by Mr. Mitchell on a holiday for the express purpose of seeing W. G. bat, and thereby having our own ideas improved. It was a drizzly cold morning, and W. G. in a thick overcoat had a spirited argument with 'Mike' as to the weather and the ground being fit for cricket, the former, caring little about standing as a model for us, thinking it was not; and the latter, caring little as to the particular match, thinking it was. I must have seen but little of W. G. between then and '72, except in Canterbury in the week, but in '72 I had a two months' experience of his comradeship during the tour in Canada and the States of Mr. R. A. FitzGerald's team, the first amateur eleven that crossed the seas on a cricketing tour, and a right good eleven it was, the best strictly amateur team, I should say, that has ever been made up for that purpose. W. G. and poor Cuthbert Ottaway went in first, and generally put on 100 before the first wicket fell, a pretty good start, with the 'Monkey,' Alfred Lubbock, and Walter Hadow to follow on; and then what a bowling side it was, Appleby dead on the off stump every ball, and Billy Rose, about the best lob bowler I ever saw, at the other end, and W. G. and C. K. Francis as changes. But the history of the tour, is it not all written in 'Wickets in the West,' by that prince of cricket reporters, Bob FitzGerald himself? So

I will not reproduce the time-honoured allusion to W. G.'s speeches, but content myself with bearing grateful witness to the kindly sympathetic consideration which characterised his comradeship. That tour commenced and cemented a friendship between us which I value at the highest.

From about '76 to '86 I saw a good deal of the old man's play in the big matches, and I shall never see such all-round play again. There may arise a bat as good, and at point and to his own bowling a field as good, and, of course there have been and will be bowlers as good, but I doubt one generation producing two such all-round cricketers. And remember, my young friends, that this super excellence was not the result of eminent physical fitness only, it depended a good deal also on the careful life the old man led. He did not play brilliantly despite how he lived, as some, whose all too brief careers I can remember, did, but he regulated his habits of life with such care and moderation that his physical capacity was always at its best, and has lasted in the most marvellous manner. I shall always hold that W. G. was the best and pluckiest field to his own bowling I ever saw. The ground he used to cover to the off—and with the leg break of course the majority of straight balls went there—made him as good as a twelfth man. He used to have his mid-on nearly straight behind the bowler's arm so as to cover the balls hit straight back. I fancy I've noticed that he has not tried for long leg catches so much since poor dear Fred Grace, the safest catch I ever saw, went home, but it may be only fancy. And then the hot 'uns I've seen him put his hands to, half volleys hit at ten yards distance, low down, with all the momentum of a jump in and a swinging bat, catches that looked like grinding his knuckles against the sole of his boot, but I never saw the old man flinch. And that reminds me of a rather humorous incident when England played the Australians at the Oval late in the year in 1880. We had seen very little of them that year, as, in consequence of the affair at Sydney in '79, they could get no good matches arranged, but late in the year the sore was healed and a match arranged.

Percy MacDonnell was in and Fred Morley bowling, and for some reason, obscure to both of us I should think ever since, W. G. and I agreed that he should go silly mid-off. The wicket was not a slow one, and, under any circumstances, Percy MacDonnell was not the sort of bat to stand close up to on the off side. Well, presently Fred bowled one of his half volleys on the off, MacDonnell gave it the full swing of his powerful shoulders, and the first thing that everyone realised subsequently was that it had hit the old man. He had had no time to stoop, or dodge, or move a finger, but luckily for him, it hit him on the heel of his boot, and he was none the worse. I saw W. G. blink his eyes and look at the batsman, in that searching way that others besides myself must have noticed I should think, and he stayed there till the end of the over—after that we thought he might be more useful further back.

I always thought the old man depended rather too much on the umpire for leg before, particularly when I was on the opposite side. He crossed the wicket so far to the off himself that he could not in many instances judge with any accuracy whether the ball pitched straight or not, and I don't think a bowler ought to ask for leg before unless he is pretty sure as to the pitch. I remember one day at Canterbury, the wind was blowing pretty strongly across the ground, and W. G. was lobbing them up in the air to get all the advantage of the wind. I kept on fetching them round to sharp long leg—I never hit him square—or trying to, and every time the ball hit my leg he asked, and every time he asked Willsher shook his head, and the old man was getting almost savage, when, at last, I got my left leg too much to the off, and the ball went through my legs and bowled me. Of course, W. G. held that was proof positive that all the others would have hit the wicket too, whilst I held that that was possible, but that none of them had pitched straight.

Another reminiscence connecting him with Canterbury Week is that weary day—or day and a half I might say—when he made his 344. We had got a big score in our first and only innings, and had got M.C.C. out for something small. I thought it rather odd, for the wicket was all right, and our bowling was not very deadly, and my forebodings were well founded. It did not matter what we bowled for that day and a half, most balls went quite impartially to the boundary. Mr. Foord Kelcey always declared in after years that about five o'clock on the Friday evening, all our bowling being used up, and he and poor dear old 'Bos' (Mr. C. A. Absolom) went on permanently!

On the whole, however, I think in those days we used to get rid of W. G. pretty luckily when we met him, but he gave us a severe taste of his quality at Clifton one year, over a century each innings. When he had got 98 second innings I thought perhaps a bad lob might produce results. Henty was no longer a member of the Kent team, or he would have gone on, as he always did when we were in serious difficulties, without taking his pads off, but either Mr. Patterson or I could bowl quite as bad a lob as he ever did, so one of us, I forget which, went on, and sure enough something did result. The old man hit a fourer, scored his second century in the same match for the second time in his career, and stumps were drawn. Some people said I did this on purpose to let him get his second century, but that allegation was not founded on absolute knowledge, and a bad lob when a man is well set is sometimes luckier than a good ball.

A lucky selection came off in one Gentlemen v. Players' match at the Oval. I was not playing myself, but I saw the ball bowled. The captain of the Players' team had been asked whether there was anybody in particular they wanted to play, and he—either Dicky Daft or Bob Carpenter I think—said they would like to have Emmett, because he might bowl Dr. Grace out early, and sure enough Tom bowled him, and first ball I think.

I have referred to poor Fred Grace's fine fielding, and I recall an incident at the Oval in a match we played late in the year for the benefit of the sufferers by the sinking of the 'Princess Alice,' an excursion boat. Fred was bowling, W. G. was point, and I was mid-off. The batsman skied one so high on the off side that we three had quite a little conversation which of us should have it. It was a horribly cold day, and I had no particular fancy for it, and when Fred said he would have it I was quite ready to resign knowing he was certain to hold it, which he did.

I do not know whether it is fancy, but I shall always believe that W. G.'s later style is quite different from what it was between '70 and '80. Now he plays the regulation back and forward strokes, but at that time he seemed to me to play every good length straight ball just in front of the popping crease, meeting it with a perfectly straight bat every time, but a kind of half stroke only possible when great experience of the bowling, a very clear eye, and great confidence are combined. Remembering how many straight balls he used to place on the on side in those days, and the improbability therefore of the full face of the bat being given to the ball at the moment of impact, his extraordinary accuracy of eye can perhaps be realised.

I did not expect when I left England in 1890 ever again to play in a first-class match with my old friend; and—though but for a broken finger I might have done so at Gravesend this year—I fear my expectations will be realised, but I had the opportunity of taking a part in paying him what I know he holds to be as great a compliment as ever was paid him—viz., the decision of the Marylebone Cricket Club to give its support to the National Testimonial which was so enthusiastically started this year. I gave my vote for that decision, not merely because I regard W. G. as the most prominent exponent there has every been of the finest and purest game that has ever been played, but also because the old man is the kindest and most sympathetic cricketer I have ever played with. As I said in proposing his health some years ago at a banquet the Kent County Club gave in his honour, I never knew a man make a mistake in the field but what W. G. had a kind word to say to and an excuse to find for him, and I doubt if I could conclude with anything in praise of my old friend which would be truer or more gratifying to his feelings than that.

LORD HARRIS

YIELDING to none in admiration of the 'hero' of a hundred centuries, and to none in love for the game in which he is so proficient, I am bound to say I was not altogether pleased with the *Daily Telegraph* testimonial. A national testimonial in honour of the greatest cricketer the world has ever seen, on his completion of a performance which may be a 'record' for all time, was indeed fitting. Surely the greatest cricket club in the world—the M.C.C.—was the proper initiator of the testimonial to the greatest cricketer. Day after day, as one read of the flood of shillings pouring in, accompanied by such varied correspondence, one could not but feel a little alarm for the dignity of our great game. But whether the means adopted for raising the testimonial were the right ones or not, the fact remains that it was an enormous success, and showed that the personality of W. G. Grace had taken a deep hold upon all classes of the English people. The enthusiasm was such as has probably never before been kindled concerning the exponent of any modern form of athletics.

The first occasion I ever played against W. G. was at Cambridge in the summer of 1878, and this was the first time I ever saw him play. I remember being desperately anxious to get him out, but I was disappointed, and on my telling him what pleasure it would give me to get him out, he laughingly replied, 'It's only a question of time; if you go on long enough you are bound to get me out.' I was not, however, successful on that occasion, but I shall never forget the kindly encouragement I, a young cricketer, received from W. G. the first time I met him. It was not, however, his batting, oddly enough, which struck me as so wonderful, it was his bowling. Never, as far as I know, did any bowler give the same peculiar flight to the ball as W. G. does, and well justified is the remark I have often heard him make of a newly-arrived batsman, 'Oh, he's a young one, is he? I think I ought to do for him,' and he generally does.

W. G. has, so it goes without saying, a thorough knowledge of the game, and I recollect well in the summer of 1878 an incident which well illustrated the fact. North v. South was being played at Lord's. Barlow, the Lancashire professional, was batting, and W. G. was fielding point. Now Barlow had a trick of tapping the ball away after he had played it, and occasionally, in order to excite a laugh from the onlookers, would scamper down the pitch for a yard or two and then back again. On this occasion he just stopped the ball and it lay by his crease; he then tapped it towards point, and perhaps thinking he would hustle that fielder, he went through his performance of dashing down the pitch and back again. He must have been thoroughly upset by the action of point, who, ignoring the ball, quietly asked the umpire, 'How's that for hitting the ball twice?' and out Barlow had to go—a lesson which he never forgot. It was, I think in that very match that W. G. hit two consecutive balls from Alfred Shaw clean out of Lord's Cricket Ground. It is true the wickets were pitched slightly on the south side of the ground, but they were both glorious knocks; one went clean over the tavern and the other pitched right on the top of it.

One of the finest innings I ever saw W. G. play was his 152 against the Australians in the match England v. Australia at the Oval in 1880. Certainly he was batting on a good wicket, but his timing of the ball on this occasion was absolutely perfect, and the crispness of his strokes perfection. W. L. Murdoch made 153 in the second innings of this match; a very fine performance it was, too. I afterwards heard a discussion between some of the Australian team as to whether Murdoch was a finer batsman than Grace. A. Bannerman, the little Stonewaller of his side, clinched it by saying, in his brusque way, 'W. G. has forgotten more about batting, than Billy (Murdoch) ever knew.' And A. Bannerman was a very fine judge of the game.

It is during the annual week at Scarborough that W. G. is perhaps, seen at his best. The cricket, of course, is good, but there is a sort of holiday aspect about it which is absent from the more serious county and Gentlemen v. Players matches that take place earlier in the season. I always used to think W. G. hit harder and oftener at Scarborough than elsewhere. I recollect one occasion when he was playing for a team called,

I think, the Gentlemen of England against the Zingari. The latter had a good batting side, but were very weak in bowling. The wicket was good and the Gentlemen won the toss. As the Zingari went into the field we all thought we were in for a long day's fielding. W. G. and C. I. Thornton came in first; H. W. Forster and I began the bowling. I thought it possible that Thornton's hitting might have an effect on Grace, and it did. In the first over Thornton hit me out of the ground, and not to be denied, W. G. did the same, the very first ball I sent down, but it was too merry to last, and they were both caught in the long field before 30 was up on the telegraph board.

Why has the name of W. G. Grace sunk so deeply into the hearts of all branches of the community? Firstly, because of the national love for the glorious game, and secondly, because of his wonderful skill and the unusual number of years he has maintained the position and name of 'champion.' It is as a batsman that he has earned this proud title, and it may be of interest to linger for a few moments on the characteristics of his style and play which in their combination have met with such phenomenal success. First of all, W. G. Grace obeys the fundamental rule of batting that is always instilled into young players as the first element of good batting; he keeps his right foot rigid and firm as a rock, and never does he move it during the actual stroke. (Alas! I never could grasp this rule myself or act up to it!) It is an exception, even to slow bowling, for W. G. to move his right foot. Once I remember (I wonder whether he does) him breaking this rule. During the compilation of one of his hundred centuries, in a match against the Australians at Lord's, he rushed out to hit the slow leg break bowler (Cooper), missed, and after a somewhat undignified skurry back, just got the benefit from the umpire, a man subsequently not loved by the Australians.

The position W. G. takes up at the wicket is one eminently calculated to assist him in the marvellous accuracy of his placing on the leg side. The right foot points slightly in front of the crease, thus enabling him to face the leg and body balls and have the greater command over them. If it had been Grace's practice to stand with his right foot pointing towards or in the direction of his own wicket (as many good batsmen have done and do) we would never have seen the accurate placing on the leg side which, in my opinion, has done more than any other of his great batting qualities to place him in the position he has so long held. Let anyone try for himself, and he will at once see the commanding power that Grace's position on the left side gives, and how cramped and 'hunched' up he feels in the other. Grace's defence, of course, is excellent and his position at the wickets in this relation is worthy of note. He stands with the right leg as near as possible on the line to the leg stump, without, of course, being in front. And every time he plays forward, the left leg and the bat go together, so that should the ball not meet the bat there will be no space between the bat and the leg for it to pass through. How often, whilst enjoying that great cricketing luxury of seeing W. G. in his happiest batting vein, one has occasionally shuddered at the sight of that massive leg coming out straight in front to an offstump ball.

This art of playing with the left leg close to the bat is one that must be thoroughly mastered before any man can become a really first class batsman, and W. G. Grace is a master of it. Though using his left leg in this way when playing forward he is not one of those products of modern days, viz., a batsman who uses his leg on the off side instead of his bat. We should be sorry to think of our great batsman as one of these feeble, faint-hearted players, who frightened of losing their wickets, dare not use their bats, and who too timid to try to score, have done so much in many districts to disgust spectators, not with cricket, but with their own wearisome antics. What sort of bowling is W. G. Grace best at? I do not think that any cricketer of experience would hesitate in answering the question. Great, of course, to all styles when at his best, his power of playing fast bowling was the greatest feature of his game. The leg strokes already mentioned, his great height, the quickness of his hand and eye, all combined, gave him at times complete mastery over fast bowling. Bumping balls on the offstump, to a batsman of ordinary height perhaps the most difficult to dispose of, he punishes by hard cuts to the boundary.

What sort of bowling does W. G. like least? I have never asked him this somewhat searching question, nor if I did is it likely that the champion would care to give himself away. His answer probably, accompanied by a hearty laugh, would be somewhat in this fashion: *Like least, indeed? Why, I love them all.* Of course he does: but I have an opinion that on a hard, fast and true wicket, the slower the bowling the less it is to his liking. His great size prevents him getting quickly to the pitch, and a very slow bowler always has terrors to a fast-footed player that do not present themselves to a quick-footed and active batsman. Whilst discussing W. G. as a batsman, we must not lose sight of another of his great qualities, viz., patience. Never flurried because runs are not coming quite quick enough, never excited because they are coming quicker than usual, he keeps on simply playing the correct game, and even after the hundred goes on the same as before, with his mind fixed upon the two hundred.

It would be impossible, in a short article such as this is, for me to do anything like adequate justice to the merits of the great William Gilbert Grace. There have been some who for a short period have given reason for the belief that his position as champion batsman was being dangerously assailed. I allude to such names as W. L. Murdoch, A. Shrewsbury, and A. E. Stoddart. That belief was, however, but fleeting. W. G. Grace has proved his batting powers to be immensely superior to every other cricketer. He is, though nigh on fifty, still the best, and I sincerely hope he will continue for many years to give us all the pleasure of enjoying his magnificent play.

A. G. STEEL

MR. W. G. GRACE AND THE SURREY CLUB[1897]

BY THE SURREY COUNTY CRICKET CLUB COMMITTEE

Dr. Grace again featured heavily in the text of the 1987 Wisden, once more on the theme of money but this time in very different circumstances. For some time England's premier professionals had considered themselves hard done by in the matter of payment for Test match appearances. In the Oval Test of 1896 against a strong Australian side, matters came to a head with the threat of strike. Five members of the England side demanded a fee of £20, double their rate till now. The ultimatum to the Surrey Club was inspired in part by a genuine sense of grievance at being underpaid, but partly also by a well-founded suspicion which could not be proven that Grace, although an amateur, was receiving payment in excess of anything the professionals were receiving. Three of the strikers withdrew before the game but the remaining pair, Lohmann and Gunn, stood their ground and refused to play. Both the Surrey Club and the editor of Wisden felt obliged to comment on the affair.

VARIOUS rumours having gained currency as to the amount of money allowed to Mr. Grace for expenses when playing for England at the Oval, the following official statement was made public on August 10—the opening day of the third test match.

'The Committee of the Surrey County Cricket Club have observed paragraphs in the Press respecting amounts alleged to be paid, or promised to, Dr. W. G. Grace for playing in the match England v. Australia. The Committee desire to give the statements contained in the paragraphs the most unqualified contradiction. During many years, on the occasions of Dr. W. G. Grace playing at the Oval, at the request of the Surrey County Committee, in the matches Gentlemen v. Players and England v. Australia, Dr. Grace has received the sum of £10 a match to cover his expenses in coming to and remaining in London during the three days. Beyond this amount Dr. Grace has not received, directly or indirectly, one farthing for playing in a match at the Oval.

Signed on behalf of the Committee,
C. W. Alcock.'
August 10, 1896.

SOME CURRENT TOPICS [1897]

BY THE EDITOR

BEFORE the next issue of WISDEN'S ALMANACK, the present rule as to the follow-on will have been amended by the M.C.C., but it may not be out of place to devote some space to the discussion of a question that has excited great diversity of opinion. In common with most people who see a good deal of cricket, I felt sure that the plan of raising from 80 to 120 the number of runs involving a follow-on would fail to meet the difficulty raised by the incident that occurred in the University match of 1893. On a carefully-prepared modern wicket, 40 runs amount to very little, and it was inevitable that, given the same circumstances, the action taken by Mr. F. S. Jackson and Mr. Cyril Wells in 1893 would be repeated. It was a little curious that at such a short interval the repetition should have come in the University match, but really there was nothing unnatural about it, such a thing being always most likely to happen in matches that both sides are peculiarly keen to win. That events did not last July at Lord's justify Mr. Frank Mitchell and Mr. E. B. Shine in the course they took is altogether beside the question. The follow-on having been avoided, it looked as if Cambridge, on going in for the second time with a lead of 117 runs, had the game practically in their hands. No one could foresee the collapse of the Light Blue batsmen, or that Oxford, on a wicket improved instead of spoilt by rain, would, in the last innings, score over 300 runs, and so win the match. Except for Cambridge's 507 against the M.C.C. a week before, such a feat in the last innings was, I think, without precedent in first-class cricket. Bigger totals have been obtained in the closing stages of some matches, but they have not led to victory. Into the question of whether or not Mr. Frank Mitchell was justified in instructing Mr. Shine to bowl no-balls, so that Oxford should not follow on, there is little need for me to enter. The whole matter was threshed out in a long correspondence in the columns of *The Times,* diametrically opposed views being expressed by the most eminent authorities. Briefly I may say I am strongly on Mr. Mitchell's side, and that I think the angry demonstration against the Cambridge eleven in the Pavilion at Lord's, was quite illogical. Angry demonstrations, in matters far more serious than cricket, frequently are. As a matter of fact, Mr. Frank Mitchell, in what he believed to be the best interests of his side, only did in a palpable way what is often done less openly. For instance, at Canterbury, in August, in order to prevent Kent from following their innings, George Giffen, for the Australians, intentionally bowled three half-volleys in succession without a word of protest being raised. However, the M.C.C. have determined to prevent any further repetition of such an incident as occurred in the University match, and at the time I write these lines, they are only awaiting an expression of opinion from Australia before calling a special meeting to deal with the alteration of Law 53.

The alternative propositions for amending the rule are—that the follow-on shall be at the option of the side which in a three days match has gained a lead of 120 or more runs; and (2), that the follow-on shall be abolished altogether, with the necessary corollary, that captains shall have power to put the closure rule in force, either at any time or not earlier than some specified time previous to the last day of the match, instead of being restricted, as they now are, to the last day. On these two propositions, the opinions of all the leading counties have been communicated to the M.C.C., the balance of opinion, so far as I know, being in favour of the total abolition of the follow-on. On this point, however, I speak with reserve, as the views of all the counties have not been made public. Personally, I much prefer the optional plan, which is supported by two of the oldest and most influential counties—Surrey and Notts. The abolition of the follow-on is admirable in theory, but I am sadly afraid that in this country—with matches happily restricted to three days—it would lead to a large increase in the number of drawn games. Only a very daring captain would, with the ground in good order, declare his innings closed while there was time for the opposing side to make the runs in the last innings, and the inevitable result would be a lot of tedious play to save the match. The one strong argument against the optional plan is that it gives a second choice of innings to the side which had already had the advantage of batting first, but in my judgment this is by no means so unfair as a good many people seem to think. As Mr. Courtenay Boyle urged in a very able letter to *The Times,* the follow-on rule was originally framed with the object of saving time, and was never intended to benefit the side which had fallen 80 runs short of the opposing score. Indeed, when the rule was made, 80 was not a very bad total. As Mr. Boyle pointed out, the state of things then prevailing has entirely passed away, and in discussing the question of the follow-on, one must bear in mind the present development of the game. Rightly or wrongly, the majority of modern captains consider it a disadvantage—on hard wickets—to have their bowlers kept at work through two successive innings, and it is certainly contrary to the spirit of the game to penalise the side which has by superior cricket gained on the first innings a substantial advantage. Hence the desire for a change in the 80 runs rule, which found voice in Australia before the University match of 1893 made the question a burning one. Strong opposition to the optional plan comes from Middlesex, and as this means the opposition of Mr. V. E. and Mr. I. D. Walker, one is bound to treat it with the utmost respect. The Middlesex Committee favour the plan of extending the 120 runs to 150, and failing any agreement to that, they support the total abolition of the follow-on.

Nothing in connection with cricket has for some years past caused so much excitement as the so-called strike of the professionals, on the eve of the England and Australian match at the Oval. Happily the storm subsided almost as soon as it was raised, the players quickly withdrawing from the position which, without thoroughly weighing the consequences, they had taken up. I thought at the time, and I think still, that the players were right in principle, but that their action was ill-judged and inopportune. To my mind it was, to say the least, ungracious of the Surrey men to raise a difficulty with their own committee after accepting ten pounds each for the England matches at Lord's and Manchester. That they felt this themselves was made pretty clear by their speedy submission. Out of their revolt, however, I hope and believe that good will come. With England and Australia matches attracting such immense crowds of people, it is only right that the professionals should be liberally rewarded for their services, and I hope that when the Australians pay us their next visit, it will be agreed to pay every professional chosen for England in the test matches, a fee of twenty pounds. An arrangement to this effect, made at the annual meeting of county secretaries at Lord's, in December, would avoid all difficulties. In this connection, it is interesting to recall the fact that the Surrey Club, without, so far as I know, any pressure being brought to bear upon them, paid twenty pounds each to Alfred Shaw, Morley, and Barnes, in 1880, on the occasion of the first England and Australia match in this country.

A subject which is just now exercising the minds of county committees is that of winter wages for professionals, Yorkshire's arrangement to pay two pounds a week, from September to April inclusive, to their ten regular players, having excited a feeling of anxiety, not to say alarm. It is clear that only clubs with a large amount of money—Yorkshire's experiment will cost roughly £600—will be able to act with such liberality, and there is a fear that young players will drift away from their own counties to Yorkshire in the hope of participating in the benefit. Surely, however, this danger is more imaginary than real. There must always be a limit to the number of professionals for whom room can be found in one county eleven, and the law of supply and demand may be trusted to keep things tolerably straight. Moreover, the Yorkshire Committee are strongly averse to playing any but native-born men. All the same there is certainly a danger that the liberality of the Yorkshire executive will breed dissatisfaction in counties where such a winter wage as two pounds a week is out of the question. This matter of payment in the winter months is no new thing, however, the Surrey Club having for some time past, in a less public way, remunerated many of their professionals during the off season. The earnings of the players have certainly not risen in proportion to the immensely increased popularity of cricket during the last twenty years, but to represent the average professional as an ill-treated or down-trodden individual is, I think, a gross exaggeration. The field of his labours has widely extended, and as regards the Oval, Lord's, Manchester, and various Yorkshire grounds, the Benefit match, which is the special prize of a professional cricketer's life, is a much bigger thing than it was years ago. There is plenty of room for further improvement, but, taken all around, things are certainly far better than they were. Into the thorny question of amateurs' expenses I do not propose to enter, for the good and sufficient reason that I do not possess the necessary information. No doubt there are some abuses, but as a famous cricketer—a county captain and quite behind the scenes—has assured me that he does not know more than half-a-dozen men, playing as amateurs, who make anything out of the game, the evil would not seem to be very widespread. Mr. W. G. Grace's position has for years, as everyone knows, been an anomalous one, but 'nice customs curtsey to great kings' and the work he has done in popularising cricket outweighs a hundredfold every other consideration.

FIELDING IN 1900 [1901]

BY D. L. A. JEPHSON

For the next two seasons the standard of essay-writing in Wisden declined somewhat; there were one or two passably interesting accounts of overseas tours, but as these were primarily exercises in the reporter's art, they could hardly be described as literary specimens. There was a sudden upsurge in 1901, when there appeared in the pages of the Almanack one of the most intriguing figures of his time. Digby Loder Armroid Jephson (1871–1926) was one of the last considerable lob bowlers, a pugnacious batsman and, in the years around the turn of the century, captain of Surrey. He scored several centuries for the county, and in the Gentlemen-Players match at Lord's in 1899 took 6 wickets for 21 with his lobs. A prolific performer in club cricket, Jephson was clearly one of those men for whom life meant cricket. For a time he was active on the London Stock Exchange, but in time he abandoned such a resolutely non-cricketing profession and took to journalism and coaching. But Jephson's real fascination lies in his verse, which he published in cricket journals and once or twice between covers. A sentimental versifier whose main theme was the sad transience of youth and fond recollection of games gone by, he published 'A Few Overs' in 1913, in which he rhapsodised in the vein of:

Give me a day in a golden June
and the sun in a turquoise sky . . .

Do you remember the day, old friend
(You were then but a slim-built chap),
That you stayed the rot, keeping up your end,
And they gave you your old brown cap?

As a writer on cricket, Jephson had an artist's insight into the subtleties of slow bowling, but it is revealing how completely Bosanquet's pretence that the googly was a pure accident took in Jephson, revealing also that even though he is writing prose, Jephson retains the occasional grandiloquence of the poet in full flight.

MUCH has been written with regard to the batting of the past season, and much has been written with regard to the bowling; much praise, and rightly too has been bestowed on the one, and on the other a modicum of commendation. To write in the same congratulatory vein of the fielding necessitates the pen of a ready writer, the pen of a Defoe. As these are not numbered among my possessions, it is a difficult task. To write well of the fielding in 1900 is but to forge a romance that exists nowhere, save in the writer's brain.

Taken as a whole fielding has been bad, thoroughly bad. Men stand in the field to day like so many 'little mounds of earth,'* or waxen figures in the third-rate tailor's shop. The energy, the life, the ever-watchfulness of ten years ago is gone, and in their place are lethargy, laziness, and a wonderful yearning for rest. To day a ball is driven through so-called fieldsmen, and instead of a simultaneous rush to gather it, to hurl it to one end or the other, the two 'little mounds of earth' stand facing each other with a lingering hope in their eyes that they will not be compelled to fetch it. There are, unfortunately, but a few counties, regarded as sides, to which the above censure does not apply.

The two northern counties, the two best elevens of the year fielded well, perhaps as well as any teams it has been my pleasure to play against, but the majority of the rest are absolutely outclassed by many a local club throughout the country. Naturally on every county side there are exceptions to this general sloth, men who believe that the game does not wholly consist in the making of a hundred runs, or the taking of five wickets; men who delight in chasing the ball with the possible chance of saving a run, and who never 'slack' however long their outing may have been. These are the members of a team that help to win your matches, the fieldsmen whose energy, pluck and endurance go far to remedy your deficiences in other parts of the game.

The success of Yorkshire is due, in a very large degree, to their fielding. There are many fine fields on the side, and an article of this description would be void of all interest if mention were not made of Hirst and Denton, perhaps the finest mid-off and the finest out field of the year. The one is in front of you, and you may as well attempt to drive through a brick wall as pass those hands of iron; and the other, hovering on the edge of the green circle, has made you run many a three when you were crediting yourself with a four. They are cat-like in their activity; before the bat has struck the ball, by some strange intuition, they divine the direction

*A timid, though euphonious paraphrase of 'Clods of Dirt;' a definition given by an old cricketer, of many latter day fieldsmen.

it will take, and move, whilst the so-called fieldsman—the little mound of earth—stands openmouthed, watching the ball go by. All through the season their catching has been good and their ground work perhaps better; their fielding has been full of life, full of vigour. And of Lancashire the same may be said. Here there are many good fields, and again two stand out above their fellows—A. C. MacLaren, the captain, and Tyldesley. A. C. MacLaren is ubiquitous, his presence is felt everywhere, and it is a daring youth that shirks when he is in command of a team. He is full of nerves, he can scarcely stand still as the ball leaves the bowler's hand, and it is only on the fall of the coveted wicket that the stern features relax and he rests for a moment. In all positions in the field is he good, exceptionally good; and so marvellously keen is he for the downfall of the unfortunate batsman that on occasion he has been known to bowl, but rarely, I am sorry to say, with marked success. At the present time he, G. L. Jessop, and A. O. Jones, are in all probability the three players that can fill more places in the field, and fill them splendidly, than any other first-class cricketers. Tyldesley, like Denton, is always to be found in the outfield, and there is little to choose between them. Both have the same untiring energy, both go for catches, however seemingly impossible they may appear, preferring to miss rather than to stop the ball first bound, as is the method adopted by the so-called fieldsman—the 'little mound of earth.' Again, both throw well, with a low quick return that invariably reaches the wicket-keeper or the bowler after pitching but once. Not with the terrible inaccuracy, the inaccuracy of length and direction that characterises the efforts of a very large majority of the players of to day.

It is impossible with the space at my disposal to give anything approaching a complete account of the fielding, or rather the misfielding of the county elevens of 1900. Therefore in this article I am not able to deal with the work in this respect, of all the various sides that played in the Championship Competition. Mention must, however, be made of the good fielding of Gloucestershire and of Kent. Both are young sides and both are strangely aware of the importance of this branch of the game, that in so many teams is regarded as an aggravated nuisance, knowing well that many a game has been won, not by brilliant batting, or sensational bowling, but the unflagging exertion in the field. G. L. Jessop, besides having saved dozens of runs, runs that the restful field would willingly have given to the other side, has thrown out thirty or so batsmen. Readers of this will perhaps remark to themselves—'It is all very well, but how many runs has he lost shooting at the stumps?' Yes, very likely many have been lost, but think a moment. What is a four or many fours on a good wicket compared to the dismissal of Ranjitsinhji, Fry, Abel, or Hayward. Again, rare instances occur of a ball being thrown in well so that the wicket can be broken by the bowler or the stumper, arriving the fraction of a second too late. The batsman is in, whereas had the wicket been hit he would have walked slowly, miserably, probably discontentedly, to a seat in the pavilion. I am not advocating indiscriminate throwing, but if there did not exist this terrible inaccuracy of length and direction in the returns of the majority of the fieldsmen of to-day, many a wicket would have fallen that stood for hours piling up tedious fours.

Looking back calmly and dispassionately on the past season, there is another feature that strikes the interested spectator, namely, the growing inclination on the part of certain fieldsmen to remove themselves as far as possible from the *dangerous* ball that travels at *too great a speed*. Discretion has ever been considered the better part of valour, and perhaps this is the right view for the great batsmen and the great bowlers of a side to take, but it is emphatically not the plan of campaign for the privates of an eleven. For fieldsmen numbered among these last, I should strongly recommend a study of the fielding of Albert Trott, one of the finest fields at slip or in near proximity to the wicket that I have ever seen. There is no funk here, the big strong hands flash out, they give with the ball, it is held, and many a fine batsman has walked disconsolately away, who would have stayed to all eternity had he but selected a fieldsman of discretionary valour.

Another feature that presents itself is that the lethargy, the laziness, the wonderful yearning for rest, are more noticeable in our great batsmen than in our great bowlers. A great batsman having produced a colossal score seems content with his performance, he loafs in the field, and when not loafing he peacefully slumbers. Sometimes, fortunately for the side on which he plays, he drifts into the slips and sustains a rude awakening when the rising ball is faintly touched and he receives it on the wrists or on the ankle, as the case may be. Naturally for a while, so long as the pain is acute, he is awake, and perhaps during this lucid interval he makes a catch or two, but then again the yearning for rest is felt, and peacefully he dozes. It were a good thing for cricket if many a great batsman could be confined to the slips, for there there is always this chance of a sudden shock, a sudden realization that he is in the field to do some work.

The same idea of rest, of *dolce far niente* pervades many of the great bowlers of to-day, but not, I think, to so great an extent. This is probably due to the fact that they know and feel keenly the disappointment of a missed chance, a chance that they have been bowling over after over to obtain. Feeling this they do not sleep, they do their best to help their fellow workers in the field. We have all felt it, this clinging desire for rest. It may be that we are tired, that we play too much cricket; it may be the subtle influence of a bright June day, or the soothing light from the soft great turf; but from whatever cause it springs it has been with us in a more pronounced form this season than ever before in my experience of the game. We nearly all do it, we cricketers who are not included in the category of great batsmen or great bowlers, and its effect on matches is prodigious.

Personally I shall never forget missing a well-known player through sleeping at extra slip. I missed him when eighteen, and he remained with us the rest of the live-long day, making nearly three hundred with not a vestige of a chance. For several ensuing matches I endeavoured to keep awake.

Though few men have this year raised themselves to the front rank of fieldsmen, there is one whose efforts should not go unrecorded, and this is Vine, a fair all-round cricketer, but one whose fielding should ensure him a place in almost any side in England. He is full of life, full of energy, he is fast on his feet, he throws straight and hard, he catches well and possesses the same strange intuition of the ball's direction that belongs but to fine fieldsmen. In most matches, should he take no wickets, make no runs, he will have saved a goodly number, and in all probability have assisted at the downfall of some of the other side. And there is yet another whose right is plain to be included in a list of splendid workers, and he is Victor Barton, perhaps the finest cover point of the day, though run very close in this position by Johnny Briggs, who is nearly as good to-day as ever he was. Barton has the easiest and surest return of almost any county cricketer I have ever seen, and he never tires.

Of the fielding of the 'Varsity Elevens, I am not in a position to write having seen comparatively little of them. From what I saw, I should say Cambridge were a really good team in the field, their ground work being very clean, J. Daniell in all positions especially noticeable. Oxford were also good and in R. E. Foster we have one of the finest short slips in the country.

A large number of cricketers no doubt will object, and object strongly to my strictures on our fielding in 1900. There are many good fields that owing to lack of space I am unable to mention, but as I said at the commencement of this article 'there are exceptions on every side to this general sloth,' men who have energy and endurance that will carry them through a long day's outing. Doubtless all these are numbered among the little band of hard workers, the exceptions to the general rule. It is impossible for all of us to be fine fields, for to be a fine field is to be equipped with physical advantages that only a few possess. The keen, long sight—the long, quick stride—the ability to throw hard and straight—the strange intuition to divine the flight of a ball—the pace at which it is travelling—its direction—the power to hold it—*all* these gifts are given to but a few. Therefore let those of us, we who to-day stand like 'little mounds of earth,' like waxen figures in a third rate tailors shop, put energy, motion, life into our fielding; let us sleep not—let the lethargy, the laziness, the wonderful yearning for rest become as shadows of the past and there will be but few drawn matches, but few new rules required in our great national game.

ON THE PREPARATION OF WICKETS [1905]

BY A. C. MACLAREN

Jephson was back again in the 1904 Almanack discussing a point of batting technique raised in Ranjitsinhji's 'Cricket'. However, curbing his poetic flair rather too well, Jepshon achieved no more than a humdrum efficiency. The next readable essay to appear turned up in 1905, and, in view of what was to follow soon after, the choice of subject and author seems slightly risible. 'On the Preparation of Wickets' by A. C. MacLaren is a bold, opinionated blast from one of the rather too confident amateurs of the period.

Archibald Campbell MacLaren (1871–1944) was a batsman of classic style and a captain of dictatorial tendencies which did not always give the results he expected. Rendered immortal by the purple prose of Neville Cardus, MacLaren was inclined to outbursts of choler, often in connection with the condition of pitches, and once set in his attitude, nothing could move him. At the time he composed his article on pitch preparation, he had already given a spectacular demonstration of his obduracy in a crisis. The Lancashire–Gloucestershire match at Old Trafford in July 1895 was ruined through the torrential rain which persistently defeated the attempts of the batsmen of both sides to score runs. At the close of the second day, with the game balanced on a knife-edge, Lancashire requiring 45 runs to win with 5 wickets in hand, the heavens opened and the ground became waterlogged. The Gloucestershire captain, W. G. Grace, thinking it a pity that so keenly contested a game should not be fought to a finish, proposed that the final session be played on a fresh pitch. MacLaren refused and the game was abandoned as a draw, to MacLaren's evident relief but nobody else's.

Highhandedness on quite a different plane followed in July 1907 at Lord's. when once again prospects of play were bedevilled by heavy rain. On the afternoon of the second day the umpires pulled up stumps at five o'clock, after which a few of the spectators walked across the pitch. MacLaren then issued a statement to the Press:

> Owing to the pitch having been deliberately torn up by the public, I, as captain of the Lancashire eleven, cannot see my way to continue the game, the groundsman bearing me out that the wicket could not again be put right – A. C. MacLaren.

Wisden mildly commented: 'Rolled next morning for the regulation ten minutes, the pitch showed little trace of the treatment to which it had been subjected'. In the light of these antics, the choice of MacLaren as an expert on the nature of cricket pitches does have its comic overtones.

IT was only recently that steps were taken to prevent some of our groundsmen from using other materials than the heavy roller and the watering can in their preparation of cricket pitches. The groundsman had brought the art of preparing wickets to such a pitch of perfection that the poor bowler had little chance of success in fine weather, with the natural result of huge scores and drawn games, or rather unfinished games. Last season this super-excellence of wickets was not so manifest, since there was less talk about drawn games owing to more matches having been finished than formerly in a run-getting season. Many of us have, for the last four or five years, been convinced that the one and only way to improve our game, or possibly to bring it to the standard of excellence of a generation back, was the expulsion of those shining billiard table pitches which would play as well on the last as the first day of the match – pitches which must always be a temptation to even the unselfish batsman to take too long in getting a sight of the ball and, with that accomplished, to be too long at the crease for his runs. There are plenty of men on every side to-day who know how many they ought to get before the last man is sent back, and the moment when it is necessary to force the game which will be converted into a win provided all will play the game to enable the bowlers to have time to dismiss their opponents, who have to play the by no means easy losing game. Selfishness on the cricket field is seldom seen except, when the wicket is perfect, and one man alone is sufficient, provided he be selfish, to undo all the good work of the other ten. Here is the man who is a nuisance to the game, and who causes people to suggest alterations in the implements of the same, when the abolition of the perfect wicket would be the means of ousting this player from the side, without a change in his methods, for the bowler seldom fails against this type of player except on the perfect wicket. Until five years ago, any batsman who could make his century in a county match, was, in my humble opinion, a good player, but owing to the too perfect wicket of the last few seasons, making it impossible for good bowlers to hold their own against only moderate batsmen who lay themselves out for runs, my appreciation of certain centuries of late years has been considerably less. More runs are made to-day, not because the batting has improved, but owing to the fact that the wickets have been over prepared – result, there have been fewer good bowlers annually, with a corresponding increase of good batsmen – enabling the good player to knock the ball about with such demoralising effect that, when the fair batsman comes along, the bowler has no reserve power left, resulting in this player to-day making far more runs than he would have done ten years or so back. Large scores undoubtedly improve one's confidence, hence we have a lot more good batsmen than used to be the case, making it far more difficult for our bowlers than formerly, when there were fewer matches and not so many good batsmen on one side, to say nothing of the absence of the unnatural wicket that we have seen in the past few seasons. Good batsmen have not to fight for their runs, which come along more easily than used to be the case. The greatest mischief caused by these too perfect wickets is the compulsory cricket on the third day of the match without the remotest chance of a finish. This is the time, above all others, when our bowlers get ruined, having to bowl for some four or five hours without that enthusiasm so necessary if one is to be successful. This gruelling work, with no fitting reward at the end of it, is quite as fatiguing as the work meted out, at times, to some of our good bowlers who have to bowl so many hours at the nets to whatever duffer comes along. The after effects of these performances are so telling that it is not long before some of these bowlers acquire a mechanical sort of style with no variation whatsoever, making it impossible for them to become bowlers in the true sense of the word. It is absolutely necessary for us to finish more games if we are going to bring out any bowlers, and this will never be accomplished if our groundsmen continue to make such perfect wickets as are seen to-day. The very lengthy list of matches which Yorkshire, Surrey, and Lancashire have to get through is bound to tell, in fact, has already told its tale on the bowlers of the above counties. By the first week in August the Lancashire bowlers were bowled to a complete standstill, and this could also be said of the Yorkshiremen, whilst one does not require telling what overwork has done for Surrey. I have read that no one wants to see Australian cricket in England, but it can always be said of Australian cricket that the interest is kept up to the last, no matter how many days be required to bring a match to a conclusion, there being no sign of slackness on the part of the players, although they play in some matches which last double the time of ours and are decided under tropical conditions. The excellence of the Australian attack in England has been due, in no small measure, to the fact that our Colonial friends have never been sickened of bowling by playing season after season in matches, out of many of which all interest is taken owing to the fact that, long before the last ball is bowled, it becomes patent to all that no definite result can be possible. Although the bat has the mastery of the ball on the good Australian wickets, yet the very paucity of first-class matches causes the lengthy games to be welcomed, good cricket being witnessed throughout, which is more than can be said of some of our first-class matches. Here it is as well to point out that the perfect Australian wicket is not one whit better than the perfect English wicket, indeed, many of us prefer to bat on our good wicket, which allows us more time to watch the ball. The following are, in my opinion, the best batting wickets we have. Trent Bridge, fearfully overdone with marl, giving bowlers no chance whatsoever; Canterbury, when Lancashire played there, a naturally perfect wicket with no artificial aid; ditto Taunton and Bath; Oval, very good wicket, used to be artificially doctored, making it impossible for the bowler to break or bounce the ball; Leicestershire, another wicket far too good, over-marled; Birmingham, a naturally perfect wicket; Derby ditto; Worcester, naturally perfect wicket; Leyton, a perfect wicket, but naturally so; Hants, perfect. Other wickets there are which are not so heart-breaking from a bowler's point of view, such as:– Lord's. – A peculiar wicket often playing better on the second than on the first day; not infrequently breaks up on third day. Brighton. –

Good, but nothing like so perfect as formerly, breaks up at times. Yorkshire – Grounds good without being too good. Lancashire. – Possessed of life, enabling bowlers to send in a good one occasionally. A little marl has been added; generally considered a good sporting wicket. Gloucestershire – Good wicket at Bristol; at Gloucester bad.

The southern wickets, in many instances, have more than a week's preparation, being well rolled and watered continually, whilst such a thing as a coarse piece of grass or weed is almost unknown. One frequently sees two other wickets prepared besides that upon which the match is being played. These, being in reserve for the following three days, will receive attention every morning and evening of those days upon which a match is taking place. Now these wickets, natural ones too, are too good for our cricket as it is now played, and that our cricket is not so exhilarating to watch as formerly the poor gates of to-day tell us, for the British public likes a finish, which will not be seen as often as it should be, not even with a vast amount of improvement in catching, which is as good as it ever was, at any rate in the last fifteen years. The same state of things is bound to exist until the wickets in fine weather receive considerably less attention at the hands of the groundsmen. I was much impressed last season by conversations with many of our bowlers concerning some of the perfect wickets upon which they had to bowl for half of their matches. For the most part these men stuck to their work against big odds very well indeed, and one could scarcely help feeling sorry when they good-naturedly grumbled at the perfect wickets. Success, no matter how little, inspires a bowler with a certain amount of confidence which improves a man considerably, but repeated gruellings without wickets will certainly have the opposite effect and cause a bowler to wonder if he ever could bowl at all. These men ought to be considered, for if they are not, the public will not come to our matches as formerly. The bowler of old had not to bowl against so many good batsmen in one match, had no chance of getting stale owing to the far fewer matches of those days, and lastly the wickets were nothing like so uniformly perfect. In Lancashire that gloss so frequently seen on southern wickets is not even noticeable from the pavilion before our matches start, because the wickets are not over-rolled. Our groundsman has also tough weeds to contend against, finding it impossible to get all of them up, thus causing a ball to kick up at times, with the result that batsmen play a rather more forcing game than they would do provided they could trust the wicket, as a batsman can when playing on three out of every four of our grounds. I consider that Old Trafford provides an ideal wicket and one for our three day matches about which no bowler should grumble, since his chance is about equal to that of the batsman. My last request at the end of last season was that our wickets should for the forthcoming season be as near to the standard of last season's as possible. The over-preparation of a wicket is a distinct handicap to a good side, since it will often save a moderate side from defeat. Had Lancashire played upon the same billiard table at Old Trafford as are met with at Trent Bridge, we certainly would not have had half so good a record as we actually did put up, likewise our wickets would not have suited Notts – a very uneven batting side. In my opinion, an ordinary county ground which is properly looked after, can produce an excellent wicket with but a couple of good rollings, whereas five out of six groundsmen are not satisfied until the wicket has been so thoroughly watered and well rolled day after day that the turf is as hard as adamant on the day of the match, with no earthly chance of the pitch breaking up. Is it surprising that our bowlers get sick of a hard season? The flighty bowlers such as Hirst, Hargreave, Hallows, Blythe, and J. Gunn, are the only type of bowlers to get good wickets on hard going, and their flightiness vanishes more or less as soon as the ball loses its gloss. Braund and Bosanquet, of course, may get anyone out, but the latter especially is more than expensive when it is not his day out, and that must always take a considerable time for a captain to find out, especially when he knows the length bowler with the overdone off-theory style will be of little use to him. These length bowlers have been absolutely compelled by the very excellence of the wickets to bowl well outside the off-stump on the chance of getting the batsman to cut a wrong one, about the only possible way of sending a good man back when facing this type of bowler, who would certainly bowl straighter if the wicket would occasionally render him sufficient assistance to permit him to break the ball enough to beat the bat. If we only gave our length bowlers a fair wicket instead of a billiard table, spectators would see freer cricket from batsmen who prefer to thoroughly tire a bowler out and then wait for instead of making their own opportunities, for the man who goes in for defence has a very poor show against a Jack Hearne spinning the ball on a hard wicket. With less perfect wickets to play upon, the game would not last so long, nor would it be robbed one bit of its science, which assuredly it will be if ever stumps are lengthened or widened and bats lessened.

SOUTH AFRICAN BOWLING [1908]

BY R. E. FOSTER

In 1908 there appeared one of the most instructive disquisitions ever to be published in the Almanack. By this time the stratagems of Bosanquet had passed into the common stockpot of bowling technique, as more and more bowlers began to grasp the essence of Bosanquet's revolutionary methods of spinning a ball. By 1907, when the South African touring party arrived in England, the new style of slow bowling had so taken root that virtually the entire attacking plan of the visitors was invested either in the googly or variations upon it. The South African battery included no fewer that four bowlers who deployed the leg-spin grip in Schwartz, Vogler, White and Faulkner. The quartet attracted great interest, and much was expected of them in the Tests. In the first game at Lord's, outstanding batting by Braund and Jessop carried England past 400, although Vogler took 7 wickets, including that of the England captain, R. E. Foster, stumped for 8. The second Test, at Leeds, was a game of modest scores made memorable by the match winning performance of Colin Blythe, whose left-arm spin took 15 South African wickets for 99 runs. Foster made only 22 for twice out. The final Test at the Oval was another draw, Foster at last enjoying some success with scores of 51 and 35. It was, in the circumstances, an excellent idea of Pardon's to invite Foster to describe the subtly differing techniques of the four South Africans from the viewpoint of someone obliged to work them out.

Reginald Erskine Foster was one of the world's great batsmen of the golden age. The most gifted of the seven Fosters of Worcestershire, he is one of the few Gentleman-cricketers to have performed the coveted hat-trick of his social class: centuries for Oxford against Cambridge, for the Gentlemen against the Players, and for England against Australia. His 287 at Sydney in 1903 remains the highest innings by an Englishman in a Test in Australia. In spite of his outstanding athletic gifts, Foster was not robust enough to enjoy a full career, and after 1907, when he captained England against the South Africans, he never again enjoyed a full season. His last county appearance was in 1912. Foster was also an outstanding Association footballer, playing for the full England side several times, and captaining them from right full-back in a match against the embryonic German side, giving him a distinction which will never be challenged, of being the only man to captain his country at football and cricket. In 1914, after intermittent illness and bouts of convalescence, he died of diabetes at the age of 36. Because he never grew old, Foster remains an unblemished symbol of the Edwardian ideal, a carefree virtuoso whose life appears to have been one long romp under the sun. To this day he cuts an impressive figure in the photographs of the England tourists in Australia in the winter of 1903–4. With an oddly equivocal expression on his face, peering out from under the brim of an extravagant sun-hat, his body draped in a strikingly modern-looking jacket, he embodies all the pathos of a young man mercifully ignorant of his own impending fate.

THE cricket season of 1907 will always be remembered by two distinct features. 1.—The extremely bad weather. 2.—The South Africans' bowling. The less said about the former the better, though the rain and the consequent soft wickets did raise a very interesting question; namely, would the South Africans have fared better in a good dry season? Now, looking at their performances against the counties, it seems difficult to conceive how they could have improved on their magnificent record, however good and fast the wickets might have been. Before their arrival in this country we were told that they must have hard wickets to really suit their particular kind of bowling, but the way they bowled, not only in representative games, but against the counties on sticky wickets, was a revelation to many a good judge of cricket. The feature of their bowling on these wickets was the extraordinary pace at which the ball came off the pitch. This was to be expected on fast wickets, but no one had foreseen that the same thing would happen on really slow ones. Truly, as one old hand said in the Test Match at Leeds, it was like playing Briggs through the air and Tom Richardson off the pitch. Now, the opinion of English cricketers who went to South Africa with the M.C.C. team in 1905 is, that there is all the difference in the world between our fast good wickets and the South African matting wickets, and this lies in the varying height in the bound of the ball. On the matting the ball nearly always had to be played about chest high, a fact enormously increasing the difficulty of dealing with such bowling. On our fast wickets the ball may turn very quickly and go either one of two ways, but it nearly always comes at the same height; and I maintain that the English team would have got any amount of runs under such conditions, and more than that, the South Africans would not have done so well in a dry season. Had the Test Matches been played on matting it quite possibly might have been another matter, though it is open to question (their batting being rather a weak point) if the bowling could have carried them to victory in representative games. The South African bowlers could be hit on a good wicket, and it is possible that a little more enterprise might have spelt success. Jessop showed they could be hit, in a magnificent display in the first Test Match, on a good wicket; but he also showed, at Leeds and the Oval, that they could not be hit on a bad wicket, for not only did the ball turn too quickly, but it came a different height and pace. The result of a comparison of the dangers presented by the South African attack on fast and slow wickets seems to point to a preference for the latter, and I know this to be the opinion of most of the players who represented England against them.

Now let us turn to a detailed description of the bowling. The interest in the attack of the South Africans is centred round four men—Schwarz, Vogler, Faulkner, and White. These men all bowled with a leg-break action, and could make the ball come in from the off. Though England can claim the 'proud originator' of this style of bowling in Bosanquet, it has been left to South Africa to improve it—I will not say perfect—as I am convinced that this style is capable of still further improvement, which in time will be brought nearly to perfection. Bosanquet taught Schwarz, and Schwarz taught the others, and the others are better than their mentors, as Bosanquet has practically given up bowling in this way, and Schwarz, possibly because he finds he can get as many people out as he wishes, only breaks the ball from the off, but always with a leg-break action. His has been a great achievement this year, of which he and the South Africans may justly be proud, for he is top of the bowling averages, having taken 143 wickets with an average of 11.51 apiece, a performance that speaks for itself. It is rather hard to explain his great success, as, though his bowling is the most difficult to hit of the four bowlers mentioned, it is much the easiest to play, because he only breaks one way, and the batsmen have never got to think of the possibility of the ball breaking the other way. The ball comes very slow through the air, and having hit the ground goes off at the most extraordinary pace. There is nothing very deceptive in the flight, but the break varies from six inches to eighteen inches, and on sticky wickets he is quite capable of breaking a yard. Now a bowler of this description, you will say, must bowl many loose balls; certainly he does, but the pace the ball comes from the wicket imparted by the spin, makes it very difficult indeed for the batsman to place it accurately between the fielders, six of whom are placed in various parts of the one side, and hitting at random at such bowling courts disaster, and I am sure is one of the causes of his success this year. In addition to this reason Schwarz is extraordinarily deadly to the last four of five batsmen, and the man who goes in for his county side in rather a humble position seems to have no notion how to play such bowling. He is a great bowler, but I am convinced he gets many more wickets than he should. Play him with your legs—old pavilion critics forgive, but we have to deal with bowling you never had to trouble about—don't hit at him, place him for one's and two's, and wait for the real bad one which you will occasionally get and can score off. Very often a bowler of Schwarz's description will suffer at the umpire's hands, but it must be well nigh impossible to tell if the batsman is out when a ball comes so quickly off the pitch, and knowing how much the bowler is capable of making the ball break; finally, I cannot help thinking that Schwarz would prove more deadly could he control his break—*i.e.*, break nothing to a foot, and I believe that he would get many good batsmen out with the ball that does not break at all.

Of the remaining three of this interesting quartette, Faulkner and White can be considered together, but Vogler claims our attention all to himself. He was undoubtedly the finest bowler of a very good lot, indeed many good judges consider him the best bowler in the English cricket season of 1907. He has rather a hesitating run up to the wicket, but in the last few steps never gets out of his stride. The ball is well concealed from the batsman before delivery, and the flight and variation of pace are very deceptive indeed. With a new ball, Vogler makes the ball swing quite a lot and often starts bowling fast medium off-break, with a swerve. He then will have two slips and a short leg, and perhaps no man out in the country. With the newness worn off the ball he will settle down to his ordinary slow mediums, in which case his field will be, with the exception of three men, disposed of on the onside of the wicket. Vogler, like Schwarz and other bowlers who have cultivated this particular type of bowling, imparts that spin to the ball which enables it to leave the pitch at such a wonderful pace. His usual ball is the leg-break, but once in two overs perhaps he will bowl what the South Africans have designated 'the wrong 'un.' Now it is almost impossible to see this ball coming; it seems to the batsman that the ball is delivered in identically the same manner and yet it comes the other way, *i.e.*, from the off. After very careful watching the only difference one can detect, and this is possibly fancy, is that the hand seems to be turned farther over in the action of delivery. The ball seems to come more out of the back of the hand, and the batsman may be able to see almost the palm of the bowler's hand. But it is almost impossible to notice any difference, and I was told Sherwell had said that Vogler was the bowler he found most difficulty in detecting. Vogler's ordinary leg-break will turn from two or three inches up to eighteen inches, but the other one coming from the off rarely breaks more than three or four inches and frequently comes perfectly straight through, and in this case will come even faster off the pitch than the balls that turn. This possibly is due to the bowler intending to bowl the off-break, and through not quite turning the hand or fingers sufficiently, imparts a top spin. This makes the ball come straight through very quickly and is one of the most difficult balls to deal with—lbw so often resulting. Vogler bowls a slow yorker or well pitched up ball that is very deceptive in the flight and seems more to quiver than swing in the air. He clean bowled C. B. Fry with this ball both at Leeds and at the Oval in the Test Matches. As will be seen then, Vogler is a bowler of infinite variation, unbounded resource, and what is better than all, of great natural ability. He can bowl for a long time and does not seem to tire or lose his length. His performances at Lord's this year against a very strong M.C.C. XI. and again in the first Test Match were as good as anything seen at headquarters for years. Vogler's average for the season works out at 133 wickets for 15 apiece, and in Test Matches he was, taken all through, much the best and most consistent bowler on the South African side, though actual figures bring Faulkner out above him, due mainly to a great performance in England's first innings at Leeds. Schwarz does not come out so well, a third of his total number of wickets being obtained in the last innings at the Oval when the English side were risking wickets in order to obtain runs quickly, another instance of the argument that Schwarz cannot be hit recklessly. In Vogler the South Africans possess undoubtedly a bowler of the highest class, and in the writer's humble opinion the greatest bowler playing cricket in either hemisphere at the present time, and we may dismiss him with many congratulations on his great performances, and many thanks for the great interest and pleasure his bowling has afforded this summer to all lovers of cricket.

Faulkner and White are to all intents and purposes the same bowler. They deliver the ball from practically the same height, and the flight, pace, and break are almost identical. But Faulkner is certainly the more dangerous bowler, and, if there is any difference, comes through the air and off the pitch a shade faster, and is undoubtedly capable of bowling a more unplayable ball. His performance at Leeds in the first innings against England is surely the greatest that had ever been achieved in this unorthodox style of bowling. Gordon White it is true comes out with a better average, having taken 72 wickets for 13 runs apiece against 73 wickets for 15 runs each, but Faulkner did not get into form till practically July and was hardly ever called upon. These two bowlers in the ordinary way deliver much the same ball as the English batsman is accustomed to expect and receive from a leg-break bowler of the Braund-Vine type with two notable differences—*(a)* the ball comes from the pitch at a far greater pace; *(b)* the terrible 'wrong 'un.' In the first case as has been said above, this characteristic is evident in each of the four bowlers under consideration, and the reason for it is very difficult to explain. A possible cause may be found in the fact that ordinary leg-break bowlers deliver the ball chiefly by the swing of the arm and allowing the ball to come from the back of the hand, whereas the South Africans seem to deliver the ball with a flick, relying entirely on finger and wrist for spin. In the second case both bowlers can effectively bowl the ball that comes from the off with a leg-break action, but again in a measure differ. Faulkner makes the ball break quite a lot from the off and practically always makes it break; White on the other hand makes the ball break comparatively little and very often comes straight through, therefore Faulkner is more likely to clean bowl a batsman and White to get him lbw. Neither has a deceptive flight, and it is possible to see the off-break coming in both cases occasionally. Indeed I venture to think that with more practice against such bowling, batsmen would soon find far less difficulty in seeing the break and possibly might never be at fault. In Vogler's case and in future artists of his class that may arise (as this type of bowling and the art of concealing a break will greatly improve), I doubt if the batsmen will ever be impossible to deceive.

Before passing to what must be henceforward termed the ordinary kind of bowlers, it may be interesting just to see if this new type of bowling is likely in the future to improve or deteriorate batting from the spectator's point of view. Personally, I think it will deteriorate batting. For this new kind of bowling is a very great invention, and it is possible it may completely alter cricket, and no one who has not played against it can realize the difference it makes to a batsman and his shots. It must again be reiterated that this type of bowling is practically in its infancy, and if persevered with—as it surely will be—must improve and become more difficult to deal with. Now a batsman when he goes in may receive a ball which either breaks from the off, perhaps from the leg, or again may come straight through very quickly. If he survives half-a-dozen overs he ought to be getting set, but such bowling never allows a batsman to get really set, because he can never make or go for his accustomed shots. The ball just short of a half volley he is accustomed to drive between cover and extra cover fearlessly, now bothers him, and prevents him doing so, owing to his inability to discover which way and how much the ball is going to break. And as this bowling improves the difficulty will become increased, till those beautiful drives we are wont to expect from some of our great batsmen will become a thing of the past. Hayward was stumped in both the first two Test Matches, playing that shot through the covers, and after experiences such as these will give up attempting the stroke. No! such bowling will enormously increase defence at the expense of safe scoring shots such as drives and cuts, and scoring will be confined to hitting. Many people may maintain that this will be a good thing, but if Hayward's off-driving and Tyldesley's cutting are to be seen no more and such strokes to be a lost art to future generations, cricket, as far as batting is concerned, must lose a great deal of its attractiveness.

And finally let us turn to the ordinary bowlers. These comprise, Sinclair, Kotze, Nourse, and Snooke. Sinclair is a very fine bowler, and had he played on any other side would have done a great deal better. He never had a chance, and was not put on unless the quartette were unable to get a side out, which was a very rare occurrence. I think he might have been used more, though Sherwell had a very difficult task, having really too much bowling at his command. Sinclair has a nice easy run up to the wicket, and a great command over the flight and pace of the delivery. He uses his great height well, and though bowling quite medium could send down a very fast 'Yorker'—a useful and often fatal ball. The members of the English Team had a high opinion of his bowling and were secretly delighted he was not called upon more. His spin enabled him to break the ball on nearly any wicket, and on a pitch that suits him he is very difficult to deal with, as he makes the ball get up very quickly from the pitch, as well as come back sharply.

Kotze had a very unfortunate experience, the wet season rendering him of little value to his side. It is impossible to criticize his bowling as he hardly did any, but he did not seem to be very dangerous and rather to have decreased in pace since his last visit to England in 1904. But he continues to have such great success in South Africa that the cold and wet weather in this country this summer never probably allowed him to get loose or into form, and had it been a summer of hard wickets he would undoubtedly have been a very useful member of the side. Nourse is a fast-medium left-hand bowler with a big swerve, and occasionally makes the ball break back off the wicket. He bowls absolutely naturally, and might get a wicket any time—but ought not to defeat a batsman who had defied him for three or four overs. Snooke is a fast, right-hand bowler and gets up rather straight from the pitch; but as the two last mentioned were not called upon to any extent, they can hardly be classed among the regular bowlers of the side.

This brings to a close a brief description of the South African bowling, which from its varied nature and novel characteristics affords a most interesting study to the cricket enthusiast. Taken as a whole they were undoubtedly a magnificent bowling side, to be compared with advantage to any Australian side that has visited England in recent years. Had their batting been of the same calibre, England might well have come off second best.

In conclusion, they have won the admiration of everyone with whom they have come in contact, not only for their cricket capabilities but because they have played the game in the right spirit, being led by a man who has only the best interests of cricket at heart. And all will agree that it has been the greatest pleasure to have met and played with the South African Team of 1907.

PART TWO

1915 – 1939

NOTES BY THE EDITOR [1915]

BY S. H. PARDON

There follows a disappointing decline in both the standard and the frequency of the essays in Wisden. Although the game itself was enjoying what more than one historian has defined as its very richest years, and although to dip into the Almanacks of the period is to saunter through a cricket-lover's paradise, the writing in Wisden, confining itself for the most part to accounts of overseas tours, was too functional for its own good. Whether Pardon was simply doing his best to hold down the size of the Almanack, or whether he had run out of ideas for pieces, or whether he was holding the purse-strings a little more tightly, it is hard to guess, but it was not until 1915 that an essay was included which commends itself to the modern reader. Ironically this exception was Pardon's own editorial feature, which has triumphantly withstood the ravages of time, although perhaps not quite for reasons which would have pleased its author.

By the time Wisden went to press for the 1915 edition, it was clear to most thinking men that the Great War was to be no six-month escapade, but a long, savage, obscene slaughter. Soon the pathetic cricketer-poet who had greeted the war by likening his own condemned generation to those who 'turn, as swimmers into cleanness leaping', would find his own place in the Wisden death notices, by which time the euphoria of the swimmers would have been superseded by the disenchantment of Graves and Sassoon. Even in 1915, the section following Pardon's editorial was a list of cricketers who had died in 1914; the list was much longer than usual, hideously extended by casualties sustained in the fighting in France. And yet Pardon, trying desperately to put a brave face on it, talks of the possibility of a sudden resumption of the first-class game: '. . . but in the happy event of the War coming to an end at an earlier date than the experts expect . . .'. Poor Pardon, and poor cricket, hardly knowing what had happened to their world. What had happened was that the old life, of comfortable assumptions and the golden sovereign, of intimations of immortality and the impregnable imperial fortress, was already blown to smithereens. The deaths of cricketers would soon be so commonplace that Pardon would find himself editing an Almanack consisting almost entirely of obituaries.

Pardon as he prepared the 1915 edition was in a bizarre predicament. Surrounded as he was by the collapse of a civilisation, he had to concentrate on the collapse of Lancashire on a wet wicket in Manchester. Obliged despite himself to relegate cricket to a footnote in the national life, and sensing that the tragedy taking place might yet prove of a magnitude too terrible to contemplate, he was obliged to perform an editorial duty founded on assumptions no longer valid. His job was to turn a deaf ear to the shrieks of grief and the reverberations of the guns, and to tabulate the lineaments of normality, the events of an ordinary cricket season, for we have to remind ourselves that the season of 1914 had not been disturbed by crisis until very nearly at its end. For this reason alone, the 1915 edition would show no reduction in size. And yet, even as Pardon and his staff so meticulously transcribed the sensations of the previous summer, the world which had produced them was lying dead beyond resuscitation. It is an interesting exercise, trying to conjure the image of some young infantryman sitting in a dugout up to his calves in mud, or perhaps picking off from his greatcoat fragments of his best friend's brains, or practising his fielding by throwing stones at the rats, and then to guess at this young man's feelings as someone thrust into his hands the 1915 edition of Wisden, its buff covers seeming like the distilled sunlight of a world but dimly remembered, even though so close in time. What would his thoughts have been as he thumbed through the 534 pages and looked up his own deeds, performed in a world long vanished and yet only a few months past? Would he have been amused by the irony of the announcement on the inside cover, telling that at Nevill's Turkish Baths in Northumberland Avenue 'the soothing tonic character of the Bath renders it peculiarly suitable for all nervous troubles'? Would he have been tempted to write for further details to the Railway Passengers Assurance Company, who had, it was said, paid out nearly £7,000,000 in compensation for accidents and illness? Perhaps not, but in the sense that the 1915 Wisden recorded deeds suddenly bereft of any social context, it remains the most dramatic in the entire series. Under such terrible circumstances, Pardon's effort to maintain the demeanour of normality is a prodigious performance.

WRITING in the early days of the New Year it is impossible to take other than a gloomy view with regard to the immediate future of cricket. Never before has the game been in such a plight. One may take it for granted that, in any circumstances, county cricket, as we have known it for the last forty years or more, will be out of the question this season, but in the happy event of the War coming to an end at an earlier date than the experts expect, we are sure to see plenty of games of a less competitive character. Indeed, as all the fixtures were provisionally made last summer, the counties might try something in the nature of a modified programme. However, it is idle to speculate in January as to what will happen in May or June. I hope no attempt will be made to close the game down entirely. All the counties are asking their members to keep on with their subscriptions, and in return matches of some kind should from time to time be played on the various grounds. Cricketers have made a splendid response to the call to the colours. They cannot all go to the front; some of them have duties that must keep them at home. To my mind, it would be a great misfortune for any county ground to be closed for the whole summer. I had thought of preparing for *Wisden* a list of the cricketers who have joined the Army, but the number is so great that I could not be at all sure of accuracy. Any accidental omission might have involved protest and correction. After the War, whenever that may be, cricket will, no doubt, go on as before, but it will naturally take some time for the game to recover completely from the blow it has received.

Turning to the past season, it was pleasant to find Surrey winning the Championship, a distinction that had not fallen to them since 1899. Some people thought that when, in deference to public opinion—W. G. Grace himself was the chief spokesman—Surrey cancelled their last two matches, the Championship would have to remain in abeyance for the year, but this view received no countenance from the M.C.C. It would have been iniquitous if Surrey had been robbed of the position they had so fairly won. When, at Surrey's own request, the question was brought before the M.C.C. committee, the matter was promptly settled, Middlesex disclaiming any notion of objecting. Surrey had a fine eleven, but to make their side complete they needed a little more bowling. The enforced transfer to Lord's of the return matches with Kent and Yorkshire when, in the first days of the War, the military authorities took possession of the Oval, involved serious disadvantages. Indeed, the Kent match, as a benefit to Hobbs, was such a failure that the Surrey committee have decided not to treat it as a benefit. They will give Hobbs another match as soon as circumstances permit, his subscription list in the meantime remaining open. This generous action on Surrey's part—not hitherto made known—will please everyone. Hobbs is not only the best bat in England at the present time, but also the most attractive and popular.

Apart from the heavy toll imposed by the War, the casualty lists including many young officers who had gained their colours at the public schools, death was very busy among cricketers in 1914. To mention only the most famous names: Joseph Makinson, Canon McCormick and B. B. Cooper, died full of years. A. G. Steel and J. H. Brain were still in middle age, and three great players of our day, R. E. Foster, Albert Trott and A. O. Jones passed away prematurely. W. O. Moberly, one of the batsmen who helped the Graces to make Gloucestershire invincible in the 'seventies,' was not exactly an old man, but he had reached the age of sixty-three.

The death of R. E. Foster, together with the success for Oxford and Surrey last summer of D. J. Knight, sets one thinking of the wonderful things done by Malvern batsmen during the last twenty years or so. Until P. H. Latham played for Cambridge in 1892, no Malvern cricketer had ever appeared in the University match. Since Latham's time we have seen in addition to the Fosters, six of whom have won distinction in first-class cricket, C. J. Burnup, the late W. H. B. Evans, S. H. Day, A. P. Day, F. T. Mann, and now Knight, not to mention one or two others who failed to fulfil their early promise. No school, I should think, has in the same space of time produced so many good batsmen since Eton in, roughly speaking, twenty years, turned out R. A. H. Mitchell, C. G. Lyttelton (now Lord Cobham), Alfred Lubbock, E. W. Tritton, C. J. Ottaway, Lord Harris, C. I. Thornton, A. W. Ridley, G. H. Longman, Alfred and Edward Lyttelton, Ivo Bligh, Walter Forbes and C. T. Studd. The Eton record, extending from 1857 to 1879, is without parallel in the history of public school cricket. Beyond putting R. E. Foster out by himself at the head of the list, I would not attempt to place the Malvern batsmen in any strict order of merit. Most people, if asked the question would give second place to H. K. Foster, but Burnup, on his form for Kent in 1906, and W. H. B. Evans at his best, have very strong claims. A. P. Day did not have the advantage of going up to Oxford or Cambridge but, stepping straight out of school cricket into the Kent eleven, he made over a thousand runs in the first season in county matches.

One of the most notable feats last season was that of Sir T. C. O'Brien in the match at Attleborough, between Mr. Lionel Robinson's Eleven and Oxford University. O'Brien became famous as a batsman in 1884 and yet, after an interval of thirty years, he hit up scores of 90 and 111. For a man of nearly fifty-three this was a big performance. I happen to know that O'Brien has a poor opinion of most modern bowlers, contending that in their craze for the swerve they have lost much in spin and accuracy of length. In the match at Attleborough, as another famous cricketer of the last generation put it, he gave the swervers and slingers of the Oxford eleven a good deal to think about.

At the Oval, in August, I was asked to mention in *Wisden* a record which, so far as I know, has escaped the notice of all the statisticians. R. G. Barlow told me that he played first-class cricket for twenty-years, and that he was then completing his twenty-first season as an umpire. Judging from appearances he is likely to go on for many years to come. He was born on the 28th of May, 1850, and would, I fancy, be very pleased to play a single wicket match with any man of his age in the United Kingdom. In the course of a brief talk he recalled, with some pride, that not long ago he bowled out John Tyldesley and Sharp at the practice nets.

As to the future inter-change of visits between English, Australian, and South African teams, everything for the time being is, of course, in abeyance. The proposed tour of the Australians in South Africa this winter was cancelled soon after the outbreak of the War, and, at a subsequent meeting of the Australian Board of Control, the following resolution was unanimously passed:—

'With regard to the proposed visit of an English team to Australia in 1915–16, and the request of the South African Association that the Imperial programme should be put forward a year, so as to allow Australia to visit South Africa in 1915–16, the Board is of the opinion that, owing to the gravity of the situation in Europe, the matter be left solely to the Marylebone Cricket Club, to decide as to sending a team to Australia in 1915–16, or when they would be prepared to send a team to Australia. Further, that the South African Association be informed that their request cannot be dealt with until the wishes of the M.C.C. are conveyed to the Board.'

The most memorable event in the season of 1914 was, to my thinking, the dinner given at the Hotel Cecil by the M.C.C. in June to celebrate the Centenary of the present Lord's ground. Nothing could have illustrated more forcibly the greatness of cricket. On every hand were men whose names are familiar wherever the English language is spoken. No other game or sport could have produced such a company. Half a century of English cricket was fully represented, and in every speech there was a note of unswerving devotion to the game. It was a peculiarly happy circumstance that Lord Hawke, who has played cricket all over the world, should, as president of the M.C.C. for the year, have had the privilege of being in the chair. One may be sure that he appreciated the honour.

A TRIBUTE TO GREGOR MACGREGOR [1919]

Born 1869 – died 1919

BY D. L. A. JEPHSON

When cricket, and the rest of British life, picked up the pieces in 1919 and tried to put them together again, Sydney Pardon, the connoisseur, was much troubled by hints from spectators that they did not always grasp the nature of the spectacle they were witnessing:

> It is to be feared that a good many people who find their pleasure in watching cricket are very ignorant of the game. In no other way can one account for the unseemly 'barracking' that sometimes goes on. A particularly bad case occurred in the Middlesex and Yorkshire match at Lord's in August. J. W. Hearne, playing as well as he has ever played in his life, was doing his utmost to save Middlesex from defeat and yet a section of the crowd hooted him. A remedy for this sort of nuisance is not easy to find, as obviously the batsman cannot leave the wickets. A stoppage of the game, however, with all the players staying on the field, might have the effect of bringing the malcontents to their senses.

As the essence of a malcontent is that he has no senses, we might be pardoned for being shocked at Pardon's naïveté. *But these were still early days, and there were those, including Pardon, who believed that the game they loved was in command of its own destiny. And indeed, there were ways in which nothing seemed to have changed. Although there was no essay in that first post-war edition, there was a return by D. L. A. Jephson, writing in memoriam of the Middlesex and England wicket-keeper Gregor MacGregor. In strict terms Jephson's eulogy is an obituary notice rather than a formal essay, but the whole approach preferred by Jephson is of the discursive essayist, musing poetic, sighing for a lost time, grieving for the loss of a much-loved friend.*

To many, who like myself were at Lord's last year during the 'Varsity match and saw and chatted with Gregor MacGregor, the news of his sudden death in a nursing home came almost with the force of a physical blow.

I have known MacGregor and played cricket with him for more years than the average man cares to count. I have played with him in games which men label 'first class'—in games of the country house, or 'brown sherry' variety, as they are often derisively called, and I have played against him in College and county cricket, and whether with him or against him or under him, he was always the same,—even-tempered—imperturbable—at times perhaps bordering on the cynical; rarely if ever depressed by fear of disaster, or over-elated with the joy of success.

As a captain he never bustled or hustled his side—he was silent, determined, full of supreme self-confidence, but not with that aggressive, assertive confidence that lessens the value of many, who otherwise would make excellent leaders of a side. His knowledge and sound judgment of the thousand and one aspects of the game were almost unrivalled.

He was a pessimist at the start of a day—*he was an optimist* all through it!

I played with him at Cambridge in 1890 and under him there in 1891. I played against him in that fine, clean, keen cricket the Surrey v. Middlesex matches, and this I will say, speaking with that truth that is only given to 'babes' and fools to utter, that he never asked: 'How's That?' *unless* the man were out. And there is no finer compliment—no finer praise—no finer tribute to say of one of the greatest wicket-keepers that ever lived than to say that he never asked in vain.

Some men behind the 'sticks' led away by the excitement of a close finish—the rapid advance of defeat or the approach of victory—snatch at an appeal—but MacGregor never did—he was a grand *clean* stumper—clean in every sense of the word—a stumper, absolutely 'frillless.'

He never gesticulated—he never jumped about like a jack-in-the-box or as a badly regulated monkey on a stick—he was the personification of quietude.

In the world of sport there have been pairs, P. M. and A. M. Walters, the great Corinthians for example, and hosts of others in their different games, but in all my forty years I have never seen that machine-like precision—that foreshadowing of the possible—that existed between Gregor MacGregor and Sammy Woods. The faster Sam bowled, the nearer the sticks stood Mac, and he took the five and a half ounces of leather, cork and string, as if it were a ping-pong ball! He took it on the off or the on-side with equal facility, and he would throw the ball back, time in and time out, with the suggestion that he was a little tired at the simplicity of it all!

One of the most wonderful things connected with MacGregor's wicket-keeping is the fact that he never hurt his fingers. Now, I have looked with keen interest at the hands of many of our great stumpers, and some of them are as the knarled roots of trees—twisted—curved,—battered joints protrude everywhere. I looked at MacGregor's hands—and they were untouched—unmarked. 'Why?' I asked him one day at the Oval—and this was his answer: 'As a boy I learnt to bend my wrists backwards, so that I take the ball with my fingers pointing down—the result being that if I do not take it clean, my fingers are simply bent backwards—not driven in at the tips.' In other words the front of his hand faced the ball—*not* his finger tips, and this is the reason why he never broke down.

Even-tempered as MacGregor invariably was, I well remember one occasion on which this usual tranquility broke down—the reason I have forgotten. Cambridge were playing Surrey at the Oval in June 1891. As a rule he was chary of tendering advice to his bowlers, but in the second innings of Surrey, on a none too easy wicket he remarked in his quiet way to our great fast bowler: 'Let 'em go, Sam.' And then for the first time I saw MacGregor stand back—and he was right, for on his day and in the right mood, Sammy Woods was a real fast bowler. Surrey required 122 to win. Sam 'let 'em go'! As he started to bowl the majority of the famous eleven developed a strange desire for the company of the square leg umpire and 'edged' in his direction, and the stumps, unguarded, were hurled with fierce velocity to MacGregor who carried them back, with never a smile, and silently placed them, re-bailed, in their original position. Surrey were out for 103, of which number Jack Shuter made 51—he was one of the few who stood up—he faced the bowling, as that parallelogram of a man, George Hirst, would have done. As we walked back to the pavilion, a faint, very faint smile illuminated for a moment the dark features of MacGregor—'Well bowled, Sam,' was all he said.

But silent, imperturbable as MacGregor usually was, occasionally his splendid keenness broke through his cold reserve. Surrey, as was often the case, were hard pressed by our old rivals Middlesex, and on the morning of the third day at the Oval, seemed certain to lose the match. There had been some rain and the wicket was slow and easy, and with all their side to bat, Middlesex required only 150 or so to win. From the very start the game swung in their favour—the ball cut through and runs were as plentiful as fallen autumn leaves. At the interval they had made 120 odd for three. At lunch I noticed that several of the amateurs had not even changed, so certain were they of the runs. I whispered to MacGregor: 'Mac, I should like to make those fellows change.' And he smiled. After lunch, after forty-five minutes of a hot sun, a wonderful change came 'o'er the spirit of their dream.' Hayward and Lockwood and the sticky wicket caused a rapid search for garments—wicket after wicket fell and MacGregor arrived only to be run out by Turkey Rawlin in his first over! As he passed Rawlin in the middle of the pitch, seeing he had no earthly chance to get in—he shouted in a voice literally broken with emotion: 'Great Scott, Turkey, what *have* you done?'

His whole thought was for his side. No man could stop a rot better than he, and this he knew. But on this occasion his openly expressed fear was groundless, as Billy Williams, that rough and ready cricketer, made 17! and Middlesex won by one wicket.

The last time I had the pleasure of playing against MacGregor, the last time I ever played in a first-class match, was for Surrey v. Middlesex at the Oval in June, 1904. For the first and only time in my life I did the 'hat-trick' and Gregor MacGregor gave it me. Bosanquet had been stumped by Strudwick, and Nicholl bowled, and then MacGregor arrived—he took guard and then he slowly scraped forward, a thing I very rarely saw him do—the ball pitched on the leg stump and did just enough to beat the bat.

In the end Middlesex won by seven wickets, and in Surrey's second innings MacGregor stumped three and caught two. I was one of the two—c MacGregor b Bosanquet, 0—So my old captain and I were quits. It was our last meeting in the cricket field, and the last cricket match that a man plays in is the one he never forgets. I shall never forget my last duck! I shall never forget MacGregor—for indeed he was, because of his great knowledge of the game—his persistency of purpose—his very silence, a terribly hard nut to crack.

Wishing for another opinion than my own as to MacGregor's captaincy, I wrote to an old friend of mine who played under MacGregor for Middlesex for many years. This is his reply:—

'As a captain, MacGregor required a lot of knowing—he was dour—he said very little, but he had the gift of getting the very best out of those who understood him—those who did not understand him mistook his attempt to disguise his own keenness to win, for pessimism. MacGregor was a curious study in character. When a big effort was needed and it depended on the effort of one man, he would say just the right word to that man to make him feel his responsibility, at the same time conveying his own belief in the fact that he would not fail. As to words he was parsimonious, but he always said the right thing at the right moment. In this way MacGregor was a better skipper than many gave him credit for—it was all done so quietly, and few knew of it except those who played under him in the field.

'When I first played with him he asked me where I was in the habit of fielding. I replied slip or mid-off or mid-on, anywhere close in. That was enough! I was generally put in the out-field after that! No doubt he thought it was good for my training and discipline. Then one day there was a vacancy at short slip, a left-hander was coming in, and as more than one regular member of the side refused the position, Mac beckoned to me: 'I think you like short slip?' I jumped at the chance, being only too delighted to get out of the long-field which I detested. I beamed all over: 'Yes, I do like short slip'; and as I went to my place I saw the old hands grin and among them was Stoddart (this was his last match for Middlesex). Stoddart was among those who had refused, remarking: 'that his life was not insured!' I wondered why they smiled—I was not left wondering long! Trott was bowling to Tyler of Somerset. I took up my position, preferring to fall forward, than to be too near for my focus, then I was pulled up by Mac and Trott two or three yards, till I could almost shake hands with the batsman. Trott bowled three slow ones, and of the fourth all I knew was that my right hand was touching my ear, and the ball was in it. It was Trott's *fast* ball!

I turned round to meet laughter everywhere.

In the pavilion the voice of Sammy Woods greeted me: "I say, old chap, do you always catch 'em like that?"

"No, Sammy—and I don't want to again." And looking at MacGregor I saw a rare sight, I saw him smile.'

As a batsman MacGregor was of the useful, not ornamental type—a splendid stop-gap—a fine breakwater against a sea of adversity—he was a 'no-stroke' player, but he made as many runs as he wanted to. He always played back in preference to pushing forward—he watched the ball when he was batting, almost as closely as when he was behind the stumps, and he once made 73 not out against the greatest pair of bowlers in the world, Turner and Ferris, who were backed up by a man who could also bowl a little, Hughie Trumble!

Rest in peace, old friend. You were a great stumper—you were a great cricketer, and you saw in the grand old game more than a circus show on which men may find it worth while to spend sixpence—you saw in it, as C. B. Fry says 'a physical fine art full of plot-interest, enlivened by difficulties,' difficulties that through the long, long years you successfully overcame.

THE GOOGLY [1924]

The Scapegoat of Cricket

By B. J. T. BOSANQUET

For the next few seasons, new readers of Wisden might have been forgiven for assuming that the Almanack consisted in its entirety of facts and figures, and that, apart from the editorial comments and the obituary notices, it was impossible to settle down to read Wisden as one might read a novel or a collection of short stories. Nothing remotely resembling a readable piece of prose is to be found in the immediate post-war editions. The events were fascinating enough, but Pardon evidently felt that the figures spoke for themselves. In some cases they did not. The extraordinary episode of 1921, in which the ageing A. C. MacLaren led a bits-and-pieces side to victory over a till-then invincible Australian eleven led by Warwick Armstrong; the emergence of a great new batting partnership between Hobbs and Sutcliffe; the rise of Maurice Tate; the eccentricities of Lionel Tennyson, whose childhood recollection of his poetising grandfather as 'a beard at the foot of the bed' was certainly worth a thousand words. All these themes and a hundred others might have made pretexts for the most readable asides.

Or, approaching the problem from a different angle, did it never occur to Pardon that England was bursting with famous writers who would have been as thrilled as schoolboys to write a piece for the world's greatest sporting publication? We can only imagine what might have happened had someone had the wit to ask J. M. Barrie to spare a few thoughts as to why he was a better slow bowler than Arthur Mailey, or what might have come of an invitation to Sir Arthur Conan Doyle to contribute his recollections of playing cricket with Doctor Watson. Why did nobody, over a period of seventy years, ever ask P. G. Wodehouse to recall his bowling partnership at Dulwich College with N. A. Knox, and describe the moment in the Tonbridge match of 1899 when he dismissed the great Kenneth Hutchings? But Pardon simply did not run his Almanack on these sub-literary lines, though it would have been a priceless bonus for posterity if he had. But then, with the 1925 Almanack, events suddenly took a startling upward turn.

An accomplished dancer, diner, hammer-thrower, billiard player and guest as well as a richly talented all-round cricketer, Bernard James Tindall Bosanquet (1877–1936) was the exemplar of the gentleman athlete who lobs, glides and pots his way to social acceptance. After a spectacular sporting education at Cambridge, Bosanquet graduated with ease, first into the Middlesex eleven and then into the England side, spending several of his winters on cricketing tours and his summers in an endless round of country housing, where his good manners, impeccable background and games-playing virtuosity made him one of the more eligible sporting bachelors of his generation, and where his affable generosity as a tipper endeared him to many a butler and gentleman's gentleman. But there was, lying concealed somewhere beneath Bosanquet's slender, elegant hide, a genetic imp which was always likely to prompt him at any moment to attempt the reconciliation of apparent opposites. His uncle was the celebrated philosopher Bernard Bosanquet, champion of Hegelian obscurantism and a close ally of F. H. Bradley, that professional thinker whose ruminations on the relationship between Appearance and Reality were to shatter the comfortable certitude of a whole generation of Johnsonian pragmatists who believed, in their innocence, that if you kicked a stone you stubbed your toe.

The metaphysical streak came out in the cricketer in the 1890s when Bosanquet, attempting to invent a new game whose dual purpose would be to beguile wet country house mornings and perspiring fast-bowling afternoons, began the series of empirical experiments destined to flower some years later into that rampant heresy, the googly, or, as Australians eponymously prefer, the bosey. This ball adheres so spectacularly to Bradleyian doctrines that its appearance as a leg-break is belied, much to the dismay and bewilderment of the batsman, by the reality of an off-break. The effect of Bosanquet's dazzling deception was to deprive, more or less overnight, the self-confidence of batsmen raised on the sternly utilitarian principle that, when confronted by a slow bowler, once you 'read' the wrist and deduced therefrom the direction in which the ball, on striking the ground, was sure to spin, you were able to select your stroke accordingly, throwing yourself into it with all the narcissistic flourish of an egotist posing for a portrait painter. Batsmen famed for their instinctive aggression at the crease were rendered introspective by the threat inherent in Bosanquet's serpent of a delivery; before long other bowlers had acquired the secret and were becoming googly specialists. All the canons of batsmanship were suddenly called into question; accepted methods underwent radical amendments, and there were those whose concerted voice became louder as the season plick-plocked by, who openly accused Bosanquet of having, by so drastically reducing the confident flourish of stroke-play, committed a crime which not only constituted a breach of aesthetic morality but also a blatant example of foul play.

In 1924, by now long since retired from the first-class game but still the object of lingering vituperation, or at any rate so he believed, Bosanquet was stung at last beyond endurance by accusations that by his heresy he had corrupted the innocence of batsmanship, and responded in the most remarkable way. Torn between vehement denial that his invention was anything to make such a fuss about, and an understandable pride in both its stark originality and its subtle undermining of first principles, Bosanquet took up the cudgels in his own defence by publishing an essay in 'The Morning Post'. The diatribe incorporated contradictions which would surely have drawn a few admonitory tut-tuts from the avuncular eminence lurking somewhere up in the rich foliage of the family tree, for the declamation swung between the opposing poles of passionate protestations of innocence and equally passionate contrition for guilt. Bosanquet's attempt to disarm his enemies by defining the googly as 'merely a ball with an ordinary break produced by an extra-ordinary method', was hardly worthy of the scion of a family renowned for its relentless dialectical mastery, for, by the same reasoning, what is the three-card-trick but an ordinary effect produced by extraordinary methods? As for Bosanquet's concluding remarks, in which he begs the cricket world's pardon, it was so unique a departure for any famous cricketer to compose a public confessional that after it had appeared in 'The Morning Post', the astute Sydney Pardon took care to pick it up and bestow upon it some degree of permanence by reprinting it in the Almanack of 1925, where it has lain buried ever since.

THE visit of the South African team has revived interest in the googly. Poor old googly! It has been subjected to ridicule, abuse, contempt, incredulity, and survived them all. Nowadays one cannot read an article on cricket without finding that any deficiencies existing at the present day are attributed to the influence of the googly. If the standard of bowling falls off, it is because too many cricketers devote their time to trying to master it, instead of carrying on with the recognised and hallowed methods of bowling. If batsmen display a marked inability to hit the ball on the offside, or anywhere in front of the wicket, and stand in apologetic attitudes before their wicket, it is said that the googly has made it impossible for them to adopt the old aggressive attitude and make the old scoring strokes.

But, after all, what is the googly? It is merely a ball with an ordinary break produced by an extra-ordinary method. It is quite possible and, in fact, not difficult, to detect, and, once detected, there is no reason why it should not be treated as an ordinary 'break back.' However, it is not for me to defend it. Other and more capable hands have taken it up and exploited it, and, if blame is to be allotted, let it be on their shoulders. For me is the task of the historian, and if I appear too much in the role of the 'proud parent,' I ask forgiveness. In view of many conflicting statements, it may be of interest if I recapitulate the inception and development of the googly.

BIRTH OF THE GOOGLY

Somewhere about the year 1897 I was playing a game with a tennis ball, known as 'Twisti-Twosti.' The object was to bounce the ball on a table so that your opponent sitting opposite could not catch it. It soon occurred to me that if one could pitch a ball which broke in a certain direction and with more or less the same delivery make the next ball go in the opposite direction, one would mystify one's opponent. After a little experimenting I managed to do this, and it was so successful that I practised the same thing with a soft ball at 'Stump-cricket.' From this I progressed to a cricket ball, and about 1899 I had become a 'star turn' for the luncheon interval during our matches at Oxford. That is, the most famous batsman on the opposing side was enticed into a net and I was brought up to bowl him two or three leg-breaks. These were followed by an 'off-break' with more or less the same action. If this pitched on the right place it probably hit him on the knee, everyone shrieked with laughter, and I was led away and locked up for the day.

RECOGNITION

During this and the following year I devoted a great deal of time to practising the googly at the nets, and occasionally bowled in unimportant matches. The first public recognition we obtained was in July, 1900, for Middlesex v. Leicestershire at Lord's. An unfortunate individual (I believe it was Coe) had made 98 when he was clean bowled by a fine specimen which bounced four times. The incident was rightly treated as a joke, and was the subject of ribald comment, but this small beginning marked the start of what came to be termed a revolution in bowling.

From then on progress was slow but sure. We achieved marked success at Nottingham in August, and attracted a certain amount of notice, and my old friends Gregor MacGregor and 'Plum' Warner were fully alive to future possibilities. At that time I myself always endeavoured to convey the impression that the result was unintentional and accidental, as I did not wish batsmen to be too much on their guard. I even persuaded 'Plum' not to write about it, which he nobly refrained from doing for nearly a year! By that time, however, human nature had to be served, and, following on other successes I obtained, he and others began to write it up, and considerable attention was attracted to it as a new development.

THE SECRET

At this stage I would like to say that it was in reality nothing new in itself. Many leg-break bowlers (including Attewell and E. R. Wilson to my knowledge) had dismissed batsmen with balls which, intended to break one way, had done the opposite. The sole difference was in achieving this result at will; and although leading cricketers and the more knowledgeable critics appreciated that this could be done, it was some time before the ignorance and prejudice of others was overcome. The Googly after all (bowled by a right-handed bowler to a right-handed batsman) is nothing more nor less than an ordinary off-break. The method of delivery is the secret of its difficulty, and this merely consisted in turning the wrist over at the moment of delivery far enough to alter the axis of spin, so that a ball which normally delivered would break from leg breaks from the off. That is all there is to it.

To revert to ancient history, from the moment it became generally recognised that a ball could be bowled which left the batsman in doubt as to which way it would break, the fun began. I must confess that in the beginning I persevered with the Googly chiefly because I found that the lot of an average fast-medium bowler on a county side was not a happy one. It generally meant being put on under a sweltering sun, on a plumb wicket, when the other bowlers had failed and the two batsmen were well set. If one was lucky enough to get a wicket, the original bowlers resumed, and unless the same conditions recurred one was not wanted again. If the wicket was difficult, one was never thought of. As a result, partly from a natural disinclination to work hard on hot days (how much more pleasant to walk slowly up to the wicket and gently propel the ball into the air), and partly, I hope, from a sneaking ambition to achieve greater things, I persevered with the Googly. It took any moment of perseverance, but for a year or two the results were more than worth it, for in addition to adding to the merriment of the cricketing world, I found that batsmen who used to grin at the sight of me and grasp their bat firmly by the long handle, began to show a marked preference for the other end!

PUZZLED AUSTRALIANS

Contemporary history has recorded the progress of the Googly from this period onwards, and I do not propose to enlarge any further on my personal connection with it. There are a few incidents, however, which stand out vividly.

There was the first time it was bowled against the Australians—at Lord's late one evening in 1902—when I had two overs and saw two very puzzled Australians return to the Pavilion. It rained all next day, and not one of them tumbled to the fact that it was not an accident. The first Googly ever bowled in Australia, in March, 1903; Trumper batting, having made 40 in about twenty minutes. Two leg-breaks were played beautifully to cover, but the next ball (delivered with a silent prayer), pitching in the same place, saw the same graceful stroke played—and struck the middle-stump instead of the bat! W. Gunn stumped when appreciably nearer my wicket than his own! Arthur Shrewsbury complaining that 'it wasn't fair.' These are a few impressions.

There are two or three bright patches I can recall, as, for instance, in 1904, when in three consecutive matches I got five wickets in each innings v. Yorkshire, six in each v. Notts, and seven in each v. Sussex (including Fry and Ranji). There was one week in 1905 in which I had eleven wickets v. Sussex at Lord's (and got 100 in each innings. The double feat is still a record); and during the next three days in the first Test match at Nottingham I got eight out of nine wickets which fell in the second innings, the last man being out just before a thunderstorm broke—and even then if Trumper could have hobbled to the wicket it meant a draw! This recalls the fourth Test match at Sydney in 1904, in which at one period in the second innings I had six for 12, and then got Noble leg-before, and never appealed. The last man was in, and the match won, and there were reasons!

I have the balls used in these two matches, both presented to me by my old friend Dick Lilley, the best wicket-keeper in a big match we have known. There is a good story of Lilley (whom I last saw pigeon-shooting at Monte Carlo in 1914!) in the Gentlemen v. Players match at the Oval, in 1904. I got a few wickets in the second innings. Then one of the 'Pros' came in and said: 'Dick's in next; he's calling us all a lot of rabbits; says he can see every ball you bowl. Do try and get him, and we'll rag his life out.' Dick came in. I bowled him two overs of leg-breaks, then changed my action and bowled another leg-break. Dick played it gracefully to fine leg, and it removed his off-stump! I can still hear the reception he got in the dressing-room.

If the preceding lines seem egotistical, let the following be my excuse. Last year a great pal of mine, with whom I have played a lot of cricket, said at a dinner-table: 'I know old Bose invented the Googly and that sort of thing, but did he ever get any wickets?' I can truthfully say that after 1905 he didn't, and one over subsequently bowled at Harrow elicited about a quarter of a column of ribald comment in a newspaper, which finished the Googly so far as I am concerned, and I had better finish this article.

SYDNEY PARDON [1925]

BY C. S. CAINE AND OTHERS

At the end of 1925 there occurred at last the event which the proprietors of Wisden must have been dreading for so long. Sydney Pardon had been at the helm at the offices of the Almanack for so many years that most of its readers could not recall a time before him. When Sydney took over on the death of his brother Charles in 1891, Tennyson was not the Hampshire captain but the Poet Laureate; Thomas Hardy was still working on 'Tess of the D'Urbervilles' and nobody had heard of Rudyard Kipling. There were no cinematograph, no X-rays, no wireless telegraphy, no flying machines. Mr. Gladstone was waiting in the wings to take over the administration of the Government from Lord Salisbury, and the Manchester Ship Canal was still under construction. In cricket there were only nine clubs in the County Championship, the six-ball over was unknown, Dr. Grace had yet to reach the apex of his fortunes, and Test sides would travel as a matter of course from hotel to ground in a horse-drawn brake. By the time of Pardon's death, British life had been transformed by a ruinous war: the game had matured, if that is the right word, into a major form of entertainment; and the annual sales of Wisden were as steady as a rock and slowly rising. At least there would be no breach of continuity, for Pardon's successor was his old colleague from the early days of the Cricket Reporting Agency, C. Stewart Caine. And just as Sydney Pardon's first editorial chore had been to preside over the farewell to Charles, so it fell to Caine to compose a valedictory to Sydney.

SYDNEY Herbert Pardon, for thirty-five years editor of 'Wisden's Cricketers' Almanack,' died on November 20 after a few hours' illness. Born in 1855, he had recently completed his seventieth year, and yet at that age was as full of enthusiasms as he had been half a century before. Possessed of an extraordinarily good memory, he had a mind stored with interesting information on many subjects, and was always a fascinating companion for young and old. While the game of cricket played the biggest part in his life, he was also a close student of the drama, a devoted supporter of good music, and a keen follower of racing. These were the four things in which he chiefly delighted, and it was always a proud recollection with him that on each of these four subjects he had written special articles for 'The Times.' His journalistic experience extended to many forms of sport outside cricket. Upon athletics, rowing, boxing and billiards, he was a mine of information, and used to charm his friends with descriptions, always illuminating and happily phrased, of happenings in bygone days—the running of George and Cummings, the sculling of Hanlan and Trickett, the billiards of John Roberts and William

Cook. His joy in racing was peculiarly his own—not the bringing off of a bet successfully, but the triumph of one or other of the big breeding strains, as, for instance, that grandsons of St. Simon, or some particular line of Galopin's descendants, had done honour to their pedigree.

A playgoer from his earliest days, Sydney Pardon rarely missed seeing anything in the way of serious drama during a period of fifty years, and was always a fine judge of acting, rather contemptuous of stage accessories, and insistent upon the most polished elocution. Of plays and players during his life-time, and even of those before that period, his knowledge was encyclopaedic, and he was equally well-informed about musical matters. Upon this phase of Pardon's acquirements, a leading musical critic wrote:—'His detailed and accurate knowledge of the events in cricket had its parallel in regard to music. He could tell you, off-hand, of events in the operatic world, and these not only within his personal experience, but in past history. One often went to him for information as to when and where some eminent vocalist made her appearance in this country, and in what opera, and rarely was he found wanting.'

Despite his remarkable attainments in other directions, Sydney Pardon will be chiefly remembered for his writings upon cricket, and his long association with 'Wisden's Almanack.' Taken as a small boy to Lord's and the Oval, he developed an absorbing interest in the game, and by the happy accident of circumstances he was able to realise his ambitions while still a young man. Keen and accurate, well-balanced in his conclusions, and gifted with a particularly graceful form of expression, he rapidly built up a name for himself. Steadily his reputation grew until at length all leading cricketers were glad to have his opinions upon the big questions of the day. In years—now happily long distant—when throwing had become very rife, and threatened to invade the best of county elevens, Sydney Pardon fought a great battle for fair bowling, and had no small share in bringing about a healthier state of affairs. Spending his youth in an atmosphere that presumed the superiority of the Englishman in every walk of sport, he mourned over any England failure, yet, however keenly he might feel, nothing but sound and gracious criticism ever emanated from his pen. He treated his calling as a trust, and no power on earth could have made him write anything of which he was not absolutely convinced.

So interesting and pleasantly instructive a companion, Sydney Pardon had naturally a very wide circle of friends in the theatrical, musical, sporting and journalistic worlds. A strong individualist, always level-headed in his judgments, even when his personal sympathies were concerned, and a man of perfect integrity, he had great charm of manner, and by his always interesting speech and never-failing kindness he contributed in no small measure to the happiness of all who knew him. Possessed of mental powers of no common order, he strove untiringly for half a century to give consistently of his best, and certainly his long career brought much honour to his profession.

An old friend asked: 'Why didn't he write his reminiscences? They would have made a fine book.' Undoubtedly he could have produced a volume, full of interesting information about famous people and outstanding events conveyed in attractive style, and invaluable for its absolute accuracy. It was not to be. Sydney Pardon, in the busy life of a Fleet Street journalist, had neither the time nor the inclination to attempt anything of the kind. All he knew was generously at the disposal of his companions, but, if, with his passing, much has been lost, he has his monument—and he would have desired no other—in the many 'Wisden's Almanacks' which he produced with such ability and loving care.

C. S. C

Below are some of the many tributes paid at the time of Sydney Pardon's death.

LORD HARRIS:—'I am concerned to hear of the death of Mr. Sydney Pardon, my old friend, and, I might almost say, my old colleague of the cricket field, for we have had very intimate relations for many years. He is a great loss to the cricket world, for he had a most retentive memory and was therefore able, in pursuing his profession, to inform each generation correctly of incidents and players of the past. He had a facile pen, and to me his accounts of matches were always most readable and his criticisms most fair. He was, too, a great judge of the game, and I would as soon have had his opinion on difficult points as anyone I have known. I do not know if he was ever himself a player, but he knew how the game should be played, and was a staunch advocate of the classical style, and a fearless critic of the reverse. There will be many who will miss him much, but none more than I.'

MR. A. J. WEBBE, the old Harrow, Oxford and Middlesex captain:—'I received only on Friday morning a most charming letter, in which he said that it was sad to think it was fifty years since he and I first met on the old Prince's Ground. For those fifty years, he has said and written nothing but kind things. I shall always remember him with gratitude and affection. What a loss he will be. He was a power in the cricket world and all for good. We cannot think of 'Wisden' or, indeed, of cricket generally without him.'

LORD HAWKE:—'The loss of Sydney Pardon is to cricket journalism nigh irreparable. His knowledge of the game, his retentive memory of the old days, made his articles sought after by all the best papers and they were eagerly devoured by a devoted following. A more kindhearted man I never knew. Is that surprising when his two greatest hobbies were cricket and music? I am not sure but that latterly music did not come first.'

MR. P. F. WARNER:—'He had such a sane and sound outlook on all cricket matters. He wrote with a charm that was peculiar to himself and had an amazing aptitude for saying a great deal in a few words. I cannot recall in any of the biographies which he wrote—a marked feature of 'Wisden'— an unkind word about any cricketer. Criticism was sometimes imperative but the charitable touch was never wanting. On all questions which agitated the cricket world during his long editorship—to ventilate which the pages of 'Wisden' were always open—his views were always balanced, one might almost say, judicial. Towards all cricketers with whom he came in contact he showed an amiability of which I, personally, had more than one proof during a long illness. He was a most interesting and many-sided talker. His knowledge of cricket, racing, the drama, the opera, was full and complete and made him at all times a rare companion. His death is a great loss to the cricket world.'

MR. F. E. LACEY, Secretary of the M.C.C.:—'All at Lord's are very grieved. We feel we have lost a great supporter, as well as an old and valued friend. His knowledge of cricket was wonderful and he always used his influence in the best interests of the game.'

MR. H. D. G. LEVESON-GOWER, of Winchester, Oxford and Surrey:—'His loss to cricket will indeed be severe. No better judge, no fairer critic, no better writer, ever existed.'

JACK HOBBS [1926]

ANON

The death of Sydney Pardon was certainly one of the dominant events of 1925. An even greater one was attended by mounting national excitement as the Surrey and England opening batsman Jack Hobbs steadily approached the record set by W. G. Grace of 126 centuries in a career. Hobbs, 43 years old as the season opened, had already made 111 hundreds, which meant that in order to surpass Grace, he would have to perform a second record-breaking feat by scoring 16 centuries in a season. The closer he crept to the two records, the more tense did the usually phlegmatic Hobbs become. Day after day the newspapers speculated on the likelihood that this might be the moment when the record was finally lowered. Each time Hobbs was dismissed for less than a hundred, his critics spoke of 'another failure'. By the time he arrived in Taunton in mid-August to play for Surrey against Somerset, he had made 14 of those required hundreds. The nation watched and held its breath. In the first innings the record was equalled as the master-batsman made 101. As he reached three figures, the game stopped, the players from both teams clustered round in congratulation, and the Surrey captain brought out a drink for the hero of the moment, 'who raised the glass high and bowed to the crowd before partaking of the refreshment'. In his autobiography published some years later, Hobbs disclosed that because his captain, Percy Fender, was well aware of the record-breaker's dedicated teetotalism, the glass had contained lemonade. In the second innings Surrey required 183 to win, and their opening pair, Hobbs and Sandham, knocked off the runs without loss, Sandham judging the situation to a nicety and ensuring that Hobbs reached 101 not out. The achievement was doubly remarkable in view of the fact that the Great War had robbed Hobbs of four full seasons of his prime. Despite his age, he was to continue opening for the county for a further nine seasons, by which time he had set a mark never likely to be surpassed, of 197 first-class centuries.

GREAT as his successes had been since he first appeared for Surrey in 1905 when, with scores in his first two matches of 18 and 88 against the Gentlemen of England and 28 and 155 against Essex, he showed himself at once a batsman of remarkable ability, John Berry Hobbs surpassed himself in the summer of 1925. Never previously had he made 3,000 runs in one season or headed the batting averages, but he accomplished both those feats, his aggregate amounting to 3,024 and an average of 70.32 placing him above all his rivals. He seized the occasion, too, of the Gentlemen and Players match at Scarborough to put together the highest innings of his career, beating his previous best—226 for Surrey against Notts at the Oval in 1914—with 266 not out. Furthermore, whereas until last summer the largest number of hundreds he had obtained in one season was eleven—his total in 1914 and again in 1920—and the record for any batsman was thirteen—made by C. B. Fry in 1901 and equalled by Tom Hayward in 1906 and by Hendren in 1923—he eclipsed those performances by reaching three figures on no fewer than sixteen occasions.

These achievements, however, notable as they were, counted for little compared with Hobbs' triumph in first equalling and then heading the number of centuries which stand to the credit of W. G. Grace. That the 'Grand Old Man's' record of 126 hundreds was likely to go, Hobbs speedily demonstrated. So far from the strain of the Australian tour having any ill effects upon his powers, he jumped into form at once, playing such wonderful cricket that at the end of a dozen matches he had ten centuries to his name. A few small scores ensued but an innings of 140 for the Players at Lord's being immediately followed by one of 105 against Kent at Blackheath, Hobbs by July 20 was within one of Grace's total. Then came what must have been a nerve-wracking time even for one so well-balanced as Hobbs. He found himself the most talked of man in England, pursued by interviewers and photographers, and day after day, while the coveted century eluded his powers, he was referred to—whatever score he made—as having 'failed again.' For the time being the performances of one individual were, in many quarters, actually allowed to overshadow the game as a whole. Hobbs managed to survive all the embarrassing attentions showered upon him but, according to those watching him closely, he became rather weary-looking during the four weeks which elapsed before August 16 when with an innings of 101 against Somerset at Taunton he at last equalled Grace's record and on the following day beat it with 101 not out.

Grandly as Hobbs batted in 1925 there yet were times when something seemed to have gone out of his game. He who had often in the past shaped in the first over as though he had batted for an hour, generally found it necessary to play himself in with some care, as, perhaps, was not surprising now that he is in the 'forties.' Yet, whatever might be noticed at the start of one of his innings, once he had settled down, he was usually as adventurous as of old. Certainly he had not to drop any of his special strokes, although many of these demand supreme quickness of foot and wrist.

That Hobbs, during the forthcoming season, may show himself in something like the form of last summer will be the fervent prayer of all followers of the game. The great occasion is at hand and we look to him to 'speak with the enemy at the gate.' It would be a glorious climax to an historic career were he, by his batting, to play the outstanding part in so long-delayed a triumph of England over Australia. Curiously enough while more than 2,000 runs (including nine centuries) stand to his credit in Test matches with Australia, he has played only ten innings for England against Australia in this country. He did quite well in 1912, scoring 224 runs in four innings, but in 1921 he figured in only one of the five encounters and, attacked with appendicitis during the progress of the struggle, he did not bat.

In view of that disappointment a real triumph for him next summer would be singularly appropriate. Certainly it will not be his fault if he cannot give of his best for he has been at much pains during the winter to keep himself in condition. Still, whatever the next few months may have in store—whether success or failure attends his efforts—Hobbs will go down to posterity as one of the greatest figures in cricket history. A masterly batsman under all conditions, possessed of exceptional grace of style, remarkable in the variety of his strokes, ready to run any risk for his side, and a superb field, he has been at once the wonder and delight of all cricketers of his generation.

RECOLLECTIONS OF MR. F. R. SPOFFORTH [1927]

BY LORD HARRIS, THE EARL OF DARNLEY, AND MR. C. I. THORNTON

It will be remembered that many years before succeeding to the editorship, Caine had been quoted to the effect that Wisden should be 'essentially a work of reference', and there must have been those who wondered if this meant that the Wisden essay was about to undergo formal interment. Fortunately for everyone, Caine was to prove gloriously untrue to himself, and to publish essays which retain to this day their historical interest and easy readability. Although the world was already embarked on what the greatest comic artist of the age was soon to describe derisorily as modern times, the coverage of cricket in print remained markedly quaint. On the facing page to the Hobbs eulogy there appears an advertisement for a national newspaper. Headed 'A Way to See Cricket', it proceeds:

> The wonders of Press Photography are perhaps as clearly demonstrated in Cricket Pictures printed in the DAILY MIRROR as in any of the marvels of the modern Camera. To see a ball actually striking the stumps, with the bails simultaneously flying in the air is a frequent feature in photographs printed in the pages of the DAILY MIRROR . . . lovers of cricket this season who want to know the styles and methods of the Australian cricketers cannot afford to miss a single copy of THE WORLD'S GREATEST PICTURE PAPER.

Marginally more archaic than the literary style of this piece of advertising copy was the reputation of the original demon bowler Frederick Robert Spofforth, who had first toured England with the Australians in 1878 and terrorised every batsman he encountered. A ferocious fast bowler who exuded deep antagonism with every delivery, made five tours of England and eventually settled down as a professional with Derbyshire, Spofforth in retirement shed the old minatory aspect and became a rather genial gentleman who enjoyed some success as a tea wholesaler. His death at Surbiton in the middle of the 1926 season, when he was 72 years old, prompted Caine to ask some of the demon's old adversaries what they thought of him.

I WAS talking to Mr. Noble early in the season at the Oval, and he told me that Spofforth was seriously ill, and then put to me the astonishing question, 'Was he a great bowler?' It was about equivalent to asking if W. G. was a great bat. 'About the best I ever played,' was my reply; 'but did you never see him?' It was another shock to find that Noble, with whom I had never played, had never seen him bowl. Later on I went down to see Spofforth, and we had a chat about old times; he was keenly interested in past as well as present times, but as I left the room he said, 'The doctors say I shall see the first Test Match; but I made my reputation in May; you knocked me out in May; and I shall go out in May.' He actually passed away in the first days of June.

Now what he described as my 'knocking him out,' was a very curious coincident. If anyone cares to look at the Cricket Records of 1885 and 1887, he will find in Australians v. Gentlemen of England, at Lord's, in 1884: F. R. Spofforth absent 0, and absent 0, and in 1886, F. R. Spofforth retired hurt 0, and that he did not bowl at all in the second innings.

I have recorded in 'A few Short Runs,' and I can but repeat that on each occasion I hit a ball back which injured his right hand; and he always said that he was never the same bowler after the second injury. He followed up his ball very far, and as I probably jumped in, he was very close, too close to put his hand in exactly the right place; else he was ordinarily a very good field to his own bowling, but so full of nerves, that a hard blow made more difference to him than to many.

An amusing illustration of this sensitiveness occurred at Canterbury, in 1886, in Kent v. Australians. I was in with G. G. Hearne, who would always run at a nod from me. Old Spof had been rather upset about the wicket keeping; a ball was thrown in badly from long field, which hurt him; he went dancing about wringing his hand, and at last danced on the opposite side of the wicket to where the ball was lying close to the wicket, and we ran, much to the amusement of the crowd.

It is a common misconception, amongst those who did not see or play him, that he was a very fast bowler. He may have been in Australia before his first visit to England, in 1878, but he was far too knowledgeable on our slower wickets, and 1878 was little better than a mud lark, to depend on pace. He could bowl a very fast ball, and did, as often perhaps as once an over; but what he depended on was what he termed the 'judgment' ball; medium pace, but with great variety of pace, and therefore of flight, and a strong break from the off. He could break slightly from leg, I believe, though I cannot remember his doing so; and the rumour went round amongst us who had to face him for the first time, that if he was going to break from the off, he held the ball at the tips of his fingers; if from leg, in the palm of his hand. In my opinion what deceived the batsman, was that he came up at a great pace and then bowled a much slower ball than his pace up to the wicket led one to expect. Consequently the batsman played rather too quickly, cocked the ball up a bit, and he was so close up, and judged the direction the ball would come off the bat so well, that he brought off the catch and bowl very frequently; and if it did not come off in his direction, the break would take it round to silly mid-on, where Boyle was waiting for and seldom missed it. Indeed, with Spof bowling, Blackham at the wicket, and Boyle at short leg, the forward type of play on slow wickets almost certainly led to disaster. That he was a great bowler cannot be disputed, his performances on the tours he took part in were astonishing, as shown elsewhere in this volume.

There were two signs which pretty clearly indicate what the public thought of him; his title 'The Demon' Bowler; and that he was singled out amongst cricketers for a Cartoon in 'Vanity Fair.' In after years there were quite a number of cricketers similarly honoured by that paper, but in his day it was a rarity.

I have said that he came up to the wicket very fast, and he followed up straight down the wicket, thus, left foot on or about the popping crease, right foot well on to the half volley pitch, and then both feet plump on the awkward pitch; and when wickets were soft, he undoubtedly made a mess of the pitch. In those days we were not so particular as cricketers are now; we took such happenings as the 'rubs' of the game; but in his case we used to remonstrate, and Spof's indignation was deep seated and high voiced. 'Look at my heels, no spikes,' was his retort; which was true, but the heels were high.

At Sydney in 1878–79, we had made a very good start. I was in, and could not imagine why they did not put Evans, a most accurate bowler, on to bowl at the hole Spof had made. At last they did, and I said to Murdoch, who was keeping wicket, 'This innings is over,' and we were out for some 40 more. Evans kept on finding the broken spot. He was much more thought of than Spofforth in Australia, and was a much better cricketer all round; but was not successful when he came home, partly due to ill-health. Spofforth was of no great worth as a bat, and was never conspicuous in the field; he seemed to concentrate on his bowling, and I think did really study his opponents' weak points, and work at them; and in after years it was interesting to get him to talk about his performances, which, when we met at Lord's, he was quite ready to do.

I was playing for ten years abroad and at home against those great medium pace Australian bowlers, Allan, Garrett, Palmer, Giffen, Turner, and Ferris, as well as Spofforth, and I have of course also played such great English medium pace bowlers as Alfred Shaw, Watson, Jim Lillywhite, Lohmann, C. T. Studd and W. G. Grace, and I am quite satisfied and always have been that Spofforth was the most difficult of them all, because he concealed so well the pace of the ball. What he could have done on the easy wickets of the present day, no one can say, but I am sure he could have adapted his bowling to them; and does it matter? What we must judge performances by are the circumstances and conditions of the time when they were done, and taking those as the criteria, I do not see how any bowler can be held to be better than was F. R. Spofforth.

HARRIS

I well remember the first time that I encountered the Demon bowler – in the Cambridge v. Australian match, at Lord's, in 1878. We had all been warned by our captain, the Hon. Edward Lyttelton who had, I think, recently made a big score against the Australians, to watch Spofforth's bowling hand as he came to the wicket. If the wrist was bent, one was to expect a slower ball with break back; if the wrist was straight, a very fast ball, and not improbably a 'yorker.'

In some of the accounts recently published of Spofforth's bowling it was said that he was never a really fast bowler. I believe this statement to be quite incorrect. If my memory does not deceive me, there were two very distinct stages in his bowling. When he first came to England in 1878, his bowling was very fast indeed, almost as fast as the fastest we have seen, with occasional very well disguised slower ones, which were very deceiving to the batsman and caused many a premature forward stroke and retirement of the batsman – caught and bowled.

After 1878 he greatly moderated his pace, and relied more on the fast-medium ball of wonderfully good length and considerable break back, with the occasional variation of the very fast one, including a particularly deadly 'yorker.'

I should imagine that the nickname of 'Demon' arose from the terrifying aspect of his final bound at the wicket when delivering the ball – long lean arms whirling through the air from a commanding height, and a long stride coming down with great force and damaging effect on a very awkward spot for a breaking-back ball bowled from the other end. The long arms seemed to be whirling round at much the same speed whether the ball was coming fast or slow, and he had practised these disguises of pace to great perfection.

Some of his bowling success may be traced to certain physical attributes of an unusual character – very tall, 6ft. 3in., broad shouldered, but unusually lean and sinewy and carrying very little weight. A year or two ago, he told me that at his best he only weighed 11 stone 7 lbs. His early life on horse-back in the Australian bush gave to him the lasting power which made him incomparably the best stayer of any fast or medium pace bowler that I can remember. Though of so comparatively light build, he was exceptionally strong, and one of his feats was to support Bonnor, weighing over 16 stone, on the calf of his leg, held horizontally backwards at right angles to the upright leg – no mean feat. He and Bonnor were the two fastest hundred yards runners in the Australian elevens of those days, one weighing some 5 stone more than the other.

In addition to these physical features, no bowler that I ever saw had a more graceful, spacious sweep of the arm, and his delivery gave a most satisfactory sensation of perfection of pace and power combined. Unlike most of the modern fast bowlers, his run up to the wicket was only of average length, and his pace and power owed nothing to the impetus of an abnormally long run.

One of the very best bowlers that the last 50 years have seen, unquestionably; possibly the best of all. A cheery and amusing companion, withal, amongst his fellow cricketers. Fond of a good story, and, like many of his compatriots, not inclined to understatement. His old cricketing friends will cherish a very kindly recollection of his unique personality.

DARNLEY.

I first met F. R. Spofforth on the Orleans Club ground at Twickenham where the Australians of 1878 met a team which I had got together. My side included I. D. Walker, W. Yardley, W. N. Powys, D. Q. Steel and three professionals – Fred Wild, the Notts wicket-keeper, Arnold Rylott of Leicestershire, and Ted Barratt of Surrey. Barrett took twelve wickets and when the game was left drawn we wanted only 75 to win and had eight wickets to fall. In the 'seventies' and 'eighties' I knew Spofforth well and played a lot of cricket with him. He was a first-rate judge of the game and certainly the best bowler of the 'dodgy' class I ever saw, as he varied his run up to the wicket and you could never tell what paced ball was coming along. Still he never stuck me up as much as did Ferris and Giffen. To get Spofforth and E. M. Grace on a side was to ensure a pleasant day's cricket if not necessarily a successful one. Spofforth was at his happiest at country matches where his stories – always told with an air of sincerity – used to amuse people immensely. One special one that never failed to please used to be given in the following circumstances. I would say to him at lunch 'How did you learn to be such a fine short-slip, Spoff?' And he would reply 'When I was quite young I made a boy, when out for a walk, throw stones into a hedge, and as the sparrows flew out, I caught 'em.'

C. I. THORNTON.

OXFORD MEMORIES [1928]

BY LORD HARRIS

It was only a matter of time before George Robert Canning, fourth Lord Harris (1851–1932), be asked to contribute to Wisden. Harris had captained Eton, Kent and England, become President and Hon. Treasurer of the M.C.C., and had always conducted himself as though English cricket were part of his patrimony. A bigot who always protested his own rectitude with absolute sincerity, a hypocrite who would have been genuinely astonished to be accused of any such failing, a successful politician and diplomat so obtuse that he, a West Indian born, could bar Ranjitsinhji from the England side because the Prince had been born in India, and then fail utterly to see the absurdity of his own case, Harris appears to have been a sort of moral imbecile who took up a long succession of bogus ethical positions without ever perceiving the faintest trace of self-delusion. In his own time Harris was a forbidding character, but in retrospect he appears distinctly comic to an age immune from the wrath of his disapproval. In 1921 he had published a volume of memoirs entitled 'A Few Short Runs', in which time and again he demonstrated his wonderful gift for being brusque, rude and callous while remaining convinced he was the very model of an English gentleman.

The same gift for unwitting self-parody comes through in his retrospective essay on his years at Oxford. Instead of the predictable dreaming-spire sentimentality in which almost all of his contemporaries would have indulged, Harris produced a positive pageant of death and disaster, grumbles and disapproval, all inspired by a curious inability to understand that people have feelings and that a nostalgic essay in Wisden is not perhaps the best place to ruffle them. Harris, happy in his work, maladroit to the brink of genius, briskly dismisses Oxford as a dreary and boring cricket centre and goes on to hint that it was only his father's selfish insistence on dying at an inconvenient moment that cost his son the captaincy of the varsity side. He adds in passing that this one of his old friends was bald and that one spoiled by success, this one lazy and that one clumsy. Finally, after remembering that he too is an Oxford product, Harris bursts into poetic effusion, leaving us with the insistence that there is nothing quite the equal of your Oxford man. And which particular Oxford man, we wonder, did his lordship have in mind?

MY first recollection of the Oxford and Cambridge match at Lord's was in 1863 and 1864 when I saw Mr. R. A. H. Mitchell play one of his finest innings on a difficult wicket. The story was told that when Voules, better known as Rat Voules, came in Mitchell said to him, 'Now, Rat, steady for the first hour,' and that, during my career in first-class cricket, was a maxim that I always kept in mind. After that for six years, being at Eton, I saw no Varsity matches though some of my comrades in the Eton Eleven had the luck to go to Lord's in 1869 and saw the finish of the celebrated Cobden match, when Frank Cobden in three balls disposed of the last three Oxford wickets with only three runs to get. I found at Christ Church several of my old comrades and throughout my residence at Oxford I enjoyed my Christ Church cricket a great deal more than the University cricket. I have elsewhere recorded how I got into the Oxford eleven by a piece of luck. I happened to be a member of the Marylebone Cricket Club and Mitchell, who was then our coach at Eton, wrote to the Secretary of M.C.C., Bob FitzGerald, to give me a place – and to me, that I must play. I had to face some very good bowling, Sam Butler, a very fast and very terrifying bowler, and C. K. Francis. I scored a duck in my first innings but got over 100 in the second – rather a rarity in those days – and made them sufficiently well to get me a place against the Gentlemen of England in the next match when I scored 67 not out and 64, got three wickets, and fielded well. That secured me a place in the Eleven for that year, but I was not successful in the Lord's match. W. N. Powys, one of the fastest bowlers I have ever played, was in great form. However, we had very much the best of it for Sam Butler was quite irresistible, getting fifteen wickets for 95 runs – all ten in the first innings.

Cricket on the Magdalen ground at Oxford was not an exhilarating occupation. The weather at Oxford in May is generally pretty detestable and the ground being close to Cowley Marsh was, I always thought, a dreary place. What remains more distinct than anything perhaps about Varsity matches was my re-introduction to Russy Walker whom I had seen playing at Lord's when I was some years younger. He had got on a pair of very wide flannel trousers (one turned up at the bottom) with a harlequin stripe, a harlequin shirt, and a wide-brimmed hat turned up on one side! David Buchanan in those days was a celebrated slow left-hand bowler. He was about the height of 'Tich' Freeman, very bald, and of no use at all either with the bat or in the field but a really good bowler. However I had been so well instructed by Mitchell and Dupuis at Eton in the correct way of playing a slow bowler breaking away to the off – either run out and take the ball full pitch or play back – that he caused me no trouble.

In my third year I was very unlucky. I was a very good long-field catch and used to practise long-field catches assiduously, but doing so that Spring in the cold weather I bruised the bones in the palm of my right hand and it hurt me so much to bat that I had to give up my place in

Bob Thoms (*top left*), blue-serged and watch-chained, majesterial from the crown of his billycock to the soles of his sensible boots. The umpire in excelsis, and a subtle contrast to S. H. Pardon (*top right*), man-about-town, whose straw boater, double-breasted waistcoat and natty striped pants proclaim the connoisseur of other things besides cricket

BELOW Alan Gibson Steel, once a schoolboy phenomenon, goes out to bat with the best-loved Englishman for Prince Albert's XI v. Charterhouse School in 1903

Lord Harris, the first West Indian to captain England, partnered by Sir Samuel Hill-Wood (*left*), soon to become chairman of Arsenal FC

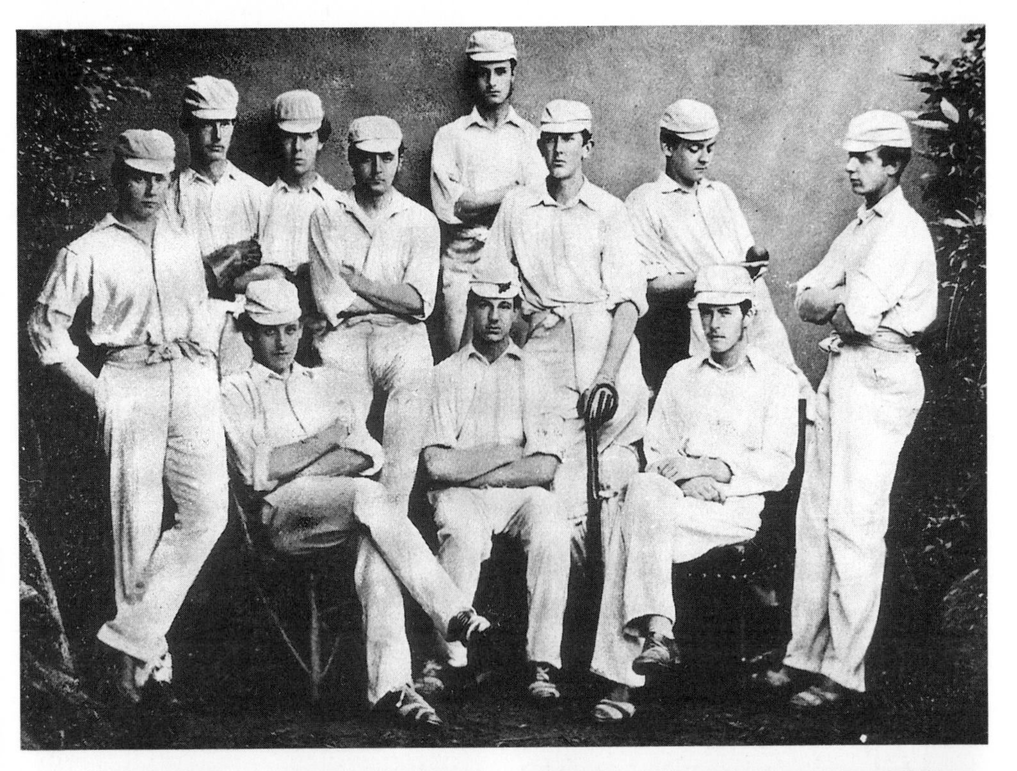

TOP The Eton Eleven of 1871. The beanpole at the back is the Hon. R. H. Lyttelton. His captain is G. H. Longman

BELOW LEFT D. L. A. Jephson (*right*) with A. O. Jones and W. G. Grace. Perhaps Jephson's diffidence comes of knowing that The Doctor disapproves of literature because it is bad for a batsman's eyesight

BELOW RIGHT A. C. MacLaren, captain of Harrow, Lancashire and the Gentlemen, who never went to Oxbridge but captained England with a dictatorial relish

TOP Sir Francis Eden Lacey, MCC Secretary 1898–1936. His super-efficiency resolved the muddle at Lord's, but Wisden said "the new broom swept a little too clean"
BELOW Lord's in the 1930s. The Warner Stand has not yet arrived to rob the northwest corner of its rusticity. The period is given away by the impressive array of men's hats

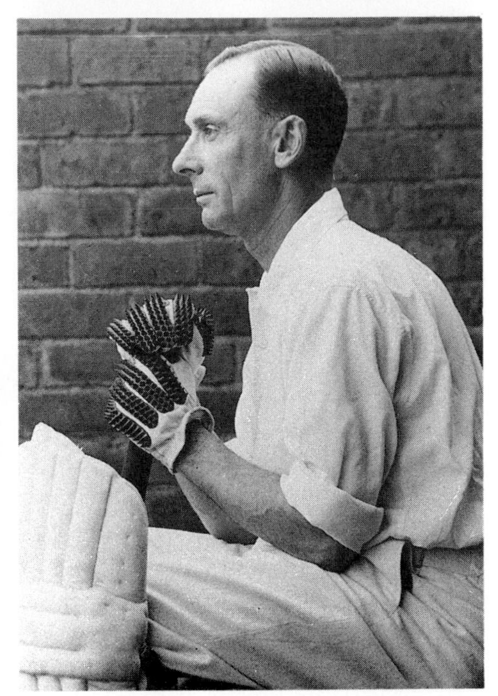

TOP LEFT Martin, Lord Hawke, Lincolnshire's most famous cricketer, ready to defend the castle walls against the onslaught of the Philistines
TOP RIGHT Frank Chester, a teenage prodigy who lost his right arm in the Great War and went on to become the world's most respected umpire
BELOW LEFT Dr Evatt, safe at last in the haven of the United Nations, thinks back to the *real* complexity when he was examining the Laws of Cricket
BELOW RIGHT Hobbs in the early 1930s. The Master's course is almost run by now. Perhaps he is thinking of the last peak to conquer: the 200th first-class century. In the event he never bothered

B. J. T. Bosanquet. Fresh from ballroom and billiard room, the Great Deceiver, a minatory air about him, unveils his secret weapon

TOP LEFT H. D. G. Loosen-Gore, the Surrey Shrimp, looking less like a famous cricketer than a cross between Erich von Stroheim and Peter Lorre, stares out of the shadows

TOP RIGHT Between 1914 and 1936, Tich Freeman took 3,776 wickets for 69,577 runs. When at last he retired, he called his house "Dunbowlin". No wonder

BELOW LEFT Sir George Allen, seen here when the Lord's crowds knew him as Gubby. Eton, Cambridge, Middlesex, Gentlemen, England, and President of MCC

BELOW RIGHT Patsy Hendren in the 1930s, trying to be serious for once as he contemplates his approaching retirement. The idolised clown–virtuoso looks understandably wistful

TOP Trent Bridge in the 1930s, described by Sir Neville Cardus as "a lotos-land for batsmen, a place where it was always afternoon and 360 for 2 wickets"
BELOW The most defensive field setting in cricket history: the Oval, 1939–45, converted into a PoW camp

the Eleven. That contributed to my not being selected for the Captaincy of 1874. My father had died and I was down at the time of the annual meeting when the Officers were selected. It is quite possible that under any circumstances Billy Law would have been selected Captain, but, anyhow, I being absent and it not being known whether I was coming up again, he was elected Captain and I, Treasurer. We worked together most harmoniously the following term with an Eleven which had no distinct merits about it, but developed into one of the finest fielding sides I have ever seen, with some useful bats and bowling.

We played the England Eleven that year on the Christ Church ground where one ball from Allen Hill flew up within an inch of my nose and over the wicketkeeper's head to long stop, and Tom Emmett, as he passed me at the end of the over said to me 'I reckon you smelt her.' Tom Hayward, the Cambridgeshire, not the Surrey, crack, had a fit in the match, and I think never played again. In the match at Lord's that year my father-in-law having asked me to put something on Oxford for him, I was haggling about the odds with Charlie Thornton during lunch, standing out for 6 to 4. Cambridge had made a very good start on a dry wicket. It came on to rain and we went in to lunch. Just before the first ball was bowled when we resumed, Thornton ran down to me as I was fielding close to the rails and laid me the odds I asked for. The first ball got a wicket and we won in one innings. I caught the last man out at long leg and Billy Law gave me the ball with the scores engraved on a silver band.

I remember being full of enthusiasm and zeal that last year, but I cannot remember that I enjoyed 'Varsity matches as I did Christ Church matches on our own ground. There I was playing with the friends of my youth and of The House on a really good ground. For Bullingdon cricket I cared not a jot: it was not business-like enough for my temperament: to start cricket at one o'clock and go to lunch – and a very elaborate one – at 1.15 did not appeal to me.

Of those with whom I played I suppose not many will be recognised now as players of distinction; but then we thought much of the following:– I have alluded to Sam Butler. At Eton, Mitchell brought him up from Aquatics where he was bowling slows to Upper Club, and taught him to bowl fast. He was a very fierce bowler, drew himself up on his toes, rushed at the wickets, and flung the ball at you – a fling is not an inappropriate expression, for his great feat in the 1871 match spoilt him. He thought pace was all in all, and to keep it up resorted, in the few years of cricket left to him, to a very doubtful action.

C. K. Francis, my comrade in the Gentlemen of England Eleven to Canada, 1872, had a beautiful action (tho' it was sometimes questioned) with much spin, and was a very good cricketer all round, but a little lazy.

E. F. S. Tylecote was of the highest class as a bat and wicket-keeper, and after our Oxford days we played together for Kent. He was a most courageous and hardy wicket-keeper in days when gloves were little better than the bare hand. He told me recently that what he suffered from far more than blows, was cold hands. The wicket-keeping gloves in his days were very hard and dry, and keeping them wet improved the chance of holding the ball. Sometimes a piece of ice could be seen at the foot of and behind the wicket for that purpose.

Walter Hadow distinguished himself by scoring over 200 in a Middlesex County match in 1871 – a very rare feat in those days. He was, or thought he was, pursued by a malicious fate; one example of this occurring on our trip to Canada when his brand new dressing bag was dropped in the St. Lawrence.

Another fine fast bowler was Cecil Boyle. He did not keep up cricket for long; he went out to South Africa with the Imperial Yeomanry, and was almost the first man killed. But the tower of strength in the Eton and Oxford Elevens of my time was C. J. Ottaway. He was a genius at all games, and of great mental ability; a very correct and patient bat, with no brilliant strokes, but all made with great care. He died soon after leaving the University – leaving a marked blank in the athletic world.

Although Oxford cricket has not remained to me as an entirely joyous reminiscence, Oxford itself and its life there have. There one made the friends of one's life and I subscribe loyally and whole-heartedly to the lines:

'And thro' all the strife and turmoil of life
  Be he Parson, Lord or Squire,
He's as well known to all in the Cottage and the Hall,
  As the Vane on the old Church spire.
You may search the whole batch you'll ne'er find his match
  That have been since the world began,
Be he sober, be he mellow, you'll ne'er find a better fellow
  Than the thoroughbred Oxford Man.'

MY YEARS AT CAMBRIDGE [1929]

BY GEORGE H. LONGMAN

Having inflicted irreparable damage to the image of Oxford cricket by disclosing that its cricketers were not above gambling on the outcome of matches, Harris gave way in the following season's Almanack to George Henry Longman (1852–1938), who, being a Cambridge man, may be said to have redressed the university balance. Longman had played four times for Eton against Harrow, four times for Cambridge against Oxford, several times for the Gentlemen against the Players, and after leaving university represented Hampshire for several years. An excellent bat, Longman was also renowned as a fielder, and one of his catches in the deep, in a Gentlemen-Players contest at Prince's Ground in 1876, was described in Wisden as 'the catch of the season . . . a catch in a thousand'.

Longman's essay is a delight from first to last, because he happens to possess the priceless asset of charm. Having disarmed the reader with his very first remark, which amounts to arraigning himself on a charge of dimness, Longman goes on to raise a succession of genial ghosts, and even manages to imply, without giving the slightest offence, that a certain posthumous Mr. Smith was perhaps not quite the world's greatest batsman. Among the memorable images rising out of Longman's essay are those of the fat man armoured against fate at Lord's by a basin, a towel and a sponge 'for the purposes of mitigating the effects of the heat'; the reaction to the vocabulary of scholarship by the professional J. C. Shaw; and the harmless attempt by the author to wriggle out of his student commitments for the sake of the game. The attempt failed, it must be said deservedly, but the essay succeeds gloriously.

After he ended his playing days with Hampshire Longman became a Surrey member, rose in 1926 to the presidency which he retained for three years, and then became Hon. Treasurer until his death, which occurred under circumstances benign for so committed a sportsman. On August 18th, 1938 Mr. Longman, by now 86 years old, enjoyed a game of golf which must have been more strenuous than he realised. The following night he died in his sleep, a lapse of decorum which Lord Harris would no doubt have found regrettable.

My recollection of Cambridge cricket, which commences as far back as 1872, must of necessity be somewhat dim, and this dimness is immensely increased by the loss of my old friend, Mr. A. S. Tabor, with whom my cricket career, both at Eton and Cambridge, was so closely connected, and whose powers of memory would have been of immense assistance.

One thing which has impressed itself on my memory very particularly is the extreme cold of certain early May days at Fenner's, with a strong N.E. wind blowing, and I particularly recollect having a catch from Mr. C. I. Thornton's bat out in the country on such a day, which mercifully stuck in my hands.

Another recollection concerns College examinations. In those days there were certain so-called 'May' examinations, and in 1872 the days of those examinations clashed with those fixed for one of the University matches. Mr. Thornton, who was then Captain of the Cambridge Eleven, was very anxious that I should play for the University, and informed me that when he was in the same position he went to his tutor, Mr. Blore, told him that he knew nothing about the subjects, and that Mr. Blore had excused him from sitting for the examinations. In the innocence of my heart I called upon Mr. Blore and the interview was as follows:

Mr. Blore: 'Good morning, Mr. Longman, what can I do for you?'

Mr. Longman: 'Well, sir, the fact is that the May examinations take place on the same days as those fixed for one of the University Cricket Matches, and I thought perhaps I might be excused from sitting. The fact is, I don't know much about the subjects.'

Mr. Blore: 'Mr. Longman, if you do not know much about the subjects, all I can say is you ought to. Such a request never was made before and I trust it never may be again. Good morning.'

Such is life!

Well, in process of time my old friend and companion in arms, Mr. A. S. Tabor (now, alas, no longer with us) and I – both freshmen – were given our Blues, and, Cambridge having won the toss, we were selected to go in first for Cambridge in the Oxford match. I took the first ball – a fast yorker on the off stump – which I just managed to stop. The Reverend G. R. Dupuis, who for many years, together with Mr. R. A. H. Mitchell, looked after the cricket at Eton, remarked at the time that if he had wanted to bowl me out that was the ball he would have bowled. The wicket was good, runs came steadily, and we were so successful that the hundred was hoisted on the telegraph board without the loss of a wicket – an achievement which had never before been accomplished in the history of the match. As the hundred went up I caught Mr. Tabor's eye, and I have always felt that that was the supreme moment of my cricket career.

One cannot give an account of this match without saying one word of admiration for the extraordinarily masterly innings of Mr. Yardley, who made 130. He ran me out, but I think he was justified, as I was tired and getting runs very slowly.

The other individual performance which I would like to mention is that of Mr. Powys, who obtained six wickets in the first innings and seven in the second; in both Oxford innings my cousin, Sir Edward Bray, the late County Court Judge, and Mr. Powys shared the wickets.

In my judgment Mr. Powys was in 1872 the fastest and one of the best left-handed bowlers in England, but he never again bowled with the pace and spin he achieved in that year.

There is an incident which showed supreme captaincy. In the second innings, when Mr. Powys was bowling to Mr. Ottaway from the nursery end, Mr. C. I. Thornton placed himself in a then very unusual place, about level with the long-stop and about three yards on the leg side, where, sure enough, he caught out Mr. Ottaway, off quite a good stroke from a ball of Mr. Powys's, which, but for Mr. Thornton's intervention, would have gone to the boundary.

One recollection of this match might be of interest, viz: that Mr. R. A. H. Mitchell, who as everyone knows, was a tower of strength to the Oxford side during his Oxford career, was heard to say at the beginning of the match that he hoped those boys would get a few before they were out. When 20 and 30 went up without a wicket he began to get a little uneasy, and I think that his love for his two Etonian cricket pupils soon became overwhelmed by his loyal partisanship for Oxford – and quite right too.

The one other recollection to which I shall refer only came to the knowledge of Mr. Tabor and me two years ago, and was as follows: An ardent Oxonian was sitting in the pavilion at about 1 o'clock on the first day of the match, and up to him came another Oxonian with the eager question: 'Well – how is it going?' 'Going!' replied his friend, 'there are two . . . little freshmen in, and they've got the 100 up without a wicket.'

This match is ancient history, and all cricketers know that we won in one innings. In spite of that, however, I cannot help feeling that Oxford were quite as strong a side as Cambridge, if not stronger. Anyone looking through the list of names of the Oxford Eleven will see that it contains those of Mr. C. J. Ottaway, Mr. W. H. Hadow, Mr. W. Law, Mr. E. F. S. Tylecote, Mr. C. A. Wallroth (an extremely good batsman), Lord Harris (then the Honble. G. Harris), Mr. C. K. Francis, Mr. A. W. Ridley, and last, not least, Mr. S. E. Butler, at that time an extremely good fast bowler. All of these gentlemen, with the exception of Mr. C. A. Wallroth, represented the Gentlemen at Lord's in the Gentlemen v. Players match at some time during their cricket career.

The 1873 match was won by Oxford by three wickets and was chiefly remarkable for the extreme value of Mr. Ottaway's batting for Oxford, but there occurred one hitherto unrecorded incident which, to my mind, immensely emphasised his value. In the second innings, during the stand made by Mr. Ottaway and Mr. C. E. B. Nepean (which certainly decided the match) the following incident occurred:- A ball from, I think, Mr. Tillard, pitched on Mr. Ottaway's toe, causing him excruciating pain, but his bat was so close to his foot that all we fieldsmen, with the exception of Mr. Tabor, thought he had played the ball. Mr. Tabor, fielding at mid-off, did not like to appeal, but after the over he asked the umpire what decision he would have given if he had been appealed to on the question of Mr. Ottaway's being out l.b.w., and the reply came quickly: 'I should have given him out, sir!' Mr. Ottaway did not wince in the slightest degree until the next ball had been bowled in spite of being in great pain. This was heroic, and I have little doubt was the turning point of the match. Had Mr. Ottaway been given out, I think we might have won.

With regard to the Cambridge side, I think it should be mentioned that Mr. Goldney, who was given a place in the Eleven as a fast bowler, only bowled two overs during the entire match.

In the 1874 match we were entirely out-played, and so far as the Cambridge side is concerned, Mr. Tabor's score of 52 in the first innings was the one redeeming feature. He certainly played extremely well.

No picture of Cambridge cricket in the '70's would be complete without some reference to the Rev. A. R. Ward. He was President of the C.U.C.C. during the whole of my Cambridge career and was, I believe, chiefly instrumental in preserving Fenner's Ground to the University, though this was completed before I went up. He was very anxious to eliminate the word 'Fenner's,' and took a great deal of trouble to establish the name of the ground as 'The University Ground.' This desire of his had so great an effect on me that I always write and speak of it as 'The University Ground' even now. I believe, however, that to-day the ground is usually described as 'Fenner's.'

He took an immense interest in Cambridge cricket and at his house in Jesus Lane dispensed hospitality to cricketers with no grudging hand. He was also a well-known figure at Lord's, could always during Oxford and Cambridge Matches be found on the top of the pavilion watching every ball bowled, and during hot days was provided with a basin, a large towel and a sponge for the purposes of mitigating the effects of the heat which were bound to be great in the case of a man of his very large build.

One season we were rather short of bowlers and the following conversation took place between Mr. Ward and J. C. Shaw who was engaged that May Term to bowl at the nets on the University Ground.

> Rev. A. R. Ward: 'We are a bit short of bowling this year and I think we shall have to enrol you as an undergraduate. Do you know your Greek Testament?'
>
> J. C. Shaw: 'Wort's thot?'

The 1875 match was, to my thinking, one of the best contested games ever played. Oxford won the toss and made 86 runs before a wicket fell. I believe this start was chiefly due to the fact that while the wicket where the ball pitched had been covered, the run-up to the wicket had not, so that whereas Cambridge bowlers had to bowl on a wet run-up the ball pitched on a perfectly dry wicket. This start practically won the match.

In the last innings the two incidents which, I think, sealed the fate of Cambridge were: one, the magnificent catch by Mr. A. J. Webbe, which brought Mr. Edward Lyttelton's innings to an end, and the other, the catch by Mr. Pulman which disposed of Mr. Sims. Mr. Pulman judged the catch extremely well and held it in spite of the ball being wet. When it came to the last wicket I was anxious to give Mr. A. F. Smith a little sal volatile before he went in, but he declined it, saying that he was all right. When he came back to the Pavilion he confessed to me that though he did feel all right until he got outside the Pavilion, he then felt sick. Poor old fellow, he has departed this life and on the principle of *de mortuis* we will make no further remark about his innings. I feel firmly convinced that, if Mr. Macan could only have got to the other end, he would have made the seven runs off Mr. Ridley's lobs.

May I end on another personal note? The Rev. Hon. Edward Lyttelton wrote an article two years ago describing this match, and his last sentence was this: 'Has George Longman ever got over it?' I will reply to that question, even at this distance of time, by telling him that considering the match only occurred 53 years ago, he must be patient, but that I am going on as well as can be expected.

AUSTRALIAN TOURS AND THEIR MANAGEMENT [1930]

BY SIR FREDERICK TOONE

Longman's essay apart, the 1929 Almanack is revealing in the way its editor so generously paid tribute to his helpers in producing what was the sixty-sixth edition of Wisden. In a brief gracious preface, Caine apologises for having trimmed down the 'Births and Deaths' in the cause of economy, and goes on:

> In preparing the Almanack, I have received great assistance from Mr. Hubert Preston—my partner—and from Mr. W. H. Brookes . . . . Mr. S. J. Southerton, who in other years has helped in producing the Almanack, is prevented from doing so on the present occasion owing to his absence in Australia reporting the matches of the M.C.C. team.

Caine's curious choice of words implies that he shared, and was willing to share, his editorial authority with Preston. Whatever the truth of that, the cover of the Almanack states without equivocation that the editor is Caine, but the list of helpers is interesting in its confirmation of how tight a circle controlled the editorial policy of the publication for so many years. Brookes and Southerton were each to succeed Caine before long, and the mention of Preston introduces for the first time a dynastic element destined to play a role very nearly as dominant as that of the Pardons. Whether it was Caine or one of his assistants who had the idea of inviting the manager of England touring sides in Australia to contribute an essay it is impossible to guess, but none of the editorial committee could have had the faintest suspicion that the sentiments expressed in this article were soon to be reduced by events to a sour joke.

Frederick Toone (1868–1930) was one of those Yorkshiremen who, without being as talented as cricketers themselves, dedicated their lives to the welfare of those who were. His first official post was as Secretary in 1897 to the emergent Leicestershire County Club. In 1903 he moved to the same post for Yorkshire and remained there until his death. He was particularly popular among the Yorkshire professionals, who were well aware of the great industry and resource with which he nursed along their benefit funds. Each year he produced the 'Yorkshire C.C. Year Book', and, in his younger days, spent much of the winter playing rugby for the Leicester club. It was only natural that so stalwart and experienced a managerial figure should at last be invited to supervise the England touring party to Australia. In the event his three trips proved to be models of tact and decorum, from the speechifying at colonial cricket dinners to the niceties of etiquette dominating shipboard life. For these reasons it was merciful that so

sober and resolute a man should have died too soon to know of the events of 1932–33, when all the good work which he and others had contributed to the cause of Anglo–Australian sporting goodwill was swept away in a few weeks, largely owing to the extraordinary abrogation of authority, not by one England manager but by two.
After the Bodyline catastrophe, life was never again quite the same as Toone describes it in his recollections. But for the moment the English cricket Establishment could still bask for the last few hours in the russet glow of ancient concepts and outmoded ritual. Toone's managerial hat-trick may be seen as the very last Edwardian administrative performance, roundly applauded by all. Indeed, so unanimous was the approval for the tone of his conduct that on his return from the last of his Australian visits, in the spring of 1929, he was knighted for what Wisden calls 'his great work in helping to promote the best relations between the Commonwealth and the Mother Country'. Any last lingering doubt that Toone represented the dying fall of an epoch is dispelled by the whiff of period musk attached to his recklessly romantic definition of cricket, borrowing the half-crazed pantheism from Lord Harris but adding aromatic refinements of his own. The fact that most of what Toone is prepared to claim on cricket's behalf ought to be true, even if it is not, only adds to the sad pathos of the whole performance.

It is but natural that when for the first time one is entrusted by the M.C.C. with the management of a tour to Australia, he should feel impressed with the sense of responsibility and be anxious to justify the confidence placed in him by the rulers of the game. The success of a tour depends, to a very large extent, upon the preliminary arrangements at headquarters, and, of course, it is the manager's duty faithfully to carry out the intentions of the authorities he represents. As manager of the three tours in which I have had the privilege of representing the M.C.C., I have, naturally, appreciated the great work done beforehand by Lord Harris, the Selection Committee, and those indefatigable secretaries, Sir Francis Lacey and Mr. W. Findlay. They have done everything possible in advance to ensure the smooth working of the undertakings and, although I have had no experience beyond the tours in Australia, I think the work and foresight of those at home have been of the greatest value in all tours, not only from a cricket point of view but also from the imperial standpoint. So far as I am personally concerned, I have from the very outset regarded these tours primarily as imperial enterprises, tending to cement friendship between the Mother Country and her Dominions. Players, therefore, selected to take part in them—and this has always been borne in mind by the M.C.C.—should not be chosen for their cricket qualities alone. They must be men of good character, high principle, easy of address, and in every personal sense worthy of representing their country in all circumstances, irrespective of their work on the field.

The tours it has been my privilege to manage were those of 1920–1, 1924–5 and 1928–9. The three captains who have shared the responsibilities of the visits are Mr. J. W. H. T. Douglas, Mr. A. E. R. Gilligan and Mr. A. P. F. Chapman. And here let me say that with all three I had the most happy relations. Nothing but absolutely good sportsmanship was the keynote of all our proceedings. Not a wrong word was spoken on any of the tours; nothing but the greatest good feeling prevailed among all the players. Sunshine is lovely in Australia but it was never more lovely than the feeling which prevailed in defeat as well as in victory. Australia is a happy country and the cricketers privileged to visit and to play there are assured of five and a half happy months. They make very many friends whom they leave with regret. The travelling arrangements for these tours, including the selection of the hotels at which the team will stay, are made on the other side but they have to be ratified by the M.C.C. The carrying out of these arrangements, of course, devolves upon the manager, who makes it his first duty to see that the comfort of the players is properly provided for. This, indeed, is the constant consideration of the manager and it necessarily involves some degree of tact and not a little patience. No trouble must be spared; no little detail overlooked. The health of the players, too, must be a special managerial care. No illness, or mishap however slight, can be neglected. An expert masseur always accompanies the team, and is constant in his attentions. The need of such services can be judged when it is said that, apart from the strains of continuous match play, we had on the last tour to spend between twenty and thirty nights in the train, the longest journeys being from Perth to Adelaide which occupied about four days—ie., three nights on the train—and, after the last Test, from Melbourne to Perth. The whole tour means a round journey of between 40,000 and 50,000 miles.

Though one does not like to stress it, managing an Australian cricket tour is hard work. An avalanche of letters has to be dealt with, a mountain of data about plans and itinerary removed. Not the least of this work has reference to the social side of the tour. A very great deal of tact is required in this connection for the offers of hospitality are innumerable and one has to be very careful that the comfort, the convenience and personal wishes and health of the players are properly considered without giving the least cause to any host to feel slighted. I must say here that the Governor General and State Governors have always been extremely cordial and eager in welcoming the teams I have accompanied. Lord Forster during my first and second tours took a very great personal interest in the progress of the team and their individual and collective performances. The spirit of imperialism which animated the party had a very ready response from their Excellencies and the Australian public at large.

From what one could gather there can be no doubt that the Australian Board of Control is the constituted authority to which the Australians as a body look to guide the game in the proper channel. The Board has the finger on the pulse of Australian cricket. Its authority is recognised throughout the States. There may be differences of opinion. There always will be. We have them at home. But the great thing to be recognised is that the members of the Board do their best for the game and its exponents. The trustees of the various grounds have done wonderful work in building up some of the finest enclosures in the world. The arrangements for the accommodation of members and the public and for getting them to and from the grounds are on a scale not to be beaten for efficiency anywhere. During the last tour I was asked to give my definition of cricket, and as it roused considerable interest, and I believe was received with approval, I may be forgiven for including it in this, I fear somewhat sketchy, contribution to 'Wisden's ' immortal pages.

'It is a science, the study of a lifetime, in which you may exhaust yourself, but never your subject. It is a contest, a duel or melee, calling for courage, skill, strategy and self-control. It is a contest of temper, a trial of honour, a revealer of character. It affords a chance to play the man and act the gentleman. It means going into God's out-of-doors, getting close to nature, fresh air, exercise, a sweeping away of mental cobwebs, genuine recreation of the tired tissues. It is a cure for care, an antidote to worry. It includes companionship with friends, social intercourse, opportunities for courtesy, kindliness, and generosity to an opponent. It promotes not only physical health but mental force.'

It would be remiss on my part if I did not state how deeply I have felt the confidence which the M.C.C. reposed in me in offering me the appointment of manager of three consecutive Australian tours. As I have mentioned, the success of those tours, so far as a manager can make them, has been due in the first place to the care and foresight by which the ground was prepared in advance. My work has been to carry out the wishes of the M.C.C., and to cultivate the real spirit of cricket, and this I have endeavoured to do to the best of my powers. My grateful thanks are also due to Lord Hawke and to the Members of the Yorkshire County Cricket Committee for giving me the necessary leave of absence which the management of the tours made necessary.

LORD'S AND THE M.C.C. [1931]

Thirty Years of History

BY SIR FRANCIS LACEY

Someone just as oblivious as Toone and the editor of Wisden to the rumbling hints of the storm to come was Francis Eden Lacey (1859–1946), the next administrator to be invited to reflect on his career. Lacey, a model of his class, who had captained Sherborne School at cricket and football; who had played for Dorset while still a schoolboy; who had won Blues for Cambridge at football and cricket; who joined Hampshire in 1879 and captained them for six years; who set a county batting record in 1887 with an innings of 323 not out against Norfolk, ascended to the secretaryship of the M.C.C. in 1898, at a juncture in the club's affairs when financial chaos was drifting towards ruin. Lacey proved to be the man of the hour. A barrister by profession, a parsimonious martinet by inclination, he brought to the administration of Lord's an efficiency which won him the grudging respect rather than the affection of many of those who fell under his sway. Even Wisden, not generally given to strictures regarding the great panjandrums of the M.C.C., commented in its obituary on Lacey that 'the new broom swept a little too clean, perhaps'. But there is no denying that within a few years Lacey had cleansed the Augean stables of the club's finances and placed the general running of the ground and its facilities on a firm footing of business efficiency. It was Lacey who in 1902 introduced Easter classes at Lord's for the sons of members, Lacey again seven years later who presided over the formation of the 'Imperial Cricket Council'. In 1926 he became the first commoner ever knighted for services to any sport.

Lacey's essay on the condition of Lord's reads less like a literary gesture than an inventory in a divorce case. Every nuance of the prose betrays his profession, just as his style of supervision of the ground reflected a tendency to the impersonal and even the draconian. If his message published in Wisden is to be taken at its face value, then no faint ripple of dissent ever disturbs the smooth surface of Cricket's affairs. Lacey's world is serene, placid, a world of balanced books and no unbalanced serfs, in which cricket, even though it may be the king of games, has to be administered like any other business concern. Yet again, the reader can see the terrible risks which any commentator takes in claiming that everything in cricket's garden is lovely. At the very moment that Lacey was mixing his bromides for the readers of Wisden, plots were being hatched calculated to render everything Lacey thought he stood for passé to the point of risibility. Unlike Toone, Lacey lived on to witness the desecration of Eden, although there is no record of his having commented on the crisis. This is perfectly understandable, for Sir Francis, having retired from the Board, was no longer obliged to defend the splendid beliefs with which he rises to what must have been for him a recklessly exultant climax in his review of the world of cricket. Sadly, Sir Francis, who was, judging from contemporary memoirs as well as the photographic portraits, a bit of a cold fish, lacked any trace of a sense of humour, otherwise he would have been reduced to hysterical laughter at the mores of the Edwardians, who gave him a knighthood and gave W. G. Grace nothing.

CHANGES are frequent in these days but it is doubtful if any place has changed more completely than Lord's Cricket Ground in the last thirty years or any institution grown more in administration than the M.C.C. which owns it. Taking the physical condition first, the only part remaining of the earliest history of Lord's is the match ground. Its turf was brought from Dorset Square and North Bank over 100 years ago and, except for a complete system of drainage supplied about 20 years ago, the usual operations of upkeep, the addition of two tanks for conserving rain water and the work of earthworms, it is the same. The tanks were made on the north and south sides to catch the rain water falling on the large stands. The value of these additions was soon shown. They provide suitable water for preparing wickets and an opportunity of reducing water rates. It is almost imperative, especially in a large town, to have an independent water supply in case of drought.

All else has undergone improvements and additions to meet the requirements of the public and the members. Outwardly the hotel (in early days called 'The Tavern'), the members' luncheon room and the pavilion appear to be unchanged. Internally these buildings have been brought up to date. The hotel is the centre of the refreshment department and from it are dispensed refreshments to different parts of the ground. Its excavations extend from the hotel proper to the members' entrance. When the refreshment business was taken over in 1898, the hotel and its accommodation were found to be unsuitable and inadequate for the business it was required to carry on and bakeries, cold storage and other facilities were provided and now, although it is impossible to serve every individual in a large crowd at the same time, the conduct of the business compares favourably with any ground that has the same problems to solve. The shop adjoining the hotel was built some years later for the purpose of finding employment for some of the staff in the 'off season' and in order to reduce the loss which, owing to overhead charges, has to be faced during that period. The addition to the pavilion, on the north side, was made so as to give the Press the best position from which to watch the game in progress and in order to improve and extend the professionals' quarters below.

ADDITIONS AND FINANCES

All the present stands and seating accommodation were built within the time under review. The large mound stand followed a decision of the Committee in 1898 to give more spectators an opportunity of seeing Test matches. This involved removing the tennis and racket courts to a site behind the pavilion. Many mourned the loss of the ivy-mantled wall of this old building and the large clock it held, which offered an invitation to ambitious batsmen to reach its face with a square-leg hit. Owing to the growing popularity of Test matches these familiar and attractive features were sacrificed out of consideration for the public. The stand has answered its purpose. It is only when it is unoccupied that it offends the artistic eye. As the popularity of the big matches grew an increased demand for accommodation for entertaining arose. This was, to a great extent, satisfied by building luncheon arbours on the north, south and east sides of the practice ground. The erection of the members' extension and its south west tower followed and all the covered seating on the ground floor was replaced subsequently by buildings of a more permanent and less dusty character. The new grand stand (replacing one built in the middle of the last century) and the cantilever stands on the east side of the match ground, recently erected, were constructed from the plans of Sir Herbert Baker and have made a substantial addition to the seating capacity of the ground.

On the death of Dr. W. G. Grace, the champion cricketer, in 1915, the Committee decided to erect a memorial in his honour. This took the form of memorial gates at the members' entrance on the south-west side of the ground.

Finance is not usually regarded as a matter of general interest; but those who are under the impression that the M.C.C. has always been a rich club will be surprised to learn that in 1898 there was an overdraft at one bank, a loan from another bank and the balance of the purchase money of the freehold of the match ground, bought in the middle of the last century, still owing. The purchase money had been advanced by Mr. W. Nicholson, a member of the committee and in his day a famous wicket-keeper. These liabilities had to be faced in spite of the fact that £40,000 had been raised by the election of 200 life members to meet, in part, the erection of the large mound stand and the removal and building of the tennis and racket courts. In the year above mentioned the property of the Club consisted, besides the match and practice ground, of two leasehold houses in Grove End Road, two freeholds and one leasehold in Elm Tree Road and a leasehold in Cavendish Road West. Now the M.C.C. owns as freeholds all the houses abutting on the ground from St. John's Wood Road to 22, Elm Tree Road, the Secretary's official residence. Flats for housing several of the club staff, whose services may be required at short notice, have recently been built on the north side of the practice ground.

The improvement in the financial position has enabled the club to set aside a sum of money for financing, or helping to finance, tours in different parts of the Empire, thereby enlarging its responsibilities towards Empire cricket and increasing its opportunities of strengthening family ties. Cricket finance, however, has always its problems and difficulties owing to increasing expenses and rates and taxes. Although stronger financially than it has ever been, M.C.C., after a few bad seasons or a decrease in the popularity of the game, might easily find, unless a large reserve is provided, that its work in promoting cricket in this country and elsewhere in the Empire would have to be curtailed. Exchanges of visits have done much to give birth to an Empire sense and it is to be hoped that a sufficiently large reserve may be secured to enable M.C.C.'s work to be continued ad even increased.

THE PROFESSIONAL STAFF

M.C.C. professionals, 30 years ago, were recruited from the County Cricket Clubs which then needed help. These clubs often sent up promising but inexperienced youths. If these youngsters turned out well they were claimed for county matches, except when representative M.C.C. matches such as those against Australia or South Africa, were played. If they did not come up to expectations they were left under the parental influence of M.C.C. When the counties played only eight home and away matches, this arrangement could be tolerated. As the counties increased their matches, however, M.C.C. found itself left with elderly or second-rate players only. In these circumstances it was found necessary to train young players at Lord's conditionally on M.C.C. having first claim on their services. The members of the professional staff used to be given a 'benefit' match in rotation, subject to an agreement to retire on receipt and to the approval of the M.C.C. Committee with regard to the investment of the proceeds of the match. The fixture allotted was the Whitsuntide match at Lord's and the money taken fluctuated with the weather, the game more than once producing nothing. It was accordingly decided to give on retirement £500 in lieu of a match and this is always granted now on the old conditions, even when the professional has given all, or nearly all, his services to his county.

Most of the professional staff are taught the principles of coaching so that they may be available for the Easter classes. These Easter classes are held during three weeks of the Easter holidays when the M.C.C. gives instruction in every department of the game to the sons of members and to boys introduced by them. The classes were first held 25 years ago for about ten sons of members. They are now attended by nearly 200 boys a day and Lord's, for this purpose cannot take more.

The Middlesex C.C.C. has for many years used Lord's for its home matches. As, however, other county clubs thought that Middlesex was unduly favoured, a carefully considered agreement was drawn up dealing with the equities of the case and creating a situation to the mutual advantage of the M.C.C. and the Middlesex C.C.C. Under this agreement Middlesex pays a fair rent and its proportion of expenses and its members are granted facilities in Middlesex and other matches.

A COURT OF APPEAL

Membership of the M.C.C., limited to 6,000, has naturally increased by slow degrees. It is now, roughly speaking, about 1,000 more than it was 30 years ago and, owing to wastage, it may be many years before the limit will be reached. The increased membership and the fact that the M.C.C. is regarded as the Court of Appeal throughout the cricket world, entail a very large and wide range of correspondence. Enquiries and requests for decisions in disputes and difficulties, often couched in quaint language, are received even from remote parts of the Empire. These show a loyalty to the club such as cannot be enjoyed by many institutions. Correspondence connected with the Laws of Cricket and interpretations thereon became so voluminous that a pamphlet giving decisions and interpretations on all the Laws and Rules in cricket and its conduct, about which there can be reasonable doubt, was published by the M.C.C. This has a large circulation.

When the war came in 1914 the Committee felt that any tendency towards scare or morbidity should be resisted and an outward show of 'carrying on' was allowed. But the ground and its buildings were, at once, placed at the disposal of the War Office and, the offer having been accepted, were used until the end of the war as accommodation and a training ground for the military. The policy of the Committee was directed towards providing games for soldiers and sailors in training and on leave and for boys too young to serve. Contrary to the usual custom of changing the President each year, Lord Hawke remained President until after the war, and he and the Treasurer (Lord Harris), although doing everything possible to serve their country in other ways, helped and directed in the administration of the changed conditions of the Club.

TOURS AND THEIR CONTROL

While the physical outlook at Lord's was altering a less conspicuous, though more valuable and potent growth was taking place in the influence and responsibility of the M.C.C. Tours abroad became frequent and on them, especially on those to Australia, public interest was focused. It was generally felt that tours of such importance should be controlled and conducted by some responsible body. Under pressure, the M.C.C., somewhat reluctantly, accepted responsibility. These tours involved money liability as well as administrative responsibility and for these reasons there was no competition for the honour. Of recent years tours to Australia have given a satisfactory return and the county clubs have shared in the profits. For some time previously M.C.C. was out of pocket; but the deficit was honourably made good by the Australian Board of Control. There can be no doubt that Australian cricket has benefited considerably by visits from home.

Other Empire tours, financed, or partly financed, by M.C.C., have visited India, Egypt, Canada, The West Indies, New Zealand, Ceylon and South Africa. The South African Cricket Association has been particularly helpful as it has generally guaranteed all, or nearly all, the expenses of a tour to that country. Only those in close touch with the network of interest created by these visits can fully appreciate their value in making friendly relations and understanding.

NEW GOVERNING BODIES

In proportion as interest in Imperial cricket increased responsibility in selecting sides and organising Test Matches, in England, also increased. In order to secure the best advice and the willing co-operation of the County Clubs, the M.C.C. convened a meeting composed of representatives of these clubs and the constitution of a Board of Control of Test Matches at Home was established. This was in 1898. Besides passing rules as to the conduct of Test Matches and selecting grounds on which they should be played, it was agreed that there should be an apportionment of profits, if any. One of the leading counties moved that M.C.C. owing to its position and the work it did for cricket, should not contribute to the pool from profits from a match at Lord's. This proposal would have been passed had not the Rt. Hon. Alfred Lyttelton, M.P. (then President of M.C.C.) intervened and stated that M.C.C. wished to share equally with the county clubs. The equality arrangement was passed and has held good ever since.

Cricket legislation and control had been in the hands of the M.C.C. for over 100 years. The idea of a more democratic form of government had already taken root in the minds of the M.C.C. Committee and another meeting of the county was called and an Advisory County Cricket Committee brought into being. This Committee, on which all the first class counties are represented, with three nominees appointed by the Minor Counties' Cricket Association, is consulted on cricket matters of importance and meetings can be called by the counties themselves.

Arrangements, so far, enlarged the duties and advantages of clubs at home only. The M.C.C., owing to its close connection with clubs and cricketers throughout the Empire, realised the importance of bringing these forces within the network of cricket organisation and invited the largest clubs outside England to form governing bodies and to send delegates to an Imperial Cricket Conference. At least one meeting of this Conference is held yearly. The above mentioned consultative bodies, with the M.C.C., now control and manage Home and Empire cricket and the organisation thus created has proved its value in many ways. The M.C.C. still remains the Parliament of Cricket, holding its position by general consent, and the county clubs in framing their rules have invited it to accept the responsibility of a Court of Appeal. The M.C.C., apparently, assumed the position of head of cricket at the end of the eighteenth century and it is significant that through such a long time of change and criticism it has been free from any serious attack. This is, no doubt, due to the constitution of the M.C.C. Committee on which can be found famous cricketers and men of the highest repute in business and in other activities. The Committee has been trusted and has never failed to aim at securing the best interests of the game as a whole and to preserve the spirit in which it should be played.

FIFTY YEARS OF YORKSHIRE COUNTY
[1932]

Happy Memories

BY LORD HAWKE

Although the departure of a humorous essay was not to occur to the editor of Wisden for a few seasons yet, readers of the 1932 edition were able to revel in the false dawn of a contribution by Martin Bladen seventh Lord Hawke (1860–1938), a well-intentioned bungler who was to Yorkshire cricket what the Duke of Plaza Toro was to military science. Continuing his policy of deferring to the great public figures of cricket, Caine turned to Hawke and invited him to give an account of the history of the

Yorkshire county side. The upshot was yet another remarkable exposition by the Yorkshire President of the elusive art of playing straight to one's own slapstick excesses. Hawke had trodden the conventional path to his present eminence, Eton and Cambridge, where he had captained the side in the last of his three appearances against Oxford, in 1885, and into the Yorkshire eleven in 1881. Two years later he was appointed captain of the county side, and held the post for the next twenty-seven years. During his captaincy he was appointed President, and remained so until his death thirty years later. He captained England, served as an England selector, became President of the M.C.C. during the years of the Great War, served as Trustee of that club for twenty-two years and as Treasurer for eight. He was also one of the most spectacular noodles in the history of codified team games, making even Lord Harris seem like Albert Einstein by comparison.

Hawke really did have a breathtaking talent for self-revealing idiocies, and in his essay for Caine gave copious evidence of it. He begins his address by scattering exclamation marks all over the place, nudging the reader into respectful approval as it were. He then achieves the first of his priceless strokes by telling us that when in 1865 five Yorkshire professionals went on strike, they did so not because of anything to do with the Yorkshire club but because of 'a supposed grievance against Surrey'. There follows a passage headed 'Discipline and Fellowship', which must have been especially amusing to the left-arm bowler Bobby Peel, who, thanks to Hawke's comprehensive grasp of the principles of Christian charity, was expelled from the first-class game for life. But how forgiving Hawke is about this whole episode, saying of his victims that 'I bear them no malice'. Further laughter is to come when Hawke tells us: 'I am a firm believer in the right kind of friendship between the captain and the professional members of a county eleven', although regrettably he does not go into details and describe the operation of his iron rule that before any Yorkshire player became engaged to be married, he was obliged to bring the lady to Hawke, so that the captain could decide whether or not the marriage struck him as a good thing.

The richest comic effect of all may be found in the section entitled 'The Board of Control', in which Hawke describes how his two star players, Wilfred Rhodes and George Hirst, were invited to tour Australia under the captaincy of A. C. MacLaren in 1902–3, but were prevented from accepting the invitation by Hawke, who, regarding all the professionals in the club much as he regarded his cook or his under-gardener, refused on their behalf. Hawke's blackguardly behaviour on this and many other occasions is one more proof of the proposition that it is always better to parley with a scoundrel than with a congenital idiot.

THE Editor of Wisden's has kindly asked me to give an account of my own time with Yorkshire County Cricket but before I take the plunge, which I am very pleased to do in these columns, it may be of interest if I enter into a few details of the early days of our County Club.

SHEFFIELD THE EARLY HOME

There would seem to be little doubt that the origin of the Yorkshire County Cricket Club is to be found in the series of matches between Sheffield and Nottingham which began in 1771. Though there were only twenty-six of such games, the last one being played in 1860, the fact that leading players of both counties took part in them gave to Sheffield the sort of right that is due to custom of being regarded as 'the' home of the game in Yorkshire. They were, by the way, evidently keen enough on the game in my county in those days, as the first match, in 1771, began at 9 a.m.! And, in 1784, in the York rules I see that a fine of 3d. was levied on any member who was 'not within sight of the wickets each morning before the Minster strikes five o'clock.' Report has it that one of the Notts players was in the habit of rising before daybreak and riding on horseback all the way to Sheffield to play! Nearly all these matches, however, were played for money—that of 1800, for example, for 200 guineas. In that year the second match took place on November 3rd, 4th and 5th! These early games were played at Sheffield on Darnall Ground, the Hyde Park Ground, and at the present ground at Bramall Lane, where the first county match was Yorkshire v. Sussex in 1855. In the first Sheffield-Notts match at Bramall Lane there played for Sheffield (totals:—Nottingham 130 and 93 against Sheffield 146 and 78 for six, Sheffield winning by four wickets) M. J. Ellison whom I succeeded in 1902 as President. Ellison held a record which must be very bad to beat, viz., that he shot grouse on the first day of the grouse-shooting season for seventy successive years. He was the second President of our County Club, a post he occupied from 1863 to 1898. Mr. T. R. Barker was the first President in 1863, though I understand he never attended a meeting.

FORMING THE COUNTY CLUB

A meeting at the Adelphi Hotel, Sheffield, on March 7, 1861, was the real beginning of the County Club. How soon they got busy is shown by the fact that the Secretary at this meeting, Mr. W. Whittles, was instructed to write to the players selected to play Surrey at the Oval to ask them their terms. Our out and home first two Surrey matches, in 1861, resulted in Surrey winning at the Oval and we at Bramall Lane. That, and the next year's efforts, ended on the resolution being carried on January 8, 1863:—

'That a County Club be formed.'

Sheffield, however, did not have it all her own way, as in 1863 Bradford played Notts, and in 1864 Kent decided not to play Yorkshire owing to a Kentish doubt 'as to who were the proper parties to get up Yorkshire County matches.'

Mr. George Padley was the first Secretary but he resigned in 1864, when appointed Borough Accountant, and was succeeded by Mr. J. B. Wostinholm, who served from 1864 to 1902. Mr. Wostinholm was followed by F. C. Toone, of whom more anon. Thus, from 1863 to date the Yorkshire C.C.C. in sixty-eight years has had only two Presidents and four Secretaries, including among the latter the present one, Mr. Nash, who was appointed after Sir F. C. Toone died in 1930.

There followed in 1865 the strike of five of our professionals. The strike was not due to any friction with the County Club, but was mainly on the ground of a supposed grievance against Surrey. The professionals suspected Surrey of having instructed John Lillywhite to 'no-ball' Edgar Willsher, who was a member of the All England Eleven of which our George Anderson and others were members. One result of this strike was that Yorkshire did not win a game in 1865 and arranged no matches in 1866. Another result was that all five professionals took the proper course in 1867, and ever since then, sixty-four years ago, complete harmony has existed between the Club and her players.

DISCIPLINE AND FELLOWSHIP

That, when captain, I had to act decisively and promptly in the case of two professionals who I desire shall remain nameless, is well known in the world of cricket. I had to act as I did in the best interests of the Club and, as I believed then and believe still, of the game everywhere. I bore, and bear, them no malice. That they reciprocate this feeling I know. My action, I believe, worked for the good of the game and the sobriety of its players, and not only in my own county. In the days of which I now write the trouble was not the player but the hangers-on, who, mainly for the sake of being seen talking to a famous cricketer, pestered professionals with their attentions and, worse still, by their offers of wholly unnecessary drinks. I am glad to think, however, that this evil has grown so much less as to be almost stamped out, and am proud to think I may have done something to help in such a matter.

Here I must add something about the origin of the tea interval. Prior to its introduction onlookers were used to seeing odd players leave the field for a few minutes, the fielding side continuing one-short. Those absences were sometimes not beneficial only to the tea trade! The authorities weighed up this matter, with the desirable result that there was introduced a regular tea interval at a fixed hour. It is very rare now for a player to leave the field under any pretext, and that is, I think, one point at least to the credit of the tea interval.

In regard to discipline generally, I am a strong believer in the right kind of friendship between the captain and the professional members of a county eleven. Between that and the kind of familiarity which only breeds contempt and therefore naturally weakens the playing power of an eleven by undermining the absolute authority—and it must be absolute—of the captain, there is a very wide margin. I believe I am the only captain who held an annual party for the whole county eleven at his own residence. To myself and my family this was always one of the jolliest days of the year, and I only hope my 'boys' enjoyed themselves at Wighill Park as much as we did. An amusing incident occurred at our little family party in 1906, after the season when we had lost the Championship by one run, our last wicket falling l.b.w. We were, of course, discussing the Championship when one of my sisters turned to Ringrose, who was next to her, and remarked, quite innocently:—'Who *was* it who was leg before, *do* tell me?' Poor Ringrose! It can surely not be possible for anyone to blush a deeper pink than he did, as he had to own up that he was the culprit.

I must give now a few of the facts and figures concerning what I may call the behind the scenes management of the County Club in my time.

Our professionals are handed a small printed brochure which gives in full all the facts of our 'Regulations relating to Players.' In these the position with regard to match fees and talent money is plainly set forth, showing that professionals who have got their county caps get £2 more per match, away or in Yorkshire, than is paid to players who have not yet won their cap. The fee is at present £15 away and £11 at home for those with caps. For an Australian or South African match the professional receives £12, and in all cases £1 extra per won match. Twelfth man is paid the same, but no fee for a match won. It is a hard and fast rule with us that a professional on gaining his cap joins the Cricketers Friendly Society. A similarly definite rule is that professionals are not permitted to write to the Press in any form whatsoever. We have made a solitary exception in the case of articles on 'hints how to play,' etc., by Sutcliffe. But I think we are on sure ground in putting out of the way of our professionals the temptation to be paid for signing their names to articles which they do not always actually write.

In the matter of bonuses we have instituted in my time the system whereby players who have played regularly for five years get a bonus of £250 if their services are no longer required. If they have played for more than five but less than ten years, our Committee guarantees them not less than £50 for each subsequent year above five. We reserve the right to grant permission to our players to go on foreign tours and, if they go, they have to insure themselves against accident or illness.

THE BOARD OF CONTROL

It may not be generally known that the action the Yorkshire County C.C. Committee took about thirty years ago, on my strong recommendation, was the cause of the formation of the Board of Control, soon followed by that of the Australian Board of Control, which two bodies ever since, under the aegis of M.C.C., have managed the interchange of English and Australian tours so admirably. Our action in refusing permission to Hirst and Rhodes to accompany the privately managed tour of a team which without them could not be possibly considered to be representative of England, thus bore good fruit. I based my refusal, in which my Committee supported me unanimously, upon the sound grounds, as I and they thought, that it was not cricket that all the profits of these tours, to obtain which English representative professionals did their full share, should go to individuals and to the benefit of Australian cricket only. It was and is, in my view, a wholly untenable proposition that the talent and labour of English professionals in Australia should be valueless so far as English County Cricket Clubs are concerned. So we refused Hirst and

Rhodes permission to go on the tour of 1902–03, paid them £184 each as compensation, and had the great satisfaction of seeing the formation of the two great controlling bodies for international cricket. I feel obliged to refer to this matter here because I have heard it was rumoured that Hirst and Rhodes were financially losers by our refusal. I have yet to know of the professional cricketer who has served Yorkshire faithfully who has not been a financial gainer by the fact. I had also the further personal amused satisfaction of knowing that the next time I played at Sheffield after our refusal to release Hirst and Rhodes for that tour, a reward of one sovereign was offered by a member of the Lancashire County C.C. to their fast bowler:—'if you bowl his lordship for a duck'! Unfortunately, the member did not have to fork out.

PLAYERS AND THEIR BENEFITS

On the subject of our professionals and finance let me say that between 1870 and 1901 the sum of £13,298 was paid to fifteen professionals as Benefits money, and between 1903 and 1923 a further sum of £15,483 was paid under the same heading to twelve professionals. Since George Hirst's £3,703 benefit in 1904, which was not a half-penny more than he deserved for he was by far the greatest all-round county professional of all time, and Wilfred Rhodes' £2,202 in 1911, both records have been broken by the £4,016 benefit of the late Roy Kilner in 1925.

In 1911 we resolved that the Committee guarantees £1,000 benefit to players of not less than ten consecutive years. A player accepting a professional engagement elsewhere without first getting the Committee's sanction forfeits his right to a bonus. Another institution in my time was that on November 16, 1921, we raised the match fees by way of response to the general demand for a higher standard of living. Speaking generally with regard to Benefits, it is the case that in the old days a player received very few subscriptions and the result of the gate after paying expenses left little profit. Now Benefits are run on much more methodical lines. The gate is always insured: there is a secretary in each large town, and numerous collecting boxes are issued throughout our large county. Instead of paying twenty-five per cent, for the use of the ground the player is allowed a ten per cent reduction. All of which is an advance on the older method.

I have already referred to the early history of the Club ere I became interested in it, and it is now fifty years last September since I played my first match for Yorkshire. It was in 1883 that I took over the captaincy from that genial old soul, Tom Emmett. Since 1886 I have been a Member of Committee, I was elected Vice-President in 1893, and I became President in 1902.

Regarding developments in management, and referring to our great success on the field, I say unhesitatingly that the latter could never have been obtained without the keen interest of the Committee and the *esprit de corps* of the team. It will be noted how for years Sheffield dominated cricket in the County; indeed Sheffield was the Committee. Even when they did recognise that to do any good in serious competition with other rising counties they must admit to their councils, representative of places other than Sheffield, they retained a very large and dominating vote, *viz.* fourteen out of a Committee of nineteen. I wish to be fair to Sheffield and state here that they always worked in no jealous spirit. They were always ready to play the best men, no matter what part of the county these lived in. It was an old friend of mine, Major Shepherd (I have happy memories of his presiding in 1908 at my second presentation), who was the moving spirit in stirring Sheffield up to have outside representatives on the Committee; also to have representative matches played in other large cities.

In those days the town to which a match was allotted ran the match, paid the expenses, and took what profit there might be. That method could never produce a sound financial position for the Club, so the ground was hired by the County Club who assumed all responsibility for the match, at the same time giving ten per cent of the gross takings to the ground. This percentage has varied from ten to thirty-five per cent and now we can say it is practically fixed at twenty-five per cent. At the end of the year we consider a further bonus to each ground, and in many cases it is earmarked to improve the accommodation, not only for our members, but also for the public. Having set ourselves to get a reserve fund of £20,000 we now allot to the grounds, bar a small balance, all the profits of the year. I think we have proved ourselves to be very wise in the allocation of matches to different grounds; ours is the largest county, and by dividing out matches between the large towns we increase our membership. In the old days of Sheffield I do not suppose our membership was ever more than 150, but with the allotment of matches outside it reached the large total of 3,000 in 1902. As showing the remarkable difference in our turnover in a period of forty years, while it was £909 in 1891, it was £34,826 in the Test Match year of 1921, and £16,324 in 1931, which was almost a record for a bad-weather season.

GREAT SECRETARIES

It was in 1902 that our Secretary, Mr. J. B. Wostinholm, who served the county so well for thirty-five years, retired. Here, may I say, that by all other Secretaries he was considered a hard-headed old Yorkshireman, because he always fought hard for the best date. And I guess he succeeded!

Great as was his work, we were to find in his successor, Mr. F. C. Toone, even, I venture to think, a greater Secretary—the very best that any county could ever have. Toone raised the number of subscriptions from 3,000 in 1903 to over 7,000 in ten years. What is more, he was a very true friend of all the players and one to whom they could always turn for advice. Toone's capacity for organisation of Players' Benefits was wonderful, a thing which had to be seen to be believed. It was a sad day for Yorkshire when, fairly early in life, he passed away. I cannot help thinking that the great Imperial work (and hard work it was) as manager of three Australian tours hastened his end. He was honoured by his King with a Knighthood for his wonderful management of these tours, and we in Yorkshire felt pleased indeed that we were able to lend him to M.C.C. for the purpose. We were so proud of his honour and success. I have said that Sir Frederick Toone raised our subscriptions up to over 7,000, but I am sure he would have been the first to admit that he only did so by the success of the Eleven on the field.

LEADING PLAYERS

It is not possible to name even a quarter of those who have made Yorkshire history and those whom I do not mention must not think they are forgotten.

Hirst, surely, must come first. What a hero! Two thousand runs and two hundred wickets in a season is surely a county record—not that I like records—I hate 'em! Yet the public always knows when a batsman has scored his one, two or even three thousand runs and applauds accordingly, forgetting all the time that a man may be playing for his own record and not for his side. Never in my long career would I give marks when I could see a man was playing for records which were detrimental to his side winning the match. I shall never forget when we had all agreed to get out in order to force a win—it was before the declaration rule came in—one batsman was determined to bat on. We were truly annoyed until old David Hunter said to me, 'Let me go in; I'll run him out!' I have wandered away a bit from Georgie. Was ever anyone such a trier? Slack fielding he abhorred. Woe betide 'Scofie' if he missed a catch, and wasn't Haigh himself frightened. However, with all his keenness Hirst was loved by the team and always had a good word for a youngster.

Ted Peate and Bobbie Peel, our great left-hand bowlers, had all too short careers before they made way for Wilfred. Peate's eight wickets for five runs against Surrey in 1883 at Holbeck, where we dressed in a tent in those days, is a county cricket record, and was about the greatest bowling feat I ever saw. Rhodes' numerous fine performances are too many to mention, but the manner in which he made himself from a last-wicket batsman to a No.1 with Hobbs will never be beaten. Georgie at Eton and now Wilfred at Harrow—lucky schools—ere long may they both produce some England players, is my heartiest wish.

What a bowler, too, was our 'Scofie' Haigh. No one could spin the ball or nip in a real fast Yorker better than he. Alas! I think he was a bit lazy about the latter, and many a time I had to remind him of it! Sure enough he produced it, and bang went the wicket.

I had always a warm corner in my heart for John Tunnicliffe. He had not a great benefit and never got his deserts, but, as my right-hand man, he was charming to work with. His high moral character had a great deal to do with the success of the side. He was a good and ready speaker, and we always enjoyed listening to him at the annual Wighill outing.

SUTCLIFFE AND HOLMES

Sutcliffe and Holmes, the heroes of our first-wicket stands, and the former for years one of the mainstays of our England Eleven. Nobody I know trained, and trains, harder or more conscientiously than Sutcliffe. I ascribe much of his great success to that fact. Rhodes also deserves mention in the same category. It was told of him that once on the way back from India he took a glass of stout, but said he, 'It gave me rheumatism so I didn't have a second.'

In the case of Holmes, we in Yorkshire shall always consider we had a few seasons back a little bone to pick with the Selectors for passing over such a brilliant field and resourceful batsman on any wicket. It was, perhaps, his misfortune to be generally regarded only as one of a first pair.

Macaulay, who has taken nearly 1,500 wickets in only eleven seasons, must not be forgotten. Verity, too, stepping into Rhodes' place, has already taken over 200 wickets in less than two seasons. There is also decided promise in the fast right-handed bowling of young Bowes.

Last, but not least, I cannot forget our David Hunter. It was hard luck he never played for England, for he was one of the greatest keepers of the day. On one occasion at Leyton I had to leave early to catch a train and I told Georgie to take command. Poor old David, how hurt he was! I forgot he was senior player and never thought he wished to be troubled with the captaincy. Later, however, he had his chance and captained jolly well. His successor, Dolphin, was also a fine wicket-keeper.

YORKSHIRE'S AMATEURS

The above are some of our great Players, and I am the last to forget the help we received from Ernest Smith, Arthur Sellars, F. S. Jackson, F. W. Milligan, T. L. Taylor, Frank Mitchell and Rockley Wilson. We have often been accused of not playing Amateurs and that we are practically a Players side. My answer is that whenever we have an Amateur good enough he has always been asked to play. Did we not always welcome with open arms Smith and Rockley Wilson during August when, owing to scholastic duties, they could not play earlier?

Our greatest amateur was undoubtedly Stanley Jackson, who was 'Jacker' to everyone from his Harrow days. He was a great batsman, great bowler, fine fielder—a great cricketer to the core. He took 506 wickets for 19.18 runs for us and made 10,405 runs with an average of 33.78 during the seventeen years he played for Yorkshire. Few who remember him as a batsman know that he was once No. 10 in the batting order for Yorkshire! This is how it happened. Though he had just taken seven for 42 against Middlesex somebody had run him out for a song and he did not seem keen to play in the next match at Chesterfield.

'Why,' I argued with him, 'you've just got seven of 'em out at six apiece! You must come.' So he came all right. Next day as I was writing out the order I asked him where he'd like to go in, so he said, 'Oh! don't know. Treat me as a bowler.' So I wrote him down No. 10. Brown and Tunnicliffe then proceeded to make 554 for the first wicket. I was No. 3 that day in Jackson's place. As they walked out to bat I put on my pads. I took them off for the lunch interval; I put them on again and took them off again for the tea interval. Again I put them on, and sat another couple of hours. Such is cricket!

I have never seen 'Jacker's' equal at bowling for his field. I remember on one occasion when we were 'in the cart' at Bradford against Surrey how precisely he bowled for his field, and how he apologised to me for having bowled a ball not intended. Though his grand batting for England is probably best remembered, he was a bowler of the very highest class, with a graceful, flowing delivery of a kind but rarely seen nowadays.

Since those happy days 'Jacker' has passed through more serious times in Bengal. There, a couple of years ago, he and I were the guests of honour at the dinner to us of the Calcutta Cricket Club given at the Bengal Club. We both made speeches, and when he got up to speak first he said across the table to me, 'I've got first innings to-day, old man. You bossed me often enough in the past, but I'm boss here!' One of our greatest cricketers; what a pity Australia never saw him out there in his heyday.

Ernest Smith, really fast in his time, took 284 wickets for 23 runs each, and made 4,781 runs for 20.81 per innings often when badly wanted. One of his greatest innings was that at Leyton when, in saving the match, he batted an hour for 0. That was the innings in which our Georgie was in for five hours for 96 and then said he got out by accident!

Rockley Wilson, of the perfect length, took 196 wickets for Yorkshire for 15.70 runs each, playing only in August, and the claims of business prevented T. L. Taylor playing for more than seven years, during which he made 3,951 runs for an average of 35.27.

In conclusion I must not omit to mention, as an instance of the 'roughing' that we old cricketers had to put up with, the reply given to me by the man responsible for the arrangements of the first county match ever played at Dewsbury, about the year 1882. On my hinting to him that the arrangements were somewhat primitive and that I saw no such thing as a bath, he appeared to have received the shock of his life as he replied, 'We old cricketers never had baths!'

An interesting fact concerning our eleven is that since I retired from the captaincy in 1910 we have had eight captains, all but two of whom have been captain of the winning side in the Championship in their first year. I am aware that it is not good for a side to be always changing its captain, so I hope that now that we have a really good cricketer as captain in Greenwood he will lead us to victory on many more occasions as decisively as we won last year.

THE UMPIRE'S POINT OF VIEW [1933]

Some Experiences and Suggestions

BY FRANK CHESTER

The Hawke contribution may have been the most amusing item in the 1932 edition, but it was certainly not the most prescient. When we turn to Caine's editorial notes, we find a man uneasy at the prospect to come, although it is no more than a vague disquiet which is exercising his mind, something he cannot quite put his editorial finger on, or perhaps cannot muster the courage to express in words. But it says something for Caine's perspicacity that he sensed his own misgivings at all. After discussing prospects for the coming tour of Australia and bemoaning the loss of Hobbs to the international scene, Caine discusses batting candidates before arriving at the growing shadow of his own perturbation:

> There remains the big question who shall captain the side. A year ago everything pointed to the probability of the post being offered to Jardine. The old Oxonian not only possesses the experience born of a tour in Australia but can look back upon a series of fine performances . . . On the other hand he does not seem to have impressed people with his ability as a leader on the field. Whether Jardine lacks some of the essentials for a successful captain or not, the impression appears to be widely entertained that Chapman, were he in form, would again be given charge of the team. Unhappily Chapman has apparently lost his judgment in batting.

In the light of what was soon to happen, the final deposition of Chapman from the England side, the rise of Jardine in his place, the calamities which befell that appointment, the spectacular demonstration of Caine's mild-mannered shrewdness in suggesting that perhaps Jardine might have lacked 'some of the essentials for a successful captain', these editorial comments possess a wisdom which can only be appreciated in hindsight. Meanwhile Caine set to work on what was to prove the last Almanack of his life, selecting as his guest essayist one of the tragic survivors of the Great War who rose above his disabilities to win a different kind of fame. It is revealing that even though the horrors of the war had by now receded, Caine in his editorial annotation cannot bring himself to be any more specific regarding the nature of his subject's misfortunes than to write that he was 'badly wounded'.

Frank Chester (1896–1957) joined Worcestershire as an all-rounder at the age of 16, and displayed such precocious talent that in the following season he scored three centuries for the county and took 44 wickets. As Sydney Pardon commented,

'Nothing stood out more prominently than the remarkable development of Chester, the youngest professional regularly engaged in first-class cricket. Very few players in the history of cricket have showed such form at the age of seventeen and a half. Playing with a beautiful straight bat he depended to a large extent on his watchfulness in defence. He bowls with a high, easy action . . . Having begun so well, Chester should continue to improve and it seems only reasonable to expect that he will be an England cricketer'. Chester continued his advance in the following season, and then, when the war began, fought with the British Army in Salonika, where he was so badly wounded that he lost his right arm just below the elbow. Yet by 1922 he was standing as an umpire in the County Championship, and, by the time of his retirement in 1955, he had officiated in forty-eight Test matches. It was Chester who first introduced the gambit, soon to be followed by others, of bending low over the stumps as the bowler delivered the ball. Respected for giving decisions, as Wisden put it, 'without fear or favour', he was generally regarded as the man who had raised umpiring to its highest level. Both Bradman and Hobbs rated him the best umpire they had ever played under, and his partner on so many occasions, F. S. Lee, said on hearing of Chester's death, 'There is a great deal for which umpires have to thank him'. One fascinating suggestion Chester makes in his essay, which has never been aired since, is the co-opting on to selection committees of the occasional umpire, on the grounds that he sees as much of the game as anybody, and perhaps more.

IMAGINE the feelings of an umpire just appointed to the list, anxious to 'make good' and denied admission to a ground at which he had been instructed to officiate. That was my experience in 1922 at Northampton. It all occurred because of my youthful appearance—I was little more than twenty-five at the time. When I told the gateman I was one of the umpires, he treated it quite as a joke. 'You have made a mistake,' he said, 'this is a first-class match.' Happily, he consented to fetch the club secretary, and after explanations and apologies the twenty-five year old umpire was passed through.

Since then I have umpired regularly each season—we get an average of twenty-two matches each year. Sound eyesight and good hearing are, of course, the first essentials but knowledge of cricket and—more important—knowledge of the Laws of the Game is imperative. Don Bradman has said that he considers our umpires the best in the world, but it must be remembered that we have a big advantage because more cricket is played in England than anywhere else.

People have asked me, 'Why don't the Selectors take some of you umpires on their Committee when they are picking the England team? You are on the field all through the matches in which you are acting as umpires, you see everything that goes on and can spot the good players.' That suggestion is not for me to discuss here, even if we certainly get an excellent view of all that happens. Umpires are often asked whether they have any suggestions to make regarding the game, as well as for an opinion on various experiments tried in recent years. That is a gesture which all umpires appreciate.

At the time of writing, everyone seems to be discussing our bowling in Australia—the so-called 'leg-theory' bowling. If it is of the character described in the cables, I do not agree with it; it is sure to make cricket a good deal slower and may keep people away. It is said our bowlers are aiming to hit the leg stump, but to hit the wicket you do not pitch half way and there is a danger the practice may lessen interest in the game.

The bowler to whom the term 'leg theory' was first applied used to bowl the swinger. The best player I ever saw do this was A. Jaques, the Hampshire amateur (killed in the War) between 1912 and 1914 when I played for Worcestershire.* He could swing an old ball. He stood 6 ft. 3 ins. in height and bowled medium pace, placing nearly all his field on the on-side and pitching on the wicket or outside the leg stump. As he could make the ball swing in and also get on an off-break, he cramped the batsmen so much that many of them lost patience and were out. W. T. Greswell, of Somerset, was another very good 'leg theory' bowler.

Still, spin bowlers get most of the wickets nowadays, not those who swerve. Freeman, Sam Staples, Parker, V. W. C. Jupp, Goddard, Verity, James Langridge and Mitchell (Derbyshire) generally finish with well over 100 wickets each season. We should not hear so much of pitches being over-prepared if we had more spin bowlers. In my opinion, pitches are no better now than they were during my playing career. I could mention some county grounds where the pitches before the War were much better than they are at the present time. It was a big help to the bowlers when the larger wicket was adopted. With the new stumps in use, I have seen a large number of batsmen out from balls which, before the alteration in the size of the stumps, would have just missed the mark. Also, the experimental rule regarding l.b.w. and 'the snick' has been a very good one, and, I think, has come to stay.

Why do not bowlers make more use of the bowling crease? The late J. W. H. T. Douglas used the crease more than any other bowler I have seen and I am told that Walter Brearley used to bowl from varying places between the stumps and the return crease. Suggestions have been put forward that a new ball after 150 runs have been scored, should be allowed. This would certainly help bowlers of the fast and fast-medium pace and swing bowlers, but personally I do not favour such a change. Cricket is just as popular as ever. It is the uncertain weather we get during

* Qualifying for Worcestershire at the age of sixteen and a half, Frank Chester a year later—in 1913—scored 698 runs, playing three innings of over a hundred, and took forty-three wickets. 'Wisden' of 1914 said of him: 'Very few players in the history of cricket have shown such form at the age of seventeen and a half.' The following season, he scored 924 runs, making 178 not out against Essex at Worcester. A very promising career was interfered with by the War, Chester being badly wounded and so prevented from playing further cricket. Appointed to the umpires' list in 1922, he has stood in thirteen Test Matches in this country.

the summer months that keeps so many people away. When we get a good summer the 'gates' are always better.

Perhaps in the near future special rules for certain grounds will disappear. I should like to suggest that definite times for the luncheon and tea intervals be in force everywhere. The hours of play—11.30 to 6.30—are ideal.

While it may not be considered within the province of an umpire to suggest tampering with the rules, there is one matter which I think merits very close consideration. Where a batsman, not out overnight, is not present on the ground to resume his innings next morning and the two minutes grace has lapsed, he can according to the existing laws bat with the consent of the opposing captain. Surely, unless an unanswerable explanation of excuse is given, the batsman should be ruled out without the captain of the opposing side being approached on the point. An incident touching on this rule occurred last season.

Another curious occurrence at a match in which I was standing umpire took place some years ago. A batsman deliberately ran after a ball and kicked it; then he started to run. I informed the batsman he could not run and no runs were allowed, but afterwards I was 'called over the coals' and told there was no law whereby a man should not kick the ball. My defence of the action was that this was unfair play and that, had it occurred again, I should, had I been appealed to, have given the batsman out for impeding the wicket-keeper.

It has often struck me as curious how in some matches one of the umpires is constantly dealing with appeals while the other man receives hardly any. I remember one match in particular, at Dover, when the late Harry Butt was my colleague. Altogether, he gave twelve batsmen out, but meanwhile I did not have an appeal made to me. Butt called to me jokingly, 'It is about time you earned your money.'

Out in Australia, I have read, umpires are using special 'over' watches. Umpires scarcely need anything so elaborate. Personally, I use stones to count, some umpires use a special machine with six levers, others coins and some their fingers. Whatever the method is, it becomes automatic. There is nothing else automatic about an umpire's job. We need to be very much on the alert the whole time.

THE BOWLING CONTROVERSY [1934]

Text of the Cables

BY C. S. CAINE

Caine lived just long enough for his misgivings about Jardine to be confirmed in the most alarming way. The notorious Adelaide Test match of January 1933, in which Jardine pursued tactics of unprecedented ignobility, was defined in the Almanack as 'probably the most unpleasant ever played'. But this editorial comment was not Caine's but Sydney Southerton's. Caine died in April 1933, just as the Almanack for that year was appearing in the shops, complete with the open questions about Jardine. In his attempt to review the events of the 1932–33 tour and to evaluate the accusations being flung about by both sides, Southerton's attempts at a judicious neutrality tip him over to the English side perhaps inevitably. Like most English commentators who were not witnesses to the Bodyline excesses, he seems unable to grasp what actually happened, and even invokes the figure of Fred Root as an example of the new tactics. In the end he comes down in favour of sanity, rationality and a sense of proportion, but yet again the orotundities of speakers at cricket dinners give rise to the smiles of posterity. Southerton's précis of the Recorder of Gravesend's sentiments as passed on to the West Indian touring side has ironic overtones in view of what was to happen during the 1933 season, when the West Indian bowlers, evidently impressed by the defence of Bodyline mounted by so many English armchair experts, decided that it would be acceptable for them to use it in their contests with the host nation. The biter being bit, howls of protest rose up, and Bodyline was seen from fresh perspectives, especially at Lord's, where, in the match between the tourists and Middlesex, Patsy Hendren took defensive measures typical of his deflating humour. As Kenneth Gregory wrote many years later:

> When the West Indian Martindale was hurling down bumpers in 1933, Patsy Hendren persuaded his wife to fit protective side-pieces to his cap, the outcome being Sherlock Holmes looking in three directions.

This is the only laugh ever to come out of the ugliest confrontation between batsmen and bowlers of the pre-war period.

Or at any rate the only intentional laugh. There were to be several of the unwitting kind. Although it was Jardine who ran amok on the field, ultimate responsibility for the conduct of the tourists fell on the manager, or in this case the managers. Whether or not the selectors had subconscious fears that the usual dangers of a tour were doubled by the appointment of Jardine as captain, they committed themselves to the unusual step of appointing two managers, one of whom, the Somerset amateur R. N. Palairet, seems never to have lifted his head above the parapet from start to finish of the entire episode. The other manager, Pelham Warner, had been a resolute opponent of Bodyline tactics when they appeared in their embryonic stage in the County Championship, but in Australia his disapproval mysteriously lost its voice, and Jardine, brushing the ineffectual Warner aside, became his own manager. This made three in all, none of whom had the slightest idea either of what they were doing or of what they should have been doing. In later years Warner buttered his own path to salvation, and, in a history of Lord's published in 1946, raised a huge laugh with: 'The question was not understood in this country'. Five years later, clearly intoxicated with the exuberance of his own pomposity, Warner surpassed himself in his autobiography, remarking loftily of Bodyline: 'I do not propose to discuss it here. It would serve no good purpose'. What Warner meant, although he was too coy to say so, was that it would serve no good purpose to Warner, who, despite his total failure to implement the authority of a tour manager, despite having presided over the most disgraceful tour ever undertaken by any English touring side, came out of it all smelling so overpoweringly of roses that before he died he was knighted, as the citation wittily put it, 'for services to cricket'.

As for Jardine, his powers as a comedian proved in the end to outclass even those of Warner. When the fires lit by Bodyline had died down, Jardine disappeared, at first from Test cricket, finally from all first-class cricket. Among the hobbies with which he beguiled the longueurs of premature retirement was writing. In 1936 he published a book called 'Cricket', in which, apart from a brief disquisition on the career of Bonnie Prince Charlie and an insistence that cricketers should always brush their teeth before starting a match, Jardine achieves a pair of one-liners worthy of inclusion in any comprehensive anthology of English humour. One is 'the play's the thing', and the other, breath-taking from a man whose malapert policies very nearly ended the imperial peace, is the advice that 'cricket is only a game'. That Jardine really did stir the muddy waters of imperial politics is confirmed by the candour and honesty of later commentators, especially E. W. Swanton, who in his autobiography 'A Sort of Cricket Person' reproduces the text of a letter written by Warner in 1934 to Sir Alexander Hore-Ruthven, the then Governor of South Australia. Discussing the possibility that Jardine might again captain England, Warner writes:

> I say 'No' unless he makes a most generous public gesture of friendliness, and then I am not sure I would trust him. He is a queer fellow. When he sees a cricket ground with an Australian on it he goes mad! He rose to his present position on my shoulders, and of his attitude to me I do not care to speak.

This is the closest Warner ever came to shouldering any of the responsibility for the insane act of appointing as an England touring captain someone who 'when he sees a cricket ground with an Australian on it he goes mad'.

Further revelations are to be found in Geoffrey Moorhouse's 'Lord's', in which he notes that 'one of the few things quite clear about Warner is that he came to detest Douglas Jardine as a result of his experiences alongside him in Australia'. Moorhouse then addresses himself to the most interesting of all the unanswered questions about the Bodyline crisis, and hints at at least one alarming answer:

> How did the lachrymose Manager and Chairman of Selectors absolve himself from any of the stigmas which were attached to English cricket at this time, and especially to all who toured Australia in the winter of 1932–33? We do not know. For one of the most arresting features of the whole episode is the dearth of relevant material. As Manager of that tour, Warner submitted to the MCC Committee a report on all that had happened from the moment the party left home until the day it returned. That document, quite simply, has vanished from the archives at Lord's. So has every letter he wrote from Australia to Findlay or anyone else in the hierarchy of MCC. The protective coating, it seems, has insulated him rather well from historical research.

But perhaps after all not quite well enough. No matter how much documentation has been spirited away, the one incontrovertible fact remains that Warner presided over a tour which did more damage to the image of the game than any other ten tours before or since.

There remained one body of involved men who might have borne witness, the professionals who accompanied Jardine and Warner on that tour, and who received their orders from them. But they were hired hands, and to have implied any criticism of their paymasters would have meant professional disaster. Every one of the paid players held his tongue—until 1946, when Hammond, W. R., having been transmuted by expediency into Mr. W. R. Hammond so that the myth of amateur captaincy could be maintained a little longer, published a newspaper article on the eve of his departure to Australia as captain of the first post-war English touring side. The time for Hammond to fear victimisation was long since past. He was immune by now even for the cricketing panjandrums, and was already contemplating the retirement which followed a few months later. In his newspaper confessional, Hammond said that had Bodyline tactics continued in the first-class game, he and other famous England players would have left the game altogether, and added that in his opinion only good luck was responsible for nobody being killed by it. Hammond's belated burst of candour seems inexplicable except that from all reports he had long since become disillusioned with the game and wearied of its bromides. His behaviour as captain on the 1946–47 tour was to prove curious to say the least. The rest of the party complained that they hardly saw him except on the field of play, where he performed so lamentably that it soon became quite clear that this great all-rounder had lost his appetite for the game. In such a mood, Hammond may well have felt it his moral duty to say his piece concerning an episode which had preyed ever since on the consciences of everyone involved in it.

There was a quaint postscript to all this. It is not strictly accurate to say that Jardine played no further part in English cricket after 1937, when he made his last appearances for Surrey. In May 1946, at the Oval, a one-day game was played between Surrey and an Old England side whose ranks included Jardine. He duly reached his half-century, and the Wisden report suggests that he had lost nothing either in his technical command or his aloofness: 'D. R. Jardine, wearing his Oxford Harlequin cap, was as polished as ever in academic skill'.

DURING the tour of the M.C.C. team in Australia in 1932–33, exception was taken in that country to the methods adopted by certain of the visiting bowlers, and long correspondence by cable between the M.C.C. and the Australian Board of Control followed. Below will be found, in chronological order, the text of these cables, together with—in proper sequence—a short report of meetings bearing upon the subject.

FROM AUSTRALIAN BOARD OF CONTROL TO M.C.C., JAN. 18, 1933

'Body-line bowling has assumed such proportions as to menace the best interests of the game, making protection of the body by the batsmen the main consideration.

'This is causing intensely bitter feeling between the players as well as injury. In our opinion it is unsportsmanlike.

'Unless stopped at once it is likely to upset the friendly relations existing between Australia and England.'

FROM M.C.C. TO AUSTRALIAN BOARD OF CONTROL, JAN. 23, 1933

'We, Marylebone Cricket Club, deplore your cable. We deprecate your opinion that there has been unsportsmanlike play. We have fullest confidence in captain, team and managers and are convinced that they would do nothing to infringe either the Laws of Cricket or the spirit of the game. We have no evidence that our confidence has been misplaced. Much as we regret accidents to Woodfull and Oldfield, we understand that in neither case was the bowler to blame. If the Australian Board of Control wish to propose a new Law or Rule, it shall receive our careful consideration in due course.

'We hope the situation is not now as serious as your cable would seem to indicate, but if it is such as to jeopardize the good relations between English and Australian cricketers and you consider it desirable to cancel remainder of programme we would consent, but with great reluctance.'

FROM AUSTRALIAN BOARD OF CONTROL TO M.C.C., JAN. 30, 1933

'We, Australian Board of Control, appreciate your difficulty in dealing with the matter raised in our cable without having seen the actual play. We unanimously regard body-line bowling, as adopted in some of the games in the present tour, as being opposed to the spirit of cricket, and unnecessarily dangerous to the players.

'We are deeply concerned that the ideals of the game shall be protected and have, therefore, appointed a committee to report on the action necessary to eliminate such bowling from Australian cricket as from beginning of the 1933–34 season.

'We will forward a copy of the Committee's recommendations for your consideration, and it is hoped co-operation as to its application to all cricket. We do not consider it necessary to cancel remainder of programme.'

The committee appointed consisted of Messrs. R. J. Hartigan (Queensland) representing the Board of Control; W. M. Woodfull, V. Y. Richardson and M. A. Noble.

FROM M.C.C TO AUSTRALIAN BOARD OF CONTROL, FEB. 2, 1933

'We, the Committee of the Marylebone Cricket Club note with pleasure that you do not consider it necessary to cancel the remainder of programme, and that you are postponing the whole issue involved until after the present tour is completed. May we accept this as a clear indication that the good sportsmanship of our team is not in question?

'We are sure you will appreciate how impossible it would be to play any Test Match in the spirit we all desire unless both sides were satisfied there was no reflection upon their sportsmanship.

'When your recommendation reaches us it shall receive our most careful consideration and will be submitted to the Imperial Cricket Conference.'

FROM AUSTRALIAN BOARD OF CONTROL TO M.C.C., FEB. 8, 1933

'We do not regard the sportsmanship of your team as being in question.

'Our position was fully considered at the recent meeting in Sydney and is as indicated in our cable of January 30.

'It is the particular class of bowling referred to therein which we consider is not in the best interests of cricket, and in this view we understand we are supported by many eminent English cricketers.

'We join heartily with you in hoping that the remaining Tests will be played with the traditional good feeling.'

The Australian Board of Control, meeting on April 21, 1933, considered a proposal submitted to them by the special sub-committee set up to consider the question of 'body-line' bowling and cabled M.C.C. asking that body to give the proposal their consideration. The cable read as follows: 'Australian Board adopted following addition to Laws of Cricket in Australia, namely:—

'Any ball delivered which, in the opinion of the umpire at the bowler's end is bowled at the batsman with the intent to intimidate or injure him shall be considered unfair and "No-ball" shall be called. The bowler shall be notified of the reason. If the offence be repeated by the same innings he shall be immediately instructed by the umpire to cease bowling and the over shall be regarded as completed. Such bowler shall not again be permitted to bowl during the course of the innings then in progress.'

'Law 48a shall not apply to this Law. Foregoing submitted for your consideration and it is hoped co-operation by application to all cricket.'

FROM M.C.C. TO AUSTRALIAN BOARD OF CONTROL, JUNE 12, 1933

'The M.C.C. Committee have received and carefully considered the cable of the Australian Board of Control of April 28th last. They have also received and considered the reports of the Captain and Managers of the cricket team which visited Australia 1932–1933.

'With regard to the cable of the Australian Board of Control of April 28th last, the Committee presume that the class of bowling to which the proposed new law would apply is that referred to as "body-line" bowling in the Australian Board of Control's cable of January 18th. The Committee consider that the term "body-line" bowling is misleading and improper. It has led to much inaccuracy of thought by confusing the short bumping ball, whether directed on the off middle or leg stump, with what is known as "leg-theory."

'The term "body-line" would appear to imply a direct attack by the bowler on the batsman. The Committee consider that such an implication applied to any English bowling in Australia is improper and incorrect. Such action on the part of any bowler would be an offence against the spirit of the game and would be immediately condemned. The practice of bowling on the leg stump with a field placed on the leg side necessary for such bowling is legitimate, and has been in force for many years. It has generally been referred to as "leg-theory." The present habit of batsmen who move in front of their wicket with the object of gliding straight balls to leg tends to give the impression that the bowler is bowling at the batsman, especially in the case of a fast bowler when the batsmen mistimes the ball and is hit.

'The new Law recommended by the Australian Board of Control does not appear to the Committee to be practicable. Firstly, it would place an impossible task on the umpire, and secondly, it would place in the hands of the umpire a power over the game which would be more than dangerous, and which any umpire might well fear to exercise.

'The Committee have had no reason to give special attention to "leg-theory" as practised by fast bowlers. They will, however, watch carefully during the present season for anything which might be regarded as unfair or prejudicial to the best interests of the game. They propose to invite opinions and suggestions from County Clubs and Captains at the end of the season, with a view to enabling them to express an opinion on this matter at a Special Meeting of the Imperial Cricket Conference.

'With regard to the reports of the Captain and Managers, the Committee, while deeply appreciative of the private and public hospitality shewn to the English team, are much concerned with regard to barracking, which is referred to in all the reports, and against which there is unanimous deprecation. Barracking has, unfortunately, always been indulged in by spectators in Australia to a degree quite unknown in this Country. During the late tour, however, it would appear to have exceeded all previous experience, and on occasions to have become thoroughly objectionable. There appears to have been little or no effort on the part of those responsible for the administration of the game in Australia to interfere, or to control this exhibition. This was naturally regarded by members of the team as a serious lack of consideration for them. The Committee are of opinion that cricket played under such conditions is robbed of much of its value as a game, and that unless barracking is stopped, or is greatly moderated in Australia, it is difficult to see how the continuance of representative matches can serve the best interest of the game.

'The Committee regret that these matters have to be dealt with by correspondence and not by personal conference. If at any time duly accredited representatives of Australian Cricket could meet the Committee in conference, such conference would be welcomed by M.C.C.'

FROM AUSTRALIAN BOARD OF CONTROL TO M.C.C., SEPT. 22, 1933

'We note that you consider that a form of bowling which amounted to a direct attack by the bowler on the batsman would be against the spirit of the game. We agree with you that Leg-theory Bowling as it has been generally practised for many years is not open to objection. On these matters there does not appear to be any real difference between our respective views.

'We feel that while the type of bowling to which exception was taken in Australia, strictly was not in conflict with the Laws of Cricket, yet its continued practice would not be in the best interests of the game. May we assume that you concur in this point of view and that the teams may thus take the field in 1934 with that knowledge?

'We are giving consideration to the question of barracking and you may rely upon our using our best endeavours to have it controlled in future tours.

'We are most anxious that the cordial relations which have so long existed between English and Australian cricket shall continue.'

FROM M.C.C. TO AUSTRALIAN BOARD OF CONTROL, OCT. 9, 1933

'The M.C.C. Committee appreciate the friendly tone of your cable and they heartily reciprocate your desire for the continuance of cordial relations.

'In their view the difference between us seems to be rather on the questions of fact than on any point of interpretation of the Laws of Cricket or of the spirit of the game. They agree and have always agreed that a form of bowling which is obviously a direct attack by the bowler upon the batsman would be an offence against the spirit of the game.

'Your team can certainly take the field with the knowledge and with the full assurance that cricket will be played here in the same spirit as in the past and with the single desire to promote the best interests of the game in both countries.

'The Committee much appreciate your promise to take the question of barracking into consideration with a view to ensuring that it shall be kept within reasonable bounds.

'Your team can rely on a warm welcome from M.C.C., and every effort will be made to make their visit enjoyable.'

FROM AUSTRALIAN BOARD OF CONTROL TO M.C.C., NOV. 16, 1933

'We appreciate the terms of your cablegram of October 9 and assume that such cable is intended to give the assurance asked for in our cablegram of September 22.

'It is on this understanding that we are sending a team in 1934.'

A joint meeting of the Advisory Country Cricket Committee and the Board of Control of Test Matches at Home, at which the county captains were present, was held at Lord's on Thursday, November 23, 1933, to consider the replies received from the counties to the M.C.C.'s circular letter in regard to fast leg-theory bowling.

A decision was reached that no alteration of the Law was desirable. It was agreed that any form of bowling which is obviously a direct attack by the bowler upon the batsman would be an offence against the spirit of the game.

It was decided to leave the matter to the captains in complete confidence that they would not permit or countenance bowling of such type.

FROM M.C.C. TO AUSTRALIAN BOARD OF CONTROL, DEC. 12, 1933

'Reference your cable of November 16th, you must please accept our cable of October 9th, which speaks for itself, as final.

'We cannot go beyond the assurance therein given. We shall welcome Australian cricketers who come to play cricket with us next year. If, however, your Board of Control decide that such games should be deferred, we shall regret their decision.

'Please let us know your Board's final decision as soon as possible and in any event before the end of the year.'

FROM AUSTRALIAN BOARD OF CONTROL TO M.C.C., DEC. 14, 1933

'With further reference to your cable of October 9 and your confirmatory cable of December 12 in reply to ours of November 16, we, too, now regard the position finalised. Our team will leave Australia on March 9.'

FROM M.C.C. TO AUSTRALIAN BOARD OF CONTROL, DEC. 14, 1933

'Thank you for your cable. We are very glad to know we may look forward to welcoming the Australians next summer. We shall do all in our power to make their visit enjoyable.'

BY THE EDITOR

Had the foregoing cables been the medical history sheets of a person suddenly afflicted by some mental or physical trouble a doctor would have experienced little difficulty in tracing and analysing the disease from its onset to its cure. In like manner cricketers can gather from the cables almost the whole course of the disturbance brought about between the M.C.C. and the Australian Board of Control over the question of fast leg-theory bowling. I have purposely omitted to use the expression 'body-line bowling.' It may have conveyed to those to whom it was presented at the outset the meaning the inventor of it wished to infer, but to my mind it was an objectionable term, utterly foreign to cricket, and calculated to stir up strife when the obvious aim of everybody should have been directed towards the prevention of any breach.

Happily the controversy is now at an end, and little reason exists, therefore, to flog what we can regard as a 'dead horse.' But, obviously from the historical point of view, something on the subject must be said. I hope and believe that the ventilation of either grievances by the Australians, and the placatory replies of the M.C.C. will have done much towards imparting a better spirit to Test Matches which of recent years have become battles rather than pleasurable struggles. A false atmosphere has pervaded them. During the last few tours of M.C.C. teams in Australia, and the visits of the Australians to this country one could not fail to detect a subtle change taking place in the conduct of Test Matches—reflected unfortunately in the style of play of the cricketers themselves. The *result* of the contests was given a prominence out of keeping even with the importance of Test Matches, and the true sense of perspective stood in danger of disappearing altogether.

There is no need to enter into some of the reasons for the hostility with which D. R. Jardine in particular and certain of his team were received by the huge crowds in Australia. Animosity existed and was fanned into flame largely by the use of the term 'body-line' when Larwood and others met with such success against the leading Australian batsmen. To such an extent had real bitterness grown that the storm burst during the Third Test Match at Adelaide. The dispatch of the petulant cablegram by the Australian Board of Control even placed the completion of the tour in jeopardy. Saner counsels prevailed, and, although tension existed for months afterwards, the M.C.C. for their part never lost their grip of the situation and, what was even more important, refused to be stampeded into any panic legislation. Whatever individual opinions were held at the time the M.C.C. Committee, as a whole, naturally stood by the captain of their Team in Australia. They had heard only one side of the question.

And now, what of this fast leg-theory method of bowling to which not only the Australian players themselves, but a vast majority of the people of Australia took such grave exception? With the dictum of the M.C.C. that any form of bowling which constitutes a direct attack by the bowler on the batsman is contrary to the spirit of the game everyone must unquestionably concur. D. R. Jardine, on his return to England, stated definitely in his book that the bowling against which the Australians demurred was not of this description, and Larwood, the chief exponent of it, said with equal directness that he had never intentionally bowled at a man. On the other hand, there are numerous statements by responsible

Australians to the effect that the type of bowling adopted was calculated to intimidate batsmen, pitched as the ball was so short as to cause it to fly shoulder and head high and make batsmen, with the leg-side studded with fieldsmen, use the bat as a protection for their bodies or their heads rather than in defence of the wicket or to make a scoring stroke. Victor Richardson, the South Australian batsman, has said that when he took his ordinary stance at the wicket he found the ball coming on to his body; when he took guard slightly more to the leg-side he still had the ball coming at him; and with a still wider guard the ball continued to follow him. I hold no brief either for Jardine or Larwood or for Richardson, Woodfull or Bradman; but while some of the Australians may have exaggerated the supposed danger of this form of bowling I cling to the opinion that they cannot all be wrong. When the first mutterings of the storm were heard many people in this country were inclined to the belief that the Australians, seeing themselves in danger of losing the rubber, were not taking defeat in the proper spirit always expected from honourable opponents. I will confess that I thought they did not relish what seemed to me at that stage to be a continuous good length bombardment by our fast bowlers on to their leg-stump. This idea I afterwards found was not quite correct.

There is nothing new in leg-theory bowling. The most notable exponent of it in recent years was Root, of Worcestershire; to go back to just before the War A. Jaques, of Hampshire, often exploited it with success; and to delve deeper into the past an Australian—no less than the famous Spofforth himself—would at times bowl on the leg-stump with an off-break and two fieldsmen close in on the leg-side. Root and Jaques were, however, medium-paced bowlers while Spofforth, even if he had a very destructive fast ball always at command, could not truthfully be classified as a fast bowler consistent in the pace of say Larwood, Knox, Richardson, Lockwood, or Kortright. Moreover, Root, Jaques and Spofforth almost invariably bowled a good length, so that the ball could be played either in a defensive manner or with the idea of turning it to leg, and when the batsman made a mistake in timing or in placing he usually paid the penalty by being caught.

That type of bowling, however, is very different from the kind sent down at top-speed with the ball flying past the shoulders or head of the batsman who has only a split second in which to make up his mind as to whether he will duck, move away, or attempt to play it with the bat high in the air. Against one sort a perfectly legitimate and reasonable stroke could be played without any apprehension of physical damage; against the other it seems to me that by touching the ball in defence of the upper part of his body or his head a batsman would be almost bound to be out. One would not accuse Hammond or Hendren of being slow on their feet, yet Hendren at Lord's on one occasion was not quick enough to get out of the way and received a crashing blow on his head, while last season at Manchester Hammond, in the Test Match against the West Indies, had his chin laid open, and on resuming his innings was caught off a similar kind of ball. We saw in that particular match at Old Trafford what I should conceive to be a somewhat pale—but no less disturbing—imitation of Larwood in Australia, when Martindale and Constantine on the one hand, and Clark, of Northamptonshire, on the other were giving a demonstration of fast leg-theory bowling. Not one of the three had the pace, accuracy of pitch, or deadliness of Larwood, but what they did was sufficient to convince many people with open minds on the subject that it was a noxious form of attack not to be encouraged in any way.

Cricketers whose memories go back to the days of the bad wickets at Lord's, are I think a little too prone to emphasise the fact that W. G. Grace and other famous batsmen of that era were often struck so frequently on the body that after their innings they were covered with bruises, but I should like to suggest that the blows they received were to a large extent caused by good-length balls getting up quickly off the rough turf. I certainly can find no trace in the course of a good deal of research among old reports and comments on these matches that the fast bowlers of those days like Tarrant and Jackson continually dropped the ball short with the idea of making it bounce.

Fast bowlers of all periods have delivered the ball short of a length on occasions—sometimes by accident, and sometimes by intention to keep batsmen on the *qui-vive*—but in modern days some of our bowlers of pace have become obsessed with the idea that it is necessary to do this three or four times in an over. I desire none of my readers to get the impression that I am against fast bowling. Nothing is further from my thoughts. I like to see fast bowling, the faster the better, but I do like to see it of good length and directed at the stumps.

The Australians without any doubt thought that during the last tour they were being bowled at, and small wonder that edging away as some of them unquestionably did they found themselves bowled when, instead of the expected short-pitched 'bouncer,' occasional good-length straight balls came along and beat them before they were in a proper position to defend their wickets. It is, to say the least, significant that G. O. Allen, whom nobody would place quite in the same class as Larwood, enjoyed many successes and for the most part obtained his wickets by bowling with which we in England are familiar. Surely, with his extra pace, Larwood could have done as well as Allen and so have prevented that bitter ill-feeling which led a good many people in this country to the belief that the winning of The Ashes had been gained at too great a cost to the relations hitherto existing between England and Australia.

For myself, I hope that we shall never see fast leg-theory bowling as used during the last tour in Australia exploited in this country. I think that (1) it is definitely dangerous; (2) it creates ill-feeling between the rival teams; (3) it invites reprisals; (4) it has a bad influence on our great game of cricket; and (5) it eliminates practically all the best strokes in batting. Mainly because it makes cricket a battle instead of a game I deplore its introduction and pray for its abolition, not by any legislative measures, but by the influence which our captains can bring to bear and by avoiding use of the objectionable form of attack take a great part in wiping away a blot. Early last season I heard Mr. Weigall, the Recorder of Gravesend, deliver a great speech at a dinner to the West Indies team, in which in beautifully chosen phrases he exhorted them always to look upon cricket with the idea that the game is of far greater importance than the result. If that lesson is driven home to all our cricketers we shall hear no more of the kind of bowling which so nearly brought about a severance of the cricket relations between England and Australia.

THE HOBBS ERA [1935]

BY JACK HOBBS

The obvious essay theme for the 1935 edition was the retirement of Jack Hobbs, who contributed a typically self-effacing account of his thirty years in the game. Both the details and the tone of voice of this farewell address are highly reminiscent of his 'My Life Story', published in the same year. This raises the issue of who the real author was, both of the autobiography and the Wisden essay. During his career Hobbs had rented out his authorial prestige to a sizeable quantity of schoolboy ephemera like 'The Test Match Surprise' and 'Between the Wickets', on one occasion even subjecting himself to the farce of posing for the editor of 'Chums', in mufti, 'at the desk on which "Between the Wickets" was written'. There would appear to have been a whole platoon of ghosts haunting the journalistic career of Hobbs, the best-known of them being a writer called J. T. Bolton, who acted as the cricketer's alter ego *in the years from 1930 to 1950. If the autobiography and the Wisden essay were indeed the work of Mr. Bolton, then it must be said that he hit off the diffidence and honest modesty of his client to such perfection that Tolstoy himself could hardly have done better. Then again, perhaps after all this is an authentic Hobbs composition.*

MY career in first-class cricket having, after a very happy period, reached its end, I gladly comply with the request of the Editor of *Wisden's Almanack* to jot down some personal impressions which may be of interest to present and future readers of the book.

The honour has been done me of referring to the period of my active participation in important cricket as 'The Hobbs Era,' and I should like to say at once how mindful I am of this distinction. Roughly thirty years have gone by since I first played for Surrey under the residential qualification, and nothing has ever occurred to cause me the slightest regret that I took the advice of Tom Hayward and migrated from Cambridge to London. Without blowing my own trumpet I can say that when I went to the Oval I knew pretty well my own capabilities; it was just a question as to how great I should find the difference between first-class and Minor Counties cricket. The feeling was strong within me that I could make good, but I little thought then that I should achieve the success in an even higher sphere of cricket than that to which I was then aspiring, or that I should be the first man to beat the record of that wonderful batsman, W. G. Grace, in the matter of making centuries. However, this article is not meant to be a statement of what I myself have accomplished; the purport of it is to give in some slight degree my ideas on the changes that have come about in the game—whether of improvement or otherwise—and the points that have struck me as being worthy of mention.

THIRTY YEARS IN CRICKET

The era to which my name has been given by you, Mr. Editor, covers first-class cricket from 1903 to 1933. The War came to rob all of us of four solid years of the game, and although I played a little last summer I think that I really finished in 1933 when at 50 years of age after, roughly, 30 seasons at the Oval, I was beginning to feel that the strain of the game day after day was getting just a little too much for me. There was also the fact that younger players were knocking at the door, and that it did not become me, having had a longer innings than most cricketers of modern days, to stand in the way of promising recruits who wanted to feel that their positions in a county eleven were secure. So even though I scored one century last season I still fall short by three of the two hundred I had fondly hoped to obtain. Records after all are ephemeral; they are only made to be beaten by somebody else, and while it is nice to think that one has accomplished something out of the common there are other and more important considerations to bear in mind. The new leg-before-wicket rule, which is being tried experimentally may, if adopted, have a far-reaching effect on batsmen, but at the back of my mind there is the impression that someone will come along one of these days and surpass the 197 hundreds which now stand to my credit.

Before my time there were other epochs in our great game. The days of top-hats, when Alfred Mynn, the 'Lion of Kent' and other famous men were in their prime, are now far distant. Then came the Grace period when that marvellous batsman stood out head and shoulders above everybody else; the Hon. F. S. Jackson, Ranjitsinhji, G. L. Jessop, Tom Hayward, C. B. Fry, A. C. MacLaren, George Hirst, J. T. Tyldesley, Victor Trumper, M. A. Noble and others too numerous to mention were contemporaries in what has been described as the 'Golden Age' of cricket. It will be seen therefore that my own follows in a natural sequence in this recurring cycle.

IS CRICKET BETTER?

As to whether during the past thirty years cricket generally has been better or worse than those periods to which I have referred is not perhaps for me to say. Cricket was at its very best in that Golden Age when almost every county had one, if not two or three outstanding personalities either as batsmen or bowlers.

I do not agree, however, with the oft-repeated statement that cricket nowadays is not what it used to be, and I would ask why, when in the ordinary affairs of every-day life as well as in most other games we have gone ahead, cricket should be singled out as an example of deterioration in all-round form and skill? We know that, in a broad sense, wickets are more favourable to run-getting, and while I do not hold with the over-preparation of pitches and the use of various forms of 'dope' to achieve perfection and make the batsman's task easier, it must always be remembered that, with a heavier programme now necessary owing to the increase of first-class counties since the days shortly before my advent, cricket grounds are subjected to far harder wear.

But it should not be overlooked that there were several county enclosures before say 1900 where the wickets were really good, and one has only to look up the records to find that big scores were made at the Oval before swerve bowlers came into existence, and when length, allied to spin, was the first consideration. All wickets were not bad, as many people seem to think. The one important difference between those of my early times and those of the present is that you very, very rarely see a real 'sticky' wicket nowadays. Over-preparation is the cause of this, and probably the system in use at certain centres of covering the pitch completely before the match has also had something to do with it. That, however, brings you to another consideration, that of finance. Many county clubs are often hard put to it to make both ends meet. If rain not only prevents play for a long time but in the end hastens the completion of a match, measures have to be adopted to mitigate undue loss of time.

Efforts have been made more than once, because of the heavy programmes and constant play day after day, to limit first-class matches to two days. I am not altogether opposed to this; in fact I would ask: why not two-day matches of one innings each? That would give a lot of our professionals a much needed rest and, as far as I can see, the main argument against this would come from professionals themselves because they would not be able to earn quite as much as they do now. Possibly, however, that is a question which time will solve.

SOME CHANGES

I have always regarded it as curious that while most of the changes in cricket in my thirty years have been in favour of the bowler, such as the smaller ball and the wider wicket, bowling generally, in my opinion, has deteriorated. There are very few outstanding bowlers of real class to-day, and I remember that just after the War, when admittedly things had changed a good deal, bowlers opened for their sides who weren't considered prior to 1914. Everyone nowadays seems to want to bowl the in-swinger. This is absurd, for my experience is that this particular ball is not so dangerous as the one which goes away from you. It has led to what I should call 'negative cricket.' Bowlers adopting this method try rather to keep the batsman quiet than to get him out. The result of this is that back-play has developed to a large extent and on-side play has increased out of all proportion, to the detriment of off-side batting. But then it must be remembered that it is very difficult indeed to drive an in-swinging ball on the off-side, and with bowlers keeping just short of a length, as modern bowlers do, the natural tendency of a batsman, at any rate since the War, has been to step back and play the ball to the on.

In regard to this it would seem that the new leg-before wicket rule is going to make things difficult for opening batsmen, and the in-swinging ball is more dangerous under this rule than the off-spinner. You can see and, to a degree, anticipate off-spinners better, and an in-swinger seems to come off dry ground much quicker. That, therefore, is one of the big changes I have noticed in the style of batting during my era. In my early days youngsters were taught to play forward, and it was the accepted theory that one only played back when the wicket was soft and the ball was turning. Now, batsmen play back on a hard wicket largely because, as I have said of the preponderance of in-swinging bowlers who keep just short of a length. Consequently, young bowlers, seeing that this type of attack cannot be driven to the off, very rarely try to make themselves spin bowlers pure and simple. I know, of course, that it is not given to everyone to keep such a perfect length as J. T. Hearne or Albert Relf used to. They would bowl all the afternoon and scarcely give you six balls that you could hit with safety.

While bowling, particularly as regards length, has gone back, batting in a certain way has advanced. The means have been found to contend with the swing, but at the expense of many of those glorious off-side strokes for which our predecessors were famous, and it is only when an over-pitched ball comes along that you can drive it to the off. Even then, when it does come, your feet may be wrong and you are too late to get into position.

There is one point about the improvement in batting to which I should like to draw attention, and that is that it is not confined to those in the first half of the order. Even in my early days we seldom expected or saw the last four men stay very long. Nowadays Numbers 8, 9, 10 and 11 all come in, not so much to have a wild swipe, but to play for runs; and they very often obtain them. This, of course, may be considered to be partly due to the difference in bowling. Back-play, too, has been the means of driving the off-spinner largely out of the game, and figures clearly show that batsmen, even when allowance is made for a great deal of extra cricket which they play, generally get far more runs now than they used to do.

ON FIELDING

It is a little difficult to say definitely if fielding has improved. Individually it may not have done, but collectively I think it has. Thirty years ago, the positions of mid-on and short-leg were both known as 'Mugs' Corner.' The captain looked round and almost invariably put his two incompetent fieldsmen in those places. I have never agreed that mid-on's was an easy job. You have to watch the batsman and anticipate his stroke, and you have to be quick off the mark when you field there. Only in recent years have we awakened to this fact, while men like 'Bill' Hitch made short-leg an honourable position in which to field. Hammond is my ideal fieldsman. He would be great anywhere, and Mitchell of Yorkshire runs him very close. No matter where they are put these two men can be right at the top, and it has often struck me that Hammond's fielding would very likely have been far more extensively talked-of had he been an outfielder, while it is certain he would do wonderful work at cover-point. With regard to the placing of the field there can be no question at all that this has engaged the attention of captains to a far greater degree than it used to and consequently it is better. The Australians, for instance, have developed the study of this to such an extent that they are now much better than we in England at placing their fieldsmen to stop runs, and the increase in on-side strokes by batsmen has led to two or three men being placed on the leg-side when in my early days there was only one. This is not meant as a reference to 'body-line' bowling. My views on that are well known. I deplore its introduction. I think it has done great harm to the game, because it fosters a spirit foreign to the traditions of cricket and which certainly never existed when I first came on the scene.

I think the development of the county championship in regard to the number of counties now competing is rather to be regretted. There are too many counties—some of them, I am afraid, not quite up to the best standard—and we in England have got a false opinion of the strength of our cricket. The trouble is that, against the weaker counties, players get plenty of runs and wickets and they are thought at once to be Test Match cricketers. It is much harder now to pick a team for a Test Match than it was thirty years ago. The field of choice is so much wider and the all-round standard consequently more on a level—especially in the County averages.

HAMMOND AND HENDREN

Since I started, the hook and the leg-glide have become common strokes, and I always had the idea too, that before my time it was considered rather *infra dig* to hook a ball round to the leg-side. Nowadays, batsmen will step right across and hook a ball from wide of the off-stump round to square-leg. Hammond is the great exception. He won't hook. He considers it a dangerous stroke and I remember once, the first time I saw him, he persisted in playing balls which the ordinary batsmen would have hooked, hard back either to mid-on or mid-off. But then Hammond, as a batsman, is a law unto himself. He can step right back and force the short ball to the off, but not many men possess such power of wrist and forearm, and quickness on the feet, to be able to do that. Pat Hendren is my ideal batsman, for I think he has every stroke for all sorts of wicket against all types of bowling. Had he played thirty or forty years ago he would, I think, have been equally effective.

We saw last season one noticeable feature about the batting of the Australians in the power they put into their strokes. When young, they are taught first to hit the ball; we in England are taught defence. The wickets in Australia are, of course, easier as a general rule than ours. They are the same pace and the ball comes along at a uniform height. Because of this Australian batsmen are for the most part more confident.

'SWINGERS' AND 'GOOGLIES'

I have already said that one of the most notable changes in cricket with regard to bowling has been the introduction of 'swing' or 'swerve.' No doubt long before my time bowlers were able to, and probably often did, make the ball swing, but it was not known then how this was brought about and quite likely when it occurred bowlers put it down to an extra strong current of air or some outside influence of a similar kind. The secret of being able to make a ball move about in the air was acquired during my era and at the present time almost anybody with any knowledge of bowling can send down swingers of one sort or the other. It is all a question of how the ball is held in the hand at the moment of delivery and bowlers of this description now come under the general heading of 'seam-up bowlers.' Shortly after I began to play first-class cricket came the googly, known in Australia as the 'bosie' because it was first discovered by B. J. T. Bosanquet. The South Africans were quick to realise the deadliness of this ball once a command of length had been gained. On the matting wickets in their country they soon perfected it and in G. A. Faulkner, A. E. Vogler, Gordon White and R. O. Schwarz they produced the finest array of googly bowlers ever seen together in one team. W. G. Grace did not, I think, play in an important match against googly bowling but obviously he must have been so very good that he, like many of us later on, would have mastered it. He would have played every ball on its merits.

While on the question of bowling I am definitely of the opinion that during my career the art of flighting the ball has steadily deteriorated. We have nobody now so good at this as Colin Blythe. He was one of the world's greatest bowlers of his type, and, unlike most of the present-day exponents, was never afraid of being hit. Of fast bowlers the only ones of recent years at all comparable with those giants of the past have been Larwood and McDonald. Being a member of the same county side I only played against N. A. Knox in Gentlemen and Players matches and games of a similar description, when he was probably past his best, but I think he was the best fast bowler I ever saw. He brought the ball down from such a great height that he could often make good length deliveries rear up straight.

The widening of the wicket, which previously had often been advocated, did not, when it came into general use, help bowlers to the extent that had been anticipated and, although a batsman, I personally am all for still wider wickets. When the alteration was made I thought at the time that the decision had not gone quite far enough—not far enough, at any rate, to achieve its main object of putting the bowler on more level terms with the batsman. Events have, I think, proved me to be right.

CHEAP ENGLAND CAPS

The past thirty years have brought with them a remarkable increase in tours to this country and visits abroad of English teams. As the Mother Country of cricket, England, as represented by the M.C.C., have naturally considered it politic to foster the game overseas but I am of opinion that, on the question of elevating countries like South Africa, West Indies, New Zealand and India to the same rank as Australia in the matter of Test Matches, we have been premature. The vast host of cricket followers throughout the world know in their own minds that there are only two really top-class cricketing countries—England and Australia. Far be from me any idea of throwing cold water on those countries who aspire to the highest status in cricket but when we think that of the numerous teams which have come from South Africa not one has ever won a Test Match in England it makes me wonder why they are put on the same plane as Australia in being allotted five 'Tests.' I am not forgetting that they, as well as the West Indies, have beaten England in their own Countries. I should not be averse to them having three and I would give the others I have mentioned one each. The honour of wearing the England cap with the three silver lions on it has, I am afraid, become rather cheap since its inception. These Caps should have been awarded only to cricketers who have appeared in England against Australia.

During my years of first-class cricket I do not think captaincy has improved. With one or two exceptions there has been too much chopping and changing about but, of course, other considerations have to be remembered, for amateurs do not find it so easy to spare the time for first-class cricket as their predecessors did. I have often thought that it was a mistake for counties to put an amateur into the team merely to act as captain when he has had little or no experience of county cricket. We had an example last season in Maurice Tate, of how well a professional could acquit himself as leader of a side, but I definitely always prefer to see an amateur rather than a professional captaining England if his cricket ability entitles him to a place in the eleven.

The umpiring has improved all-round, and I should say the two best umpires I have known are 'Bob' Crockett of Australia, and Frank Chester. Umpires nowadays are younger than most of those who officiated when I started, and naturally their eyesight and hearing are better.

In the last quarter of a century—and perhaps during a longer time—there has come about a great change for the better in the relations existing between amateurs and professionals. County committees have realised that both on and off the field their players are all members of the same team and professionals are not, as was largely the case some years ago, relegated to incommodious dressing-rooms with no amenities, while, as a general rule, amateurs and professionals now take their luncheon and tea together in the same room. The natural consequence of this, of course, has been a pronounced improvement in the bearing of professional cricketers off the field. The average professional nowadays can, I think, hold his own as a man in any company.

AUSTRALIAN CRICKET [1935]

Its Control and Organisation

BY THE HON. MR. JUSTICE HERBERT V. EVATT

(of the High Court of Australia)

Immediately following the Hobbs valedictory there appeared an item by a writer who is granted full typographical honours: 'The Hon. Mr. Justice Herbert V. Evatt', then of the High Court of Australia, but later to assume more elevated powers and to exercise them in so controversial a way that one wonders whether Mr. Southerton, had he been cursed with the gift of prophecy, would have invited Mr. Evatt to tread the hallowed halls of Wisden at all. Herbert Vere Evatt (1894–1965) was a professional jurist and politician who became a member of the Labour administration which acceded to power in Australia in 1941. Evatt, a great booster for the United Nations, helped write its charter and served a term as President of its General Assembly, where he became renowned as a champion of the rights of small nations. But the most controversial aspect of his career, the one which would have given Lord Harris apoplexy, was his defence of the rights of the Australian Communist Party to continue to exist. His opponents said that it was because of Evatt's attitude during a 1954 alleged Soviet espionage case that the anti-Communist wing of his party seceded, bringing about the decline of the Australian Labour Party from power. Evatt's desire that Australia should work for a greater degree of independence from the Mother Country is reflected in his obvious conviction that Australian cricket administration was not only more democratic than Britain's, but more efficient and much more desirable. This was perhaps the only issue on which he and his opposite number in the Conservative Party, Robert Menzies, came remotely close to agreement.

OCCASIONALLY, comments are made which show a lack of knowledge of the conditions under which cricket is organised and played in Australia, and I send these notes to the Editor of '*Wisden*' in the hope that they may serve to clear up some misapprehensions.

METHOD OF CONTROL

The controlling body is the Board of Control, to which delegates representing the six States of the Commonwealth are appointed annually. New South Wales, Victoria and South Australia each send three delegates, Queensland two, and Western Australia and Tasmania one each. Then there are the Associations in the several States. The controlling body in each State comprises delegates from affiliated clubs. As any player or resident may join a district club in (say) Sydney or Melbourne, he has the right of taking part in the election of his club delegates to the State Association just as, in turn, the Committee of the Association elects representatives on the Board of Control. In form, this is a very democratic system of control, because the members elect the delegates, and the delegates choose the representatives on the Board. In practice there is perhaps an inevitable restriction of membership of the supreme Board to those club officials who have been Association delegates for many years. The Board of Control assembles only four or five times a year, whereas the State Association committees meet frequently and at regular intervals.

The Australian system of control of cricket is therefore 'representative' in character, quite the reverse of the M.C.C. In practice, the M.C.C. may voice the opinion of the English clubs and players quite as effectively as the Australian Board, but their Committee is elected annually by the members of the Marylebone Club.

LEADING MATCHES

New South Wales, Victoria, South Australia, and Queensland play each other twice in a season for the Shield presented by Lord Sheffield. As this means twelve Sheffield Shield matches a season, Melbourne, Sydney, Adelaide and Brisbane each see only three Shield games, so that there is no surfeit of high-class cricket. The other two States, Tasmania and Western Australia, participate in only a few matches. A second grade competition between these two States and the second elevens of the four Sheffield Shield States has been suggested recently but not adopted. A great difficulty in the way of big cricket in Australia is the enormous distances between the largest cities.

In the cities, the major part of cricket is confined to club games, which are organised on a district basis, and residential qualifications are imposed. The standard of club cricket is difficult to gauge. There has been a tendency to increase the number of clubs, and it is suggested that the standard has declined. As to the attendances these are relatively small in comparison with football crowds. Some at least of the clubs in Sydney and Melbourne might reasonably hope to defeat the weaker English county teams. Last season for instance, Bradman and O'Reilly played with the same Sydney club, and one Melbourne club had five or six Test players.

The leading Australian players take part in a very limited amount of first-class cricket and this should always be remembered when comparisons are made between the performances of the players of England and of

Australia. Some statistical enthusiast could probably show that, although Hobbs has scored 197 centuries and Bradman only 51, the latter's proportion of centuries to innings is much higher. A representative Australian player's games are confined to Sheffield Shield and club cricket except, of course, when a team from abroad visits Australia.

GAMES WITH TIME LIMIT

The club games are restricted to two Saturday afternoons—about four hours play on each afternoon. Some years ago, the Sheffield Shield rules were altered to confine the duration of those games to 4 days, with several hours play on the fifth day if necessary. Finally, four days were allotted with 5½ hours play on each day. Originally, and for several seasons, the Sheffield Shield games were played to a conclusion, however long they might take.

The time limit has been a great success. First innings points are awarded but are of small value in comparison with an outright win. A very great proportion of the games are finished in the four days. The rate of scoring has certainly increased, and wickets fall more rapidly. Personally, I am satisfied that it was the necessity of quick scoring in the interests of his side some years ago which developed in Bradman that vehemence, not to say ferocity, which characterises much of his recent batting.

The Australian Board would probably disagree with any attempt to fix a time limit on Test Matches in Australia; but I definitely think that if the experiment of a 5-day limit were tried, most of the Tests would be concluded and the cricket would be more sporting. The five days would, with our shorter hours, correspond to a four days Test in England. The success of the Australians in four days Test in England in 1930 and 1934 is partly accounted for by their having adapted themselves under the newer Sheffield Shield rules, to time-limit matches. The eight-ball over still obtains in Australian cricket and there seems to be no tendency to revert to the six-ball over.

PROFESSIONALISM

Whilst a number of representative cricketers earn their livelihood from sports businesses, there is practically no professionalism in the English sense. This does not mean that our Test players are not paid. For matches in Australia they received about £30 each; for tours in England they receive about £600 each, in addition to expenses. In the days of the privately conducted tours of England, larger sums were on occasion received. The payments for Sheffield Shield games are almost nominal, whilst all the players bear their own expenses in club cricket.

COUNTRY PLAYERS

Many of Australia's greatest players have been country as opposed to city players. The State Associations spend a good deal of time and money in fostering country cricket by sending city teams to the country and by arranging 'Country Weeks' in the city. Bradman and McCabe received opportunities in this way and quickly succeeded. The handicap of distance is a serious one in country districts but a great deal is being done to overcome it.

SCHOOL CRICKET

This is very well organised by the school authorities. In Australia the bulk of primary education is controlled by the Educational Department of the State itself and this facilitates control. The older boys attending secondary schools are well catered for whether the schools are controlled by the State or privately. The Association keeps a keen eye on this training ground for its future representative players. For instance, the late Archie Jackson played cricket for his State school in the Balmain district of Sydney and, by reason of his success in combined matches, was chosen to play with his district club at the age of 15 and with his State at 16 or 17. He represented Australia at 19, and scored a century in his first Test Match.

BARRACKING

When English critics speak of Australian barracking, they are apt to overlook the crowds' very generous treatment of nearly all of our English visitors. Hobbs' reception from the Sydney crowd, first in December 1924 when he beat Victor Trumper's record of six Test centuries, and later in December 1928, when he was given a presentation, was quite wonderful. Players like Hobbs, Douglas, Gilligan, Kilner, Chapman, Parkin, Hendren and Tate, were idols of Australian crowds. It is a great mistake to judge the Australian spectators by the reaction of some of them when many of their players were repeatedly hit in 1932–3 as a result of an entirely novel method of fast bowling. Unfortunately a section of the press exaggerates every trifle. It becomes an 'incident,' then a 'dispute,' and it ends in an 'international episode.' In February 1920 for instance, in the Fifth Test at Sydney, Hobbs, who had a bad leg, was fielding at cover when Macartney drove a ball for four. Hobbs was allowed by two other English players (at mid-off and extra-cover) to limp to the boundary in order to return the ball. Some of the crowd chaffed, not Hobbs, but his two, apparently, inconsiderate colleagues. One or two English papers misunderstood what had happened and asserted that Hobbs himself had been barracked about his injury. It is all very well to counsel silence, but nothing in the world will prevent occasional comment by some of the spectators.

TRIAL OF A COUNTY SECRETARY [1936]

Forty years of cricket management

BY R. V. RYDER (SECRETARY, WARWICKSHIRE COUNTY CRICKET CLUB)

The 1936 edition saw yet another new name inscribed as editor, that of Wilfrid H. Brookes. The death of Sydney Southerton had come about quite suddenly in a style which many cricketing veterans must have envied, at a cricket dinner, among friends and admirers, with a drink in his hand. Southerton had supervised the production of only two editions of Wisden, and it is a sure sign of the final passing of the old Cricket Reporting Agency nucleus that between 1933 and 1940, eight editions of Wisden were produced by four different editors, a marked contrast to the thirty-five successive editions produced by Sydney Pardon. Southerton's death evidently struck his obituarist, Hubert Preston, as so sublime that the writer disdains to use the word at all, reverting instead to the monumental masonry of 'his life ebbed away'.

The first thing an observant reader would have noticed about the début of Brookes in 1936 was that an altogether more lively approach was being used than ever before in the history of the Almanack. In Brookes' first edition were no fewer that three items of prose composition and a fourth so extraordinary in the context of the Almanack as to cause a raising of more than one pair of true-blue eyebrows. In terms of readability, the recollections of the Warwickshire County Club Secretary, Roland Vint Ryder (1873–1949), are outstanding. In his recollections Ryder makes a point always overlooked by the more casual follower of cricket, which is that Warwickshire by no means encompassed the life of its chief city, Birmingham. In Ryder's words, Birmingham had made 'giant strides which have taken her into three counties'; his own circumstances reflect this geographical confusion clearly enough. Ryder was born in Yorkshire and spent most of his early years in his father's printing business in Staffordshire before becoming, in 1895, Assistant Secretary to Warwickshire; eight years later he succeeded to the secretaryship and remained in the chair until his retirement in 1944. In his youth Ryder represented Staffordshire twice, and was prominent in club cricket.

Ryder's energy sometimes pushed him above and beyond the call of duty, as in 1903 and 1904, when, in an effort to avert a major financial crisis in the county club, he organised a special appeal fund which raised the £3,000 required to stave off disaster. In 1906 further desperate measures were called for, at which Ryder took to the streets of Birmingham and its purlieus in a one-man recruitment drive for club membership. This campaign was a spectacular success, bringing in 600 new annual subscriptions. In the light of these passionate espousals of a cause he loved, it is no wonder that Ryder on his retirement was presented by a grateful club with a cheque for £1,608 and an inscribed silver salver.

Ryder's memories incorporate several delights and one or two surprises. Among the pleasures is his ability to evoke the recent yet long-gone past of horse-drawn cricketers, and spectators so fanatical in their devotion to the game that they were capable of breaking into a ground and demanding that play commence. Among the surprises is Ryder's recollection that had he only taken to the streets a little more often, the county might have enjoyed the services of one of the greatest all-round cricketers of the age. One other pertinent fact is that it was he who first suggested that the prevailing arrangements, whereby Championship matches were commenced on Mondays and Thursdays, should be amended so that starts could be made on Saturdays and Wednesdays.

I AM attempting at the request of the Editor, to give the reader an insight into County Cricket organisation from the management point of view together with impressions of change during the past 40 years, the period I have acted as Secretary to Warwickshire.

Unhurried leisure was the keynote of the game, and, for most of the time, of its organisation in my early days. Cricket had fewer rivals; there were plenty of interested people to enjoy this popular pastime. A county secretary, with the programme comprising no more than 18 to 20 first-class matches, really had time to take a deep breath in between games and devote a little quiet thought to his many problems.

Fixture-making, for one thing, was an unhurried business, commencing in September, through the agency of the penny post, and culminating in a visit to Lord's in December where the silk hat and frock coat were *de rigueur*. Most matches started on Monday, and I may say many of my Sundays were far from days of rest.

One of the outstanding changes in cricket organisation during my time was the decision to begin matches on Saturday, and in this connection it is interesting to me to recall that I drafted the motion which was first submitted to the Advisory County Cricket Committee on January 13th, 1913. Seven years later, Saturday starts were introduced to the great advantage of first-class cricket.

In the days when Monday starts were the rule our groundstaff was smaller, so we frequently had to scout round for the occasional player engaged perhaps with a local club, and persuasion was often needed to get a business man or a schoolmaster to fill a gap. The need of persuasion many times found me spending Sunday in a hansom cab trying first this man and then another. The telephone had no place then in team collection. I imagine my Committee regarded it as a luxury!

We even worked a Test Match—and our first too—without the help of this sometimes blessed invention. And thereby hangs a story which will tell eloquently of the trials which beset a county secretary.

TEST MATCH PLAYED ON 'A SWAMP'

It was in 1902 that a Test Match—England v. Australia—was allocated to Birmingham for the first time. This meant fitting up the ground to accommodate more people than had ever before patronised a cricket match at Edgbaston. It meant many other things and I was to find out they mainly concerned the club secretary. Quickly we got to work—many months in advance of the date. New stands were erected, and thousands of seats carted to the ground. Committees of all kinds were hard at work for months. There were, indeed, 36 meetings of the General Committee that year!

It was an anxious time as the day drew near. Had we thought of everything? (Events were to prove we hadn't). Details had been carefully thought out. Sixty gatemen were required. Sixty police were ordered for duty. There were 90 pressmen to accommodate. The catering staff approached 200. As I recall the occasion it astonishes me to realise that my clerical staff then consisted of myself only, and that besides the non-possession of a telephone a typewriter was something else we did not have. But to continue.

It was our custom at the time to await payment of membership subscription before issuing the member's card. The Test Match started on May 29. You can perhaps imagine what happened. Crowds of members delayed payment until they arrived at the match on the first day. At the end of the day I solicited the help of a friend, and eight hours after stumps were drawn I balanced up and as I crawled home between 2 and 3 a.m. thanked my lucky stars I lived near the ground.

But worse was to come. The last day of the match was Saturday, May 31st. Torrents of rain fell overnight, and at 9 a.m. the ground was a complete lake. Not a square yard of turf was visible and play was, of course, out of the question that day. The head groundman agreed; I paid off half my gatemen and dispensed with the services of half the police. It proved a 'penny wise, pound foolish' action. The umpires arrived; the players arrived—the captains were there. I have never known any men more patient, more hopeful than those umpires and captains. They just sat still and said nothing most effectively. At two o'clock the sun came out and a great crowd assembled outside the ground. What I hadn't thought of was that two umpires and two captains would sit and wait so long without making a decision. The crowd broke in, and to save our skins we started play at 5.20 on a swamp. The main result of our promotion to Test Match rank was that at the end of the season we had to appeal to the public for £3,000 to repair our finances!

THE DAYS OF THE HORSE

And apropos of the changes cricket has undergone in the past forty years let us turn to the following account of the scene outside the ground during that memorable Test.

'At the corner of the road it was amusing to come across an imposing but obviously excited coachman (with a pair of restive horses) trying to ascertain from a humble pedestrian the whereabouts of the County Cricket ground, the while a lady, cool, composed and statuesque reclined in a tandem. Every minute a hansom dashed up, carriages and pairs were as common as blackberries in autumn, and bicycles crept in and out everywhere.'

Yes, I remember it all very well. Not a single motor vehicle reached the scene of *that* cricket encounter. Horse transport was the thing in those days. What quaint reading is afforded now by the perusal of this extract from the Warwickshire Committee Minutes of April 26, 1897:—'A member wrote suggesting that accommodation should be provided for horses as many members had to travel long distances.'

WARWICKSHIRE LOST WILFRED RHODES

And while my thoughts are on those old Minutes let me quote another recorded in 1897, one which will probably bring a sigh of regret as well as a smile to Warwickshire members whose eyes may fall upon it. This entry, dated October 4, reads: 'It was decided that on account of the heavy expenses already incurred in connection with next year's ground staff an engagement could not be offered W. Rhodes of Huddersfield.' If we had only known!

When I took up my work in Warwickshire forty years ago, the team under the captaincy of Mr. H. W. Bainbridge had just won promotion to first-class rank. It was well equipped for the struggle on which it was entering and was a force with which to be reckoned for ten or twelve years until the temporary deterioration in 1909 and 1910 which was blotted from the memory by winning the Championship in 1911.

From the start Budget balancing was a difficult business. At first I don't think I fully realised my responsibilities. In this connection there was a Finance Committee! Little did I know then how much of my life was to be spent in staring at figures, and adding them up again. However, if the reader will pardon the disgression, I frequently found time for a knock at the nets and I played a great deal of Club and Ground cricket. Once or twice I was included in the County side—in matches outside the Championship Competition.

CRICKET FINANCE

Cricket finance to some of us, has always been 'a thing of shreds and patches,' varying a little perhaps in texture and colouring but failing generally to provide that protection and comfort which is the lot of the well-breeched. We shiver at the thought of rain—especially at Whitsuntide and on August Bank holiday. A wet Holiday Week may mean the difference between making ends meet or heavily increasing a bank overdraft. There are one or two Counties which never have to meet trouble of this kind; playing success has earned them this exemption from anxiety. The problems of the Counties differ. There are clubs which have several good grounds within their boundaries. Matches can therefore be allocated to towns wide apart. The County exchequer is not dependent on one public. The fact that Birmingham has never quite risen to the needs of Warwickshire cricket remains something of a mystery.

For one thing we are awkwardly situated geographically. Birmingham's giant strides have taken her into three counties. A condition of my appointment was that I 'must live near the ground,' with the result that for most of the time I have lived in Worcestershire! From Warwickshire's point of view, with so many Birmingham people living in Worcestershire and Staffordshire, the position as it bears on County qualification is a nightmare. The value of Lancashire's membership has risen as high as £10,000 in a season. We in Warwickshire have never exceeded £4,500 and a very large proportion of that comes, of course, from the Birmingham area. The smaller Warwickshire towns contribute very little. Coventry, thriving and pulsating with energy, produces crowds of active cricketers but not a single ground equipped to accommodate a County match. Many Warwickshire matches have been played in Coventry during the past 25 years but the cost of providing temporary equipment is a very heavy extra charge and this has led to a suspension of the fixtures in that city.

In 1906 cricket interest fell away in Warwickshire. There was a heavy slump in membership. It was clear something must be done to repair the damage, so I spent the winter months in a personal canvas of the city and suburbs and secured 600 new members.

PLAYERS AND PITCHES

Two hundred players have represented Warwickshire in first-class cricket during the past forty years. Thousands have been tried out at the nets and in Club and Ground matches. Many indeed have been called but few chosen. We could have done with Wilfrid Rhodes.

When I came to Edgbaston in 1895 the wicket was a marl prepared pitch. W. G. Grace and A. C. MacLaren were at the top of the batting averages, 51 each. Not all County grounds were 'doped' with marl. The only two Yorkshiremen who scored a thousand runs that season—Tunnicliffe and Brown—averaged 27 and 26 respectively. By 1904 C. B. Fry's average was 79 and there were quite a number of 60's. In 1932 Sutcliffe and Leyland headed the Yorkshire list with 87 and 60. Marl had found its way into Yorkshire.

So the procession of happy successful batsmen continued. Well, at last something has been done through the new l.b.w. experiment to make the conditions of the cricket fight more equal, and we may surely look forward to a further growth in cricket interest.

SUCCESS OF THE L.B.W. EXPERIMENT [1936]

BY W. H. BROOKES

The second of the readable items in the 1936 edition was Brookes' own editorial commentary, which struck a perfect balance between institutionalised prose and chatty discussion. Shades of later ages may be found in his comments on the poor fortunes of the England side at the time and the peculiar nostrums suggested by some worried gentlemen. Noting the rumbles of discontent around the pavilions of the nation, Brookes remarks: 'The happiest man in the country must have been the born pessimist. In the course of sixteen months our cricketers have lost a rubber to Australia, West Indies and South Africa in turn'. Brookes then proceeds to a spirited defence of the Selection Committee, making the astonishing claim that 'English cricket is going through a lean period'. A few pages away he produces the statistics for 1935, refuting his own argument without realising it; among the leading run-makers and wicket-takers in this 'lean period' may be found Hammond, Sutcliffe, Hendren, Bakewell, Hardstaff, Leyland, Mead and Paynter; Verity, Geary, Bowes, Copson, Farnes, Tate and Goddard. No wonder Brookes is obliged to admit that 'No selection Committee is infallible, and the present body made more than one unfortunate mistake'. Of far more entertainment value is Brookes' review of a suggestion then in the air that the esprit de corps *of England sides might be much improved:*

> In making a passing allusion to the rather widespread demands in the newspapers last summer for our Test teams to stay together at the same hotel, I do so primarily with the desire to correct statements criticising the M.C.C. on this point which is entirely under the jurisdiction of the Board of Control. To see the whole matter put forward as a novelty, when the facts are that several writers brought forward this suggestion in 1921, was rather amusing. I agree with those who urge that a manager should be appointed to take charge of England teams at home as well as abroad. To make it compulsory for all the players to stay together at the same hotel during a Test match would be a reasonable sequel to the appointment of such an official, but I cannot see that a change of procedure regarding accommodating players would bring about the advantages which many people seem to think.

Poor Brookes, snapping at the carrot dangled before him by writers from Fleet Street who, by the time the new editor of Wisden was so dutifully refuting their arguments, had forgotten all about the bedding arrangements for the England team and were away in pursuit of those pertaining to the latest film star divorcee or reverend gentleman in the dock.

The real objection to the suggestions discussed by Brookes was of course that they would cause the abandonment of the age-old convention whereby the paid players lived under one set of conditions while the amateurs lived under quite another.

In leaving his readers to the mercies of an edition which consisted of nearly 800 pages, Brookes insists that minor matches will in future have to be omitted from the canon: 'A line must be drawn to keep the Almanack within reasonable limits, and deal essentially with first-class cricket and its stepping-stones'. Having made that statement of intent, Brookes then confounds it, fortunately, by adding peripheral material of a thoroughly readable nature. His coverage of the latest amendments to the ever-shifting sands of the leg-before-wicket laws ought not perhaps be defined as peripheral, but there must have been those readers whose hearts sank at the prospect of yet another symposium on the same old subject.

ABOVE everything else in the game itself last season the experimental leg-before-wicket rule stood out as most important. A year ago *Wisden's* Editor, together with many other good judges, welcomed the change, but very naturally wished to see how it worked before confirming his approval. That he is not with us to express a matured opinion is to be deplored, but like the vast majority of players and spectators, Southerton would have felt satisfied. Those who watched cricket day after day in variable weather on all kinds of pitches could see how the game benefited from the alteration. Facts cannot be denied and we find that of 1,560 leg-before-decisions favourable to the bowler in first-class matches last season 483 were under the new rule. In the County Championship fixtures there were 1,273 instances of a batsman being out L-B-W and of these 404 were due to the operation of the amended law.

The idea held by many people in the past that on a difficult pitch off-break bowlers would have matters all their own way under the altered rule and that on fast, true turf batsmen still would hold the upper hand, was proved by experience incorrect. The skill of modern bowlers in swinging the ball made all the difference when the conditions favoured run-getting. A batsman dare not 'cover-up' to the ball that was coming wide of the off stump in the air unless prepared to pay the penalty.

The swerving ball and the break-back each took toll of doubtful batsmen, but very soon much of the uncertainty as to what to do with the well-pitched-up ball disappeared. After being a few times in trouble batsmen became alive to the need of depending upon the bat to deal with likely break or swerve—and this for the most part meant getting to the pitch of the ball. Quick footwork and the straight bat were used to solve the difficulty and if these genuine methods in the art of batsmanship failed, the bowler very rightly earned the verdict he deserved.

Sutcliffe, who anticipated the new law with misgiving, found that in practice his fears were dispelled. He was among the early converts and as the summer advanced almost everyone fell into line by acclaiming the success of this variation of Law 24. There came a decided check to those interminable first-wicket partnerships which were so detrimental to the game. It was not surprising that, facing the swerve with the ball brand new, the early batsmen found their task harder than previously. A good deal of criticism was also offered by left-hand batsmen who had to play deliveries pitching in the 'rough' of the bowlers' run up, where the ball often 'does' a lot.

The definite results reached last summer in so many matches, the reduction in scoring with consequent livening up of the game and obvious progress towards a finish pleased the majority of cricket lovers. Unrepentant players could not argue against the innovation without confessing their faults and admitting inability to remedy their own shortcomings. The fight between bat and ball became more equal than it had been for many seasons. Even on pitches still over prepared by artificial aids, bowlers knew that their efforts would not be in vain because of obstructive methods; batsmen discarded their cramped, pokey style for freedom in stroke play and the cut and off drive were brought into use almost to the same extent as when these glorious strokes gave chief charm to the game. Umpires found their duties lightened if anything; they did not have to decide that the ball pitched straight but only that it would have hit the stumps and that the 'obstruction' occurred in the line between wicket and wicket.

To emphasise how the altered rule affected cricket in all respects the following facts are of the highest value, even if other causes may have contributed to them. Definite results in the 234 County Championship matches played last summer numbered 161 as against 134 in 1934 when there were 232 fixtures—an increase of 27 victories. Of regular players Hammond again came out at the top of the batting averages but his figures fell from 76.32 in 1934 to 49.35, the smallest average to head the list since 1910 when the weather was deplorable. Allowance must always be made for loss of form, but last season only seven batsmen had aggregates reaching 2,000 as compared with nineteen a year before. Strangely enough, R. E. S. Wyatt, E. R. T. Holmes and Sutcliffe, of those who did not like the experiment, made considerably more runs than in 1934. The Yorkshireman rose from seventeenth to second in the averages. Class told.

To generalise over the whole area of cricket the number of batsmen reaching the 1,000 aggregate showed a decrease of nine to 76. Among bowlers Freeman, with his 212 wickets, did not monopolise the honours, Verity taking 211 and Goddard exactly 200, while 27 men were rewarded with at least 100 wickets as against 18 who enjoyed this amount of success a year before; also seven bowlers took 42 or more wickets at a lower cost a piece than the 17.07 with which Paine excelled over all his rivals in 1934.

The experiment has brought great gains to cricket. Our legislators can be relied upon not to act in a hasty manner and their broadcast request for the provisionally altered law to be tried in *all* cricket during

1936—a suggestion which has received widespread support—shows the desire to test the innovation as thoroughly as possible before making any permanent change in the laws. A trial over three seasons should be sufficient to determine whether the alteration goes far enough to adjust the balance between batsman and bowler. There is always the possibility that by the end of another season the batsman may have mastered the changed theories.

Following are some opinions regarding the experiment expressed by County Captains at the invitation of the Editor of *Wisden*:—

FOR

Mr. A. Brian Sellers (Yorkshire):—

'I think the new rule has come to stay. I have found it to help the bowler a great deal and that is what was wanted. There are a good many batsmen who have got out when playing at the ball which last year they would have padded off, or left alone.'

Mr. R. W. V. Robins (Middlesex):—

'I am a firm believer that, if the experiment becomes law, we shall go a long way towards obtaining 'brighter' cricket. Our wicket at Lord's last year gave the rule as big a test as any other ground in the country and in no case did I hear an umpire during the whole season suggest that it made his duties more difficult. On the contrary, many agreed that it lightened their task. It is up to the rest of the cricketing countries and all Club Cricket Associations to try the experiment thoroughly without delay. We in Middlesex were delighted with the experiment and think that it has given a very much needed filip to the game.'

Mr. W. G. Lowndes (Hampshire):—

'I think the new L.B.W. rule has, on the whole, been a success. This year, with its bad and wet wickets, may not have given it a fair trial, as it was not intended to prevent players using their legs on these wickets so much as on hard and fast pitches. I do not think it has made any difference to the player who has always been taught off-side shots playing forward.'

Mr. T. N. Pearce (Joint Captain of Essex):—

'In my opinion, the new rule has been a great success for the following reasons:—(1) It has aided the bowlers who most needed help, namely, the fast and fast-medium. (2) Batsmen have had to play forward at the good length ball pitching just outside the off stump, thereby bringing back into first-class cricket an almost obsolete scoring stroke. On the other hand, the rule has been a little severe on opening batsmen playing against the new ball.'

Mr. G. F. H. Heane (Joint Captain of Nottinghamshire):—

'The new L.B.W. rule eliminates a large amount of pad play, and it quickens up the game, with the result that more matches are brought to a definite conclusion. It provides a difficulty for left-hand batsmen owing to the assistance given the bowler by foot marks outside the off stump made by the bowler at the opposite end.'

AGAINST

Mr. R. E. S. Wyatt (Warwickshire):—

'Although there is something to be said in favour of the new L.B.W. rule, I am not in favour of it being continued. My reasons are that it encourages bowlers to bowl off breaks and in-swingers resulting in less off-side play and also affecting the hook shot. One thing in favour of the rule is that it does make batsmen play at more balls outside the off stump.'

Mr. E. R. T. Holmes (Surrey):—

'I am not in favour of the new rule being continued. From the point of view of the game, I say it has not achieved its object. It puts a premium on forward play. It has made little difference to forward players but has curtailed strokes of back players considerably. It has not helped me personally as a bowler.'

MISCELLANY [1936]

BY W. H. BROOKES

The retirement of the greatest batsman in England, the ways in which the rules pertaining to l.b.w. might be adjusted or not, these were matters of portent requiring the magisterial touch from the Almanack. But the fourth of the features included by Brookes in the 1936 edition fell into quite a different category. Clearly thinking in terms of journalistic appeal rather than of editorial solemnity, Brookes decided to acknowledge a fact about cricket well known to every man who has ever played the game or watched it with any degree of intentness, which is that very often the moments which stick in the memory are those not covered in the rules, accidents which nobody could possibly anticipate and which, having once occurred, might never happen again. A later age sometimes refers to the study of this kind of ephemera as 'trivial pursuits'. At any rate, Brookes inaugurated a brief but entertaining section headed 'Miscellany', in which we are enlightened by the news that not only are English summers no longer what they used to be but never were; that mechanistic devices to measure degrees of bad light were in the wind even in the days of comparative innocence; and that one of the laws of the universe seems to be that umpires can expect to be in constant trouble of one kind or another.

A SPARROW was killed by a ball bowled by Jahangir Khan in the M.C.C. and Cambridge University match at Lord's. T. N. Pearce, the batsman, managed to play the ball and the bird fell against the stumps without dislodging the bails. The bird is preserved as a relic in the pavilion at Lord's.

* * *

In a rain-ruined match at Nottingham, G. O. Allen (Middlesex) batted on each of three days for 6 not out. Actually his innings occupied half an hour.

* * *

Hammond of Sussex, when bowling against Kent at Tunbridge Wells, sent the ball direct to James Parks at slip who caught it as Dolphin, the umpire, called wide.

* * *

Two instances occurred during the summer of a captain permitting his opponents to alter their side after the start of a match.

At Northampton, A. W. Allen allowed India to bring in M. J. Gopalan for Baqa Jilani, who was indisposed. At Maidstone, A. P. F. Chapman made no objection to Middlesex playing Gray instead of G. O. Allen, who stood down.

* * *

Blankets were used to dry the actual pitch at Lord's during the Test Match with India.

* * *

In 1836, two professional cricketers, Wenman and Mills, defeated an Isle of Oxney XI. at Wittersham, Kent. At the end of that game it was agreed that another of the kind should take place in 100 years time.

The agreement was fulfilled on September 5, 1936, when Ashdown (Kent) and Wensley (Sussex) comprised the professional 'team.' Oxney batted first, scoring 153; then Wensley (96) and Ashdown (83 not out) made 186, and won by 33 runs.

* * *

Tokens of appreciation for his services in connection with University cricket were handed to Mr. H. D. G. Leveson Gower at a gathering of Old Blues at Lord's on July 7. Mr. A. J. Webbe (Oxford captain in 1877 and 1878) made the presentation which took the form of a jewel for Mrs. Leveson Gower and a china dinner service. Mr. G. E. C. Wood spoke on behalf of Cambridge. Altogether, Mr. Leveson Gower has taken teams to play 64 matches against the Universities; he now finds it necessary to relinquish the task. An illuminated book containing the names of the subscribers came as a specially interesting souvenir.

* * *

Mr. W. Findlay, the M.C.C. Secretary, on retiring, received presentations from Members of the Imperial Cricket Conference, the First-Class Counties, Minor Counties, and the Staff at Lord's.

* * *

After 27 years of service at Lord's, H. White, the groundman, was succeeded by Austin Martin, son of the Oval groundman.

* * *

At the end of September, Dan Hayward retired from Fenner's after being in charge since 1908. He had been connected with Cambridge University sport for upwards of 50 years. Jack Haylock, who has been at Fenner's for 26 years, is now head groundman.

* * *

In recognition of the valuable services the late Hon. F. S. G. Calthorpe rendered as one of the founders of the Folkestone Cricket Festival, a portrait of him was placed in the Pavilion at Folkestone.

* * *

As many as eight Marlborough College players were l.b.w. (four under the new rule) in the second innings against Cheltenham College at Marlborough. Altogether 34 wickets fell in the match and 16 batsmen were l.b.w.

RECOLLECTIONS OF OXFORD CRICKET [1937]

Some memorable 'Varsity matches

BY H. D. G. LEVESON-GOWER

In 1937 there was further evidence of the Almanack's tendency to attach greater importance to amateur than to professional cricket. The featured essay, entitled 'Recollections of Oxford Cricket', was written by yet another of those gentleman-athletes whose presence at the councils of the game seems to have been everlasting. Sir Henry Dudley Gresham Leveson-Gower not only basked in the glow of a hyphen, but also in the possession of a surname which required for the accepted pronunciation in well-bred circles a comprehensive grasp of the principles of linguistics, etymology, nomenclature, lexicography, terminology and palaeography. Sir Henry addressed himself as Loosen-Gore, this perversity being one more cunningly contrived bear-trap in which to ensnare the socially gauche elements of society, although the most unfortunate débâcle of Sir Henry's career, the

maladroit handling of a Surrey Club dispute involving the great all-rounder Jack Crawford, was a case of one amateur abusing another.
Loosen-Gore (1874–1954), of Winchester, Oxford and Surrey, was the captain in the Varsity match of 1896 who had to stand by and watch an opposing bowler deliberately bowl wides in order to prevent Oxford from following on. In addition to the captaincy of Surrey, Loosen-Gore appeared several times for the Gentlemen against the Players, took sides to Eastbourne to play the universities, selected sides for the Scarborough Festival, and toured with the M.C.C. in America among other places, where his name caused him to be referred to in print as 'The Hyphenated Worry' and 'The Man with the Sanguinary Name'. He served also as an England Test selector and as a legislator. In 1953 he was knighted for services to cricket, was the author of a volume called 'On and Off the Field', and, if the camera does not lie, was in the habit of sitting at the piano in plus-fours. Sir Henry is a useful proof of the cultural bonuses accruing to a university education, for it was while he was up at Oxford that his diminutive stature inspired his fellows to called him 'Shrimp', a nickname of such subtlety that it stuck to Sir Henry for the rest of his life.

THE Editor of *Wisden* has paid me the compliment of asking me to give some reminiscences of Oxford Cricket—a compliment that I naturally appreciate very much and an invitation that I readily accept. Perhaps my chief qualification to do this is that since the beginning of this century I have had the pleasure of getting up 'Teams' against the Universities, both at Oxford and Cambridge, for over twenty years at Eastbourne, and the last three years at Reigate. While there is always a certain amount of responsibility and at times anxiety in collecting sides, the reward is great, for it has enabled me year after year, not only to keep in touch with the different generations of 'Varsity cricketers, but also to retain the friendship of those who were good enough to play for my 'Elevens.' I would like to thank most sincerely the members of the Eastbourne Cricket Club and Sir Jeremiah Colman, the President, and members of the Reigate Priory Club for the use of their famous and picturesque ground.

My reminiscences of Oxford cricket date back to 1893 for although, before I 'went up,' I had with keen and boyish delight followed the fortunes of the University Matches at Lord's since the early 1880's, it was when I got my 'Blue' in 1893 that I may be said to have become intimately connected with Oxford cricket. As now, so in the past, I think every boy has his cricket heroes. My two heroes, funnily enough, were 'Cambridge'—A. G. Steel and C. T. Studd, two great cricketers. If at any time they failed—and it was seldom they did—I took their temporary lapses as a personal matter! I had the good fortune to get into the Oxford Eleven as a Freshman; and here I may say what I think is the general opinion that luck plays a very important part in getting one's 'Blue,' particularly as a batsman, as a 'Fresher.'

The Summer Term is so short—a bare eight weeks—that unless one strikes form almost immediately, one is up against very strong opposition. I make mention of this from my own personal experience, for this fortune was on my side. I have before me a list of some of those who played in the Freshmen's Match of 1893:—G. O. Smith, G. B. Raikes, M. J. Barlow, P. F. Warner, B. N. Bosworth Smith, H. K. Foster, F. G. H. Clayton, G. J. Mordaunt, H. A. Arkwright—and myself. Of these only Mordaunt and I succeeded that year in getting into the Eleven; we had the luck of a good start in the Trial Matches.

Of the four University Matches in which I took part, those of 1893 and 1896 provided 'incidents.' In 1893 C. M. Wells and in 1896 E. B. Shine gave away eight runs while bowling to prevent Oxford following-on. Being captain at Oxford in 1896 I was naturally very interested in the decision reached by Frank Mitchell in giving orders to E. B. Shine to bowl 'no balls' to the boundary in order to prevent my side from going in again. In my opinion the reception he and his team received from the members of M.C.C. and when his team went in to bat from the 'spectators,' was quite unjustifiable. His motive, no doubt, was do to what he thought was best to ensure victory; whether his policy was sound or not was entirely a matter for him as captain to decide. Personally, I should not have done it; I do not say this because we won. The moral effect of following-on in a University Match is great, and the Cambridge Eleven had not had an over-strenuous time in the field. Of all the players on both sides only G. J. Mordaunt and myself took part in both these 'incident matches.'

TRIUMPH OF THE 'LAST CHOICE'

I may perhaps be excused for going rather fully into the match of 1896. Naturally it is the ambition of a captain to win his 'Varsity match, and once again Dame Fortune did not forsake me. I had the luck at the last moment of making the right choice for the last place in my side. I left the selection till the morning of the match. G. O. Smith and G. B. Raikes, both old 'Blues,' were the candidates. I had practically made up my mind to play Raikes. He was a good all-round cricketer—useful bowler, very good slip and a sound bat. What made me alter my mind was this: when I inspected the wicket I did not think that another bowler, unless an exceptional one, would make the difference, and I decided to play the better bat of the two, G. O. Smith. Experience had taught me that you can never have too much batting in a 'Varsity Match. I took the risk of going into the field against a powerful Cambridge batting side with only four bowlers. It meant that I should have to work these extremely hard. F. H. E. Cunliffe and J. C. Hartley, my two chief bowlers, sent down no fewer than 88 and 92 overs in the match respectively. The last choice won me the match by a superb 132 when we were set 330 runs to win. Thus, G. O. Smith followed the example of Lord George Scott in 1887, for Oxford, and Eustace Crawley, of the Cambridge Eleven, in the same year. The former contributed 100 and 66; the latter 33 and 103 not out; both were last choices. P. F. Warner had a most unusual experience in this 1896 match, being run out in both innings.

Another incident during this game that I recall is a personal talk I had with an onlooker, who apparently came to watch the 'Varsity Match like one might 'The Derby,' to spot the winner with advantage to himself. During the lunch interval on the last day, when I was none too happy of our prospects of victory—three good wickets were down for just over 70—this spectator approached me and said, 'I'm afraid Oxford's prospects of victory are very poor. What do you think?' My answer, given rather abruptly, was 'We shall win all right.' 'What?' said my interrogator, 'are you sure? I have been laid 8 to 1 against Oxford, shall I take it?' 'Certainly,' I said, anxious to get away from this rather adhesive person. Ten days afterwards I received a registered envelope with a sapphire pin enclosed—and the following letter:— 'Thank you so much for your very valuable information. I collected a very nice sum but I knew it was a certainty as it came from "The Horse's Mouth." '

With the conclusion of this match my cricket career at Oxford came to an end. Of the four Oxford teams that I played with, I think the 1895 one was the strongest; although we lost this 'Varsity match, H. K. Foster played a magnificent 121 out of 196. It was during this match that I received a rather doubtful compliment from an uncle of mine, Sir Edward Chandos Leigh, who was a President of M.C.C. in the Jubilee year of 1887. I had made 73 runs in Oxford's first innings, and on my return to the pavilion my uncle, who was seated near the entrance gate, greeted me with these words: 'Well done, Schwimp (he could not pronounce his R's). Capital, capital, you played just like I used to.' I was somewhat ignorant of his ability as a cricketer beyond what he had from time to time told me so I proceeded to look up his record in 'Varsity matches. It was: 8 in 1852, 0 in 1853, 0 in 1854. A certain limited success!

Knowing that anything written for *Wisden* is handed down to posterity I was anxious to refresh my memory on some subjects and A. H. J. Cochrane, the Oxford Blue of the 'eighties, placed at my disposal helpful and interesting information for which I am much indebted. With regard to facilities for cricket at the Universities, the wickets at Fenner's and at Oxford are easy. 'The Parks' wicket has improved enormously since the War and has the reputation of being almost the easiest-paced in England. It has been said that despite its loveliness 'The Parks' is the only first-class ground in England where it is impossible to get a bath in the pavilion, that the woodwork of the pavilion has not been painted for 25 years; also the practice wickets are very moderate, surrounded by children and perambulators and with a very difficult background to the bowler's arm. In these respects Fenner's has a distinct advantage and another is that a 'gate' can be taken there, which is not the case in 'The Parks.'

A MATCH PLAYED ON TWO GROUNDS

The Oxford University ground was first used for cricket in 1881. The second fixture of that season—against the Gentlemen of England—was transferred at the last moment to the Christ Church ground where entrance fees could be demanded. The Gentlemen went in on a wicket described as having been hastily prepared. The Oxford fast bowler was E. Peake, whose efforts were marked by pace rather than precision. He got out three batsmen who were no doubt relieved to escape alive, and finally he laid out a prominent amateur with a severe blow on the side of the head. The game was then stopped and about three o'clock in the afternoon another start was made in 'The Parks.' This time Oxford won the toss and in the course of a drawn match 1,064 runs were scored for 36 wickets.

The Christ Church ground can provide an admirable wicket and the engagement with the Australians has taken place there since 1882. Here it was that in 1884 Oxford for the first and last time beat an Australian eleven. Fifty years ago one joined the O.U.C.C. and paid, if I remember right, thirty shillings subscription. The annual grant from the M.C.C. to the University Cricket Club dates from 1881. I think at first it was £150 and has been for the last few years £500. In addition to this each University has received for 1936 the equivalent of a half share of the sum given to each first-class county from the profits of Test Matches.

INTERESTING UNIVERSITY MATCHES

It is a long time since a 'Varsity match yielded a close finish. The two runs win by Cambridge in 1870 and the six runs success of Oxford in 1875 are now very distant memories. In the last decade the only thrill that one remembers was when, a few years ago, the last two Oxford men managed to stay in until the finish and had the minor satisfaction of annoying their opponents though they could not defeat them. During the present century the nearest approaches to a level result were the matches of 1908 and 1926. In the former game Oxford got home by only two wickets, while in the other, the margin in favour of Cambridge was 34 runs.

Often enough we have seen reversal of public form. The side supposed to be the weaker nearly always confounded the prophets not only by winning, but by winning easily. In 1881 Cambridge, with A. G. Steel, Ivo Bligh, the three brothers Studd and other great players had what looked like an invincible side. Steel, practically on his own one may say, had already beaten Oxford three times and was confidently expected to do so a fourth time. But the side failed completely against the fast bowling of Evans, the Oxford captain, and were beaten by 135 runs. In 1895 Oxford, with a splendid eleven, were never in it from start to finish and lost by 134 runs.

Almost every boy who has gone up to Oxford or Cambridge with a big cricket reputation has established himself in University cricket. When the famous Harrovian, F. S. Jackson, appeared depressed by doing badly in the trial matches, S. M. J. Woods, the Cambridge captain, told him that if he was worrying about his 'Blue,' he could have it at once. Whether such bold policy would always pay may be an open question; it certainly paid in the case of Jackson.

A MATCH OF FOUR DAYS

Like so many historic engagements, the University Match is more difficult to finish than used to be the case. From 1827, the year of the first match played, until 1898, there were 64 matches, and of these only two were drawn. In 1888 on the Monday the weather was so bad, with thick darkness and continuous rain that there was never the remotest possibility of play, and on the two following days, though cricket was possible, progress in the mud was so slow as to make it soon evident that a draw was inevitable. In these circumstances it was pointed out by a strong body of outside opinion that there had not been a draw for over forty years, and perhaps in order to obviate such a novelty the M.C.C. agreed to allot a fourth day to the match. As it happened there came a further downpour and the game had to be abandoned unfinished, after all.

The University match probably has lost something of its old interest and popularity, but this idea may be more apparent than real. Before the Mound stand was built a ring of ten or fifteen thousand people was about as many as Lord's could hold. Given fine weather you might get ten thousand spectators a day at the University match, but with the accommodation at Lord's increased to Test Match requirements, this is a mere sprinkling and the ground looks somewhat empty. But, while this contrast is not much to go by, it remains true that there are not the coaches and carriages, the arbours and the luncheons, at the match that there once were. It is curious that the attraction of matches like Eton and Harrow, or Eton and Winchester, seems to increase as the years go by; as opportunities for social gatherings they become more patronised every season. But, if as a cricket spectacle it holds its own, as a society function the University match is not what it used to be.

SOME COMPARISONS

How cricketers of to-day compare with the generations of thirty or forty years ago is a subject always likely to provide plenty of argument—I personally can see very little difference. Many able critics of the game deplore the decadence of modern cricket, and sigh for the glories of the past when bowlers bowled a length, and batsmen hit sixers instead of pottering about and stopping the ball with their pads. Have there not always been hitters and slow players, stylists and pad-players, steady bowlers and erratic bowlers? One must allow that shortly after the War a style of batting came into fashion which seemed to most of us far from an improvement on methods of the older school. The player moved in front of the stumps, facing the bowler, and with a short lift of the bat pushed the ball to either side of the wicket. The style was quite distinctive and many batsmen exploited it with much skill. Its advantage was that it involved close watching of the ball, but the limited swing of the bat meant a loss of power, while against fast bowling the 'two-eyed stance,' as it was then and is still called, was less effective than the usual position with the left shoulder forward. All this was fifteen years ago, but in 1936 the two-eyed stance or anything approaching it was less in evidence. Men like Mitchell-Innes and Yardley are typical high-class University batsmen, playing in what surely should be the correct style—the style handed down by tradition and coaching.

The status of the University player in relation to other first-class cricket has not changed much in the last half century. The Universities meet the first-class counties as equals, and most Blues would be worth a place, or at any rate a trial, in all but the strongest county teams. This, it may be contended, has always been the case, but what is more curious is that the proportion of Blues who after their undergraduate days are over, have the inclination and the opportunity of taking a prominent part in public cricket has also hardly altered at all. If you look at the score of any Oxford and Cambridge match, whether in 1885 or 1895 or 1925, you will find four or five names familiar in county or other first-class cricket. Hawke, Key, O'Brien, Bainbridge, Marchant, Fr/y, Woods, Jackson, Jessop, Warner, the Fosters, Ranjitsinhji and A. O. Jones, of the earlier decades have their counterparts in Allen, Jardine, Chapman, Robins, Holmes, Duleepsinhji, Turnbull and others of our own time. It is pleasant to notice that the longer first-class programme, with its exhausting calls upon a young man's leisure, and the economic conditions, with their even more exacting demands on his resources, have not stopped this valuable supply of test-match captains and county captains and players. Space will not permit of my trying to describe what I might think were the best teams that played for Oxford and Cambridge during the time I was connected with University cricket and afterwards. But I would say that the best Cambridge side that I played against was that of 1893. Of individual players, there are obviously many that I would like to mention but again space will not allow me to do so. Are they not to be found in *Wisden*?

Let us examine finally University cricket as a stepping-stone to Test cricket. If we restrict our enquiry to matches against Australia and South Africa, as being contests in which for many years we have in this country chosen absolutely our best teams, we find that since 1880, when we first played Australia over here, 63 amateur cricketers have appeared in England elevens. Of these, 33 have been Oxford or Cambridge Blues. The distinction of being selected while still in residence at the University is uncommon, and only seven of the 33 have enjoyed it. And yet four of the five English teams sent out to Australia since the War have been under the leadership of University players, A. E. R. Gilligan, A. P. F. Chapman, D. R. Jardine and G. O. Allen. If I had to choose a combined University eleven of Blues since 1919—and what a difficult task!—my nominations would be the following twelve:—G. O. Allen, H. Aston, A. P. F. Chapman, K. S. Duleepsinhji, A. E. R. Gilligan, E. R. T. Holmes, D. R. Jardine, D. J. Knight, C. S. Marriott, Nawab of Pataudi, G. T. S. Stevens and G. E. C. Wood.

The older one gets, more precious must be one's memories. Very precious to me are the memories of my Oxford days and my connection with Oxford cricket—happiest of cricket days. Never shall I forget the kindness shown to me by one to whom Oxford owes more than she can ever repay with regard to University cricket. That is, A. J. Webbe, who for so many years brought teams to play against the Universities. It was the example he set that I tried to follow and if in any way I was successful it is to him that I give my grateful thanks.

Long may the Universities continue to be the stepping stone of 'Cricket'—long may University cricketers continue to keep up the high tradition handed down to them by famous cricketers of the past.

SPIN BOWLING [1938]

BY A. P FREEMAN (KENT XI, 1914–36)

In an interview

Loosen-Gore features again in the 1937 edition, in the 'Miscellany' section which Brookes had decided to retain for a second year:

> Tokens of appreciation for his services in connection with University cricket were handed to Mr. H. D. G. Leveson-Gower at a gathering of Old Blues at Lord's on July 7th. Mr. A. J. Webbe (Oxford captain in 1877 and 1878) made the presentation which took the form of a jewel for Mrs. Leveson-Gower and a china dinner service. Mr. G. E. C. Wood spoke on behalf of Cambridge. Altogether, Mr. Leveson-Gower has taken teams to play 64 matches against the Universities; he now finds it necessary to relinquish the task. An illuminated book containing the names of the subscribers came as a socially interesting souvenir.

Rather more miscellaneous than this Social Note was the recording of a famous incident at Lord's in the match between M.C.C. and Cambridge University, news of a marathon innings of an unusual nature by G. O. Allen, and recourse to improvisation, again at Lord's, in a Test match.
The 1937 edition was the last to be bound in paper, much to the relief of regular purchasers. The paper binding was not nearly stout enough to contain the number of pages in each edition, with the result that after usage of a year or two, the book would begin to disintegrate. To this day it is a not uncommon sight among collectors to find some ancient Wisden broken up by the ravages of time into several segments, some of which find themselves drifting down a time-warp into the wrong year, so that a County Championship featuring the deeds of Jessop is followed by an overseas tour in which Hammond and Sutcliffe are prominent. The binding methods favoured for so long were clearly inadequate, but it was not till 1938 that a radical improvement was forthcoming. Until

now Wisden had been its own publisher, but now the editor's preface began:

> To regular readers of Wisden this edition—published for Messrs. John Wisden and Co. Ltd. by Messrs J. Whitaker and Sons, Ltd.—will appear rather strange, but although new features have been introduced and the contents have been rearranged, nothing, I hope, of real interest to lovers of cricket has been omitted. The major principles that have served the book so well in the past have been zealously guarded. While friendly critics have said that Wisden stood in no need of alteration, the results of a long and careful investigation showed that it was desirable to undertake certain changes, aimed mainly at making reference easier. For instance, an alphabetical order has been followed in reviewing the county season, and the division of the book into two parts—what has been called 'a quaint Victorian survival'—has been scrapped, a decision that necessitated a variation in the order of appearance of certain sections to allow a grouping of relative matter.

What Brookes did not mention was the real reason for the drastic changes. In an account of the Almanack's affairs published in the centenary edition of 1963, L. E. S. Gutteridge explains that the Almanack had been one of the casualties of the great economic Depression of the 1930s, and that 'sales had fallen to such an alarming extent that professional help was called in and the publishing of Wisden was passed over to J. Whitaker and Sons, Ltd; publishers of Whitaker's Almanack'. Response to the new design was both instant and spectacular. The cheap edition of the 1937 Almanack reflected declining popularity in a sales figure of 8,000. The first edition published by Whitakers sold 12,000 copies, and sales would no doubt have continued to climb had not the Second World War arrived. What is extraordinary is that neither Brookes nor Gutteridge mentions the favourable effect on readers of the new cloth binding, which transformed the cheap edition from a self-destructing curio to a publication of permanence.

As part of his redesigning of the Almanack, Brookes introduced a more lavish editorial policy than ever before, including four readable essays and an analysis of Don Bradman's career by Justice Evatt consisting mostly of statistics. No doubt the new binding method made it practicable to include more pages in the Almanack, which in this year totalled just under 1,000. The leading item is not in strict terms an essay but a reported interview which none the less retains the flow of a personal digression. Its author is Alfred Percy 'Tich' Freeman (1888–1965) of Kent and England, one of the most prolific wicket-takers in the history of cricket. A leg-break and googly bowler of immaculate length and deceptive flight, he stands second to Rhodes in the list of successful bowlers, with 3,776 wickets at an average cost of only 18.42 each. Some of his records will never now be lowered, especially his total of 304 wickets in the season of 1928 and his total of 298 five years later. He is the only bowler in first-class cricket to have taken 10 wickets in an innings three times, and in the eight seasons from 1928–35 took over 200 wickets on all eight occasions. In Test cricket he enjoyed nothing like the same success; in twelve appearances for England he performed moderately, and perhaps the most perceptive comment on him was by another leg-break bowler, R. W. V. Robins:

> Against other than the greatest batsmen, he was the most effective bowler I ever saw. We will never see his like again as a consistent wicket-taker. Under Percy Chapman, Freeman sometimes opened the bowling, which is astonishing in itself and almost unheard of for a leg-break bowler these days.

In attempting to confess his secrets, Freeman in his interview denies having any, but the photographs of his hand gripping the ball which accompanied the interview gave to his disquisition an aura either of sorcery or incipient arthritis. Freeman marked his retirement by naming his home 'Dunbowlin', an execrable pun but perhaps forgivable in a man who spent twenty-three years taking 3,776 wickets for 69,577 runs.

THE best piece of advice which I offer to the young bowler is: watch and experiment. To my mind, too many bowlers in modern cricket neglect to use their intelligence; their efforts are little more than mechanical. It is absolutely essential that a bowler should study the batsman, not in a casual sort of way, but with proper concentration. I am convinced that I learned most because I spent so much time all through my career in watching both batsmen and other bowlers.

I do not claim to have any wonderful secrets that may account for my harvest of wickets for Kent in season after season. When you are at the top of the tree it is easier to take wickets than in the days of less experience in the art. I know I bowled better as long ago as 1914 than when I was in my supposed prime. Never having received a day's coaching in my life, I am very sure that bowlers are born and not made. If the ability is there, it can, of course, be brought out and developed, but without natural gifts no one can hope to attain real eminence as a bowler. A length bowler will get wickets in any class of cricket. Action, length, flight, control of pace and finger spin may all be persevered with, but to rise above the common level that natural ability must be there. The experienced player should be able to tell a boy with cricket in him by the way the boy picks up a bat or bowls one or two balls.

So many cricket text-books are available that I do not think it necessary to go at all deeply into the main principles of bowling. The question has often been raised whether bowlers are given sufficient coaching nowadays. My view has been that you can only tell the pupil the 'secrets'—by which I mean the fundamental points of bowling—and he must, by thorough practice, do the rest for himself.

Given natural ability and having developed an easy run up to the wicket, a boy has a good start. No one can hope to succeed without a loose arm, for if the action is at all bad the bowler has much harder work to do. Fast bowlers like McDonald and Larwood have provided admirable examples in post-War cricket of an easy, loose run up and smooth action and the slow bowler, too, must acquire a perfectly natural run up. It is beyond all contradiction that length is the chief part of bowling, and length must be commanded before any attempt at spinning the ball is begun. When I was coaching, I used to draw a line nine feet in front of the wicket and instruct my pupils to bowl to that; I have also laid a sheet of newspaper on the wicket and told the boys to pitch the ball on it. Of course a good length to a tall batsman like Frank Woolley would be a long-hop to a player of the height of, say, Hendren. The aim must be to drop the ball just out of a batsman's reach and to give him as little time as possible to deal with it.

FINGER-SPIN

The good coach will stress the importance of learning to change pace without change of action. In my view that is one of the hardest parts of bowling. I know it is the general opinion that the leg-break is the most difficult ball to bowl but, as it is also the most deadly ball, it is worth mastering. The grip of the ball for this is a matter for the individual. I hold it with the first and second fingers round the seam, with the ball resting on the third finger and the thumb steadying the ball and I think one has more command of the ball with this grip. The seam is pointing towards slip. Some people run away with the idea that the grips for the leg-break and googly are different. That is not so. In fact my grip is the same for the top-spinner as well. The difference between the three balls is this: For the top-spinner I hold the ball with the seam pointing straight down the wicket and release it from a position half-way between that for the leg-break and googly. When bowling the googly the wrist is turned over and the ball comes over the top of the little finger from the back of the hand. In this case the ball is held with the seam pointing to fine leg. Some off-break bowlers who are supposed to spin the ball merely do little except turn the wrist. That is rolling the ball—no more. To spin the ball, you must use your fingers. Hold the ball tight with the first finger over the seam and, at the time the ball is leaving the hand, flick it with the fingers.

STUDY THE BATSMAN

If the art of studying the batsman and watching for his weak spots was cultivated more both in county and club cricket, we should not hear so many lamentations about the scarcity of good spin bowlers. It is important to study the batsman right up to the moment of releasing the ball. A movement by him before the ball has left my hand has prompted me to pitch the ball a little wide and often to get him stumped. It may take you half an hour to find out his weakness but it is worth while. Never mind giving a batsman 20 runs or so. Four wickets for 100 at the Oval always pleased me more than, say, eight for 20 on a bad wicket against a poor side. Humour the batsman if he has a particular hit but be sure you have safe fieldsmen in the position where a catch may be put up. A good captain will always consult the bowler before altering the placing of the field; otherwise he is likely to ruin the bowler's best laid plans.

I always enjoyed pitting my brains against the top-class batsmen. I preferred to bowl to Jack Hobbs more than anybody. He played every ball on its merits, took no liberties and if you got his wicket you earned it. I always knew he would play every ball as it deserved.

During the later years of my career in Kent cricket I believe I knew every batsman's weakness. That knowledge, carefully memorised, I was always ready and willing to pass on to younger bowlers in the team. When Warwickshire were playing Kent at Gravesend in the first year Douglas Wright turned out for us, I got a wicket with the last ball of an over and Bates came in to take the next ball from Wright. I suggested to Wright he should bowl a googly first ball; he did and Bates' leg peg went down. Bates said to me afterwards: 'You told him, Tich, didn't you, to bowl a googly?' and I admitted the little strategy.

Always be ready to experiment is a good motto for bowlers. If you cannot get a man out try anything. Never be afraid of being hit. If a batsman starts hitting, keep him at it; a little more flight and the batsman may make a mistake. It is when the wicket is 'dead' that you need to experiment most. At such times bowl a bit faster but not forgetting to slip in an occasional slow one with the same action. Whenever I am asked to give advice on bowling, I always urge the prime importance of these points of studying the batsman and experimenting.

THE GOOGLY

I have probably 'kidded' more batsmen out than anyone. It may seem a strange thing to say but I got a good many wickets through *not* bowling the googly. The bats knew I could bowl it and was always expecting it. Often he became so fidgety trying to watch my hand and to anticipate the googly that he got out in some other way.

A bowler cannot expect to master the googly without a lot of hard practice. When the late R. O. Schwarz came to England in 1907, round about my eighteenth birthday, I summoned up courage to ask him how to bowl the googly. His advice was, 'Just watch me, you will soon see how it is done,' and after close observation of his bowling I was optimistic enough to believe I could master it and set to work to practice bowling the googly for two years, winter and summer, before attempting it in the middle. When at last I felt confident that I could keep a length I tried the googly out in a match against Charlton Park and took eight wickets for about 20 runs. W. H. Levett, the Kent wicket-keeper, always said I bowled the googly in two ways. Actually this was not so, but I sometimes released it earlier in my delivery. Also, like Grimmett, I bowled a ball which was not an ordinary googly. Everything else was the same except that, instead of the ball coming from over the back of the hand, it came out between the third and fourth fingers. By using the second method I brought the ball through quicker because I could grip it harder.

A slow bowler, without the support of a good wicket-keeper, would probably find that half of his work was wasted. I have been lucky in playing with such a fine wicket-keeper as Leslie Ames. We made a perfect combination. He knew everything I could do with the ball. Occasionally I beat him but not often. The number of wickets which Ames took off my bowling must be something like a record. I never signalled the googly to Ames but, before he came into the team regularly I used to do so, although I know that most wicket-keepers prefer to find it out for themselves, rather than be given a signal when it is coming. Signs I used to indicate to the wicket-keeper when I meant to bowl a googly were to hitch up the back of my trousers as I walked back after delivering the previous ball or to swing my left hand, holding the ball.

OPPOSING LEG THEORY

Always try to force the batsman to make shots. That was my plan. Cricket looks so bad when a bowler's policy is aimed at 'pegging down' the batsman. I think leg-theory is a sign of weakness on the bowler's part. I only once bowled deliberately outside the leg stump and then with the idea of exposing this negative bowling. We were playing at Tonbridge and Warwickshire's slow left-arm bowler kept on dropping the ball just outside the leg stump. Kent had a bang at him, not with much success, and some of our batsman said, 'If he bowls this stuff in the return match, we will ignore it.' They did so and although the Warwickshire bowler had a lot of maiden overs he did not get many wickets. When I went on I put all my fieldsmen on the leg side and bowled a few overs outside the leg stump. One man was run out, trying to push the ball to the off, another left a ball alone and it broke and hit the off stump. I don't think a run was scored while I was indulging in this little 'retaliation.' But it did not please me a bit, because it was so entirely a case of the batsman getting himself out rather than the bowler taking wickets.

A bowler who doesn't like the job will never get on. He should never allow himself to be worried by dropped catches. As soon as you start slacking you are finished. I might have been out of the ordinary but I never got tired all the time I was bowling, no matter how long my spell with the ball. The hotter the weather, the less tired I seemed to become. It was after the day's play that I used to feel the strain. Cold weather, of course, affects the muscles and it takes a long time to get the fingers supple. I believe a good many bowlers are troubled with pains in the wrist and elbow after long hours of spinning the ball, but I can honestly say that I was never affected in this way, nor did I ever have a corn on my hand.

SOME EXPERIMENTS WORTH TRYING

In my view bowlers do not use the bowling crease as much as they should do. Obviously when this is done the batsman has to contend against the ball coming to him from different angles. I often used to bowl a yard behind the wicket and rely on the art of flighting—making the batsman think the ball is coming up farther than it really is. A slow bowler must be a master of flight. It is not easy to explain how it is done although, of course, it is combined with action and is more or less natural. One of the most dangerous balls is a good length outside the leg stump. A batsman is always liable to over-balance when trying to play this ball and there is a good chance of him being stumped if he misses it. On a sticky wicket you have to bowl almost half-volleys. On a fast wicket you must bowl a bit shorter, for a good length on a fast wicket is a long hop on a slow one. Much the same thing applies when you are bowling to a quick-footed or a slow-footed batsman.

The only time I bowl round the wicket is when I think I can take advantage of broken patches outside the leg stump made by the bowler in his run-up. A left-hander, of course, has to bowl round the wicket to get the right angle. On a wicket where the ball won't turn you must rely on length and flight.

Keep pegging away.

REFLECTIONS [1938]

BY E. (PATSY) HENDREN (MIDDLESEX AND ENGLAND)

In an Interview

The bright new Wisden of 1938 included only one sad sin of omission, the decline in quality of the 'Miscellany' feature. There were, however, consolations in plenty, including a farewell address delivered by the Middlesex and England batsman Elias 'Patsy' Hendren (1889–1962). Hendren, who played for Middlesex from 1909 until his retirement in 1937, was one of the dominant batsmen of his time and among the best-loved players of the century. His statistics, impressive though they undeniably are, cannot remotely convey the deep affection in which he was held by crowds all over the world. With 170 centuries, he stands second in the hierarchy to Hobbs, and his career total of over 57,000 runs places him third behind Hobbs and Woolley. Three times he passed the mark of 3,000 runs in a season, seven times he scored a hundred for England, and so passionate was his love of the game that once his playing days were over, he lingered on, first as coach at Harrow School, then in the same post at the Sussex Club. Finally, from 1952 to 1960 he was official scorer of the Middlesex side, giving up only when illness brought about his retirement. In his youth he was an outstanding winger for Brentford, Queens Park Rangers and Manchester City, and was chosen to represent England in the 'Victory' international of 1919.

But the roots of Hendren's immense popularity were to be found in his quick earthy humour, which could defuse the most inflammable situations.

In discussing the various ways in which a touring cricketer in Sydney might effectively cope with barracking, Jack Fingleton describes an afternoon when Hendren, fielding on the boundary, was asked by one of the bass-baritones on the Hill why so-and-so was not in the England side:

> 'Ah,' replied Patsy as he turned that incorrigible Irish face of his to the questioner, 'they only pick good-looking blokes in this side'.

Not surprisingly, Hendren made an ideal tourist. Jack Hobbs described him as 'the life and soul of the party on all our tours', and S. C. Griffith, who had played against and alongside him, remembered that 'he brought a tremendous amount of fun and happiness to everything associated with the game'. In a period when English batting was rich beyond measure, Hendren played fifty-one times for his country. The best epitaph of all was composed by his Middlesex colleague Ian Peebles:

> In the West Indies his personality, his tremendous batting and a talent for innocent and really comical buffoonery evoked a response nigh to delirium. He made a duck in his first match for Middlesex, and a duck in his last, a memory which gave him as much pleasure as that of his 170 centuries.

IT is a big pull leaving the stage, as they call it; leaving the people I have played with and the camaraderie of the game, but we all have to come to it at some time, and I thought it as well to give up while I was doing well.

You know what they say about cards: bad beginning, good ending. Well, my first county match was one in which I did not get an innings! That was in 1907 against Lancashire at Lord's, the game being abandoned before lunch on the second day. There were naturally unusual circumstances. After heavy rain, a drizzle set in, but the crowd—allowed, as they were then, on the playing-area—gathered in front of the Pavilion and clamoured for cricket. In the middle of all the rumpus, somebody got on to the pitch itself and, accidentally or not, stuck the ferrule of an umbrella into the turf. When this was discovered by Mr. Archie MacLaren, the Lancashire captain, he refused to play, even if a fresh wicket were cut out. So there was nothing for it but to pack up and go home.

The fight for the Championship in my last season, 1937, provided a great struggle, but it was not the closest in which I have been concerned. I remember in 1920, when Middlesex were under the captaincy of Mr. P. F. Warner (as he was then) for the last time, Lancashire, in celebration of winning the Championship, split a bottle or two of champagne before the result of the Middlesex and Surrey match at Lord's reached them. As a matter of fact, I started the turn of that game by catching Tom Shepherd in the deep—can see myself now running from long-off to long-on to take the ball—and, with a win by 55 runs, Middlesex gained the title.

It has been suggested that cricket at the present time does not attract spectators as it used to do. All I can say is that the kind of game Middlesex played in 1937 most certainly does not fail to attract. Many times we made 350 or more before tea, and that is a lot of runs. Then, too, we had a skipper who was always out to win. That in itself must make the game interesting and worth watching, particularly when the skipper concerned is a great fielder and one who studies the viewpoint of the spectator.

TO HELP YOUNG CRICKETERS

Anyway, I have said good-bye to all that, and I take up with confidence my new task as coach at Harrow School. I have done a good bit of coaching; I was the first to start indoor cricket schools in London. A big mistake often made in coaching is that of trying to teach youngsters too much. No two batsmen play alike, and it is no use one trying to copy another. It cannot be done.

My advice to budding batsmen if they want to keep the game alive is to play off the left foot a little more, ready to hit the half volley. The average cricketer is apt to play a bit too 'safe.' That is all very well till you have made 20 or 30, but then you must be ready to hit the ball. Otherwise what should be hundreds are only seventies.

I consider that a batsman should make a good coach for bowlers—as good, indeed, as a bowler. The bowler can show the pupil how to hold the ball, how to spin it and how to flight it; but the man towards whom the ball is coming is the one who can say whether or not the bowler is bowling well. I am in favour of indoor cricket schools. Lots of people improve their game there. They have, of course, to adapt themselves from matting wickets to turf, but winter practice cannot fail to do a lot of good to club cricketers, who in this way get the necessary exercise to commence a cricket season already loosened-up.

There is, at the moment, a scarcity of outstanding bowlers. I cannot give a reason; they run in cycles, and this is one of the 'off-periods.' Wickets, too, do not help them nowadays. We want another Maurice Tate or another F. R. Foster. We cannot expect to get another Barnes; that is too much to ask.

IMPORTANCE OF FIELDING

I must say a word about fielding, to my mind the most interesting part of the game. Good fielders make a fair bowler very good. There is nothing more pleasant for a bowler than to see people dashing about trying to save runs and improve his analysis; it puts heart into him. It is a great mistake for fieldsmen to stop chasing the ball. Too many men slacken off when a four seems a certainty. Spectators like to see the ball chased to the very end, with the resultant thrill in the point of whether the man or the ball will win the race to the boundary. Sir Pelham Warner once said he would never, if he could help it, play anybody who could not field. There is a lot in that idea.

In connection with fielding, a funny thing once happened to me when on an M.C.C. tour in Australia. Between fixtures, I was journeying into the Bush by motor-car with a colleague when we stopped to watch a cricket match. One of the players, unaware of our identity, approached and asked if, as his team was a man short, one of us would play. I had already been in the field for two and a half days, but I yielded to persuasion and, rigged out in borrowed gear, was put in the deep field at the bottom of a pronounced slope, from where I could see nothing at all of the cricket. For hour after hour I fielded there, throwing the ball back at intervals until, at long last, I caught one. I ran to the top of the hill and announced with some satisfaction that I had made a catch. To my consternation, I was informed that the other team's innings had closed and that I had caught one of my own side!

VIEW ON L.B.W.

Some important changes in the Laws of the Game have been made during my thirty years in first-class cricket. As regards the larger stumps, I do not think they have made a big difference to the real class player. Certainly the increased size of the wicket has helped the bowler a little, but when a good batsman is in, it does not really matter. The smaller ball, too, has been of assistance to the bowler, though strangely enough, while this was supposed to help in spinning the ball, there are fewer people bowling 'spinners.' Now about L.B.W., 'N.'; I am in favour of the rule being applied to the ball turning from leg as well as that breaking from the off. After all, the leg-break is the most difficult ball to bowl, and the additional reward to this type of attack would bring the spin-bowler back into the game.

Personally, however, I thought the 'snick' experiment with the L.B.W. Law better than the 'N.' rule. It put a stop to those batsmen who, given out leg before, so often returned to the pavilion declaring: 'I played it.' The new rule is not fulfilling expectations as regards improvement in off-side strokes; maybe it makes batsmen afraid to get across as they should. One thing I do think, and that is that a batsman should not be given out under the 'N' rule when playing a forward stroke to an off-break. After all, the rule was directed chiefly against the men who merely raised their bats and stepped across to play the ball with their pads. It was not intended to penalise the player employing an attacking stroke, and I am pleased to say that, so far as I have noticed, not many umpires give a man out in these circumstances.

A NOTE ON WICKETS

My opinion is that, if all wickets were the same as at Lord's, we should have more of a fight for runs. Men are too often picked for a Test match on the strength of a hundred on a 'doped' pitch. Another mistake we in England make is in preparing special wickets for touring teams. As early as the autumn of the year preceding an Australian visit, for instance, some of the ground-staffs get to work on wickets for their county's game with the touring team, who in consequence are able to play in England on something like their own wickets. If visiting sides had to bat, especially in

Test matches, on the same pitches as those upon which ordinary county games are played, there would not be so many big scores.

A DREAM COME TRUE

So much has happened during my career that I find it no easy matter to single out the happiest incident. Probably my proudest moment was when, in 1926, I completed my first hundred in a Test Match against Australia. That was a dream come true: a century at Lord's, where I had been a ground-boy! A certain incident concerning a hose, which by some strange manner of means was left running all night on the pitch, nearly spoiled it all for me.

Among the players with or against whom I have played, I shall never forget the famous 'W. G.' I first played in a charity match with him and also for M.C.C. at Charlton, and very proud I was to be in the same side with him. In one of these games, I got a hundred and the Doctor 50 odd—he was past his best at that time—and I well remember him clapping me on the back and saying in that high-pitched voice of his: 'You'll play for England one day, young 'un.' I am glad he was right. Then there was Albert Trott, one of the grandest cricketers of all time and the only man ever to hit a ball clean over the Pavilion at Lord's. In his benefit match against Somerset at Lord's in 1907, he performed the 'hat-trick' twice in one innings. He took four wickets with four balls and with the fifth dislodged a bail with a ball that went for four byes. In those days, the bail had to be *removed* before a batsman was out. Next over, he sent back three men with following deliveries, making his analysis for the innings seven for 20. At the end of the innings, Albert punched his own head and called himself names for finishing his benefit match early on the third day! Sammy Woods, captain of Somerset, and one of the 'victims,' gave him a straw hat with a hand-painted picture on the band of seven rabbits bolting into the Pavilion. Albert wore it at a good many matches during the rest of the season—to the wonderment of everyone not 'in the know.'

I cannot fail to mention J. T. Hearne, my great hero on and off the field. He was a very dear man and an outstanding example to young cricketers. I have never seen a bowler with a prettier action. He did the 'hat-trick' against the Australians in the Test match at Leeds in 1899, the batsmen concerned being Clem Hill, S. E. Gregory and M. A. Noble.

STRAIN OF OVERSEAS TOURS

I have made a good number of tours abroad, and I must confess that one gets extremely tired in the course of them. It is a big strain, especially in Australia, where there are very few easy matches. In most of the State sides there are four or five Test players, and in the Up-country matches, where the cricket is less arduous, there is much travelling to do. You have to be very strong to stand it. I had five continuous seasons of it, and as I fielded in the long field at that time, it demanded the highest standard of physical fitness. In one match at Melbourne, by the way, I once occupied every position in the field—except that of wicket-keeper, of course. My football training did me the world of good as a cricketer, and among other things it helped me to keep my pace in the deep. Personally, I do not consider the absence of a cricketer-footballer from a Soccer season when on tour is a handicap to him; it does him more good than harm.

On these tours, about seventeen players are generally taken. One can never tell if that number is going to be sufficient. As it is, four or five players sometimes do not get a game for perhaps three weeks at a time. It would, of course, be very nice if you could take enough to rest the whole of the Test team now and again, but I am afraid it would cost too much money. When on tour, amateurs and professionals 'mix' splendidly. They are all part of one team: all live together, all change together.

A lot has been said and written from time to time about separate exits on grounds for amateurs and professionals. So far as Lord's is concerned, the professionals have the option of going through the centre-gate on to the field if they care, but they probably think it too much trouble to walk along there from the dressing-room.

A CASE FOR MORE NATURAL WICKETS [1938]

BY G. O. ALLEN

Following immediately on from Hendren's farewell there appeared another Middlesex essay by one of Hendren's warmest admirers. George Oswald Browning Allen (b. 1902), at the time he published his plea for the reformation of wickets, was already a figure of considerable prestige and authority although no more than 36 years old. A product of Eton and Cambridge, he represented Middlesex between 1921 and 1950, but was one of several amateurs of the period whose predicament of reconciling the demands of the first-class game with the exigencies of following a profession was an indication of the rate at which the frontiers of privilege had been shrinking since the end of the war. A fast bowler of genuine pace and copy-book action, and a resolute striker of the ball, he had emerged with credit from the ill-fated 1932–33 tour of Australia, having refused pointblank to comply with Jardine's instructions to bowl body line. The clash of wills between the two of them seems to have been won by Allen, who was allowed to follow his own counsel.

In 1936–37 he had returned to Australia as captain of an England touring side which came within a whisker of snatching the rubber from under Bradman's nose, but some idea of how little time he was able to give to cricket on his return is conveyed by the fact that in the last three seasons before the Championship was suspended for the duration, he played only 24 innings for Middlesex and bowled less than 250 overs. It seemed as though his career was over, but in 1947–48 he stepped into the breach and captained the England tourists in the West Indies. His subsequent career as an administrator scaled unprecedented heights. For six years he was Chairman of the England selectors, served as President of the M.C.C., and then as Treasurer, in which post he remained for thirteen years. From 1974–76 he was Vice-Chairman of the Cricket Council, before resigning on a point of principle. Even in retirement, Sir George Allen as he at last became has remained a figure of wide influence, living in a house attached to Lord's, and occupying a place in the annals of the game so nebulous and yet so obvious that Neville Cardus's description perhaps comes closest to the truth: 'A shrewd, not always visible, Grey Eminence at Lord's'.

IN the spring of 1937, at the request of the Advisory County Cricket Committee, the M.C.C. appointed a special Commission consisting of three men who have had great experience of the game, to examine and report on county cricket from every angle. That such action was deemed necessary showed that there were many people in England, of whom I am one, who were not entirely happy about the present state of affairs.

It is common knowledge that in recent years there has been a serious falling-off in the receipts of county cricket, and one naturally finds oneself seeking the reason. I do not believe, as many people do, that this is due to the increase of counter-attractions; rather is it because many of the matches have become dull to watch. At the time of writing this article, the Commission's report has not been made public, but I am told that it will contain several useful suggestions for the improvement and brightening of the game.

I fear, however, that unless there is included in it a strong recommendation to county committees to consider the condition of wickets generally, one of the chief causes of the present financial embarrassment of many of the clubs will have been overlooked. The public of to-day will not watch cricket unless they are assured of entertainment, and it is therefore up to the executives to do all within their power to give them 'their money's worth.'

In the past, a more enterprising form of cricket has invariably been witnessed when the wicket has been 'responsive' and I cannot see why this should not always be the case. It is impossible for me to give an opinion as to whether the present-day cricketer is as good as his predecessor, as I was not lucky enough to have seen the old masters in action. It would appear that genius is more rare nowadays and, what is still more disturbing, that many of the players have not got that spirit of adventure and daring which in days gone by made the game a so much better spectacle than it is to-day. The standard of bowling has probably deteriorated, but I beg to suggest that this deterioration has coincided with the advent of the all too clever groundman and his modern contrivances.

Each wicket may well need a different preparation, but I consider that in recent years too much water, liquid manure and various forms of dope have been applied to many of them, with the result that the number of easy-paced wickets has increased each season. I am not suggesting that the wickets are necessarily better from the batsman's point of view than they were immediately before the war but I am certain that they are more lifeless, and it is of this that I complain.

In my opinion, easy-paced wickets, besides detracting very considerably from the pleasure of playing the game, tend to produce a form of cricket which is lacking in enterprise and interest. On such wickets, even the most menacing bowler loses his sting and, realising he has little chance of attacking the batsman, in self defence adopts negative tactics; by this I mean bowling short of a length, probably at the leg stump with additional fieldsmen on the leg side, in order to try to prevent the batsman from scoring and in the hope that he will eventually throw away his wicket in desperation.

It has apparently become fashionable just recently to accuse fast bowlers, and only fast bowlers, of adopting these tactics. This is unjust, because medium-paced bowlers are as guilty, if not more so in this respect and they have less excuse than fast bowlers, who must necessarily be at a greater disadvantage when the wicket is 'dead'. This stalemate situation has arisen many times during the last few years, and, while my sympathy has been with both bowler and batsman, the methods adopted have resulted in the sort of cricket which no one wishes to see, and for which fewer every year are prepared to pay.

SOME EXAMPLES

At Old Trafford, during the seasons 1934, 1935 and 1936, three Test Matches were played in which 3,546 runs were scored for the loss of 71 wickets, an average of 50 runs per wicket. It may be argued that this was due to moderate bowling, but the fact that Grimmett, a man of slight build and light on his feet, was able to dig a foot-hole at least three inches in depth while bowling 57 overs in a first innings tells a tale—a tale, I am sure, of the too frequent use of the watering can. The groundman who was responsible for those wickets is now in command at Trent Bridge where the wicket last season was easier paced than ever before. It looks, therefore, as if certain groundmen have certain methods and those methods are the ones which, in my opinion, are killing modern cricket. In 1936, I went to play at Northampton in a county match and as I approached the ground I noticed an odour which, I assumed, came from a neighbouring farm-yard. On enquiry, I was told that when I examined the wicket I would realise whence the smell came. That wicket was one of the easiest upon which I have ever played and the match was a dull, high-scoring affair.

I have mentioned only a few cases of over-prepared pitches in County and Test Match cricket, but it is common knowledge amongst the regular players that there have been and are many others to which this criticism applies. Owing to my close association with Lord's, I fear I may be thought prejudiced when I say that in my opinion the nearest example of the ideal type of wicket was produced there frequently last year. For some time it has been the policy of the authorities not to prepare the wicket too thoroughly, with the result that most of the matches have had a definite result and have produced play of an entertaining nature. I am not sure what instructions have been given to the groundman, but I believe that he has always been restricted in his use of all forms of dope. There have been a few wickets on which the ball has 'lifted,' but that invariably has been due to ridges which are an unfortunate characteristic of the ground.

Surprising though it may seem to many people, I have seen two of the most ideal wickets at Kennington Oval, usually considered a batsman's paradise. One was the wicket on which the England-India Test Match was played in 1936; it was fast and gave the bowlers every opportunity and encouragement. The other was that interesting stretch of turf on which Surrey played Middlesex last season. That pitch was entirely different from the one which I have mentioned previously as it could never have been described as fast, but it always gave the bowlers, and especially the spin bowlers, a fair chance.

I hope I am not being indiscreet when I say that that pitch had been intended for the Test Match due to commence on the following Saturday. The groundman had no alternative but to use it, as the one which he had been preparing for the Middlesex match for some unknown reason sank on the good length at the Pavilion end. In other words, Surrey played Middlesex on a wicket which was one week short of the preparation which the groundman had intended to give it. From every point of view it was a splendid match and surely affords strong evidence that a happy medium can be found.

Please do not think that I am blaming the groundman entirely for the unhealthy state of affairs which exists on some of the grounds. That is not my intention. I am told that many of the County Committees hold their groundmen responsible for the wickets and in such circumstances one can well understand their unwillingness to prepare anything but the most perfect wickets in case they are blamed for injuries which batsmen may receive or for wickets which do not last the full duration of a match. It is difficult, however, to believe the story which so many of them tell: namely, that if pitches are to fulfil these requirements they must be very intensively prepared and will, therefore, generally be easy paced.

It is possible that there may be one or two grounds where the turf or foundation is such that the maximum preparation is necessary in order to produce reasonable wickets, but these grounds are fortunately few and far between.

A POSSIBLE REMEDY

So far my comments have been mainly destructive and no one deplores that prevalent form of criticism more than I do. Here then, are my constructive proposals.

Under the present system many of the groundmen have too much power and that I am sure is a mistake, as some of them have become almost autocratic. I would therefore urge that all County Committees should appoint sub-Committees, who would not only relieve the groundmen of much of their responsibility, but also outline the general policy regarding the preparation of wickets. In putting forward this suggestion I may be treading upon rather delicate ground, for the preparation of cricket pitches requires technical skill. My idea, however, is not so much that these sub-Committees should interfere with the curators' technique, but that they should be in a position to put some curb on their natural zeal when they deem it advisable.

As I have said before, each wicket may well need a different preparation, and the use of modern chemicals may be sometimes necessary, but much good would result if the period over which the preparation usually extends could be somewhat curtailed. To see that this policy was carried out occasionally would, of course, be one of the duties of the proposed sub-Committees. The Surrey v. Middlesex Match at the Oval this summer is the great example of the advantage of the shorter preparation. I am convinced that, had not the groundman been prevented from giving the pitch the treatment he intended, this match would have told a different story. No one would advocate the type of wicket which might be termed dangerous, nor the type on which the side winning the toss would be certain of victory, but the game to which I have referred proved that neither of these eventualities need necessarily occur.

I contend that a bowler will always attack a batsman when he considers he has a chance and a batsman will play a more open game when he realises that he has more to do than just stay there for runs to come. Some people may argue that if more natural wickets were prepared, the county matches would frequently not last the full three days. I do not think that would be the case, but if it were so it would not in my opinion be a disadvantage. On the last day of a match, unless there is a good chance of an exciting finish, the attendance is usually so small that it is hardly worth considering. If finance must come into the argument, it is fair to suppose that a spectacular match lasting two days will probably bring in receipts as large, if not larger than a dull one lasting three days. I am not advocating the shortening of time allotted for County matches, but shorter matches, if ending early on the third day, must help regular players, many of whom clearly suffer from excess of cricket, and would so tend to raise the general standard of play.

In recent years several experiments have been put to the test in first-class cricket with excellent results, so surely, this scheme which I have attempted to outline is also worthy of a trial. In urging its adoption, I am not doing anything new. The Hon. R. H. Lyttelton has for a long time been pressing for this change of policy, and Mr. A. C. MacLaren, as far back as 1905, wrote an article in *Wisden* in which he appealed for 'a fair wicket instead of a billiard table.'

CENTENARY OF TRENT BRIDGE [1938]

BY A. W. SHELTON (NOTTINGHAMSHIRE PRESIDENT, 1933)

A famous anniversary fell due in the year, and Brookes acknowledged it by publishing a brief, brisk essay from Albert William Shelton (1863–1938), one of the loyalest servants of the Nottinghamshire County Club. The Trent Bridge ground, one of the most famous in the world, and dubbed by Neville Cardus as 'the lotus-land of batsmen' because of the apparent ease with which batsmen seemed to compile huge scores on its friendly turf, was 100 years old. So many outstanding players had passed through the gates of Trent Bridge that Mr. Shelton may have been hard put to contain himself within the allotted span of little more than 1,000 words. His mention of E. V. Lucas is certainly justified. Edward Verrall Lucas (1868–1938) was a prolific belletrist of the period, bibliophile, anthologist, biographer of Charles Lamb, and among whose greatest passions was cricket. It was Lucas, the moment he realised that the great Canadian humorist Stephen Leacock had ancestral connections with Hambledon, who hustled him down to Hampshire, where he confronted him with sacred documents pertaining to the men of John Nyren's time which meant everything to Lucas and marginally less than nothing to Leacock. It was Lucas, in a privately printed essay called 'A Hundred Years of Trent Bridge', who defined the birth of William Clarke as 'a good deed in a naughty world', and who quoted George Parr on the subject of how to make diplomatic overtures during a match:

> When you play in a match, be sure not to forget to pay a little attention to the umpire. First of all inquire after his health, then say what a fine player his father was, and, finally, present him with a brace of birds or rabbits. This will give you confidence, and you will probably do well.

Mr. Shelton could claim no such literary graces as Lucas displayed in his celebrated essay, but possessed long and intimate knowledge of the Nottinghamshire Club's history and administration. An estate agent by profession, Shelton consoled himself by devoting all his spare time to cricket, and served for more than fifty years as member, committeeman and finally as President. It was due to his industry that the Trent Bridge pavilion was so rich a storehouse of cricket curiosities and books, and because of his concern for the welfare of professional cricketers everywhere that he pioneered the insurance of benefit matches against interference by weather. Ironically, both Shelton and Lucas died in the very year of the Trent Bridge centenary, and it was the ex-President's style of departure which illustrated more eloquently than any testimony the depth of his love of cricket. On September 10th, 1938, packing his bag for his annual visit to the Scarborough Festival, he was so happy at the prospect that it was too much for him, and he collapsed and died.

In a brief account of cricket during a hundred years at Trent Bridge, it is appropriate to begin by quoting one of the inscriptions written by E. V. Lucas, C.H., which appear near the gates erected in 1933 to the memory of J. A. Dixon, captain of Nottinghamshire for many years:

'THIS THE COUNTRY GROUND OF THE NOTTINGHAMSHIRE CRICKET CLUB, FAMOUS THROUGHOUT THE WORLD AS 'TRENT BRIDGE,' WAS ORIGINALLY A MEADOW ADJOINING THE OLD TRENT BRIDGE INN AT THE TIME WHEN ITS LANDLORD WAS WILLIAM CLARKE, THE INCOMPARABLE SLOW BOWLER, LATER TO EARN THE HONOURED TITLE OF 'FATHER OF NOTTINGHAMSHIRE CRICKET.' THE GROUND, PREPARED BY HIM, WAS OPENED ON MAY 28, 1838. THE FIRST INTER-COUNTY CONTEST TO BE FOUGHT HERE BEING BETWEEN NOTTINGHAMSHIRE AND SUSSEX ON JULY 27 AND 28, 1840. SINCE WHEN AS THE SCENE OF NOTTINGHAMSHIRE MATCHES AND TEST MATCHES ITS HISTORY HAS BEEN STEADILY ILLUSTRIOUS.'

William Clarke took all ten Leicestershire wickets in 1845, a performance unequalled for Nottinghamshire, and the only occasion on which this feat has been performed in a county match at Trent Bridge. In a local match he hit the first hundred on the ground, but not until 1871 was a century made there in a first-class match and then W. G. Grace scored 116 for Gloucestershire.

Since 1838 about 370 men, born, with rare exceptions, in the county, have played for Nottinghamshire; most English cricketers of note and all sides visiting England have appeared on the ground. The Ground Staff, established in 1897, has produced many great County and England players. Each year about a dozen young professionals are engaged for twenty weeks under capable coaches.

From William Clarke, through George Parr, Richard Daft, Arthur Shrewsbury, William Gunn, George Gunn and Joseph Hardstaff, senior, may be traced the never-ceasing flow of batsmen of high skill and graceful style in the Nottinghamshire eleven. But the influence of Clarke's perfect length slow bowling (then, of course, underhand), maintained so admirably by Alfred Shaw, Flowers, Attewell, Hallam, John Gunn, the left-hander, and others, has for the time being, at any rate, become lost in the demand for speed and swerve.

From its condition when taken over by Clarke, the ground steadily became one of the best in the country and since 1899 its improved equipment has been rapid. Numerous buildings, including Ladies' Pavilion, Practice Hall, Secretary's Office and new stands have been provided at an approximate cost of £40,000 to which Sir Julien Cahn made very generous contributions. Now the ground has accommodation, largely with seating in covered or uncovered stands, for 30,000 spectators besides provision for 6,000 members. In 1934 on the Monday when England played Australia 30,250 people were present.

In December 1919 the freehold of the property, upwards of ten and a half acres in extent, including the Trent Bridge Hotel and all the buildings, was purchased. The hotel was then sold to the lessees so that the cricket ground with all its buildings now belongs to the Nottinghamshire County Cricket Club and it is hoped will remain so for all time.

Numerous representative matches of historical importance have been played at Trent Bridge including three of seven during the period from 1842 to 1885 between Nottinghamshire and England. Of these games the county won three, the last, in 1885 at Trent Bridge, by an innings and 46 runs. The ground has staged North v. South fixtures and nine Test Matches including six with Australia, who again will be met by England in this Centenary year of the ground.

The first Australian side who visited England in 1878 began their tour at Trent Bridge and Nottinghamshire won by an innings and 14 runs. Alfred Shaw and Fred Morley, bowling unchanged, sent down 187 overs and three balls with such accuracy of length that the Australians scored only 139 runs in their two efforts.

From the inception of the County competition, Nottinghamshire have won, or tied for, the Championship twelve times. Probably no other county ever had a greater match-winning eleven than were Nottinghamshire in the early eighties. In the match against Surrey in 1885 ten of the home side had already played for England against Australia or did so subsequently. The exception was Walter Wright, now the only survivor, who migrated South and played for Kent for many years. On several occasions in recent years Nottinghamshire have included ten scorers of hundreds and all the eleven who met Hampshire at Trent Bridge in 1932 were makers of centuries. Such an occurrence is unique and a photograph of the eleven inscribed 'The Centurions' Match' has its place in the pavilion among the pictures, prints, photographs and score cards of famous matches with many other historic cricket relics. This collection is considered the most extensive of its kind except the one at Lord's.

Also housed in the pavilion are some 360 volumes, all of historic importance and value, given by, or to, a member of the Committee and formed by him into a cricket library.

Space precludes mention of the galaxy of Nottinghamshire men who have played for their county at Trent Bridge, including those who have represented each of the other first-class Counties, during these hundred years, and the wonderful part they have taken in the game. To readers of *Wisden* their names, some of them immortal, are household words and their doings will be remembered whilst cricket is played.

No great Cricket Ground in these islands has a more charming situation than that of Trent Bridge. The well-wooded banks of the 'Silvery Trent' are within a bare stone's-throw and all its surroundings are most delightful and pleasant. The accommodation and amenities for public and players alike are more than ample. The playing area exceeds six and a half acres. Its well laid and seasoned turf provides extremely good wickets and it is excellent for fielding. In view of these many advantages, unanimous local opinion—widely shared by visitors—considers Trent Bridge a ground second to none in the Country—apart from Lord's. During the century of its existence, Trent Bridge has been the scene of many very stern and heroic contests, helping to make cricket history.

All first-class Nottinghamshire fixtures with one exception now take place at Trent Bridge, giving an average of 44 days' play a season. Most of the second eleven and club and ground matches are played there without charge for admission and for some eighty years leading local clubs have had their headquarters on the ground.

Throughout the summer, except on County match days, the general public are admitted to the ground without charge—a privilege, much used and warmly appreciated, which constantly revives glorious traditions and hallowed memories. May this continue so long as the best of all games is played.

CRICKET AT THE CROSS ROADS [1939]

BY D. G. BRADMAN

The 1939 Almanack was to be the last edited by Brookes, who retired for reasons which have never been explained. Certainly it was nothing to do with the current health of the publication, which maintained a sales figure of 12,000 in its cheap edition for the second year in succession. But the retirement of Brookes was symbolic, for it meant that the last vestiges of the old Cricket Report Agency were fading into history. The big attraction of the 1939 Wisden was an essay by Don Bradman with the title 'Cricket at the Cross Roads'. As cricket has always been at the crossroads, this banner must have puzzled most readers, who were not especially aware of any new crisis approaching. But Bradman was being brilliantly perceptive when he suggested in his essay that cricket must look to its guns in the days ahead because competition from other public attractions was bound to become fiercer by the year. The cricket world generally remained unaware that danger beckoned for another generation at least, and Bradman's realisation of what might be coming was typical of his observant, analytical mind.

He also lent his voice to the chorus of condemnation of doped wickets which made matches either endless or pointless; made some inscrutable remarks concerning the possibility that the luck of the toss might be replaced by a rota system; and argued against the quaintness of English score-boards in favour of the huge displays on the major Australian grounds. When he wrote these reflections, Bradman had just completed the third of his four tours of England, and returned the most spectacular statistics. He had batted twenty six times, scored thirteen centuries, including three double centuries, and ended with an average of 115.66, more than 40 points ahead of his nearest rival, Walter Hammond.

THE EDITOR of *Wisden* has honoured me by asking for a contribution from my pen. He has left the subject of the article to me, but in doing so has helpfully made suggestions regarding various phases of cricket which are to-day the cause of much discussion. As I looked through some suggestions, I conceived the title of this article. It is intended to convey a meaning but not to be misunderstood.

No matter how much we love cricket and desire to regard it as a friendly pastime we cannot disassociate its future, at least in the first-class category, from the cold, hard facts of finance. Nor can we blind ourselves to the fact that at this very moment public support for cricket (possibly excepting Test cricket, around which there is special glamour) suggests either that cricket is becoming less attractive or other forms of entertainment are gaining ground. It is a state of affairs calling for very serious consideration from player and legislator alike.

I am all in favour of 'hastening slowly' and have admired the peaceful but purposeful way in which cricket has for so long been administered in England. Nevertheless, I cannot help feeling that with the quickening of modern tempo, the more Americanised trend which is demanding speed, action and entertainment value, it behoves all of us to realise we are the custodians of the welfare of cricket and must guard its future even more zealously than its present.

No matter what we may desire individually, we cannot arrest nor impede the tenor of everyday life whether it be in business or sport. With such thoughts uppermost in my mind, my reflections are intended to convey the impressions gleaned by an Australian who will naturally view things from a slightly different angle to the average Englishman. Also my opinions are based upon experience in the middle allied to contact with administrative offices and the public.

DURATION OF TEST MATCHES

One of the most debated subjects at the moment is whether Test Matches should be limited or played out. Considerable colour has been lent to this particular aspect of cricket because of the remarkable happenings at the Oval last August. I have always held the opinion that it is futile to expect Australian teams to travel many thousands of miles to compete in a series of matches for 'The Ashes,' and yet play under conditions which allow quite a big possibility of one match deciding the rubber, especially when that result may depend entirely on the weather and be inconsistent with the degree of skill otherwise displayed. But I rather doubt whether the big issue is limited or played-out Tests. I think the first consideration is the mental outlook of the individual who can, if he chooses, spoil any game by his interpretation of its character. And secondly, would it not be a better game if, by virtue of rules and conditions, the possibility of a match extending beyond three or four days became extremely improbable?

If these problems were attended to, maybe the other one would disappear. At least, I think it very largely would. There can be no doubt that in recent years changes have taken place in the methods adopted for preparing certain English wickets. The popular term used for the latest and questionable method is 'doping the wicket.' From my experience on this tour and discussions with people who are in a position to know, **I am satisfied that some groundsmen can, and do 'dope' their wickets. The effect is to produce an absolutely dead and lifeless wicket, useless to any type of bowler and not conducive to stroke-play by the batsman.**

It is imperative that we should have wickets which are true and not dangerous (fiery wickets produce a crop of accidents, rob batsmen of confidence and drive them into less dangerous sports), but let them be reasonably natural and amenable to some fair degree of wear, not the sort upon which the world's best spin-bowlers can't turn the ball an inch until the pitch is three days' old. This difficulty with wickets mainly applies to Test matches. County matches are usually played on wickets offering some degree of equality, whilst practice wickets on most English grounds receive so little consideration that one has virtually no chance of getting real practice except in the middle. The scales are not evenly balanced, and the question of wickets needs serious consideration.

A prominent English International, writing in the daily Press, declared: 'Give me another half hour of Leeds and let me forget the Oval'. He probably conveys in that statement the innermost thoughts of the majority of the players and the public. I agree with him, if I may add 1934 and 1938 after 'The Oval.' I do that to ensure that my concurrence will not be misconstrued. At the Oval in 1934 we Australians accomplished approximately what England did in 1938, so that I have experienced both winning and losing under those conditions. People left the Oval tired of watching the unequal fight. They did it when Ponsford and I were batting in 1934. They did it when Hutton and Hardstaff were batting in 1938. Not so at Leeds. The match was one succession of thrills. People fought to get into the ground, not out of it. Their hearts beat frantically with excitement, mine along with the rest of them. Did anyone think of that curse of modern cricket—batting averages? No! It was the game which mattered. Australia won. She nearly lost and if she had it would have been a greater game still. It was stirring, exhilarating cricket. **There wasn't time to think of timeless Tests at Leeds.**

VIEWS ON L.B.W.

I believe the time is imminent when another change in the L.B.W. law should be made. When our forefathers devised this beautiful game, I have no doubt they intended it to remain a contest between bat and ball. But evidently, to use the words of an eminent politician, 'they didn't make it clear,' and the practice of pad obstruction eventually reached such proportions that it became necessary to legislate against the use of pads.

Irrespective of where the batsman's pads or feet are, I believe that if a ball is pitched in a line between wicket and wicket or on the off-side of the wicket and would have hit the stumps but is prevented from doing so by part of the batsman's person (providing the ball has not first touched his bat or hand) the bowler is entitled to be rewarded. Under the existing law, that part of the batsman's person which is struck by the ball *must be between wicket and wicket.* Those last six words afford the batsman too much latitude.

An experiment could be tried with my suggestion similar to the experiment tried before the last alternation. I am confident that it would result in further reducing huge scores, increasing off-side shots, brightening the play and reducing the effectiveness of the purely defensive 'rabbit'. The leg-side may have to be considered in later years, but it would possibly be too drastic a step to alter both sides at once. Just prior to the introduction of the last alteration in the l.b.w. rule, there was a great deal of adverse comment about it. I then stated that these hypothetical ills would be found to disappear in practice. They did—and they would do so again.

Even if we assume a reasonably severe result and found county matches ending in two days, and the leading batting average dropping from 70 to 50, what would it matter? All figures would alter correspondingly and the gates for two days would exceed what they now are for three.

An experiment is going to be made with the eight ball over. It has been used in Australia for years, has proved a great success and saved a tremendous amount of time. The only people who can reasonably object to it are the fast bowlers. Whilst their claims may be reasonable, we must consider the welfare of the game itself before any of its component parts. And in any event, if the authorities consider that fast bowlers are going to be unjustly handicapped, there may be other ways of assisting them, such as by allowing a new ball earlier than after the scoring of 200 runs as at present.

We very frequently hear a suggestion that the old method of tossing should be dispensed with. If any person has grounds for objection, surely it is I, after my 1938 experiences, but, on the contrary, I favour retention of the present method. To enable one captain to know in advance which team would have the choice of batting would pave the way to so many undesirable possibilities that I do not think it worth while discussing.

A PLEA FOR MODERN SCORE BOARDS

I do, however, counsel very urgently the need of up-to-date scoring boards of the Australian type at your principal grounds. I have just been reading an article in a leading English cricket publication by a very well-known writer. He was describing the happenings in an important match at Lord's. After telling of a glorious innings by a young player, he wrote: 'I had no idea of his identity—there were no score-cards about at the time.' Subsequently, he told how he discovered the player's name.

Such a state of affairs to an Australian enthusiast is hard to comprehend. I am well aware of the forceful argument regarding the revenue produced from selling score-cards, but I submit that 10,000 spectators who do not need score-cards to tell them what is happening are going to be a happier and more virile advertisement for the game than 8,000 who do. Cricket needs to retain its present followers and to gain new ones. Modern scoring-boards would be a big help, and any temporary loss would be recouped eventually through the turnstiles.

There are many other factors upon which I could enlarge, such as playing hours, the number of matches, and so on. They are sure to form a basis for future debate and argument, but their importance is, for the present at any rate, subservient to other problems.

Whether my suggestions prove practicable or otherwise, time alone will tell. They are at least submitted in an honest endeavour to assist in ensuring that the game we all cherish so much will be enjoyed by future generations no less than our own.

I doubt if a happier series of Test matches than the 1938 series has been played and I am quite sure the administrators of England and Australia are more closely united now than ever before. To me, therefore, it seems an appropriate time to try and achieve a greater measure of uniformity of opinion upon current cricket problems.

MY HAPPY CRICKET LIFE [1939]

BY FRANK E. WOOLLEY

The season was a sadly sentimental affair because of the retirement of yet another of the great players, who followed what was rapidly becoming a convention of Wisden and published his farewell recollections. Frank Woolley (1887–1978) was one of the most gifted cricketers in English history, a left-handed bat of unsurpassed ease and elegance, holder of the world record for catching, 1,015 dismissals, almost all of them in the slips. And although the younger followers of the game in the 1930s might have remained unaware of it, Woolley in his youth had been an outstanding left-arm slow bowler, a foil to the genius Colin Blythe, but good enough to take 100 wickets in a season eight times between 1910 and 1923, and claim 83 wickets for England in Test matches.

It was as a batsman that Woolley possessed genius. Neville Cardus, reduced to rapturous awe by the apparently effortless nature of Woolley's style, used to swear that Woolley never clumped the ball, never hit it, but merely stroked it away with the gentlest of touches. In a famous appreciation of Woolley, published when the Kent star was coming to the end of his playing days, Cardus wrote of his hero's technique that 'the very brevity of summer is in it', an odd reflection on a batsman who managed, despite the brevity, to hit nearly 60,000 runs including 145 centuries. Ruefully Cardus later confessed:

> When I read to Woolley the passage in my essay on him about the miracle that happened whenever he stayed in three hours, I think he resented in particular the sentence: 'So with Woolley's cricket; the lease of it is in the hands of the special providence which looks after things that will not look after themselves'. He said he had played many long innings, and I rather think he suspected I was casting doubt on the efficiency of his back-play.

Although Woolley firmly believed that his cricketing career was over when he composed his essay, it is touching to see how wistfully he leaves the door open to the Kent selectors by musing on the chance that Kent might yet find itself short of players and ask him back. They never did, but there remained other ways of passing back through the pavilion gates onto the field of play. It was the outbreak of war and the resultant improvisatory nature of the cricket that followed which saw Woolley enjoy one last day at the crease. On August 10th, 1940 at Lord's, a match was staged between those two receptacles for whatever cricketing flotsam happened to be passing through town on leave from more rigorous duties, The British Empire X1 and London Counties. London Counties made up its numbers with the inclusion of several veterans like Joe Hulme and Jack Durston, who emerged from retirement with predictable glee. But it was the re-emergence through the white wicket gate of Frank Woolley which roused 13,000 spectators to something more subtle than enthusiasm. The star of the opposition was Sergeant Denis Compton, and these two paragons, the survivor from a long-vanished golden age and the youthful hero of days yet to come, who now performed the most exquisite dance of the generations. Compton batted first and had reached 60 before he was caught off the bowling of Woolley. London Counties then batted and Woolley scored 38 before being caught off the bowling of Compton.

Woolley remained an impressive figure of a man right into extreme old age, straight-backed and forthright in his opinions, as handsome as ever he was in the days when he and Blythe would run through the opposition in an hour or two. In his eighty-fifth year he flew to Australia to watch the Tests, and a few months later married for a second time. His first wife had died ten years earlier, and he now took a second bride in the person of an American widow called Martha Morse. The two of them settled in Halifax, Novia Scotia, where Woolley died in October 1978, it being his ironic fate to live out his last years in a country which could have understood nothing of his greatness.

THE time has come for me to say farewell to cricket as a player, and I readily acquiesce to the invitation of the Editor of *Wisden* to record some of the greatest moments of my career. It is a severe wrench leaving the game which I have enjoyed so much. My whole life in cricket from beginning to end has been 32 years of happiness, apart from 1915–1918. I have a lot for which to be thankful, having always enjoyed good health, and I have no regrets at all.

Even my last season in first-class cricket brought me memorable days when I touched my best form, but I do think it is best to say good-bye before I fail to satisfy my admirers. I believe I could have gone on for another season or two, but I might have struck a bad patch and then many people would have said, 'Why doesn't he retire?'

I will not say that I will never turn out again, because Kent, who have always treated me kindly, might—when short of players—invite me to play and in that event I could not refuse. There were occasions last summer, however, when I felt the strain of a long day in the field, especially after I had made a big score.

DEBUT AS A BOWLER

It is delving into the dim and distant past when I made my first acquaintance with the game, but it all stands out very clearly in my memory. I never played serious cricket at school, but I was born close to the Angel ground at Tonbridge and I always took a keen interest in the game. In those days I used to wander into the ground and, after leaving school at 14, never missed an opportunity of bowling at the nets.

My heart and soul were in cricket. I was fortunate enough to bowl to Colin Blythe and he mentioned my name to the Kent manager, Mr. Tom Pawley. That was in 1902, but as I had rather outgrown my strength at that age, being very tall and thin, they allowed me to attend the ground on mornings only. In 1903 I became a regular member of the staff. Colin Blythe was without doubt one of the greatest left-hand bowlers I have ever seen. He had a perfect action and run-up. I do not think I copied him. His style was so different from mine.

Curiously enough, my first match for Kent, which was against Lancashire at Old Trafford in 1906, came about through an accident to Blythe at Brighton. Kent wired for me. I was reckoned purely a left-arm slow bowler and I shall never forget my debut. The great John Tyldesley hit 295 not out, the highest innings of his career, and some funny things happened. We lost the toss and I was put at third man. Tyldesley cut one very hard, but misjudging it altogether the ball hit me on the chest. Our captain, Mr. C. H. B. Marsham, feeling sorry for me, moved me to mid-off and to mid-on; in each place I dropped a skier, although one was off a no-ball.

Johnny Tyldesley was hitting us all over the place when he was joined by the last man, W. Worsley, the wicket-keeper, who was reckoned the worst batsman in the world. We all wanted to see Tyldesley get 300. I was bowling at one end and our captain called us together and said, 'Who can we put on the other end to bowl a maiden over to Worsley so that Tyldesley can get his 300?' The cry went up 'Put "Punter" on,' and he was told to bowl away from the stumps. His first four balls were well over to the off, but to everyone's amazement, including 'Punter' Humphries, the fifth swung in viciously and knocked down Worsley's leg stump. So Tyldesley did not realise his ambition. My analysis was one for 103 and Humphries had one for 101. He came in for some rare 'chipping' in the dressing room for having to be satisfied with only Worsley's wicket. In our first innings I was bowled third ball for a 'duck', but after a rather bad beginning I had a satisfactory last day when I made 64.

My part in the next match against Somerset at Gravesend can be best described by quoting *Wisden* of 1907 which says: 'Somerset in their second innings began well, but collapsed before the bowling of Woolley.' My bag was six wickets for 39. The following game, against Surrey at the Oval, which we won was probably the deciding factor that season in Kent winning the Championship for the first time. Again we lost the toss and I opened the bowling with Fielder. I had never seen Tom Hayward. I imagined he was a tall athletic looking man and when five wickets were down I said to Fielder, 'When does Tom Hayward come in?' He replied, 'That was the first chap you bowled out.' Actually in that innings I bowled Hayward, Hayes and Goatly. It was a comparatively low scoring match and I could do little wrong. I went in number eight, made Kent's top score, 72; then took five more wickets; Kent wanted 131 and I was in at the death. I remember being dropped by Jack Crawford when one, but I got 23 not out and we scrambled home with one wicket to spare.

Those were the great days when plenty of amateurs could spare time for cricket. I do not think there are so many good players in the game now as before the War. In the old days we were probably educated in cricket in a far more serious way than now. For the purpose of giving the younger people my idea of the difference I will put up Walter Hammond, England's captain, as an example. Before 1914 there were something like 30 players up to his standard and he would have been in the England team only if at the top of his form. I make these remarks without casting the slightest reflection on Hammond. He is a grand player and one of the greatest all-round cricketers since the War—in fact, the greatest.

I doubt whether English cricket has really recovered from the effects of the War. You see, we missed half a generation, and since then young men have found many other ways of occupying their leisure hours. Still, I believe it is only a passing phase and cricket will one day produce an abundance of great players.

TWO-DAY COUNTY MATCHES

There is little wrong with the game itself. Just a question of the way it is played. It is amazing how the public steadfastly refuse to attend the third day of a match when so often the last day produces the best and most exciting cricket. Certain sides are to blame for batting too long and leaving the chance of a sporting finish impossible. The time may arrive when the third day will be abolished. I am fully aware that in 1919, the first season after the War, two-day matches proved a failure, but then we played three matches a week and stumps were not drawn until 7 p.m. or 7.30 p.m. and everyone became weary of the experiment. I think if the counties played matches of two days' duration with a day's rest between each for travelling, it would be a step towards better cricket. We have been suffering from a surfeit of cricket. There are too many match days and the players get jaded.

Touching on another personal subject I have been asked if I can explain why I was dismissed so many times in the nineties'. The statisticians inform me that I was out 35 times between 90 and 99 and I am also told I am credited with 89 'ducks'. With regard to those 'nineties', I can honestly say that with me it was never a question of the 'nervous nineties.' Lots of times I was out through forcing the game. We were never allowed to play for averages in the Kent side or take half-an-hour or more to get the last ten runs under normal conditions. We always had to play the game and play for the team. It is a Kent tradition.

TWO '90's' IN A TEST

As a matter of fact I consider the two finest innings I ever played were in the second test against Australia at Lord's in 1921 when I was out for 95 and 93. I do not think I ever worked harder at any match during my career to get runs as I did then, nor did I ever have to face in one game such consistently fast bowlers as the Australian pair, Gregory and MacDonald. Square cuts which ordinarily would have flashed to the boundary earned only two and I believe that those two innings would have been worth 150 apiece in a county match.

I was not depressed when they got me out. I have always taken my dismissals as part of the game. In the first innings I was in the 'eighties' when I was joined by the last man, Jack Durston. It was my own fault completely that I lost my wicket. Mailey bowled me a full toss to the off, I walked down the pitch and, stepping to the on to force the ball past extra cover, I missed it and that fine wicket-keeper, H. Carter, eagerly accepted the opportunity to stump me. I was rather unlucky in the second innings when again I fell to Mailey. The ball stuck in his hand and dropped half-way on the leg side. I hit it pretty plumb between square leg and mid-on and just there was standing 'Stork' Hendry. As I made the shot he jumped in the air and up went his right hand. The ball hit him, I think, on the wrist, and he lost his balance. The ball went up ten feet and as he was lying on the ground it fell in his lap and he caught it. He was the only man on the leg side and I think the shot would have carried for six. It was a marvellous catch.

In 1934 I was the first winner of the 'Lawrence Trophy' which Sir Walter Lawrence offers each year. As it tends to encourage brighter cricket I cannot see that it does any harm to the game, although there was no idea of the trophy in my mind when I won it. We were playing Northamptonshire at Dover and were pushed for time. I seized every chance and reached the hundred in 63 minutes.

It is often argued that left-handed batsmen have an advantage compared with the right-handers. I do not agree with this contention. When the turf is worn the right hand leg-break bowlers and left-arms slow bowlers are able to pitch the ball into the footholes of the bowlers who have operated at the other end. Right-handed batsmen can let these balls hit their pads, but the left-handers must use their bats. Perhaps the new l.b.w. rule has not helped us there, but the amended law does not worry me though in my opinion it has not improved the game. As for further extending the l.b.w. rule I think it would make a farce of the game.

In many quarters surprise was expressed last season that at the age of 51 I went in Number one. Until then I had never been in first regularly, though I have always preferred that place. Beginning as a bowler made Kent place me four or five in the order and moreover the county were always rich in opening batsmen. Consequently my wish to start the innings was denied until 1938. Because Kent have experienced their bad times against fast bowling the cry has gone round that we cannot play the fast men, but I think if you search the records you will also find that Kent have hit a tremendous lot of runs off fast bowling. Perhaps our opponents, encouraged with the idea that we did not fancy ourselves against pace, have bowled with their tails up. Again I must emphasise that Kent always endeavour to play sporting cricket, and trying to make runs off that type of bowling must sometimes have contributed to our downfall. It was never a policy of the Kent team that the pitch *must* be occupied all day after winning the toss.

I cannot let this opportunity pass without placing on record how much I have enjoyed my cricket with Kent. If I was a youngster starting as a batsman I think I should like to play always at the Oval, but the Kent grounds, with their natural decorations of beautiful trees, members' tents flying their own colours and bedecked with flowers, lend the right tone to cricket. I am devoting most of this coming summer to coaching the boys at King's School, Canterbury, and look forward to the experience, especially as it is a Kent school.

CRICKET CONUNDRUMS [1939]

BY A. E. R. GILLIGAN

In capturing Don Bradman and Frank Woolley for his List of Contents, Brookes could hardly have made his editorial exit in more impressive style. And yet, from a purely journalistic viewpoint, both Bradman and Woolley might be said to have been upstaged by the third contributor to the 1939 Almanack, the most distinguished of the three Gilligan brothers. Arthur Edward Robert Gilligan (1894–1976) was a Gentleman-cricketer who enjoyed a brilliant career at Dulwich College as athlete and cricketer playing in the eleven for four years, and as captain in the last two. Then came the war, and it was not until 1919 that he went up to Cambridge, won his Blue, and took 6 Oxford wickets for 52 with his fast bowling. In the same season, going in last for the University, he hit a century off the Sussex bowling. In 1920 he joined Sussex, appearing for them for the next twelve years, serving as captain from 1922 to 1929, during which period he advanced steadily through the ranks of the country's fast bowlers. In 1924 he was made captain of England against the South African tourists, and announced his international entrance with one of the most startling individual feats ever seen in Tests. At Edgbaston he opened the bowling with his Sussex colleague Maurice Tate, and the pair of them proceeded to destroy the opposition utterly, bowling them out for 30 runs on a good wicket. Gilligan's share was 6 wickets for 7 runs.

It was later that summer that he sustained the injury which put paid to his effectiveness as an all-rounder and so tragically curtailed his athletic career. Batting for the Gentlemen against the Players at the Oval, he was struck over the heart by the innocuous medium-pace off-spin of the Worcestershire bowler Pearson. Although in great distress, Gilligan foolishly insisted on resuming his innings. He went on to make 112 in the second innings but his refusal to retire from the game proved disastrous; he later wrote of his insistence to continue with the game: 'That was probably the worst thing I ever did'. His older brother, F. W., played against him in two Varsity matches and kept wicket for Essex for several seasons, while the youngest of the three brothers, A. H. H. succeeded him as captain of Sussex, took an M.C.C. side to Australia, in 1929–30, and was to father a daughter who married the England captain Peter May. Among Arthur Gilligan's extra-cricketing distinctions was his appointment as President of the English Golf Union and of the County Cricketers' Golfing Society. But so tireless was he in the cause of cricket that he might almost be said to have enjoyed a second successful career, so prolific did he become as a lecturer and after-dinner speaker on all manner of sporting occasions. He continued to campaign in this way for cricket for the rest of his life, and in 1967 became President of M.C.C. It seems clear that in the course of his wanderings among the cricket clubs of England Gilligan heard many good cricket stories, some of them marginally taller than others. It seems just as clear that one of the most effective methods of fundraising for cricketing charities, then as now, was the organising of cricket quiz contests. It was the fruits of these labours which provided Gilligan with the raw material for one of the most diverting if exasperating features ever to appear in Wisden. In the years since, there have been hundreds of after-dinner speakers wise enough to arm themselves with a few of Arthur Gilligan's outrageous paradoxes.

WHENEVER I have given cricket talks in different parts of England, I have always devoted at least a quarter of the time to the many cricket problems and difficulties caused by wrong interpretation of the rules. During my experiences, I have collected quite a useful list of cricket conundrums which I shall discuss in this article.

First of all, I remember being asked rather an important question at a meeting some twelve years ago: 'Why doesn't the M.C.C. legislate for many of the doubtful points arising from the Laws of Cricket?' I promised that I would put this problem before the Secretary of the M.C.C. himself and accordingly went to see Mr. W. Findlay.

His answer was an excellent one, and I can think of no better way of starting my article than by setting it out here and now. He said:—'Why should the M.C.C. legislate for doubtful points arising from the Cricket Laws? Our duty is to see that the Rules of Cricket are made to cover only the rightful interpretation of the very spirit of the game, and anything which borders on unfairness can never be legislated for by the premier cricket club.'

I think that everyone will agree that Mr. Findlay's outlook on so important a question was absolutely correct and that we should not endeavour to get round the rules by what may be termed unfair methods. Therefore, I shall try to keep my cricket conundrums on amusing lines, and prove that all of them are covered by existing rules of the game.

ONE BALL: FIVE MEN OUT

Do you know how five men can be dismissed by one ball bowled? Of course, you must allow a certain amount of licence in this respect, but actually several years ago in a county match, when play was due to resume, it was found that one of the overnight not-out batsmen had taken a wrong tube-train, and at half past eleven was miles away from the 'scene of conflict'.

The umpires, on appeal, ruled that the batsman was 'absent' and could not continue his innings. There is the first man out. The next comes in and the bowler delivers a no-ball, which naturally does not count as a legitimate delivery. The striker hits it towards cover-point and calls his partner for a run. His partner, seeing that there is not the slightest chance of a quick single, sends back the striker, who unfortunately slips up and falls to the ground. The ball is returned to the wicket-keeper and No. 2 is run out, still with no legitimate ball being bowled. No. 3 arrives and hits the first ball, a half-volley, with terrific force straight back at his partner, who receives the ball right in the middle of the forehead. The ball bounces in the air and mid-off catches it easily. No. 3 is out, caught; No. 4 is also out—knocked out—and is carried off the field unconscious, and when No. 5 (who is No. 11 on the batting list) comes to the wicket, he finds he has no one with whom to bat. So there you have five men out with one ball bowled.

WHO IS OUT?

Now here is another very interesting poser. Jones is bowling to Smith, with Robinson the non-striker. Smith hits a very hard return catch to the bowler, who just touches the ball and deflects it on to the wicket. Robinson is out of his crease and the ball, without touching the ground, ricochets off the stumps into the hands of mid-on.

Who is out? Is Smith out, caught, or is Robinson run out?

I have asked over a hundred people this riddle and practically 90 per cent give Robinson run out. I put the point to two first-class umpires, Frank Chester and Jack Newman, last season at Hastings, and they replied simultaneously: 'Smith is out, caught'; and that is the correct answer. (M.C.C. *have ruled this as 'caught.'—Editor*).

What about this one? The striker plays the ball a few yards up the wicket and calls his partner for a sharp single. Mid-off dashed in and the striker, seeing that a run is impossible, turns back to his crease, but in so doing accidentally kicks the ball into his wicket. With the striker well out of his ground, the bails drop off and the umpire gives him out.

The question before you now is: How is the striker out?

When asked for an immediate decision, many people say: 'Oh he is run out.' That is wrong, because the ball has not been touched by any of the fieldsmen after the striker has hit it. Others maintain that he is out, hit wicket. Again that is incorrect, because *the ball* has broken the wicket. The correct decision is therefore *bowled*—played on. It is just the same as if the batsman had played the ball on to his foot, from whence it rebounds on to his stumps.

HALF CAUGHT?

The subject of another conundrum actually happened in a match in New Zealand. The last two batsmen are in, the last ball of the game is about to be delivered, and two runs are necessary for victory. The bowler runs up to bowl and sends down a good length ball to the striker, who takes a terrific swipe at it, sending the ball a tremendous way in the air. When it has reached the apex of its flight, the ball breaks in two pieces. Mid-on shouts 'Mine' and catches half the ball. 'You're out,' says the fielder. 'No, I am not,' retorts the batsman. 'The other half of the ball is on the ground.'

An appeal is made to the umpire, who rightly decides that this particular delivery should not count and sends for another ball, as much as possible like the one which has been discarded, and play is resumed. The bowler is so excited by the occurrence that he sends down a full toss to leg, the batsman hits it straight to the square-leg boundary, and the match is won by the batting side.

This case was sent to the M.C.C. Committee for a ruling, the result being that the umpire's action was unanimously upheld.

HOLDING ON!

I remember George Cox, the old Sussex player, telling me of the following remarkable case which was submitted to him. The batting side require 50 runs for victory and the last two men are together, with the last over of the match to be bowled. No. 11 is a complete 'rabbit', but manages somehow or other to survive five balls. As the bowler is running up to bowl the final ball, No. 11 waits till the ball is delivered, throws away his bat and, turning, holds on the bails with his hands. The ball just snicks the off-stump and travels slowly to the slips.

The batsman removes his hands from the bails, picks up his bat and says: 'Well, that is a drawn game.'

An appeal is made to the umpire, who scratches his head, and the batsman, noticing this, declares loudly: 'There is nothing in the rules which says a batsman cannot hold his bails on.'

'Oh, yes, there is,' says the umpire. 'I give you out for unfair play, Rule 43.' So the match is won by the fielding side.

Some years ago, when giving a cricket talk to the Portsmouth Umpires' Association, I was asked to give an instant decision upon this perplexing problem, and I wonder how many of you can do likewise: 'How can a batsman hit the ball twice, yet score runs and not be given out by the umpire?'

Knowing that a striker may be out for hitting the ball twice without any attempt at a run being made—that is to say, he hits the ball a second time before it touches the ground, and is out for obstructing the field—I was momentarily at a loss to give the correct answer. Suddenly, like a flash, I remembered, and said: 'If the ball has been struck twice lawfully, in defence of his wicket, and an overthrow is made, the striker is entitled to any runs that follow.'

A roar of laughter went up, and I thought I had made a mistake until the questioner explained to me that he and his colleagues had gone carefully through the rules before the meeting in the hope of catching me out!

TEST MATCH CONTRETEMPS

I have already mentioned that, if the umpires agree that a ball in use is unfit for play, they have the right to allow the substitution of another ball as much as possible similar to the one discarded.

I recall that, in the second Test Match between England and Australia at Melbourne in 1925, after only 15 runs were on the board—I was bowling at the time—I noticed that a great piece of leather had come off the ball. I immediately showed the ball to Umpire Bob Crockett, who consulted his colleague and a brand new ball was brought out.

Before lunch that day we had no fewer than four new balls with the total no more than 87. When we adjourned, we discovered that, by mistake, a wrong packet of balls had been delivered to the ground and that we had No. 3 grade cricket balls instead of No. 1. It was agreed between 'Herby' Collins and myself to play out the first innings with both sides using the No. 3 grade variety, and it is interesting now to record that we used eight new balls before the score reached 200 and Australia had seven.

I do not think that any similar incident can be brought to mind of the ball being changed so frequently in a Test or any other match. It came as quite a relief when we embarked upon the second innings.

THE MAN WITH THE WOODEN LEG

In conclusion, let me tell you of a problem which Alec Kennedy, Hampshire's noted all-rounder, propounded to members of Frank Mann's M.C.C. Team on the outward voyage to South Africa in 1922. This is it. A batsman with his back foot well within his crease hits the ball hard to cover-point and does not move out of his ground. The ball is returned to the wicket-keeper, who whips off the bails; on appeal, the square-leg umpire gives the striker out.

When I replied that it could not be possible for the striker to be given out if his back foot was still inside his crease, Kennedy said: 'Oh, yes, he can. You see the batsman has got a wooden leg!'

'But,' I expostulated, 'even if he has a wooden leg, that is still part and parcel of his body.'

Kennedy laughed and replied: 'That is quite true: but you see, by virtue of his having a wooden leg, he was entitled to a runner, and the runner was out of his ground. Rule 39 covers that.'

There are many more cricket conundrums which puzzle a great number of cricketers, all of them excellently explained in the sixpenny blue edition of the Laws of Cricket with decisions and interpretations authorized by the M.C.C., so I will not dwell upon any contained therein.

Lastly, let me commend to every cricketer a thorough understanding of the rules of the game, and let us not forget the excellent example of Don Bradman, the Australian captain, who has actually passed an umpire's examination with flying colours.

PART THREE

1940 – 1946

NOTES ON THE 1939 SEASON [1940]

BY R. C. ROBERTSON-GLASGOW

The production of the 1940 edition of Wisden presented the identical problems confronting Sydney Pardon a generation earlier, of producing a wartime publication devoted to the routines of peace. The one advantage held by the later Almanack was that because the Second World War opened with the lull, comparatively speaking, of the Phoney War, the obituary columns were nothing like so heavy with the weight of death as the tragic 1915 edition has been. There was another, very striking contrast between the worlds of 1915 and 1940. On the outbreak of the First World War there had been a demand, amounting to hysteria, for every able-bodied man to join the colours, or, if not actually getting into uniform, then at least to be seen to be thoroughly miserable. The crass assumption that the spectacle of a game of cricket was in some unspecified way an unpatriotic and even treasonable act had had two effects, the total disappearance from the fields of England of anything remotely resembling a first-class cricket match, and the acute embarrassment of a War Office overwhelmed by tens of thousands more volunteers than it knew what to do with. At least the compilers of the 1940 Wisden went about their work in the comforting knowledge that this time rather more common sense was being applied.

How would Wilfrid Brookes arrange his contents? In the event, Brookes did not arrange anything, having stepped down from the editorship after wrapping up the 1939 edition. No reasons have ever been given for his departure, but there are one or two hints of a breach of relations between the Almanack and its editor. In the past, only death had deposed the editors of Wisden and each burial had been followed by fulsome obituaries, but when Brookes died in 1955, the notice in the Almanack was terse to the point of being tight-lipped:

> BROOKES, Wilfrid H; who died in a nursing home at Putney on May 28, 1955, aged 60, was Editor of Wisden from 1936 to 1939, and for several years until the outbreak of the Second World War a partner in the Cricket Reporting Agency.

These brief notes tell us nothing, except perhaps to make a point which till now may have gone unnoticed, that by the standards of Wisden, Brookes had been a youngish man to accede to the editorship when he did. Neither is there any enlightenment offered by the preparatorial note to the 1940 edition. Instead of the Conventional encomium for the departing editor, there is only:

> At the end of the season Mr. Wilfrid H. Brookes resigned from the editorship, and from the Cricket Reporting Agency.

The note is written by Haddon Whitaker, son of the J. Whitaker whose publishing company had in 1938 taken over the responsibility for printing the Almanack. As Brookes was still only 44 years old at the time he severed his connections both with the Almanack and with the Agency, he was presumably not ready for retirement. And yet nothing more is heard of him. It must be said that Haddon Whitaker's first attempt at editing proved to be a happy event. Limited as he was by the rationing of paper, which meant that this print run of the cheap edition had to be limited to 8,000, Whitaker produced a book of nearly 900 pages, and was so parsimonious in his surrender of editorial space that even the inside back cover was packed with information. Neither did he feel fitted to contribute the traditional 'Editor's Notes'. Instead he passed on the duty to one of the outstanding cricket writers in England, Raymond Charles Robertson-Glasgow, already respected at that time as a columnist for 'The Morning Post' and 'The Daily Telegraph'. In an earlier incarnation, Crusoe, as he was usually called, appeared as an all-rounder in the Chaterhouse elevens of 1918–19, went on to play for Oxford against Cambridge in the following four seasons, became a star of the Somerset side of the 1920s and represented Gentlemen against Players five times. His subsequent career as a cricket reporter and essayist was a delightful affair, lit with whimsy and humour as well as the wisdom of long experience.

In time he published several collections of his best work, notably the series of thumbnail sketches of the great players of the 1920s and 1930s, 'Cricket Prints' and 'More Cricket Prints', and an outstanding autobiography, '46 Not Out'. Among his favourite funny stories about the game was one concerning the acquisition of his nickname. In a match between Somerset and Essex, he speedily dismissed the star amateur batsman C. P. McGahey, who returned to the pavilion and, when asked what had happened, replied: 'First ball, from a chap named Robinson Crusoe'. His death by suicide in the spring of 1965, in his sixty-fourth year, came as a tragic shock to the world of cricket.

So great was the thing which started, for us, on September 3rd last year, so pervasive of our thoughts, homes, even of our pastimes and sports, that to look back on the English cricket season of 1939 is like peeping curiously through the wrong end of a telescope at a very small but very happy world. It is a short six months since Constantine gave the England bowlers such a cracking at the Oval, like a strong man suddenly gone mad in a fielding-practice, but it might be six years, or sixteen; for we have jumped a dimension or two since then in both time and space.

It is true that throughout the season the rumble of War rolled louder and louder, that our guests the West Indies, excepting L. N. Constantine and E. A. Martindale, had to sail for home with seven matches unplayed, that in the County Championship several matches had to be abruptly cancelled; but, in a sense, it was a strangely happy season. There may have been more rain than is convenient to fast bowlers, thin shoes, or anxious secretaries; but, as is customary when great issues hang in the balance, men set themselves to a quiet but determined enjoyment. They turned to cricket as to an old friend, who gives you a seat, a glass of beer, and something sane to talk about. Perhaps some of them wondered when, if ever again, they would watch on the Mound at Lord's and borrow from a small boy in a school cap a score card to see what it was all about, and find strange entries and pencilled mysteries; when, once more, they would sit on someone else's sandwiches in the tram that sways to Kennington, or trip over the marquee-ropes at the Saffrons, or smell the sea at Hove, or argue at Old Trafford.

There was much cricket worth the seeing. The advice, both official and unsolicited, given to those who control or direct the County teams, had not, as so often before, rebounded with hardly an echo from the walls of complacency and self-satisfaction. There was a renaissance of the liberal attitude to the game and of the generous technique in batting. The fielding, if we forget a few hours of pandemonium and chaos in the Third Test, was of a high standard generally. The bowling, it must be allowed, was at least no worse than in the preceding years. There are two or three English bowlers who are nearly great, and perhaps a dozen who are undeniably good. But few of them are young, as bowlers must be young. There is hardly one man, unless some are lost in the meadows and villages, to cause the batsman to fidget with his cap-peak and shirt-buttons, the wicket-keeper's gloves to go off like an exploded paper-bag, and the spectator to suck in the long-drawn breath. Yes; there is one, K. Farnes, of Essex. But not only is he a bowler of, as it were, high-geared temperament, and difficult to stimulate to utmost powers, but also during most of last summer he was a full-time schoolmaster, and had betaken his art at half-pace to the practice-nets.

Of great leg-break bowlers there was none, in the sense that Leonard Braund and, within certain inexplicable limits, Freeman (A. P.) were great; not to mention the masters of leg-break bowling of Australia and South Africa, men who in their prime suffered but little from variation of form, who were often wonderful, and, even when they weren't, yet remained bowlers who *mattered*. Their very name was worth two or three wickets, and if they had come out of the pavilion with a gouty foot in a carpet-slipper, they would still have been feared, as the sick Napoleon was feared at Waterloo. There was nothing of that sort in England last summer, though there were some half-dozen leg-break bowlers who, if you happened upon them for a half-hour in a match, might almost persuade you into the belief that you had found the right thing at last. There was Sims, of Middlesex; with stuttering run-up but beautifully easy action, almost too easy; he could be difficult, sometimes, for overs on end; cheerful, willing, nearly tireless. Something here, surely; but the great moment and the great batsmen have too often found him wanting in the last indefinable gifts of temperament and art. Then Wright, of Kent; more dangerous, at best, than Sims; a vicious spinner of the leg-break at an unusually high speed; less potent and artful in the googly; failing, sometimes, through straining the possibility of spin and so losing length;

always clutching at the skirts of greatness, but so far never quite holding on. And Mitchell (T. B.), of Derbyshire; so natural a leg-breaker that the ball almost spins when it sees him; unlike most others of his kind, he resorts often to genuine off-break; a genius, certainly; but quixotic and unreliable, and quite happy suddenly to desert art and purpose to argue privately with invisible fate. There is none quite like him, but his value has too often been frittered away in individualism. F. R. Brown, of Surrey, a very strong player of games, had days of inspirations both as a leg-breaker and a fierce driver. He bowled very finely against West Indies for Surrey at the Oval, sustaining length, direction, and acuteness of spin for long spells. Business prevented him from playing in all matches, but his record was good; 86 wickets at 23.34, 946 runs at 33.78. Few genuine amateurs can afford to play regularly, and Brown's form for some years would have been less variable if he had had the opportunity of regular play, for, decidedly unlike some modern cricketers, he has the heart and the will for the grimmest fight, and the optimism to surmount the occasion.

There are others; some of promise and fair performance, some, I fear, unmistakably launched on the irrevocable decline that all bowlers know. Those who may think these judgments of English bowling a little harsh should remind themselves of the steep and rarely crossed hill between County and England form. The great men of the past set no easy standard.

RICHNESS OF BATTING

The thinness of the bowling was perhaps exaggerated by the richness of the batting. A strict observer, a first-class batsman of a generation ago, considers that the first dozen or so of modern English batsmen are in sum the equals at least of those of his own time, about 1905–14. The old freedom of stroke-play, especially in off-driving and straight hitting, that thing of joy which nature is always urging the real batsman to release, was more often to be found last season, and the poisonous vapours of dullness and dunce-like inaction, which hung over County grounds for heavy years, and, at one time, seemed to have settled for all eternity over Old Trafford in particular, were at last dispersing. It was Paynter who finally drove Calvinistic cricket from his native grounds. Ernest Tyldesley had begun the crusade. His art was above and beyond dry and cautious doctrines, and an eloquent rebuke to the business methods of batting. But he was almost unsupported. In 1939 such batsmen as Iddon, Washbrook, and that accomplished artist, Oldfield, completed the reformation. This new attitude, then, coupled with the loyalty of groundsmen in supporting Marylebone's suggestions for less artificial pitches, gave pleasanter hours to spectators who had deserved some compensation for the hardish seats, for the long, imperfectly explained delays, and the short, imperfectly executed strokes, to which they had, in ever decreasing numbers, become accustomed. Cricketers and committees, even under the shadow of bankruptcy, might continue to remark on the ignorance of spectators, but they could no longer ignore their comparative non-existence. This overdue change, and the discrediting of the Utilitarian method in batting, were the two great victories won by cricket in 1939. But now, of the immediate future no man can speak with more than hope.

The M.C.C. tour to India, which was to have taken place this present winter, was naturally cancelled. A moderately strong, if by no means representative, team had accepted invitations. Some of our best cricketers had decided on rest, in view of the visit to Australia, due in the winter 1940–41, and now most unlikely of achievement. Our guests for this coming summer were to have been the South Africans who, on their last visit, under H. F. Wade in 1935, gave us a rude but helpful shock. This is a severe loss. The virility and gaiety of South African teams have always been refreshing. There was an appalling interlude of funereal proceedings in the Test Matches between South Africa and England over there last winter. It will not, I think, happen again. Some notice of the deceased must be given later, but in general the matter, so far as sheer cricket is concerned, is best forgotten. It was, perhaps, nobody's fault. The pitches were often ludicrously docile, and there was an unfortunate experiment in a type of Test cricket which has been proved to be supremely suitable to only one set of matches, those between Australia and England in Australia.

At Lord's Mr. W. Findlay and Sir Pelham Warner have taken over the respective duties of Secretary and Assistant Secretary to the Marylebone Cricket Club, in the places of Lieut.-Colonel R. S. Rait Kerr and Mr. R. Aird, who are absent on military service. The Club is fortunate to be able, at temporary need, to replace two most efficient officers by men whose experience and discretion are so well tried and known. Sir Pelham Warner has given many years of much energy to the playing, the interest, and the furtherance of cricket. Mr. Findlay resumes an office which he performed with unfailing tact and conspicuous ability from 1926 to 1936.

It was announced that M.C.C. has contributed three hundred guineas to the British Red Cross Fund, and intend to arrange certain matches to be played during the summer in aid of that organisation. It is also proposed to hold the usual Easter classes at Lord's from 5th April to 24th April. More than forty matches against Schools have been arranged.

In legislation, it is unlikely, War or no War, that any further change or modification of the Rules of Cricket, or advices to captains, secretaries and players, will issue from M.C.C. for some period. The old and bald truth is that any game stands or falls not by its Laws but the spirit of their interpretation. Neglect of this truth has led, and always will lead, at best to irritation, at worst to grievous quarrels. The Over is likely to remain one of eight balls. It gave rise to discussion and correspondence, some helpful and sensible, much irrelevant but harmless, and a small but diverting section of remarkable mathematical obscurity.

THE WAR AND CRICKET

As to the possibility or impossibility of playing this summer what is generally known as first-class cricket, I cannot avoid the opinion that there has been in some quarters a deal of cloudy thinking and an over-generous flow of sentiment devoid of reason. Optimism is the thing. So is sense.

We must be prepared, as so many are at the moment compelled, to have nothing at all, or nearly nothing. But, in another sense, too, members of County Clubs must be prepared—and this is the duty of those who are left behind—to pay, if possible, the full subscription, if not possible, a part of it, to the Club to which they belong; in the words that Sir Stanley Jackson addressed to the Yorkshire County Club, 'to keep our grounds and facilities for cricket in order . . . to keep our organisation in its present efficiency ready for the happier times when the troubled world has returned to normal conditions.' On the same question the Surrey County Cricket Club began their circular to members with the same words as were used in their Report dated April 14th, 1915, the first issued after the start of the last War: **'The Committee are faced with many difficulties and uncertainties in the present National Crisis, and rely on the loyal support of the Members, as heavy current expenses have to be met whether cricket is played or not.'**

Advice on the spending of private monies is, in general, as improper as it has become unhappily necessary and frequent, but I do not feel that many will turn as lightly as they might in peace-time from helping to secure the future of a game that they love. On this point, then, agreement must, I feel, be nearly complete. But on the playing of actual, as opposed to the supporting of future cricket the divergence of view is wide. First, there are those who think that any organised cricket this summer, by those 'first-class' cricketers who are too old or too young or unfit for War service, or only temporarily available, is improper ethically. While respecting this view, I cannot agree with it. The idea of having anything remotely resembling the ordinary championship is certainly not only improper but wildly impossible. But I can see no reason or gain in wearing mental sackcloth in advance. Secondly there was—I much doubt if there still is—a view held that County cricket might take place in the form of one three-day match a week, starting on a Saturday, with certain adjustments of the Qualification Rule. But three-day cricket, in peace, was scarcely maintaining the public interest except in matches between the few best, or the locally rivalrous, teams, and how many are going to pay even six pence to watch cricket for three days between scratch or constantly varying elevens? Again, it was proposed that two-day matches might be played on Saturday and Monday. But why two-day? And why Monday? Few who remember or took part in the two-day matches in the County championship of 1919 will wish to revive them. Gaily undertaken as a bright and promising idea, they proved a dreary disaster; tiresome, unsatisfying, and financially hopeless.

Later, in December 1939, proposals came from Lancashire suggesting groupings for Regional Cricket in 1940, each group including a proportion of the Minor Counties. This carefully thought out, if perhaps over-ambitious scheme, may conceivably prove to be the basis of a simpler programme this summer. I much doubt it. As none can tell who will be available to play any cricket at all, or to what extent the severity of war may strike us, it is useless to make even provisional arrangements for any such programme.

D. G. Bradman, the Paragon, who made a century in every third innings, and whose Test average was 99.94. A shrewd tactician and administrator

TOP LEFT Frank Woolley, one of the greatest left-handers of all time. Nearly 59,000 runs, 145 centuries, 2,068 wickets, 1,015 catches, and all done with balletic grace

TOP RIGHT A. E. R. Gilligan in the 1940s – a pillar of Sussex cricket, an England captain whose career was blighted by injury, and a man who was a source of much delight to cricket lovers

BELOW The Surrey XI in 1897. And what a pity that the poet Jephson (back row, extreme right), never elegised the giant Richardson (back row, extreme left) who died a mysterious death

R. C. Robertson-Glasgow, inspired chronicler not just of the greats, but of the rabbits, the clowns of the fathers' match, the armchair heroes. And the only cricketer ever to be mistaken for Robinson Crusoe

TOP LEFT H. S. Altham, the most distinguished of all cricket historians, from boyhood in the Repton XI to the Presidency of the Hampshire Club
TOP RIGHT Hubert Preston, Editor, the last of the old school of professorial Edwardians who prospered under the tutelage of the Pardons
BELOW *Guardian, Times* and *Telegraph* crossing the seas together. Three generations of cricket writers: Cardus, Woodcock and Swanton

On January 12th this year M.C.C. issued the statement that their Committee was not prepared 'at this stage' to take the initiative in the matter of Regional Cricket, but that if the general feeling was in favour of it, they advised the Counties to ask for a meeting of the Advisory County Committee. This wise exhortation to rational procedure was wrongly interpreted by some as an expression of indifference or inertia. In fact, as the conditions then were, and, at the moment of writing, still are, only, so to speak, more so, it was the only decision that could reflect the view of the majority.

No. There is only one solution of the question, unless beyond expectation but not hope, peace returns early, and that is the improvising of one-day matches whenever and wherever possible, in the same spirit that has moved villagers to come out from under the yew-tree and bowl in the place of Tom looking after the calf and bat for Johnson delivering a telegram, and be d—d to the score and the points and the Cup! There will be plenty to play and enough to watch such games. Many would delight to see again a few early-Edwardian drives and a late-Victorian pull or two. And if most of the pence taken at the gate should go to help a greater cause than cricket, so much the better.

TEDIOUS TESTS

For the notes that follow, on the Test series between South Africa and England in South Africa, winter 1938–39, I am much indebted to an able and vigorous critic, who was an eyewitness of the five principal matches. If the original lucidity of the information should suffer from necessary compression, the fault is not his. It is probably that in the memories of those who took part in this tour little now remains except the entertainment given by a most hospitable people. Which is natural and proper. But annals demand fact; and the warmest enthusiast could not deny that much of the play in the five Tests was, as earlier remarked, laboured and tedious. The effect of this on spectators accustomed to the brisker pleasures of half-day and one-day cricket can readily be imagined. They saw their sprinters, so to speak, stretched out on a marathon, and most of them were frankly bored—and often said so. In truth, the intensity of the matches was out of all proportion to their meaning. The general standard of skill, too, was unequal to the importance artificially attached to it. The growth was unnatural. And, in the end, the Fifth Test match exploded in frustration and farce. For this there were two chief causes; the undue solemnity of proceedings, and the Test pitches which, like certain triumphs of chemistry in England, had so far overstepped perfection as to be of little use to the bowler and to impose some inexplicable narcotic on the batsman. They were plumb, but without pace. Yet the batsmen, with a few exceptions, cannot be wholly acquitted of blame. Some of them nearly slept on the pitch, and it is recorded that the number of half-volleys played by the back stroke was quite dreadful!

On the South African side Melville, the captain, well-known in England as a former captain of Oxford University and Sussex, played a beautiful innings in the Fourth Test. He had not been in form. But on this occasion he attacked that wonderfully accurate left-hander, Verity, first on the full pitch, then by hooking; probably the best innings in the series. His fielding was of the highest class and his captaincy, in most trying circumstances, sound. Dalton, a free and wristy batsman, kept to his natural style. Nourse, another attractive player, headed the Test averages for South Africa with 60.28. He scored centuries in the second and fifth Tests. Bruce Mitchell, classical and elegant as ever, averaged 58.25, and seemed happier when not called upon to open the innings. Van der Bijl, a very big man and rather slow of foot, showed an advance in ability, played the fast bowling very stoutly, and was extremely hard to shift. His average was 51.11.

On the English side the averages were generally higher. First Hammond with 87.00. It was remarked that in the Tests he used, in general, his quieter and safer method, scoring mainly from strokes off the back foot. Then Paynter (81.62). He, too, was studious; though the partnership between him (243) and Hammond (120) in the Third Test at Durban, which England won by an innings and 13 runs, produced a rare interlude of freedom and gaiety. Valentine (68.75) and Ames (67.80) brought a reviving breath of festival Canterbury to the solemnities, and from them and Hutton (44.16) came most of those strokes which flow instead of being squeezed from the bat. Nor must Gibb (59.12) be forgotten. With a concentration rarely given even to a Yorkshireman, he applied his mind and spectacles to the task. He scored 93 and 106 in the first Test, and 120 in the unfinished second innings of the fifth. He was very slow, but entirely in the fashion.

In bowling, Farnes, the one fast bowler of a high class on either side, was seldom happy with either pitch or climate. But he was accurate always: occasionally hostile. He took 16 wickets at 32.43 each. Verity, as ever, was extremely steady, taking 19 wickets at 29.05, so heading the list on both sides. Wright, though fairly steady in length, was unable to spin the ball much. Wilkinson, the other leg-breaker, could neither spin the ball enough nor find any certainty of length. Goddard did a hat-trick and Perks had one fine performance, but neither could make much of the pitches. Edrich, at a very fast medium pace, was hard-working and often useful.

The South African bowlers were facing an extremely severe task and, until they collapsed with weariness or strain in the fifth Test, acquitted themselves well. Langton we know as a resourceful and artistic bowler. Of Gordon, a tall, powerful bowler of inswingers and off-breaks, Hammond spoke with high praise, and remarked especially of his difficulty in the fourth Test, when on a damp pitch he made the ball swing very late away from instead of into the batsman.

England led by one match in the series after four had been played. The fifth was to have been played to a finish. It never ended. Some wished that it had never been begun. Player after player, especially on the South African side, became halt or incapacitated. England had been set the colossal task of scoring 696 runs to win. Quite soon, as 'soon' went in this match, with 250 for one wicket on the board, it was obvious that England stood a strong chance of winning. Langton was reduced to bowling half pace and round-arm. The athletic Gordon's powerful springs at last ran down. Newsome was only difficult with a new ball. The captain, Melville, was dead lame. But he could still speak. So on they went. The world of cricket, till now uninterested, suddenly became wildly excited at the prospect of a victory in this weird battle. The days went on, and at last that victory was almost in sight. But the boat for home was growing restive. If it were missed, it meant another week's stay; alternatively, a return by aeroplane. It has been said that M.C.C. would have granted the aeroplane. But, whatever the world was thinking, they were dead sick and tired of it over there. It had lasted for ten weekdays and two Sundays; and all that taking of guard, retaking of guard, walking, running, limping, talking, and throwing, went in the end for nothing. O bathos! But, once more, it is not perhaps the cricket that the teams so much remember; rather, the sun; and friendships renewed or made.

WEST INDIES IN ENGLAND

I think that the West Indies cricketers enjoyed their tour here last summer, cut short though it was by the War, and often interrupted by rain. They enjoy their cricket, because they mean to do so, because to them the game is a natural, yet important, sort of fun. And this pleasure they communicate, a happy gift, to the spectators. Their matches and scores are set our fair in another part of this volume, but no mathematics can recapture George Headley batting against England in the first Test at Lords, looking far smaller out there than the hundred and forty odd pounds of weight that he claims, quietly defiant, artistic in cutting, watchful on the line of the ball in defence. In the first innings he made 106 in a total of 277, in the second 107 in a total of 225. None before had ever made a century in each innings of a Test at Lord's. There were some who criticised his style of playing so many strokes off his back foot, and it is true that no batsman, however great, looks so well playing like that; but two forces had combined to push him into the more pragmatic method; weekly play in the league, and the sense that so much depended on his individual success. He was not quite so free as when he came here in 1933, but he showed himself to have no living superior in the square and the late cut. He was wonderful, too, in hooking, and in that very late flick of the ball from thigh or hips to long-leg. I can see a resemblance to Bradman in this stroke; like Bradman, too, he seems to play the ball very late, yet with certainty; but I would not dare to compare him, great batsman as he is, with Bradman in completeness of mastery. He has not, none has, quite the same iron precision or almost heartlessly perfect technique. And I don't think that Headley, as he stood 'smiling away like clockwork' at third man, ever reflected seriously on such comparisons.

England won this Test at Lord's by 8 wickets, having declared at 404 for 5 wickets. Hutton (196) and Compton (D.) (120) added 248 for the fourth wicket by fluent and masterful batting. Apart from Cameron, who flighted the ball cleverly from the Pavilion end, and took three wickets for 66 runs, the West Indies bowling was not good. Constantine for once somehow lost himself in eccentric experiments, and it was early apparent that Martindale had declined in speed. J. B. Stollmeyer, only eighteen years of age, opening the innings with his captain, R. S. Grant, made some lovely on-drives in his 59. High promise here. Bowes and Copson both bowled very finely in this match.

The second Test, at Manchester, was ruined by rain. On the first day, in the few overs available, England scored 11 for no wicket, and it needed a Marie Corelli or Ouida to describe how the torrent swirled round the chosen heroes of each country. Hutton and Fagg, the latter having, in my opinion unjustifiably, displaced Gimblett, found it almost as difficult to stand still as the bowlers found it to run. After a strange and not unexciting scramble on the Monday and Tuesday the match was left drawn, as had always seemed probable. Some harshly criticised Hammond's captaincy, suggesting that he might have forced a win. This was rather silly, if expected. Hammond does not rank among the more imaginative England captains. But he is experienced and sound, and he found the correct solutions in a quaint puzzle. At least the West Indies came out of the match with credit increased. Grant, in his 47 in the first innings, attacked the slow bowling with fierce zest. Headley, with 51, batted skilfully enough, but the best achievement was that of Bowes, who, on his thirty-first birthday, took 6 for 33. In England's first innings Hardstaff batted beautifully for his 76 in a total of 164 for 7 wickets declared.

At the Oval, in the third Test, England now leading by one match, West Indies added to the credit carried from Manchester. True, at the end, England led by 220 with 7 wickets in hand and Hutton (165) still batting, but it was something to have overtopped England's first innings of 352 by 146 runs. I should doubt if ever in the history of Test the English bowling has been so lashed and banged and rattled. Headley and Victor Stollmeyer played comfortably enough, but Weekes, the left-hander, then Constantine, 'fired indiscriminately.' Weekes scored 137 (78 by boundaries) in 135 minutes, and Constantine, soon wearying of mere unorthodoxy, began to aim for sixes over the wicketkeeper. Two, if not three, of England's best bowlers had been unable to accept invitations to play, and the land was naked indeed. At one period, when Compton and Hutton were bowling, it seemed as if all the long-hops and full-pitches in the world were being simultaneously released. Hutton and Hammond put the arithmetic right by adding 264 for the third wicket in England's second innings, and nothing was left but a formal declaration ten minutes from time on the last day.

The West Indies showed themselves to be as a team quite strong, if unreliable—Headley excepted—in batting; only moderately strong in bowling; good, sometimes brilliant, in fielding. Their chief disappointments must have been the weather and the decline in form of Martindale, opening fast bowler, and of Barrow, wicket keeper and opening batsman of the 1933 tour. Barrow had scored a century in the Manchester Test in that tour, and proved himself a sound wicket-keeper. Unhappily for his team, his batting seemed from the first to be over-anxious last season, and Sealey took his place as wicket-keeper at Manchester and the Oval. Sealey is a natural batsman of many and attractive strokes, also a witty and refreshing conversationalist; but, myself, I do not rank him high as a wicket-keeper. Hylton, tall, medium to medium fast, was a clever bowler, with a fluent action and often deceptive flight. His figures do no justice to his skill. R. S. Grant, capable and alert as a captain, took upon himself the task of opening the innings. Within the limits of his skill he performed it well, being free and venturesome in method; but it is as a short-leg that he will be remembered. Here he made some astonishing catches, and his reach was tremendous. On the administrative and social side he received tirelesss and valuable help from Mr. J. M. Kidney, the manager, whose wisdom and tact were equally appreciated among English friends and cricketers. J. H. Cameron, who captained the side when Grant was absent, showed a certain maturity of form. He was a most useful all-rounder, and had the advantage of an intimate knowledge of most of his opponents and their methods.

As to Learie Constantine, one of the few unquestioned geniuses of cricket, he shows his greatness by his gift of adaptation. He reached the age of thirty-seven soon after the last Test. And that's not young for a man who bowls, fields, and hits with the best. He no longer bowls fast as a regular habit; just a 'fizzer' now and again, to remind the impertinent. But he has kept that curious upward jerk of the head just before delivery, as if to reassure himself that the sky is up to no nonsense. He bowled every variety of medium, medium-slow and medium-fast pace. There are better bowlers in cricket to-day than Constantine, but there's none to equal him for a study in bowling craft. In the Tests there was that one lapse, at Lord's, when he reminded me of a chess-player who had somehow confounded his gambits and made a muddle of the game. At the Oval, in England's first innings, when he took 5 for 75, he was grand. His fielding, usually in the gulley, is still one of the sights of cricket, as he takes every oddity of bounce with lazy-seeming ease. As a batsman he has somewhat declined. The eye and foot are not quite so quick for those attacks on probability and text-books. But his innings at the Oval, even allowing for the ineptitude of much of the attack, was glorious hitting.

YORKSHIRE AGAIN

Our own County championship was again won by Yorkshire. Middlesex, who played six matches fewer than the winners, came second; but more than a whole unit behind. Gloucestershire, who had the felicity to beat the champions both home and away, were third. In the previous year they had finished tenth. Their bowling in 1939 was most effective. Goddard, slow-medium, alone of any County cricketer took 200 wickets (200 at 14.86 each). He was finely supported by the two younger bowlers, Scott (121 at 22.89) and Lambert (74 at 26.86). Their captain, Walter Hammond, headed the first class batting averages for the seventh successive season, an achievement that is unlikely ever to be rivalled. He scored 2,479 runs in all matches at an average of 63.56. As a team they were enterprising in idea and execution.

Essex came fourth, a rise of two places. For the seventh time in eight seasons Nichols brought off the 'double,' 1,387 runs and 121 wickets. He was most ably assisted by Kenneth Farnes during the later part of the season. Smith (R.) and Smith (P.), in their different styles, between them took 174 wickets. A varied and strong attack. Avery, a stylish batsman, advanced in ability, averaging 41.71 for 1,335 runs. O'Connor showed little, if any, decline in his powers. The playing of matches in widely separate parts of the County has proved a success. According to latest advice, the secretary, Mr. B. K. Castor, absent on War Service, has handed over his duties to his wife.

Yorkshire's victory in the Championship was assured before the programme was stopped or altered by the War. The captaincy of A. B. Sellers was once more of the highest standard, reflected in the discipline no less than in the tough optimism of his team. Verity (191 wickets at 13.13) headed the first-class bowling averages. There is nothing new that I can say of this greatest among the slower-paced modern left-handers. Bowes, fast-medium to fast, took 122 wickets at 14.48, and, to my mind has reached in the last two seasons the climax of his powers. The untidiness has gone; the vigour and control remain. Robinson, the off-spinner, showed very good form, taking 120 wickets at 19.07. This was a trio in attack of a total ability a little beyond that to be found in any other County. Hutton and Sutcliffe were a grand opening pair. The older master was occasionally absent recovering from injury, but it was a wonderful performance, in his forty-fifth year, to score 1,416 runs in 29 innings, including, at the end of May and start of June, four consecutive centuries.

Middlesex owed much to the personality and leadership of I. A. R. Peebles. Unlike some captains, he never stretched the bow too tight, but was nevertheless an observant and understanding leader, equally unworried in defeat or success. The batting, even with the brilliant Compton (D.) and the strongly effective Edrich, was never of quite the same solid quality as that of Yorkshire. It was pleasant to note the success as a batsman of J. P. Mann, of Cambridge University, son of the former Middlesex and England captain, F. T. Mann. Jim Smith was as tireless as ever in bowling, and his system of batting was, if anything, more violent and eccentric than ever.

In conclusion, I should wish to end on a note of praise for English batting. There is much to criticise in our cricket. The standard of bowling is low. In some counties the discipline of cricketers is slack. But the batting is very good indeed, and there were stars about last summer, to be seen by those not lost in the mists of pessimism and antiquity. A man could count himself happy to sit down and watch the ripening greatness of Hutton, the airy graces of Hardstaff, and the twinkling feet of Compton. While Hammond, if less flexible and destructive than he was, still looked greater than anything else that we have in the game. Besides these, there were many others last season to show that English batting had tricked its beams anew, and flamed in the forehead of the morning sky.

May I thank those friends and colleagues without whose help these Notes could not have been started: Mr. Hubert Preston; Mr. Norman Preston, and their colleagues in Pardon's Cricket Reporting Agency, who provided much matter, statistical and general; Mr. Frank Thorogood, of the *News Chronicle*; Mr. E. W. Swanton, who gave me the benefit of his observation of the M.C.C. tour in South Africa; Sir Pelham Warner and Mr. H. S. Altham, whose opinions I asked for, and received, on various subjects.

February, 1940

CRICKET IN WAR-TIME [1940]

BY MAJOR H. S. ALTHAM

There was one other essay in the 1940 Wisden, contributed by one of the most distinguished historians of the game, Harry Surtees Altham (1888–1965), C.B.E., D.S.O., M. C. Altham had played in the Repton College sides of 1905–08, had captained the eleven of his last two seasons, and had won a place in the Oxford sides of 1911 and 1912. He made his début for Surrey while still a schoolboy, but after the Great War he became a regular player for Hampshire, who subsequently honoured him by making him President of the Club from 1947 to 1965. He also served as Treasurer of M.C.C., 1950–63; President, 1959–60; and Chairman of the England selectors in 1954. But it is as a historian of cricket that his name will always be remembered. In the 1920s he embarked on a series of weekly essays in 'The Cricketer', which appeared as 'The History of Cricket' in 1926, a comprehensive and well-balanced account of the game's evolution from medieval times of the day before yesterday. When obliged to bring his work up to date in the 1930s, Altham, much occupied in his duties as housemaster at Winchester, recruited the assistance of E. W. Swanton; when a more up-to-date edition was required after Altham's death, Swanton undertook Volume Two of the 'History', completing one of the worthiest and most indispensable works in the literature of sport.

Altham, as befitted a schoolmaster, was a passionate believer in the efficacy of coaching, a cause to which he devoted prodigious energy; for sixteen years he was chairman of the M.C.C. Youth Cricket Association, and once said:

> If only we can get enough boys playing this game in England and playing it right, it is quite certain that from the mass will be thrown up in some year or another a new Compton, a new Tate, a new Jack

Hobbs, and when that happens we need not worry any more about our meetings with Australia.

Such Panglossian optimism from so shrewd a reader of the game seems astonishing, but Altham certainly believed in his panacea with sufficient passion to dedicate the last years of his life to it.

In his review of the fortunes of cricket during successive wars, Altham appears to face two ways at once, apparently approving of the shut-down in the Great War, yet acknowledging that 'there is a general feeling that the game can and should be kept going wherever possible' in the new war. Indeed, the general feeling was so strong that the continuance of first-class cricket wherever possible actually became an instrument of policy of Churchill's wartime Government. Altham's scholastic style, a pleasurable example of correctitude coloured with the occasional poetic flourish, as in his memorable description of his last peacetime cricketing recollection of 1914 when he saw in the 'blood-red sunset over the Thames an omen of the years to come', makes him one of the most accessible of all erudite writers on cricket.

So long as war was an affair of professional armies, its incidence seems to have had but little effect on cricket.

The first match of which the full score has been preserved—Kent v. All England—took place on the Artillery Ground, Finsbury (still the Headquarters of the H.A.C.) on June 18, 1744. England was then engaged in the war of the Austrian Succession, but the game was watched by 'a great company,' and amongst them the Duke of Cumberland, destined to figure in the following year on the less glorious field of Fontenoy, and Admiral Vernon, seeking, we may conclude, distraction from the memories of his defeat at Cartagena. Nor did the claims of state disturb another great patron of the game, for in 1745 we read of the Earl of Sandwich writing 'I'll to your board (of Admiralty) when at leisure from cricket.' Again in 1778 when the Empire seemed hastening to dissolution in the War of American Independence, two eminent Privy Counsellors were violently attacked in a quite unprintable lampoon for continuing to play cricket regardless of the calls of state. Fortunately Mr. Churchill was never a cricketer! When the Grande Armée was lining the cliffs at Boulogne in 1804–05, Kent mustered its militia and the Coxheath cricket ground amongst others became a military camp. But so far from war stopping cricket in England, our soldiers took their bats with them; officers of the Light Division got up a match shortly before Busaco, whilst six days before Waterloo the Duke of Richmond was playing near Brussels, only to see the game summarily ended by the appearance of Wellington himself with the Prince of Orange. The terrain of the Crimea hardly favoured cricket, but there is a pleasant story of the Battle of Alma that shows how cricket was never far from some soldiers' minds: The Guards, Rifle Brigade and Black Watch were nearing the top of the rise when a round shot came bounding along and passed through the ranks which had opened to avoid it in accordance with orders.' Sir John Astley tells how 'George Duff, a capital chap who was our best wicket-keeper, was just in front of me and I sang out "Duff, you are keeping wicket, you ought to have stopped that one", and of how he turned and smiling quietly said, "No, sir, it had a bit too much pace on. You are a long stop, sir, so I left it to you." '

The most striking reflection on cricket and the South African war is supplied by the fact that no reference whatever is to be found to it in the editorial notes of the relevant 'Wisden's.' No cricketer of high repute was killed in the war, and of the players who died on service the only memorable names are those of that fine Yorkshire player, Frank Milligan, and the great Australian bowler, J. J. Ferris. I remember, as a boy, seeing pictures of our nurses in South Africa playing cricket, and during the siege of Mafeking one of the Boer Commandants suggested to Baden-Powell that there should be a Sunday truce during which his men might come and meet the garrison in all amity on the cricket field. 'B.P.' replied that nothing would give him greater pleasure when the present match was over, but at the moment his men were 200 (days) not out and were enjoying their game very much indeed!

The outbreak of the European War of 1914–18 will always be associated in my mind with Lord's. I was up there watching the Lord's Schools v. The Rest match and can remember buying an evening paper on the ground and reading in the stop-press column the opening sentences of the speech which Lord Grey was then making in the Commons, and subsequently travelling down from Waterloo to Esher, where I was staying with the Howell brothers, and seeing in the blood-red sunset over the Thames an omen of the years to come. The younger Howell whose batting had dominated the match and for whom no honours in the game seemed unobtainable, fell in the Salient less than a year afterwards.

For most of that August county cricket was played much as usual, though the Military Authorities commandeered the Oval, and Hobbs' benefit match was staged at Lord's, but then a speech by Lord Roberts and a dignified letter to *The Times* by 'W. G.' brought the first class game to an end.

Though the 1915 'Wisden' envisaged the possibility of the occasional county cricket in the coming summer, no such attempt was made or even seriously contemplated. Every county committee had encouraged the professional staff to join the forces or to engage in some form of war work, in most cases making up to them the difference between their Army pay and allowances and their cricket wage. Yorkshire took the lead in making such war service a condition of re-engagement. But cricketers everywhere needed no urging, and at the annual M.C.C. meeting in May, Lord Hawke as President could claim that 75 per cent of first class cricketers were serving in the Army or Navy (the R.F.C. being then of course a very small body of regular specialists).

At the same meeting he announced the M.C.C.'s intention to do all they could to help school cricket and his hope that the

Headmasters would co-operate to keep the game going. This hope was realised and in one respect at least the war brought real benefit to school cricket; deprived of their usual club opposition the schools naturally turned to each other and many new inter-school fixtures were arranged. Winchester, for instance, who had for 60 years met only one school—Eton—now arranged matches with Charterhouse, Wellington and Bradfield, and this policy, continued after the war, has proved an unqualified success.

The M.C.C. played their part nobly by playing forty-four school matches, and if their sides were often rather long in the tooth this could be off-set by the youth of the school teams: for, in contrast with the far-sighted policy of to-day, no effort was made to prevent boys joining up at a bare 18 and many were fighting or had been killed in Flanders at a time when they would normally have still been playing cricket for their schools.

Of Club Cricket, in the ordinary sense of the word, there was virtually none, and the only clubs I have been able to trace as fielding sides, and then only in isolated fixtures against schools, were the Butterflies, Notts Amateurs and Herts C. & G. But there was plenty of military cricket and the county committees everywhere put their grounds at the disposal of the troops. In many cases too they had turned their buildings to war uses: Lord's accommodated various military units, whilst the staff that remained there spent part of their time in making thousands of hay-nets for horses; the pavilions at Old Trafford, Trent Bridge and Derby became hospitals, whilst the Leicester Ground provided a headquarters for a Remount Depot and a small-bore rifle range.

At the end of the season a baseball match was played at Lord's between Canadians and London Americans for the benefit of Canadian soldiers' dependants.

But inevitably the chief and melancholy feature of the War issues of 'Wisden' was the ever growing Roll of Honour of cricketers; the war was no more than a few months old when it had claimed two young officers who, as boys, had made cricket history—A. E. J. Collins, whose individual score of 628 not out, made when a boy of 13 at Clifton, still stands (in the same match he took eleven wickets), and John Manners, whose fearless hitting had alone made possible the epic Eton victory of 'Fowler's year.' But from the losses and tragedies of the War cricketers the world over were in 1915 twice distracted—by the deaths of 'W. G.' and Victor Trumper. I can remember reading of them in France and feeling no real sorrow for W. G. passing Homeric and legendary into the Elysian fields, but an almost personal pain that Trumper's gallant spirit and matchless grace should have been called so early from the world it had enriched.

In 1916 school cricket continued to develop on the lines followed the previous year and Winchester met Harrow for the first time since 1854. The M.C.C. though only able to play half as many schools as in 1915, wisely decided to revive the Lord's Schools v. The Rest match in August. This game saw the appearance of two future county captains in

W. G. Lowndes and M. D. Lyon, and of a very young boy destined to play a great role at Lord's in later years, G. T. S. Stevens. Club Cricket received a notable reinforcement in the shape of the Artists Rifles XI, who played a number of matches, chiefly with schools, and thanks to the batting of D. J. Knight and the bowling of E. C. Kirk, carried all before them.

But it was in the north that cricket of first-class standard really survived. The Leagues there kept going and a number of professionals had gravitated to them: interest in their matches was keen, as well it might be with the chance of seeing Barnes bowling at Hobbs. In the four war years the former took 404 wickets in the Bradford League for about 5½ runs apiece, whilst Hobbs in 1916 had splendid batting figures, and took 59 wickets at very small cost.

The year 1917 saw a great change in sentiment about the game; the nation had by then re-adjusted its life to the state of war and no objection was felt to an attempt to stage some exhibition matches in the cause of charity. Yorkshire had felt their way in that direction the previous year and now played four big games, whilst the M.C.C. bestowed their official blessing by staging two matches at Lord's—The Army v. Australian Army, and Navy and Army v. Australia and S. Africa; these games, if they produced no outstanding cricket, were very popular. Charity benefited by over £1,000. Two Army Commanders, Generals Plumer and Horne, wired their good wishes, and Admiral Jellicoe himself came to Lord's.

No fewer than 119 military and school matches were played that year on the Canterbury ground, and Leyton, too, saw much cricket.

The outstanding feature in the school cricket of the year was the bowling of the Wykehamist J. D'E. Firth, who took 8 for 48 v. Harrow, all ten for 41 v. Eton, and with 7 for 27 in the last innings at Lord's, pulled the match out of the fire for The Rest. Stevens made further progress, Gibson of Eton and Rotherham of Rugby foreshadowed their future powers, whilst at Uppingham Percy Chapman, though only 16, averaged 111 for 10 innings.

The last year of the war saw a further extension of the policy of 'Exhibition' matches, both in Yorkshire and in the South.

Three such games were played at Lord's, one at the Oval, and one in September at Folkestone, and if the cricket, as was natural, hardly reached peace-time level the large crowds that attended had their moments of rich reward, in one of Hobbs' very best innings, another, almost as good, by H. W. Taylor, a piece of hurricane hitting by Fender, and the heartening spectacle of 'Plum' Warner in the familiar Harlequin cap batting almost as well as ever at the age of forty-four.

School cricket flourished exceedingly and the representative match at Lord's included, besides Stevens and Chapman of the previous year, an exceptionally fine all-rounder from Malvern in N. E. Partridge, and from Tonbridge that brilliant bat and cover-point Lionel Hedges. In a further game between a representative schools side and an eleven raised by Captain Warner, Lord Harris delighted everyone by batting for half an hour with relative ease when many, half his age, had been cheaply dismissed.

In this summer a little cricket was even played in France, principally at Étaples, where the old Essex player, Charles McGahey looked after some very respectable matting wickets. I remember one afternoon match in particular which included quite a galaxy of stars, Johnny Douglas, Nigel Haig, Dick Twining, Harry Longman, Donald Knight and poor Reggie Schwartz, who died of influenza just after the armistice. That fine batsman, Colonel H. S. Bush, motored some 100 miles from 2nd Army H.Q. at St. Omer, hit a beautiful four and then off an equally good hit fell to a miraculous catch by Knight at cover, and motored back again.

The game was also played in the Near East where I believe Rockley Wilson bowled the same length as he has bowled everywhere else; but Bernard Darwin at Salonika stuck to golf.

With the biographies of the fallen filling each year more pages in 'Wisden,' it would be impossible, and where the sacrifice of all was equal, it would be invidious to pay more than a general tribute to the contribution which cricketers made to final victory, but perhaps I may make one exception. There can never have been a great cricketer less military in temper than Colin Blythe: the artistry of his bowling was but the expression of his sensitive and highly strung temperament, his physique was never strong, but when the call came, he never hesitated, and every year at the Canterbury festival his county have paid tribute at the memorial to his sacrifice.

No one, as the summer of 1918 drew to its close, could have dreamt that next May would see county cricket in full swing again, but so it was. The Advisory Committee, faced in December with the unexpected task of getting the game on its legs again and very doubtful how far public interest would respond to a full-fledged revival, decided on the policy of two day matches, but the season was not many weeks old when everyone realised that the experiment was a mistake, that the fears were unjustified, and that cricket was as popular as ever.

To-day the horizon is again dark, and it is idle to try to look far ahead, but I believe there is a general feeling that the game can and should be kept going wherever possible. With the military service act in operation, and the nation, mobilised as never before for its war effort, there is no room for the charge of scrimshanking, and where cricket can be played without interfering with the national effort it can only be good for the national morale. Of course anything like county cricket is out of the question, but the M.C.C. have arranged one or two big Charity matches at Lord's with a number of minor matches, and undertaken a long programme against the schools, with the Lord's Schools and the Rest match to end the season at Lord's. The Club Cricket Conference have decided that, with the obvious reservations, the Clubs should keep going as much as possible, and with their short hours the northern League matches will justifiably continue to offer excitement and distraction to thousands of workers. In the last war the Universities, so far as undergraduates were concerned, virtually ceased to exist; to-day they are full of vigorous life, the undergraduates cannot join up until they are of age, and are very rightly making the best of war conditions. Cambridge, fortunate in having two old Blues in residence, mean to produce a University team and have already arranged a match for Charity at Lord's; the situation at Oxford is more difficult, but it is to be hoped that they will try to manage something on the same lines.

A visit to Lord's on a dark December day was a sobering experience; there was sandbags everywhere, and the Long Room was stripped and bare, with its treasures safely stored beneath ground, but the turf was a wondrous green, old Time on the Grand Stand was gazing serenely at the nearest balloon, and one felt that somehow it would take more than totalitarian war to put an end to cricket. *Merses profundo, pulchrior evenit.*

W. R. HAMMOND IN FIRST CLASS CRICKET 1920–1939 [1941]

Walter Reginald Hammond

BY R. C. ROBERTSON-GLASGOW

By 1941 the Almanack had reverted to the starveling proportions of the editions of the first war. A mere 426 pages, and little cricket in England on which to comment, Robertson-Glasgow again contributed his notes for the previous season, but it was not until the following year that he and Hubert Preston added to the list of Wisden essays worth rescuing from their time-warp. Perhaps sensing that by the time the war was over the career of Walter Hammond would be over with it, Robertson-Glasgow composed a review of Hammond's brilliant career, buttressed by nine pages of close-printed statistics whose relevance falls outside the frontiers of a collection of essays.

SOME judge batsmen by the number of their runs, others by the manner of their making. By either criterion W. R. Hammond, England's captain, must rank among the great. For seven seasons consecutively up to the end of 1939 he headed the English first-class averages. His batting average, since he began to play for Gloucestershire in 1920, stands in all first-class cricket at 55.72, nearly 4 units higher than his nearest rival, Sutcliffe. He has made 155 centuries. But, far more than this, he has adorned cricket and entertained the public with a style of batting in which splendour of manner, grace of execution, and muscular power of stroke have been combined to a degree rarely equalled in the history of the game. 'Let's go and see Hammond,' we used to say. It was worth a journey even to see him walk out to bat; for the true stamp of greatness was printed on him.

His bowling, though never great, was good enough to be used successfully for England. He has taken good wickets in Test matches, including that of W. M. Woodfull, in the days when the batting of Woodfull was a headline. At about medium pace, Hammond had a late swerve from leg with the new ball, and at any time could tax a batsman with an awkward break-back. He had great pace from the pitch, and an action for a boy to imitate, with easy rhythm and the left shoulder pointing at the batsman just before delivery.

As a fielder he will be remembered as one of the greatest of slips, intelligent, so quick in anticipation and movement that no catch seemed difficult. In earlier times he would field anywhere, and he threw like an Australian.

Born at Dover on June 19, 1903, Hammond toured early, playing young cricket in China and Malta. Returning to England, he went to Cirencester Grammar School, where he distinguished himself by playing an innings of 365 not out in a House match. In 1920 he played for Gloucestershire as an amateur; but his qualification was questioned by the Kent authorities. He turned professional, and 1923 was his first season of regular appearance. I remember him then as a batsman of freedom and power, but still unsound in judgment and defence.

Unlike Hutton, of Yorkshire, and D. Compton, of Middlesex, he did not jump into full panoply. He batted like a very promising undergraduate, took risks and enjoyed them. But from the start he fielded like an archangel. Little, if anything, was yet seen of his bowling. In his first match, against Surrey at Bristol, he scored 110 and 92. His aggregate for the County was 1,313; average 28.54. At the Oval he made 46 and 19 for the Players against the Gentlemen. Consistency was yet to come. In 1924 his performance in figures showed little change, but he played one remarkable innings, 174 not out on a difficult pitch against Middlesex at Bristol. Gloucestershire had been out for 31, Middlesex for 74, when this happened. It was followed by some great bowling by Charles Parker—he did the 'hat-trick' in each innings—and Gloucestershire won by 61 runs.

Next summer, his defence much strengthened, he was fit to play for England. He scored 1,818 runs in all matches, including an innings of 250 not out against Lancashire at Old Trafford, when he and Dipper put on 330 for the third wicket. In the autumn he sailed with the Hon. F. S. G. Calthorpe's team to the West Indies. In the first unofficial Test, at Barbados, he played an innings of 238 not out and made five catches. His average in representative matches was 87. Here, then, was England's number three for the coming Australian Tests in England. But he fell ill, and in 1926 played no cricket at all.

In 1927 he returned, climbed the heights, and has remained there ever since. Refreshed, stronger than ever, he showed a masterful brilliance against every variety of bowling. He made 135 against Yorkshire at Gloucester, then 108 and 128 in the next match, against Surrey at the Oval; took breath at Dewsbury with 11 and 17, then roused Old Trafford with 99 and 187. In this last century he hit four 6's and twenty-four 4's, and annihilated the redoubtable fast bowler, E. A. McDonald, whose two wickets cost him 165 runs. Back at Bristol, he scored 83 and 7 against Middlesex. There were two days of May left, and Hammond needed 164 for his 1,000 runs; so, at Southampton, he made 192, and joined that old king of Gloucestershire and English cricket, who had done the same feat in 1895 in his forty-seventh year.

In the autumn of 1927 he sailed to South Africa with Captain R. T. Stanyforth's M.C.C. team. In the Tests he scored 390 runs, highest innings 90, average 40. His bowling, so far more admired by the connoisseur than remarked by the critics, yielded 15 wickets at 26 each. He was now, beyond question, an all-rounder.

He had reached the meridian of his powers. He was twenty-five years old, an athlete from top to toe, of an agile and flexible strength more often seen in Dominion than English cricketers, brimming with health and natural confidence. Each to his own view; but in the years since the last war, for skill fortified by endurance, for harmony and control of attack and defence, I have not known his like. Bradman may have been more starkly efficient, Frank Woolley have shown more charm, Hobbs a more exquisite technique; but to me, whether trying to bowl him out or to field those terrific strokes, Hammond remains the greatest of them all. Without need of reflection or memory, I can still feel and hear those off-drives.

The best know failure, and it came to Hammond in the Australian Tests here in 1930, was when he scored only 306 runs and only one century; a performance that would have set up some cricketers for life, but, in Hammond, caused a welter of theory and vapouring. Grimmett, whom he had dominated in Australia, worried him in England. The little man bowled grandly, it is true, attacking Hammond's leg stump. But it was not only Grimmett who troubled him. Some virtue had temporarily ebbed from him. He lost confidence, and tended to play off his back foot balls that he was accustomed to bang against the rails behind cover-point. It was the husk, not the body, that was batting. I doubt, too, if he was in full health. Yet even his ghost scored in that season 2,032 runs, with an average of 53. A second journey to South Africa, under A. P. F. Chapman, did much to restore him. He scored 517 in nine Test innings, average 65, and his 136 not out was the only century for England in the series.

To return to 1928. In all first-class matches he scored 2,825 runs, average 66, including nine centuries. In bowling, he took 84 wickets at 23 each. His fielding, especially at short slip to the leg-spinners of Charles Parker, was superb. The Cheltenham Festival that year was nearly all Hammond. Against Surrey he made 139 and 143, caught four men in the first innings and six in the second. In the next match, against Worcestershire, he scored 80, took 9 for 23 in the first innings and 6 for 105 in the second. Against the West Indies, in three Tests, he scored only 111 runs, average 37.

But he was soon to rob the critics of their adjectives. Sailing to Australia with the England team under A. P. F. Chapman in one of the strongest batting sides that any country had produced, he took control of the Australian bowlers. In the second Test he played an innings of 251, in the third 200. In the fourth, still untamable, he made 119 not out and 177, and his Test average ended at 113.12 for just over 900 runs. This triumph was won not by vigilance and attrition, but by exuberant and offensive batting. They could not hold that driving. In the English season of 1929 he finished second to J. B. Hobbs, scoring 2,456 runs, with ten centuries, at an average of 65. Against the South Africans, who were led by H. G. Deane, he cooled down to two centuries, both not out.

Two lean years followed. First, the season against the Australians, mentioned before; then 1931, when his average sank to 42. Probably he was stale. Even so, he played an innings of 100 not out against New Zealand at the Oval, and in all made six centuries. In 1932 he fared better, scoring 2,528 runs at an average of 56 and he more often showed that brilliancy in attack which had marked him out as a batsman apart; but, as a whole, it was evident that some of the superb contempt had left his style, which became more thoughtful; he was batting from knowledge rather than instinct. Perhaps too much was expected of him. Critics tended to exaggerate his failures and neglect his successes. He was now, so to speak, the Prime Minister, a target for any passing fool. To recover completely, he needed a month of golf at the seaside or a cricket tour round the clubs and villages. Instead, he went out to the grimmest series of Tests ever played between two countries—to Australia under D. R. Jardine.

Dismal quarrels, public and personal, arguments and recriminations produced an atmosphere wholly at variance with his free and genial temperament. Small wonder that 'he did not repeat his record-breaking achievements of the previous tour.' Great wonder that, in a style of cricket shot through with commerce and acrimony, Hammond, mixing iron with gold, scored 440 runs during the Tests, as did Herbert Sutcliffe, and alone of the side made two centuries in the series. His parting present to Sydney, scene of his greatest triumphs, was a cracking drive for six, which ended the fifth Test and heralded an exhibition in New Zealand which none but he could have given. In three innings he scored 59,227 and 336 not out. The last two were in the Tests, giving him an aggregate that was also an average, 563. In his 336 not out, at Auckland, he batted for 318 minutes, hitting thirty-four 4's and ten 6's (three off consecutive balls). A New Zealand Test cricketer, who has played against the best in Australia and England, has told me that, even allowing for the comparative mediocrity of the bowling, it was quite the most wonderful display, in power and variety, that he has ever seen. So back to England.

In summer 1933 he took part in the three Tests against the West Indies, but did nothing of note, scoring only 74 runs for an average of 25. For Gloucestershire his form was brilliant. He scored 239 against Glamorgan, 126 not out against Lancashire; then, against Worcestershire, at Worcester, for the fourth time in his career, scored a century in each innings. In this match C. C. Dacre brought off the same feat. After a double century (206) at Leicester, he played one of his greatest innings against Middlesex at Lord's, 178, which so nearly won the match against all expectation. Centuries against Nottinghamshire and Surrey followed, both at Bristol, and then, in the return match against Lancashire, at Old Trafford, he made 120. Still the spate swelled on; 231 against Derby at Cheltenham; then, to balance failure in the Tests, 264 against West Indies at Bristol. Lastly, two centuries in the Folkstone Festival, 184 for South of England v. M.C.C., 133 for England Eleven v. West Indies. At Folkestone, I remember, he took a fancy for square-cutting balls of good length off the off stump, and third man's boots nearly caught fire. So he ended that season with 3,323 runs at an average of 68.

As in 1930, so in 1934 Hammond failed in the Tests against Australia in England. It would be idle to attribute this failure to a back injury owing to which he played hardly any cricket till the middle of June. Nor was it any one Australian bowler, as has often been suggested, who overcame him. Hammond has always been a batsman of moods, and in this series his failure was as much temperamental as technical. Half England had gone crazy about the Tests. Thousands of sandwiches were cut, hundreds of articles were written. And somehow, as he moved in the middle of the turmoil, I found Hammond faintly but undeniably bored. Naughty, perhaps, but to me, I must confess, enjoyably comical. Everything was ready for the coronation, but the king refused to get out of bed! Further, it was his Benefit year.

And richly did he give of his art to Gloucestershire. In thirteen matches he averaged 126. He made 302 not out against Glamorgan, 290 against Kent, 265 not out against Worcestershire. He was as sure a draw as ever on the County grounds, and his Benefit totalled £2,650, a magnificent and unparalleled sum for a West Country cricketer, but no more than was due to one who, wisely directed and handled by that remarkable leader, B. H. Lyon, had raised Gloucestershire to an eminence it had not imagined since the golden days of the Graces.

There is little rest in modern cricket, and in the winter of 1934 Hammond was off to the West Indies under the captaincy of R. E. S. Wyatt. He did nothing great in the Tests, though in all matches he had an average of 56, with a highest score of 281 not out. 1935 was another ordinary year for him. He looked stale, which was not surprising. Indeed, English cricket seemed aweary of its life and to go through its motions because it must. A young and virile South African team, under H. F. Wade, won the Test rubber. It was the end of a rather melancholy chapter.

Hutton had only just begun in Yorkshire, D. Compton was still in the 'nursery,' young Joseph Hardstaff appeared in but one Test, at Leeds. Middle age prevailed.

In April 1936, having had his tonsils removed, he began slowly, but soon warmed to it. An All-India team visited us. Hammond played in the second and third Tests; in the second he played an innings of 167, reaching 100 in 100 minutes, mainly by off-driving of his own inimitable sort; in the third he made 217, and his Test average finished at 194. But his most remarkable innings was one of 317 for Gloucestershire against Nottinghamshire in Goddard's Benefit match. It contained but one false stroke, and the third hundred was made in 70 minutes. In this month of August Hammond scored 1,281 runs, so exceeding the 1,278 of Dr. W. G. Grace, made in the year 1876.

In the winter of 1936 he visited Australia for the third time, G. O. Allen captaining. He began with 141 against Western Australia, 107 against a reinforced Western Australian team, 104 and 136 against South Australia; and he had not yet reached his favourite Sydney. There, in the second Test, he played an innings of 231 not out. It was seriously and, for Hammond, slowly built up; but it suited the occasion. In Australia's second innings he took 3 for 29 in 127 balls, and England won by an innings. Thereafter he was less successful against an attack mainly directed, in the case of O'Reilly, at his leg stump. His next highest score was 56, and his Test average 58. England won the second Test, Australia the next three and so the rubber.

In the three Tests of 1937 against New Zealand he averaged 51, scoring 140 at Lord's. In all matches his aggregate was 3,252 with 13 centuries and average 65. During the following winter it was announced that he had turned amateur. For the Tests against Australia here in 1938 he was appointed England's captain. He had long been king among our cricketers. As a strategist he would not rank among our great leaders; but he was safe, observant and experienced. His colossal achievements commanded the respect as his sociable nature invited the confidence of every sort of cricketer.

His responsibility, so far from weighing him down, seemed quietly to elate him, and his genius reached its height in an innings of 240 in the second Test at Lord's. When he walked down the pavilion steps, England had lost two wickets for only 20 runs to the fast bowling of McCormick. From the start Hammond was 'simply and severely great,' master of each bowler and every stroke. He and Paynter put on 222 for the fourth wicket, a new record. On the next day, before a record crowd, Hammond and Ames added 186 for the sixth wicket. At length, after he had batted for just over six hours, Hammond, soon after receiving a painful blow on the elbow, was bowled by McCormick on the leg stump. His 240 was the highest score for England up till then in any home Test. But that sort of thing hardly mattered in comparison to the quality of the innings. He gave only one chance, if I may so describe a drive that split the fielder's finger.

At Leeds he played a fine first innings of 76 out of a total of 223, but failed to score in the second, Australia winning a grand match by five wickets. At the Oval, in the deciding Test, he led England to overwhelming victory. This was Hutton's match, for he scored his famous 364 in 13 hours and 20 minutes. Hammond played very quietly for 59. For Gloucestershire he scored 2,180 runs at an average of 83.84.

In the winter of 1938 he led the M.C.C. team in South Africa. This is no place for a history of those strange and often tedious Tests on chemically over-perfect pitches. The last match, in spite of lasting for ten days, was never finished. Hammond scored 609 runs in the Tests, including three centuries, for an average of 87.

Back in England for the season of 1939, which seems so far away, he showed no decline in his colossal skill. For a cricketer so widely travelled, so drenched in runs, he retained his keenness to a remarkable degree; but it was observable that his method was changing. He now played more strokes off his back foot—the first hint, perhaps, of a need to conserve energy. Be that as it may, he scored seven centuries, one of them against the West Indies in the Test at the Oval, totalled 2,479 runs for the season, and with 63.56 yet again headed the averages.

Figures must largely fill a sketch of so great a batsman, but I should like future generations of cricketers, if they turn over Hammond's pages on some peaceful evening, to think of him as something far more than a wonderful maker of runs, many more of which, we hope, are yet to flow from his bat. For, as an all-rounder, he is the greatest cricketer of this generation, not merely in centuries, in the taking of wickets, and in the making of catches, but in his attitude to the game which he, while drawing from it his fame, has enriched with a grace, a simplicity and a nobility that may never be seen again.

COUNTY CHAMPIONSHIP REVIEWED [1941]

When the press awarded honours

BY HUBERT PRESTON

Hubert Preston's account of the evolution of the County Championship served as a salutary reminder that the history of the Championship is so imprecise a chronicle that it is not even clear who the first champions were. Although Preston draws attention to the peculiarities of the points scoring systems which were in fashion from year to year, and although he rightly casts a doubt on the justice of naming Derbyshire as the 1874 champions, he does not refer to the fact that as early as 1853 the title of County Champions had been bestowed on Nottinghamshire, and that in 1864 the 'title', such as it was, had gone to Surrey. Nor is he quite accurate as to the extraordinary Billy Midwinter, when he says that Cricket's most brilliant turncoat was the first professional to appear for Gloucestershire: in fact he was the second. Nor is it doing justice to Midwinter's genius for dissimulation to say that he 'considered himself an Australian'. The whole essence of Midwinter's case is that he considered himself an Australian when in Australia and an Englishman when in England, that he considered himself an Australian when contemplating his formative years in Victoria, but an Englishman every time he remembered that his birthplace had been in the Forest of Dean, that he considered himself an Australian when representing that country against England, and was quite certain that he was an Englishman when representing that country against Australia. Among the fascinating points raised by this essay is the table listing the ways in which the Championship has been decided, with no fewer than fourteen methods of scoring being applied in a period of sixty-five years.

At a time when, by force of circumstances, County cricket is in abeyance, a survey of the Championship Competition seemed opportune and, several questions having been put to me regarding the subject, I decided to make an attempt to do justice to such an important and far-reaching part of cricket in England. An essential retrospect takes one back sixty-nine years when, without an attempt at anything like a regulated tournament, the first Championship award was made. Fascinating and enlightening, the task stirs the imagination and makes one wonder why the competition was not given definite shape from the moment of its inception.

Histories of the County clubs throw interesting light on the casual way in which the fixtures were arranged and carried out in those days. The farce of men playing for more than one county in a season having been stopped, nine counties 'considered' first class were named for the championship, fewest defeats to settle the question of supremacy, but there was no mention of the number of matches necessary to qualify, and for several years the methods of conducting the tournament look almost grotesque in the light of the care since taken in devising various plans for settling the conundrum of properly placing the counties at the end of each season. The rules, if any existed apart from the two mentioned, were so lax that fixtures could even be abandoned for personal reasons. Gloucestershire, entirely amateur, and Nottinghamshire, all professionals, were the strongest counties in 1872, but the arrangement of their matches in 1873 meant that their first meeting would have come too close to the visit of Gloucestershire to Bramall Lane, Sheffield, to permit of W. G. Grace playing in both games. The Yorkshire match was for the benefit of Joseph Rowbotham, the only Yorkshireman credited with two centuries in 1869. Rowbotham journeyed to London specially to remind W. G. Grace of a promise to play in it. W. G. who, when snatching time from his medical work, was the great attraction on any cricket ground, said

'Joe, I have promised to play for you and I will do so.' The Gloucestershire amateurs beat the Yorkshire eleven of professionals by six wickets. On the three days 23,000 people paid to see the cricket, the crowd of 12,000 on the first day being described as 'enormous.' The consequence of the Champion not being available for the Nottinghamshire match was that both engagements between these powerful sides were cancelled and were not resumed until 1875.

Yet they were bracketed as first champions. Nottinghamshire won five games and drew their other first-class County match, while Gloucestershire won four and drew two competition games.

DOUBTFUL HONOURS

In 1874 Derbyshire, the only unbeaten side, provided a more glaring instance of the unsatisfactory way of conducting the tournament. They won three and drew three of their six eleven-a-side County engagements with first-class opponents, and so became champions, although sixteen of them played Nottinghamshire. As it happened, Flint, a slow right-hand bowler, and William Mycroft, fast left-hand, dismissed Nottinghamshire, who were not at full strength, for 65 and 125; Derbyshire won by 14 wickets.

Other counties, Middlesex among them, played no more than six matches and the general uncertainty prevailing came to a head in 1883, when Nottinghamshire received the title because they lost only one of twelve County matches, although they won no more than four and drew seven, whereas Yorkshire won nine of sixteen engagements, losing two and drawing five. Yorkshire claimed the championship and their history by the Rev. R. S. Holmes states, 'That year Yorkshire was champion County,' while F. S. Ashley-Cooper, in *Nottinghamshire Cricket* wrote 'Notts were awarded first place but the distinction could clearly be claimed by Yorkshire.' *Wisden* supported this view: 'All first-class engagements reckoned, the Yorkshiremen have an undeniable claim to the championship.' W. J. Ford, in his *History of Middlesex Cricket*, pointed out that Middlesex, another all-amateur side at that time, 'lay third, but as a matter of fact no real championship existed, though the leading sporting papers, as representing public opinion, generally awarded first place to some county with the others in order of merit, but it was in 1894 that the classification became really systematic.' Derbyshire could not maintain their early claim to eminence and, as the outcome of losing all their six games with first-class Counties in 1887, dropped out of the contest through lack of fixtures.

Criticism gradually brought about a sounder state of affairs. Yet satisfaction was far from unanimous. As the result of an abortive attempt to classify the Counties into three groups, the County Cricket Council became defunct after a lively meeting and, beyond any doubt, cricket journalists were to be thanked for keeping County cricket in something like trim shape. After the 1888 season, in which the two great bowlers, Turner and Ferris, failed to bring chief honours to the Australian team captained by Percy McDonnell, Charles F. Pardon wrote in *Wisden*: 'The steady development of County cricket is the best thing for the modern practice of the game. We have had an almost ideal competition among the leading counties.' The influence and criticism brought to bear, mainly by the Press, induced the M.C.C. to take direct action in conjunction with the Counties. Then in the autumn of 1894 came the decision that 'There was no limit to the number of first-class counties, the M.C.C. having power to bring Counties into the list or remove existing ones.' The extension upset the balance of the tournament because the counties no longer played the same number of matches as they had done for a few years, when all met each other twice. Somerset, promoted in 1891, Derbyshire, Essex, Hampshire, Leicestershire and Warwickshire brought the first-class counties to fourteen and the tournament lumbered along.

The method of awarding points underwent frequent changes without lasting improvement, and even the conclusions arrived at, after prolonged meetings by the Findlay Commission in 1937, no more than recommended ways of removing grievances that had arisen chiefly because of finance, and failed to lay the bogey that always showed itself because of real or imaginary trouble spotted by some legislators; and the decimal points that came into vogue caused much irritation. Still, except for doubts as how best to reward the winners of each game, the competition proceeded smoothly. That little injustice has been done in the long run stands out clearly when we see which Counties have won the championship. Of the 17 competing in 1939 Worcestershire, Northamptonshire and Glamorgan having in turn been admitted, nine have gained the honour, and of these all but Warwickshire were enumerated in 1873. The championship came to the eight original first-class Counties in this order—Gloucestershire and Nottinghamshire (joint holders), Derbyshire, Middlesex, Lancashire (tied with Nottinghamshire), Surrey, Yorkshire, and Kent. In 1911 Warwickshire occupied first place, after which the distinction reverted to seven of the former winners, the exception being Gloucestershire. Never has the distinction come to Sussex, who completed the first nine and are the oldest-formed County club.

VARYING STRENGTH

The rise and decline of great players affected the strength of the sides to such an extent that Gloucestershire have not once finished first since 1877. That was the season when Midwinter, who was born at Cirencester and had come back from Australia, appeared as the first professional in the Gloucestershire ranks. He returned to Australia in the winter, played in the two matches against J. Lillywhite's England team and started the next summer with the Australians, captained by David Gregory. He took part in five matches, but he was induced to resume playing for Gloucestershire 'in dramatic fashion,' as Sydney Pardon used to describe. The Australians were at Lord's for the match with Middlesex; Gloucestershire, on arriving at The Oval for their game with Surrey, decided that they must have Midwinter. In order to impress a man nearly

6 feet 3 inches in height and weighing about 15 stones, W. G. Grace, the Gloucestershire captain, himself a heavyweight, and E. M. Grace, the Coroner, took with them J. A. Bush, comparable to Midwinter as a giant. In a four-wheeled cab they drove to Lord's and brought back Midwinter. Weighty argument had the desired effect! Midwinter went to and from Australia for several consecutive seasons. He considered himself an Australian and once said: 'I made a mistake in deserting the first Australian eleven of 1878.' He played for Alfred Shaw's team in the four matches against Australia in 1881 and 1882, and appeared for W. L. Murdoch's 1884 team against England at Manchester, Lord's and the Oval, so representing both these countries in matches against each other—a unique distinction.

Derbyshire, after temporarily losing their status, could not climb to the top again until 1936. Nottinghamshire, falling away after 1889—their tenth year in the lead—were unable to regain the championship until 1907, and Surrey, following a wonderful spell from 1887 to 1899, did not reach 'double figures' as champion county until 1914. Yorkshire, on the other hand, despite their many fine professionals, were not moulded into an acknowledged championship side until 1893, when the perseverance of Lord Hawke, in his eleventh season as captain, earned the reward. From that time Yorkshire have proved themselves by far the most consistent County, having been champions 21 times in the course of 43 competitions. This is the Yorkshire total in the complete list of 63 tournaments that have taken place. Nottinghamshire come next in the number of championships with 12; then follow Lancashire 11; Surrey 10; Kent 4; Middlesex 4; Gloucestershire 3; Derbyshire 2; and Warwickshire 1. The Nottinghamshire figure includes four ties; that of Lancashire three ties; Gloucestershire and Surrey each shared first place in one indecisive result. As further evidence of how the ability of the sides fluctuated, we find that of these champion counties, Gloucestershire finished last in 1891, 1893 and 1894; Derbyshire took the 'wooden spoon' in 1886, 1887 and 1924, and Kent in 1895.

THE BIG SIX

Regarding a point raised by an ardent follower of the game, 'Which are the Big Six?' I can recall a prominent Sussex official, I think Mr. W. Newham, saying years ago, 'We don't mind if we are among the Big Six.' Asking the question of Mr. H. D. G. Leveson-Gower at Lord's last summer, I received a prompt reply which confirmed my memory that the term referred to Yorkshire, Nottinghamshire, Lancashire, Surrey, Middlesex and Kent. These were the strongest counties in the old days and most sought after as opponents when the secretaries compiled their own fixture lists at the Annual Meeting at Lord's. Now these six stand out as having most championship triumphs to their names; also as match winners throughout the period 1873 to 1939 they rank supreme in this order: Yorkshire 763 victories, Lancashire 628, Surrey 591, Kent 565, Nottinghamshire 468 and Middlesex 427.

The percentage of wins as given in the appended table shows some variation in this order, namely: Yorkshire 52.15, Lancashire 45.28, Kent 44.38, Surrey 42.30, Middlesex 38.85, Nottinghamshire 38.77; but under this closer scrutiny, the six chief counties retain the clear proof of ascendancy.

THE ONLY CUP-TIE

Suggestions in recent years for a knockout competition from advocates of what they are pleased to call 'brighter cricket' take one back again to the start of the competition. In 1873 the Marylebone club offered a Champion County Cup for competition, all matches to be played at Lord's. The proposed tournament came to nothing because some acceptances of the invitation to play were withdrawn, but Kent and Sussex carried out their tie as arranged. Kent won by 52 runs in the only first-class county Cricket Cup-Tie. What became of the Cup seems an unsolved mystery.

Could that project of the M.C.C. have become an annual event, one may imagine the excitement over everything that happened in the final tie, with a climax in the presentation of the Cup to the captain of the victorious eleven. But would the tension have exceeded that at Lord's on the last day of August, 1920, when Middlesex beat Surrey in a match which decided a desperately close fight for first place? Early in the day Lancashire beat Worcestershire by nine wickets at Manchester and went to the head of the table. The position of the game in London warranted some celebration at Old Trafford of an apparently certain championship; but Lancashire's joy was short-lived. Middlesex turned the fortune of their game and fought so well for the victory necessary to give them first honours that they pulled off the forlorn hope. A wonderful catch by Hendren in front of the sight screen started a collapse that prevented success for Surrey in a valiant race against the clock. Middlesex won by 55 runs within ten minutes of time. Surrey finished third—a true index to form, though the Counties did not play an equal number of matches, an almost invariable misfortune in the tournament. The Middlesex programme consisted of 20 fixtures whereas Lancashire engaged in 28 and Surrey 24 games. Yorkshire, Kent, Sussex and Nottinghamshire followed in this order. So, Sussex were among the 'Big Six.'

CELEBRATED CAPTAINS

Besides the presence in the team of great players who were regular choices for representative matches, strength in leadership influenced the winning powers of the Counties. Nottinghamshire, during their spell of sustained superiority, when the competition was in its infancy and so few matches qualified for entry, were all professionals, led in turn by Richard Daft, W. Oscroft, Alfred Shaw and M. Sherwin. Their chief opponents were Gloucestershire, captained by W. G. Grace; Middlesex, by I. D. Walker, and Lancashire, by A. N. Hornby. These counties gave way to Surrey, guided by John Shuter who, in his sixth year of captaincy at the age of 32, enjoyed the satisfaction of taking his side to the top, and this position was maintained six times in eight seasons, while in 1889, Surrey tied with Lancashire and Nottinghamshire. Shuter retired after 1893 when the Surrey sequence was broken by Yorkshire, Lord Hawke, after being in command since 1883, becoming in his 33rd year the conquering captain. K. J. Key then led Surrey to first place three times in six seasons.

Yorkshire took the honours eight times under their first amateur leader and Lord Hawke altogether captained them for 28 seasons. In the last part of his regime, Middlesex, captained by Gregor MacGregor, gained their second success and Kent stood out with their first championship in 1906, C. H. B. Marsham being captain. Following a decade under J. A. Dixon the invigorating personality of A. O. Jones brought Nottinghamshire to the fore again in 1907 and then Kent, with E. W. Dillon in charge, finished first three times in five years. A. N. Hornby still captained Lancashire when champions in 1897 and A. C. MacLaren led them to the honour in 1904. After this 22 years elapsed before Lancashire in their most dominating period, assisted in the supremacy of the North, unbroken since 1921.

When Warwickshire in 1911 checked the long continuity of success by one or other of the 'Big Six' they could thank very largely the superb cricket shown by their captain, Frank R. Foster, who, at the age of 22, earned the description 'the best all-rounder of the year,' with the further commendation as a young leader that he bore comparison with W. G. Grace.

The loss of four seasons during the Great War caused little difference to the strength of the best counties. Yorkshire, led by three different captains, won five championships, Middlesex; with P. F. Warner and F. T. Mann at the helm, two; Lancashire four in five seasons, the first two under Colonel Lawrence Green, when given command at the age of 36 after small practice in first-class cricket. Nottinghamshire, steered by A. W. Carr, and Lancashire, by P. T. Eckersley, again proved worthy winners before another new star arose. A. B. Sellers, when only 25, found himself left in charge of Yorkshire. Despite want of experience in big matches, Sellers accepted the responsibility with such zest that his side did not lose a match under him that season, the two defeats in 1932 occurring when F. E. Greenwood filled his elected role of captain, and, apart from 1934 and 1936, the Yorkshiremen carried off the Championship until war stopped first-class cricket again. Six triumphs in eight years of the most exacting period in cricket history is the account of his stewardship that Brian Sellers can give. In both years when Yorkshire fell away the calls of Test matches depleted the Yorkshire forces; the same thing happened in 1938, but then ample talent of the necessary standard occupied the vacancies. During these seasons Yorkshire contested 224 county championship matches when led by Brian Sellers, winning 135, drawing 68, and losing 21—one defeat in every ten matches.

These figures compare very favourably with those of Surrey nearly fifty years before, when the competitors never exceeded nine, and the strain of captaincy was much less trying. Taking their last eight seasons when captained by John Shuter from 1886, the year before their first championship, Surrey played 122 matches against first-class counties. Of these they won 87, drew 11, and lost 24. Their defeats averaging one in every five engagements. Yet, Surrey were absolute champions five times and were bracketed with Lancashire and Nottinghamshire in 1889. When Shuter left off, Lord Hawke began his long stretch of prominence. Of the last 21 tournaments Yorkshire have won twelve and Brian Sellers, unless the war denies him the opportunity, can carry on once more with the prospect of adding to his county's and his own laurels.

The various changes in the method of reckoning points in the Championship matches have been as follows:—

1873 to 1886.—The smallest number of lost matches decided the order of merit.

1887 to 1889.—A win counted one point, a draw half-a-point.

1890 to 1894.—Losses were deducted from wins, drawn games being ignored.

1895 to 1909.—One point counted for each win; one deducted for each loss; unfinished games ignored. Championship decided by the greatest proportionate number of points in finished games.

1910.—Result determined by percentage of wins to matches played.

1911 to 1914.—A win counted five points. In drawn games the side leading on the first innings scored three points, and the side behind on the first innings one point. The order decided by the greatest proportionate number of points obtained to points possible.

1919.—In this season, when each match was restricted to two days of longer playing hours than hitherto, the order was decided by the greatest percentage of wins to matches played.

1920–23.—Percentage of points gained to maximum points possible. A win counted 5 points and a lead on the first innings 2. Games in which 'no result' was obtained on the first innings were ignored.

1924–26.—The method followed in 1923 unchanged except that the county leading on the first innings scored three points and the county behind one point.

1927–28.—Percentage of points gained to maximum points possible. A win counted 8 points, and a lead on the first innings 5 points, the remaining 3 being given to the side behind. In the event of a tie, or if 'no result' on the first innings was obtained, 4 points to each side, provided that in the second case not less than six hours of actual play had taken place. Matches in which six hours had not actually been played did not count, provided no result of any kind had been obtained.

1929–30.—The method agreed upon was:—Each county to play 28 Competition matches, 8 points being awarded for a win; 4 to each side in a tie game, or when the first innings scores were level in a drawn match, or when there was no first innings result, or no play at all; and, in a drawn game, 5 points to the side leading on the first innings and 3 to its opponents. The county obtaining most points to be the winner of the Competition.

1931–32.—Each county to play 28 Competition matches, 15 points being awarded for a win, and in drawn games 5 for the side leading on the first innings and 3 for their opponents. In the case of a match being finished and the scores equal, each side to count 7½ points, and in a game not being finished or the totals of the first innings level each to have 4. A match not being concluded and there being no result on the first innings, or no play, each side to receive 4 points. The county which obtained the greatest number of points to be winner of the Competition.

1933–37.—Each county to play 24 matches to qualify for the Championship Competition. Counties allowed to arrange more matches, but all must be reckoned in the Competition. No county to play another county more than twice in a season. The system of points for 1931 and 1932 remained unchanged, but the county obtaining the greatest proportionate number of points on a percentage basis entitled to be the winner of the Competition. The unit of 100 per cent. in all matches was equivalent of 15 points.

1938.—Each county to play a minimum of 24 matches to qualify for the Championship, 12 points being awarded for a win, and 4 points for the first innings lead in all matches. A side obtaining the first innings lead and then winning the match receives 12 points; if it loses the match it retains the 4 points for the first innings lead. In deciding the Championship the points gained are divided by the number of matches played, the County with the highest average being the Champion County. 'Matches Played' are exclusive of matches in which there is no play, or matches in which there is no result on the first innings.

MATCH RESULTS IN THE COUNTY CHAMPIONSHIP
(1873–1939)

	Won	Lost	Drawn	Tie	Total	Percentage of Wins	Percentage of Draws
Derbyshire	237	448	301	0	986	24.03	30.52
Essex	265	326	364	1	956	27.71	38.07
Glamorgan	71	221	185	0	477	14.88	38.78
Gloucestershire	397	515	337	0	1231	30.78	27.37
Hampshire	246	389	358	0	993	24.77	36.05
Kent	565	378	329	1	1273	44.38	25.84
Lancashire	628	256	502	1	1387	45.28	36.19
Leicestershire	179	404	341	0	924	19.37	36.90
Middlesex	427	299	372	1	1099	38.85	33.85
Northamptonshire	131	355	203	0	689	19.01	29.46
Nottinghamshire	468	248	491	0	1207	38.77	40.68
Somerset	209	446	268	3	926	22.57	28.94
Surrey	591	304	499	3	1397	42.30	35.72
Sussex	405	474	445	1	1325	30.49	33.58
Warwickshire	229	293	403	0	925	24.76	43.57
Worcestershire	170	399	296	1	866	19.63	34.18
Yorkshire	763	208	492	0	1463	52.15	33.63

9,062 matches have been played in the County Championship, of which 5,968 have been finished and 3,094 unfinished.

NOTES [1942]

BY R. C. ROBERTSON-GLASGOW

In reverting to his role of editorial annotator, Robertson-Glasgow describes a landscape exotic in its unfamiliarity, and yet affectionately remembered by those who attended the matches and familiarised themselves with the clubs he mentions. London Counties and the British Empire XI were hastily improvised portmanteaux into which might be flung any first-class cricketer who happened to be on leave and in the right town at the right time. The Army and the R.A.F., for long years such parochial fringe attractions that their very mention in the Almanack seemed out of place, were now dramatically reformed into sides of near-Test status, with the added piquancy that the vagaries of war guaranteed that often old comrades from the same club now found themselves in contention against each other. A well remembered example is that of the Middlesex twins, W. J. Edrich and Denis Compton, who now found themselves representing opposing sides in fixtures between the R.A.F. and the Army.

In view of what was to happen to English cricket in the years ahead, nothing could have been more prescient than Robertson-Glasgow's comments on the loose talk about so-called brighter cricket. Nobody could have been more forthright in his rejection of panaceas later so eagerly embraced, and nobody could have been more adamant in his opposition to the courting of those:

> who understand no batting except that which keeps the ball far, high, and often; to whom a saving innings of few runs and great artistry is as meaningless as a batch of Hittite inscriptions; who so far from grasping the tactics and art of the bowlers, or the nature of the pitch, even regard the difficult bowler as a nuisance, a fellow that ought to give way to one who can be relied upon for long-hops, full-pitches, and half-volleys.

Robertson-Glasgow died in the very year that the cricket Establishment finally bowed to the winds of circumstance and inaugurated that corruption of the game which Robertson-Glasgow so clearly, and so rightly, feared. In writing that 'such spectators are frankly not wanted in county cricket', it is almost as though he had been vouchsafed a terrible vision of chanting, drunken hordes at one-day finals, of mentally deficient exhibitionists running naked across the field in mid-Test, of the vandalising of pitches in some non-cricketing cause, of the County Championship being hawked around in the market-place. One wonders what Robertson-Glasgow would have made of the modern age, but there is no need to wonder after all, for he put his opinions into the most forceful words as long ago as 1942:

> First-class cricket is a subtle as well as a strenuous game. It is a thing of leisure, albeit of leisure today not easily found or arranged; a three-act play, not a slapstick turn. And, in practical terms, such one-day matches would be farces, though not of the sort intended by their promoters.

Brave words, long forgotten by the time when, a generation later, first-class cricket accepted the poisoned chalice of televised commercialism.

FROM time to time the dubious highbrow and the benighted Philistine raise a little clatter against cricket, grudging that devotion which they cannot inspire for their own little causes and negligible interests. But cricketers of every age and every degree of ability or ineptitude, often in the most unlikely places, seize the fleeting hour to bat and bowl. They *will* do it. They absent themselves from felicity awhile, then return with sharpened appetite, not only to play, but to discuss the game; for, as the Labour correspondent of a London newspaper remarked of the politicians—'You can't stop them talking.'

It would be an error to rate our war-time cricket on technical values. The fact that a match is played and that the friends of cricket and the cricketers gather to watch the match is of far more interest than that Hutton, after scoring 20, was out in an un-Huttonian manner, or that

Denis Compton was late for a yorker, or that Nichols's slips not only stood rather too deep but stooped rather too slowly. For most of us, the mere sight of such players is enough. It reminds us of what has been and what soon will be again. Most of the cricket in which first-class men have taken part has been played for the benefit of some war charity. Practice and time have been short. In general, players have cared little for the result, as their methods have often shown. It has been cricket without competition; a snack, not a meal. 1941 might be called 'The Spectators' Season,' for the matches scattered over the country have provided one of the few and one of the best ways of learning the news of friends scattered over the world.

These one-day matches have given such good entertainment, where at one time little or none had been expected, that some critics have urged their retention as a regular process for the first-class County Championship in peace time. I do not agree with this view. Those who urge it most strongly would, I believe, be the earliest to tire of the experiment. The new clockwork monkey in the nursery, which waves its arms and waggles its head, delights for a few short hours or days. But the children soon return to the older, if more sedate toys, the tried companions in the familiar cupboard. The faults of the three-day match are not few, but the objections to a one-day County Championship are overwhelming.

UNWANTED SPECTATORS

There is a false analogy drawn from modern sports that all spectators are in a hurry, and that, therefore, all games-players should be in a hurry too. Cricketers and cricket-watchers are not made like that. There will always be found those who understand no batting except that which keeps the ball far, high, and often; to whom a saving innings of few runs and great artistry is as meaningless as a batch of Hittite inscriptions; who, so far from grasping the tactics and art of the bowlers, or the nature of the pitch, even regard the difficult bowler as a nuisance, a fellow that ought to give way to one who can be relied upon for long-hops, full-pitches, and half-volleys. Such spectators are, frankly, not wanted at County cricket. They would do better to stay at home and write to the newspapers about it. For first-class cricket is a subtle as well as a strenuous game. It is a thing of leisure, albeit of leisure to-day not easily found or arranged; a three-act play, not a slapstick turn. And, in practical detail, such one-day matches would be farces, though not of the sort intended by their promoters.

There would be probably not more than sixteen home matches. Of these it is reasonable to suppose that a quarter would be either marred or deleted by rain. This would leave twelve days of play on home grounds. The thing is ridiculous, a mockery; members would resign in shoals; nor, I fancy, would the gate-money take much counting. As *The Times* cricket correspondent remarked, would Yorkshire, for instance, come up to the Oval on the uncertain chance of a day's cricket with Surrey? Not if I know Yorkshire. Sir Home Gordon, too, has shown that, in one-day matches between first-class cricketers, 'the later batsmen have less than a 50 per cent chance of getting an innings.' From which he rightly argues that such cricket would lead to specialization, to teams being composed of six batsmen, four bowlers and a wicketkeeper. I should even suggest that three bowlers would be enough in most cases; and I recall a match at Lord's last summer in which an England bowler never turned his arm at all, not forgotten but compulsorily idle! Cricket fostered in such an academy would be ill-prepared to face the Australians in England, let alone in the timeless Tests abroad.

The merits and weaknesses of Two-day matches are more worth considering. They were tried in the Championship of 1919, and have generally been written off as a failure. In truth, many of these matches produced fine play and a spirit of enterprise that was painfully lacking from much of the ensuing cricket in the next two decades. The chief weakness in 1919 was the scrambling inconvenience of fitting in refreshment, rest, and travel; which irritated and exhausted players, umpires and scorers alike. There is a world of difference between seven o'clock and seven-thirty as a time for drawing stumps. Spectators, as a whole, simply do not like to stay late, and are not to be tethered even by a reduction of entrance-fee in the late afternoon. Hunger begins to assail them: also the thought that wives, cooks and servants, if any, are not pleased to be kept waiting or debarred from their favourite film-star by men who stay watching 'that silly cricket.' If two-day matches were to be tried again, better arrangements of timing would be necessary, and, surely, possible.

A TWO-DAY SCHEME

A programme of 32 matches could be arranged by playing two two-day matches each week. One lot could be played on Saturday and Monday, the other on Wednesday and Thursday, the two latter days including the trade half-holiday in nearly all parts of England. Thus Tuesday and Friday would be free for travelling, and their mornings could, if wanted, often be given to practice, in the nets or fielding, or both. Or, if no journey was to be made, an occasional game could be played, in which some of the County players would join with promising local cricketers, members, their sons and relations, much to the mutual benefit, cricketing and social. For one of the most obvious weaknesses of the present system is the almost total detachment of the County cricketers from those who watch and support them. Time and opportunity are lacking for such games and society as I have suggested. This is a mistake. For, to the club an average cricketer, who might well have it in him to rise from the ruck, there is no stronger incentive to keenness and a higher standard of cricket than to play sometimes with those who, at present, are usually no more than heroes at a distance. Also, it might well lead to an increase of membership in County Clubs.

From the playing point of view the difference between Three-Day and Two-Day matches is not so complete as some suppose. The Three-Day match, in theory, allows for 18 hours of play. In practice, this often shrinks to 17, the hour being cut off the end of the third day, either for the catching of a train, or because the match has died. Again, the gates on the third day are nearly always very thin, even when there is a prospect of a fine finish. Third days of County matches are no joy to the treasurer. Two-Day matches, if played on each day from 11 to 7 o'clock, would give 14 hours. If—admittedly a large 'if'—pitches were not made to break the bowler's heart, and if—an easier thing to ask—batsmen were to play with a sensible freedom, and if captains were to use judgment tempered with adventure in the declaration of innings, there is no reason why Two-Day matches should not produce a reasonable number of finishes and a type of cricket worth both playing and watching. The old enemy, rain, might be attacked by arranging that, if two hours or more were lost on the first day of play, the match should be decided on one innings only. The whole system would more than ever depend on the captains and the groundsmen, but, even in its times of failure, it could hardly produce cricket more dismal and unattractive than is seen in those matches which, like wounded snakes, drag their slow length along and die miserably during the third day.

CHARACTER COUNTS

Yet, though the Two-Day match has much to commend it, I think that the Championship will be resumed on the old Three-Day system. Tradition and habit favour it; the chief danger being that tradition so easily degenerates into inertia and habit into self-satisfaction. It may be said that this danger was being met and overcome by most counties and captains in the two seasons before this war; and spectators appreciated the change of spirit and tempo. In the last analysis, cricket must depend on the character of its players. A thousand laws mean nothing without liberal interpretation, and, in the matter of days and hours, a half-day cricket match can be a purgatory of boredom. The stroke of the bat, not of the pen, makes or kills a match.

The enemies of the Three-Day match are apt to condemn all slow play; but I think that most spectators still relish it in its proper place; when, for instance, batsmen of great skill and control are opening an innings against able bowlers 'fresh from the stall,' or when a match is being well saved against expectation and every wile of the attacker; arts that are far removed from slow play merely for its own sake. It is not so much slowness that kills cricket and disperses the crowd as the communicated sense that the players do not care what happens; a negligence and a slackness of mind which are as likely to corrode a match full of boundaries and apparent gaiety as one that plods and groans its heavy way.

A PLAGUE OF NOISE AND NONSENSE

Your slashing reformer would away with all 'slow' play. By him the artist and the mere obstructionist are measured and condemned alike in terms of boundaries and minutes. He is a senseless glutton, who would readily choke from a surfeit of sixes and drink up to the eyes on speed. He assumes that all bowling, all pitches, are equally easy; in captaincy as in individual execution he dislikes a finesse which he cannot understand. He 'occupies the room of the unlearned,' but he cannot keep silence. He is a plague of noise and nonsense.

We often find ourselves saying that first-class cricket no longer attracts the public. We grumble at supposed decline. So it is interesting to read the remarks by Mr. Alfred Cochrane in the *Cricketer Annual*. He played for Oxford against Cambridge in 1885, 1886 and 1888; also for Derbyshire when it was 'one of the weakest of the principal counties.' 'I detect,' he writes, 'hardly any difference between the game as I played it in the 'eighties and the game as I last watched it in the summer of 1939.' To him, the ability of a contemporary cricketer does not increase with memory. 'In some cases I may even venture to question whether what seems to be the popular conception of these heroes who now like those in Homer carry fixed epithets, coincides with my own recollection.' Again, 'There are veterans who say that cricket is not the game it was in their youth, that modern batting is slow and dull' . . . 'Sentiments like these convey the impression that first-class matches half a century ago were a lively mixture of physical risks and big hits . . . that is not my recollection; the cricket of my time was much like the cricket that I watch now; as regards the standard of play, my considered opinion is that, so far from any deterioration, I should say that it has greatly improved. Not only has the general standard advanced, but the leading experts, players like Bradman, Hammond, or Hutton, can challenge comparison with any that I have ever seen. Holding these views, I cannot be expected to take much interest in proposals to alter the rules and conditions of the game, in order, as the phrase goes, to brighten cricket. There is always a risk that in searching for spectacular values you may reduce rather than increase the real attraction of the game, and that is the rivalry between two competing elevens.'

A gust of sense in these observations blows strongly enough to shake the most self-assured Nestors and Jeremiahs, and to sweep the mist from the minds of the wild reformers.

REFLECTIONS ON 1941

In the South, once again the British Empire Team and the London Counties each carried through long programmes with conspicuous success, and gave pleasure to a wide variety of players and spectators. This is not a time when records and results matter much, but the British Empire team did well to beat a Nottinghamshire side of considerable strength at Trent Bridge in June, and in August, at Bradford, they beat a Yorkshire Eleven containing nine County players by four wickets. In both these matches R. E. S. Wyatt (94 and 52) and the Essex man, H. P. Crabtree (50 and 68) distinguished themselves, and, against Yorkshire, that clever Irish and Middlesex bowler, E. A. Ingram, took 6 wickets for 26. At Lord's a strong Royal Air Force side was beaten by three wickets. But the two 'needle' matches were undoubtedly those against London Counties. At Lord's rain fell when the Empire team had lost three good wickets for only 34 in reply to the London Counties' total of 194. Three weeks later, at Reading, the Empire team scored 187 (A. V. Avery 59), then bowled out the London Counties for 120, to which Alan Watt, of Kent, contributed a fierce innings of 40. In the two war seasons these teams have met four times: British Empire has won twice, London Counties once, one match has been drawn.

The outstanding batsmen were R. E. S. Wyatt, H. P. Crabtree, A. C. L. Bennett and A. V. Avery. Of the regular bowlers C. B. Clarke, the West Indies Test cricketer, was quite the most distinguished. His spin, flight and accuracy were generally too much for his opponents, and he returned an average of 11.4, taking 98 wickets in 273.5 overs. His fielding also was brilliant. In the win over the Royal Air Force at Lord's he took 6 for 74. The ordinary club batsman could not cope with him; and against Metropolitan Police, he took 15 wickets for 58, including all 10 wickets in the second innings for 29 runs. R. Smith, of Essex, bowled magnificently against Sir Pelham Warner's team at Lord's, in late May; the first six wickets all fell to him, including C. J. Barnett, R. E. S. Wyatt, D. Compton, and R. W. V. Robins, all England players. W. E. Merritt, the New Zealand and Northamptonshire leg-break bowler, could appear but rarely, but memorably at least once when, against Nottinghamshire, on a true pitch, he took 8 wickets for 48. Just over £2,000 was raised for War Charities, including £165 for the Coventry Distress Fund. The Club was again organized and inspired by D. L. Donnelly, and had as its President Sir Pelham Warner.

LESLIE COMPTON IMPRESSES

London Counties, consisting almost entirely of Southern professionals, again played cricket that was both entertaining and successful. In A. W. Wellard and A. E. Watt they had two of the big hitters in the game; and a steadier excellence was provided by such tried men as A. E. Fagg, J. O'Connor, and the brothers F. S. and J. W. Lee. Frank Woolley and D. Compton could only play 7 innings each, but Compton finished top of the batting averages—59.33 for 356 runs. His brother, Leslie Compton, played some very fine innings, earning high praise from such judges as R. E. S. Wyatt and the well known umpire, Frank Chester. His best performance was probably his 121 not out at Coventry, in which he defended surely and drove magnificently. Considerably larger than his brother, he will, fortune favouring, surely have a good trial with Middlesex after the war, and might well become an England batsman.

The team suffered a sad loss before the season began in the death of L. C. Eastman, the Essex all-rounder; and that vast but subtle bowler, J. Durston, who holds a commission in the Home Guard, was unable to play at week-ends. A.R. Gover, taking 33 wickets at 9.5 each, showed no decline in ability as an opening bowler, and was admirably supported by the tough and persistent Watt. J. W. Lee, a clever off-spinner, finished at the top of the averages, 47 wickets at 8.19 each. Good work, too, was done by J. A. Young, the Middlesex left-hander, who has increased his pace, and by P. F. Judge, of Glamorgan. But Wellard unfortunately dropped out during the season with serious knee trouble.

Thirty-eight matches were played, and only three lost. These were, respectively, against British Empire Eleven, as before remarked, Bedford, who on that occasion had the help of L. G. Berry (Leicestershire), and J. Grimshaw (Worcestershire), and against Slough, for whom Frank Edwards, that excellent left-hander of Buckinghamshire, bowled with great skill on a wet pitch. Over £1,200 was handed over to war charities, including £350 for Coventry Hospital and £296 for Bexleyheath War Weapons Week. The arrangements for 1942 are again in the capable hands of C. J. E. Jones, the Counties Secretary.

THE ARMY AND R.A.F.

Teams representing the Army and the Royal Air Force played each other on five occasions, distributing their entertainment and skill over the country, at Lord's, Bramall Lane (Sheffield), Nottingham, Harrogate, and Liverpool. The results were: at Lord's Royal Air Force won by 5 wickets; at Nottingham, Army won by 5 wickets; at Harrogate, Army won by 8 wickets; at Sheffield, Royal Air Force won by 77 runs; at Liverpool, Royal Air Force won by 7 wickets. The Lord's match was full of good cricket, the Essex players, M. S. Nichols and P. Smith, distinguishing themselves with both bat and ball; but in vain. R.A.F. won the toss and put the Army in. This has been the general practice, captains using the two hours of Summer Time to give their bowlers the advantage of a dewy pitch.

J. D. Robertson, the young Middlesex professional, showed his skill and grace in an innings of 30. The crowd would have enjoyed more of the crisp fluency and orthodox style of this batsman. D. Compton seemed rather short of practice, and soon, mistiming a drive, was caught and bowled by P. F. Judge, of Glamorgan. P. Smith and M. S. Nichols then added 123 by sane and strong cricket, and the Army and Yorkshire captain, A. B. Sellers, followed with a typical innings of 32 not out, starting shakily, but being undisturbed. J. W. A. Stephenson, electric as ever, was run out trying to startle close third man, and Sellers declared at 261 for seven wickets, generously leaving the Royal Air Force some four hours of batting.

R.A.F. lost the England batsman, C. J. Barnett of Gloucestershire, and C. Washbrook, of Lancashire, for only 10 runs. R. J. Gregory, of Surrey, scored 30, and H. S. Squires, also of Surrey, one of the calmest and most correct of batsmen, made 54 before he was caught at wicket by S. C. Griffith of Sussex, whose form was very fine throughout. Then came what was probably the innings of the season, by L. E. G. Ames. His first 50 runs were made quietly; then he attacked with wonderful speed of foot and power of wrist. He had made 127 including 3 sixes, when the Army total was passed.

TWO STAR TEAMS

Six England players took part in this match, and, for future record, the players and their ranks may be of interest. In order of batting, *The Army*:—2nd Lieut. J. D. ROBERTSON (Middlesex); Pte. E. COOPER (Worcestershire); †Sgt. Instructor D. COMPTON

(Middlesex); 2nd Lieut. P. Smith (Essex); †Sgt. Instructor M. S. Nichols (Essex); Major A. B. Sellers (Yorkshire), captain; Major J. W. A. Stephenson (Essex); Major G. W. Parker (Gloucestershire); Captain S. C. Griffith (Sussex); 2nd Lieut. T. F. Smailes (Yorkshire); †Captain H. Verity (Yorkshire).

Royal Air Force:—†Flying Officer C. J. Barnett (Gloucestershire); Sergt. R. J. Gregory (Surrey); Sergt. C. Washbrook (Lancashire); Flight Lieutenant H. S. Squires (Surrey); †Flight Lieutenant L. E. G. Ames (Kent); Cpl. L. J. Todd (Kent); Squadron Leader R. G. Musson, captain; Sergt. C. Oakes (Sussex); Ldg. A/c. P. F. Judge (Glamorgan); Ldg. A/c J. Nye (Sussex); †Pilot Officer A. D. Matthews (Glamorgan). *England players marked †*

Sir Pelham Warner, continuing to deputize for Colonel Rait Kerr as secretary to M.C.C., again showed his unquenchable enthusiasm for the game, and an energy which does not abate with the years. He gathered teams, advised secretaries and cricketers, and exhibited an optimism tempered with wisdom. To many others, too, nameless but not unknown, cricket owes much in war time for their help, example, and refusal to admit gloom or impediment. Among the Counties, Nottinghamshire carried out a programme of 10 matches, of which only one was wrecked by rain. Trent Bridge could watch the brilliance of young Joseph Hardstaff, and sometimes saw that other and more adventurous Harris, C. B., who like his Dickensian namesake, Mrs. Gamp's friend, had seemed to be only a myth.

BATTLE OF THE BLUES

Oxford and Cambridge played a one-day match at Lord's on 28 June, Cambridge winning deservedly by 7 wickets. Oxford certainly began with the disadvantage of having played scarcely at all as a team, The Parks pitch not being available during the war; also, their captain, E. K. Scott, was unable to play on the day. But, even so, Cambridge had the stronger set of cricketers. They appeared on the field in a specially designed cap, light blue with stripes, which suggested a pleasant approximation to the real thing.

At Fenner's, during May and early June, the side, captained by that excellent opening batsman, J. R. Bridger, of Rugby, beat Cambridgeshire, Southgate, and the United Hospitals team led by C. B. Clarke, then drew with an Army team, rain interfering. These were one-day matches. An exciting two-day match with the British Empire team was left drawn. Cambridge made 217, British Empire team 199 for 6 declared; Cambridge followed with 222 for 6 declared, and British Empire just failed to score the necessary 241 in the 2½ hours available, in spite of a brilliant innings of 149 by R. E. S. Wyatt. Wyatt also scored 70 in the first innings and revived a dying match with a generous and sensible declaration. After a most pleasant two-day match, left drawn, against Sussex at Hove, the University suffered its only defeat, by Aldershot Area, by 8 wickets. Here some fine bowling by Company Sergeant-Major Gover, of Surrey, settled the issue. After term, the match against Club Cricket Conference at Lord's was drawn, the Cambridge bowling looking rather ordinary.

Against Oxford, H. E. Watts, of Downside, bowled his leg breaks very cleverly. E. Crutchley, the best of the Oxford batsmen, met him with confidence, and looked set for a good score, when he was caught off a careless drive. M. J. W. Cassy, the Oxford opening batsman, made a valuable 52, before being bowled by a leg-break from Watts that might have settled anyone. Throughout the season J. A. Dew kept wicket well, sometimes brilliantly, for Cambridge.

From time to time news came through of well-known cricketers on Service overseas. Names and places must not in these days be connected, but mention should be made of some grand bowling by the South African cricketer, R. J. Crisp, who also won high and enduring honour in a sterner game.

Notice of the death of cricketers will be found in another part of this volume; but I cannot here pass by two whom I knew well myself. First, Kenneth Farnes, of Essex: the very type and embodiment of fast bowling, tall, strong and enduring, a magnificent sight in action. His bowling was always good and, when need called, often great. Many fine performances stand to his name, none more remarkable than his 6 for 96 in an Australian innings of 600 at Melbourne during G. O. Allen's tour of 1936–37. And who that saw it could forget his attack on the Players at Lord's in 1938? At the end of the first day he sent back both Edrich and Price for 0 in one over. On the next day he was irresistible, and, in five spells, he dismissed Hutton, Hardstaff, D. Compton, Nichols, Smailes, and Pollard for 43 runs; surely the grandest fast bowling seen in this match since Arthur Fielder, in 1906, went through the whole Gentlemen's side for 90. He was gentle and courteous in manner, humorous and observant of mind and speech, and he will be sadly missed and fondly remembered by all who knew him, not least by the young cricketers whom he taught at Worksop.

Essex have lost another fine cricketer, L. C. Eastman, whose death was the result of service during enemy action. He was the 'utility man' of the County side. In batting he would generally go in first, and, though his scores were seldom large, he often so rattled the opening bowlers by his adventurous attack that batting was made easier for those who followed. As a bowler, slow-medium to medium, he relied on a combination of length, swerve, subtly varied flight, and slight spin. On a sticky wicket he could be devastating; and at all times he was apt to take that one important wicket which loosens an innings. He was an optimist; gay, companionable and witty; and would, I am sure, have made a wonderful coach for some boys' school in his retirement, for he was both intelligent and patient.

Meanwhile, schools of every sort continue to turn out young cricketers of a standard no whit below their predecessors, for all that a few critics, who stand in perpetual need of some mental cathartic, bemoan the annual decay of cricket in paragraphs whose regularity is only equalled by their idiocy. Haileybury, coached by that admirable old-rounder, A. F. Wensley, late of Sussex, were probably the strongest side among the

Public Schools. Dulwich had two excellent all-rounders, T. E. Bailey and A. W. H. Mallett, and a real fast bowler for a boy, H. P. H. Kiddle. But I hear rival coaches and supporters sharpening their swords and pencils, so will refrain from further comment on this subject.

As to the future of English cricket, I join with the old song-writer, in the search for the silver lining. It can be found.

May I again thank Mr. Hubert Preston and Mr. Norman Preston, of Pardon's Cricket Reporting Agency, for their kind help and research, and express the hope that they and many other friends will soon again be enjoying the agitated pleasures of peace-time reporting.

February, 1942.

NOTES ON SEASON 1942 [1943]

BY R. C. ROBERTSON-GLASGOW

Robertson-Glasgow's editorial comments in the 1943 edition again show remarkable perception of the social problems awaiting the game just over the horizon. At the end of a long review of the season, he closes with a section headed 'Professionals and Amateurs', seizing the nettle which the administrators continued to sidestep for another generation. Robertson-Glasgow's views on the relationships between the paid and the unpaid, on the extent to which the distinction was any longer of any significance, are understood all the better for a knowledge of his own experiences in the county game. In the 1920s, when he took more than 400 wickets for Somerset, he served under the genial John Daniell, of whom Wisden remarks: 'He possessed a forcefully picturesque vocabulary when things did not go as he expected; but because he was always scrupulously fair, his sometimes caustic criticism left no ill-effects'. A more hilarious account may be found in Robertson-Glasgow's '46 Not Out', in which his years with the Somerset eleven are seen as an interlude in a cricketing paradise through whose pavilions there echoes the sound of bellowing laughter. There seems to have been no hint of asperity in relations between amateurs like Daniell and Robertson-Glasgow, and the Club's few hired hands. Somerset in the early 1920s was still very much a gentleman's club; in the county batting averages for 1923, in which season Robertson-Glasgow took 58 wickets at just over 17 apiece, nineteen players are listed, of whom no fewer than fifteen are amateurs. In such an environment, a young man like Robertson-Glasgow might easily have felt that distinctions between paid and unpaid were necessary to the maintenance of tradition and good conduct. On the contrary, he comes out boldly for the abolition of all social distinctions, and was surely the first of the successful university players to expose the hypocrisy by which unpaid players indirectly boosted their income through achievements on the field.

EVERY critic thinks that he alone is right; otherwise, why trouble to think at all? This confidence in personal judgment blossoms best in Sport, and in cricket comes to its full and redolent flower. A man may change his opinion about a Sten Gun or the Secretary of a Club; a woman may be converted to the tone of a wall-paper or the angle of a feather; but no self-respecting follower of cricket will budge an inch from his view that A is the worst batsman who was ever invited, by mistake, to open the England innings, and that B is the best googly bowler who ever pined the afternoon away at deep long-leg. In short, no reasonable devotee is open to reason. It is too late to ask and too churlish to expect that this should be otherwise.

Those of us who can still keep ready by the mind's fire a chair for cricket's welcome, have certain matters apt for discussion. They are trivial in the face of the one great issue, but they lack neither recreative pleasure nor a bearing on what Mr. Skimpole, good simple humbug, referred to as 'Some pounds, odd shillings, and halfpence.' From a host of subjects, each one being good enough for a day and a night's talk among the faithful, I mean to take three, one at some length, two in brief.

(i) Some cricket, such as it was, in Summer 1942.
(ii) Some cricket, such as it may be, in summers to come.
(iii) The amateur and professional question.

Also, subsidiary questions may poke an inquiring head round the corner.

Cricket in summer 1942. I have an almost irresistible urge to tax the benevolence of the editor and the patience of the proprietor with the cricket which is England—matches played often in the uniform of Service, at random, at the sudden idea of someone, somewhere, with no scoreboard, a tea-interval of an hour and a half, and umpires who bowled if they happened to feel that way. I had the fortune to take part in several such games, on Sunday afternoons, after we had all discarded those curious little gaiters which illumine the extremities of the Junior Service. In most of them there stood an umpire of long experience and of an integrity that surmounted the not infrequent appeals of his favourite son. His authority was unshakeable; he gave no answers to unofficial questions; and, at the end of a certain match in which he had sent back their best batsman on a somewhat delicate l.b.w. decision, he said to me: 'the secret of umpiring is never to bandy words. Bandy, and you're done.' Only once did this principle tremble. We were using the eight-ball Over. Suddenly the scorer, if such he can be termed, shouted to him: 'Nine balls.' 'No,' shouted back the umpire, 'seven.' 'Nine,' resumed the scorer. 'Seven,' reiterated the umpire, 'and, whichever it is, it's a—odd number, and we're not going to stop on *her*.'

In the 'superior globe' of cricket, spectators watched the fun at Lord's, Brighton, Trent Bridge, Edgbaston, Leicester, Derby, Worcester, Northampton, Reading, and other towns of repute. League Cricket flourished at weekends in Yorkshire, Lancashire, Durham, and the Midlands. Perhaps the highest standard of play was maintained in the Bradford League, where teams were often enriched by three or four of the illustrious who happened to be serving in the district; and specimens were provided of a type of play, intense, competitive, and enjoyable, which may yet become the standard first-class game of future years.

Lord's, where Sir Pelham Warner ably continued as Deputy Secretary to the Marylebone Club, once more provided a farrago of cricket which varied pleasingly from the first class, or near it, to that in which 'the players were remarkable rather for their enthusiasm than for their technical ability.' Matches were played at Lord's by such teams as the Royal Navy, the Army, the Royal Air Force, Sir Pelham Warner's XI, the British Empire Team, and the Buccaneers. Of these, the Royal Navy, as in time of peace, only more so, were unable for obvious reasons to raise a team even dimly approaching their true strength; but, in Surgeon-Lieutenant K. Cranston they had a batsman, tall, powerful, and orthodox, of whom it is hoped that 'more will be heard'; and in their losing match against the Army, on July 11th, Lieutenant G. C. Newman, at number five, played a stubborn innings of 38 not out which revealed yet another quality of this easy and versatile athlete.

In this match, too, Lieutenant J. D. Robertson, the Middlesex batsman, played an innings of 102 in just over an hour and a half. Once more he showed a method and a grace that distinguish him as a cricketer of England class. The scores of the principal matches may be found in another part of this volume, but memory recalls a dashing century by Sergeant Washbrook for Royal Air Force versus Army, and for the Army in this match an innings of 81, at number nine, by Major S. C. Griffith, full of courage and driving. His wicketkeeping, too, was of the highest order. He was helped in a last wicket stand by Company-Sergeant-Major-Instructor A. R. Gover, who, as ever, maintained speed and accuracy of bowling throughout the season.

Pilot-Officer R. E. S. Wyatt showed little, if any, decline in batting skill, and none at all in keenness. Sergeant-Instructor D. C. S. Compton was sometimes to be seen batting in his own spirit of freedom, and, though he seldom interested himself in heavy scoring, his 'eye was as steady as ever.' Squadron Leader W. J. Edrich, likeminded as to freedom, batted and bowled and fielded as if each match were to be his only appearance in the season, and Flying Officer C. J. Barnett looked as usual, as if he meant to crack the screen behind the bowler.

Among the older men, Sergeant M. Leyland and Sergeant - Instructor M. S. Nichols suggested intimations of immortality, and Flight Lieutenant Ames wafted at least one spectator back to Canterbury at peace. From these scenes the great Yorkshire batsman, Sergeant-Instructor L. Hutton, was missing, because of a severe injury to his arm. Latest advice informs that he has recovered. May it be so.

The Royal Air Force had won their first match against the Army by seven wickets; but in the second, on September 5th, their bowlers were treated lightly. For the Army, Sergeant C. B. Harris (115), most whimsical of modern batsmen, after a meditative beginning, drove past the covers like flaming fire. He was kept good company by Major B. O. Allen (69). The Army declared their innings at 291 for 3 wickets. The Royal Air Force had three hours for batting. Squadron Leader W. J. Edrich hit 48 in 30 minutes, Flight Lieutenant Ames 70 in 70 minutes. A collapse followed, but a stubborn last wicket stand by R. G. Emery and Pilot Officer A. D. Matthews baulked the Army of victory. Once more, Sergeant T. G. Evans, of the Army and Kent, showed very fine form as wicketkeeper. A discovery indeed.

Cricket at Lord's abounded in tight finishes. On May 30th the British Empire team beat the Buccaneers by 2 runs on the last ball of the match. C. B. Clarke, the West Indies Test player, bowled it to G. Lambert, of Gloucestershire. Lambert drove it high and far, just on the off side. Surely a boundary. But L. B. Thompson, running from the on side of the screen at the Nursery end, made a wonderful catch.

Then, on June 27th, Cambridge beat Oxford on the seventh ball of the last over, when A. F. G. Austin, the last Cambridge choice, a slow leg-breaker, bowled the Oxford captain, W. J. H. Butterfield. Cheers and groans. Let the feelings of Butterfield be unspoken, for his 22, at number seven, had in another few seconds saved the match. Yet Cambridge deserved to win. Their start was magnificent, even contemptuous. J. R. Bridger and the lefthanded J. D. Matthews (captain) scored 118 in 75 minutes, and the Oxford bowling, never very sure, was spreadeagled. Cambridge supporters gaily recalled the feat of M. W. Payne in 1906, when 'in the first half hour of the Cambridge innings he hit to the on boundary nearly every ball he received,' and was then out for 64 in a total of 73, his partner, R. A. Young, continuing to 150.

Matthews was free and fallible, Bridger was free and safe. C. F. Anson added a fine innings of 85, and Matthews declared at 295 for 8 wickets, leaving Oxford three hours. Oxford answered with spirit, L. K. Purkiss (36) and C. P. Lindsay (61) scoring 70 for the first wicket at good pace. At 104 for 2 they seemed safe from defeat, but the militant D. F. Henley was stumped, and Lindsay was very well caught low at mid-on. On and around the field Cambridge stood on its collective toes. G. L. Robins, a lefthander, bowled A. N. Mather, the Oxford number eight. Butterfield and ten minutes remained. Bang went G. E. Dixon and L. L. Toynbee to Robins. Then Matthews, inspired by some imp or genius, gave Austin the ball for that last over to Butterfield from the pavilion end.

On July 16th there was a match between teams purporting to represent Oxford Past and Present and Cambridge Past and Present, but, since it had to be played in mid-week, few indeed of the less legendary 'Past' could help either side and Oxford won a narrow victory, mostly owing to the astute and genial captaincy of B. H. Lyon and the all-round ability of E. D. R. Eagar, and in spite of the apparent refusal of one of their team to cease from bowling.

Then, at August Bank Holiday, a crowd of 22,000 were given something good to see and talk about, for on the Monday and

Tuesday Middlesex and Essex (United) played Kent and Surrey (United). The match was in aid of King George's War Fund for Sailors. The result was a draw, but the cricket was grand and the end exciting. Middlesex and Essex were left 95 minutes to make 190 runs for victory. S. M. Brown and A. V. Avery strove to keep up with the clock, but not till W. J. Edrich joined Brown was the race level. Then D. Compton succeeded Brown, and the real fun began. Edrich was out for 73 to a glorious catch and bowl by A. V. Bedser. Twelve minutes were left for play, 34 runs were needed, when L. Compton joined his brother, who attacked Bedser and A. R. Gover with most of the known strokes and several peculiar to himself. Four balls remained to come, 4 runs were wanted; and D. Compton, going out to drive Bedser, was neatly stumped by T. G. Evans who, with 55 in the first innings of Kent and Surrey, showed that he is not only a good wicketkeeper. Most reluctantly the spectators re-assembled themselves for departure. In a match so full of skill and adventure the performance of Major E. R. T. Holmes stood out. He returned to captain Kent and Surrey after a year's absence from all cricket; also, he had recently been ill; but he scored 39 and 114 not out, making many of those drives which are the crown of batting and the joy of watching.

Among teams of less eminence but, perhaps, even intenser ardour, much obviously good, some enjoyably bad, cricket was played, and many words about old and absent friends were spoken. On July 7th a team of Eton Ramblers surely raised by, but not, for once, including, that Napoleon of Eton cricket, Colonel G. H. M. Cartwright, played a team of the Home Guard from the London District, and the Home Guard, 'with a reasonably mobile side,' avenged their defeat of 1941. For 'the domestic defenders' A. C. L. Bennett (103) and C. V. G. Haines (85) put on 123 in a second wicket stand, Bennett reaching the 100 in 90 minutes. The Eton Ramblers, 'collected with considerable difficulty,' could only answer 326 for 7 (declared) with 135; and their number eleven batsman, unbeaten for 3, remarking that he could have batted for the rest of the day, mounted his motorcycle for Salisbury Plain, whence he had set out very early that morning. The concluding hours of this match were 'further brightened by the band of the Metropolitan Police.'

For enthusiasm, and excellence of fielding, the London season's (unpresented) prize must be accorded to a team of the Royal Australian Air Force who, in beating a team from the Royal Air Force, displayed an agility, a speed and accuracy of picking up and throwing the ball, a comprehensive brio, which might have surprised even Leary Constantine in his boyhood. The bowling and batting were, certainly, not quite of the same standard; that was hardly possible. But, for those who were present, it was a scene that no man would wish, and no boy ought, to forget; an entertainment and a lesson in one.

On August 29th the match between Hornsey and Southgate produced a remarkable last wicket stand. T. Plant and R. W. Somerville of Hornsey stayed together for the last hour and 35 minutes, added 79 runs, and saved the match.

In summary, 1942 was the best war-time season that Lord's has had. In 1940, receipts for War Charities were £1,033; in 1941, £1,075; in 1942, £1,397. The 'gates' for War Charity matches totalled 89,299, as against 74,325 in 1941. All officers and men of the Services in uniform were admitted free.

Turning aside for a moment, I should like to pay a tribute, short, as he himself would have had it, to Andrew Ducat, who fell dead while batting at Lord's on July 23rd for the Surrey Home Guard against the Sussex Home Guard. His character was gentle and kind, but strong and clear. Nothing showy, insincere, or envious came near his nature. As an athlete, in his prime, he looked and was magnificent, and he was one of the very few who have played both cricket and Association football for England. I first met him in a match at the Oval against Surrey, and remember most his strong leg hitting and square cutting. I was fortunate to meet him more often, later, in the Press Box, and he used to tell me, in his quiet way, something about the footballers of his time. In football, Aston Villa, whom he led to victory in the Cup of 1920, was his chief love. Very many will miss him. He was a fine player of games, and, in his simplicity, a fine man.

Television being in a state of suspended infancy and travel in a temporary decline, I did not find it possible to see more than a glimpse of the obviously enjoyable and often excellent cricket played away from London. The copying out of scores and the embellishing of hearsay would, with reason, exasperate readers and alarm the proprietors. So, those who followed, arranged, or played the provincial cricket of 1942, must forgive the somewhat narrow space given to it. Absence of body, not of mind or heart, is the cause. But, as regards one famous old home of cricket, Brighton, I am fortunate to have before me some matter as committed to *The Cricketer* by Sir Home Gordon, who likes, when he can, to take Lord's and Hove in one day. He will, I trust, allow me a summarized use of his information.

Upon his motion, Sunday cricket was started at Hove. That marks, as they say, if not 'an epoch,' at least an advance. 'Usually,' writes Sir Home, 'play began somewhat after two o'clock.' Very many of us gratefully recall peace-time cricket around villages and towns on Sunday afternoons which might else have been spent with boredom, friend of mischief. But *Wisden* is no place for theological discussion; further, it enjoys the advantage of not opening its columns to daily correspondence.

Apart from Sunday cricket, more matches were played at Hove than anywhere else except at Lord's, three a week from the end of May to the third week in September. Here, the 'Seven Services' tournament took place, causing over twenty matches. They were played on the time-limit system, and seldom did any team bat up to the full limit. Pleasant and keen as the cricket was, most of the scoring and wicket-taking was done by first-class players of tried ability, and, so far as Sussex was concerned, no new stars, let alone comets, whizzed into the sky. The tournament was won by Royal Air Force, led by Flying

Officer H. P. Chaplin, who captained Sussex over twenty years ago and keeps a spirit ever young. The Bedser twins, E. A. and A. V., were often prominent in bowling, batting, or both, and the bowling averages were headed by H. P. H. Kiddle, one of the most promising of the younger school of cricketers. The Royal Navy team, for whom Surgeon-Lieutenant K. Cranston batted very well, came second. Bottom place was taken by the Army team, led by the tireless Captain Maurice W. Tate, the famous England cricketer. The years cannot take away his length, but they have confiscated something of that wonderful 'nip.'

LEAGUE CRICKET

In the Bradford League 'A' Division, there was a close struggle for first place between Lidget Green and Windhill. The issue was delayed till the very last Saturday of their season, September 5th. On that day Windhill beat Saltaire (memories of S. F. Barnes!) by one wicket; but Lidget Green, taking three points from Idle, kept their lead by 2 points. Against Saltaire, Windhill had in their team L. N. Constantine, W. H. Copson, D. Smith, and J. S. Buller. For Lidget Green, T. B. Mitchell, the England and Derbyshire leg-break bowler, and A. Bastow between them took every wicket that fell to their team in championship matches, a feat without parallel in the League. Bastow topped the League bowling list with 63 wickets at 6.96 each; Mitchell had 78 wickets at 8.94 each. The batting list was headed by E. Paynter, the England and Lancashire lefthander, who, playing for Keighley, champions of Division 'B,' had the extraordinary average of 138.55 for 15 innings, highest score 158. In bowling, the West Indies test cricketer, E. A. Martindale, provided the complement to Paynter's batting; and so Keighley return to Division 'A' for season 1943.

In the Birmingham League, West Bromwich Dartmouth won the championship for the second year in succession, largely owing to the skill of E. Hollies, the England and Warwickshire leg-break bowler. Once more, H. O. Kirton (Mitchell and Butlers) showed fine form as a batsman, coming first in the League averages with 68.40 for ten innings. In the Durham League of ten teams the Sunderland Police made a welcome appearance, and finished third. South Shields won the tournament for the fourth time.

Report of a Royal Navy Air Station cricket team, 'somewhere in England,' caught the curious eye; for there, at the top of the batting averages, as he is entitled to be by fame and merit, stood Major Lord Tennyson, of the Army—10 innings, twice not out, highest score 55, average 30.12. Unconsciously, if illogically, I searched beneath his name for Kennedy and Newman, Brown and Bowell, Mead and stumper Livsey; and the rigours and revels of the Bournemouth festival came back, without invitation, and were gone.

The British Empire Eleven which, when fully representative, was of strongest County standard, again gave to spectators good cricket and raised for Charity (the Red Cross, except in one or two instances) the sum of £1,500. They played 34 matches; won 23; lost 5; drew 6.

Of those who could play with some frequency, C. B. Clarke, the West Indies Test cricketer, bowled remarkably well even for him, taking 129 wickets in 323 overs at 10.17 each. His leg-breaks, delivered at unusually fast pace and with a longish run, were apt to unsettle the best and unhook the weaker opponents. Three times in one fortnight he did the hat-trick. Among British Empire batsmen, Captain A. H. Parnaby, A. V. Avery, H. P. Crabtree, H. Halliday, R. Smith, A. C. L. Bennett, R. J. Partridge, and T. E. Bailey were the most successful. R. Smith, of Essex, captained the team in most of the matches, and the committee carried such well-known names as Sir Pelham Warner and S. F. Rous. The manager, A. C. L. Bennett, joined the army during the summer, and was succeeded by C. V. G. Haines.

London Counties, of equal standing with the British Empire Eleven, again aimed more particularly at bringing attractive and powerful cricket to districts not usually, even in time of peace, thus entertained. In result, many games were won with something more than ease, but the playing mattered far more than the winning. Denis Compton headed the batting averages with 86.80, followed by Jack O'Connor, 64.25. Besides the familiar worthies of the home counties, the brothers J. W. and F. S. Lee, of Somerset, and Stuart Boyes, of Hampshire, still a fine lefthand slow bowler and close fielder, gave their help. During the winter, the constitution of the club was remodelled.

Of the Public Schools, Dulwich, Eton, Charterhouse, and Rugby had good teams, and from these four schools came nine out of the twenty-two cricketers who played in the match, Lord's Schools *v*. The Rest, on August 5th and 6th. More detailed reference to school players will be found in another part of this volume, and there is no doubt whatever that the general standard of play was up to the average; but, in the friendliest spirit, I should like to deprecate that excessive praise which, especially in time of war, when values may be forgotten, is so easily and so often accorded to very young players. The calculated belittling of any games-player makes none ridiculous but him who belittles; but thoughtless flattery makes a fool of both the flatterer and the flattered.

Of those school players who were seen at Lord's, T. E. Bailey and A. W. H. Mallett, both of Dulwich, showed promising all-round form, and their fast-medium bowling was of quality. Both, if opportunity offers, should make good in first-class cricket. Besides these, E. N. W. Bramall, of Eton, showed himself to be a stylish player of strokes, and N. D. Howard, of Rossall, was solid and sensible as an opening batsman. In varying methods, J. S. Souter, of Haileybury, G. E. S. Woodhouse, of Marlborough, G. A. Wheatley, of Uppingham, and A. S. Lovett, of Charterhouse, showed promise as batsmen, G. A. Wheatley also being an alert and crisp wicketkeeper. Among the bowlers, besides Bailey and Mallett, C. M. Wheatley, of Eton, maintained accuracy with his inswingers, and both B. J. K. Pryer, of City of London School, and R. R. Rees, of Haileybury, could look difficult with slow spin-bowling, though Pryer at present uses the leg-break hardly at all. One other cricketer, who was twelfth man for the Public Schools X1 *v.* a Lord's XI, R. J. L. Altham, of Marlborough, should be mentioned for a second innings of 116 against Rugby, in which he reproduced some hereditary skill in both defence and attack.

Good work was done by the Surrey County Club in continuing to run their 'nursery' team, the Surrey Colts, under the care and encouragement of Mr. Andrew Kempton, who wrote: 'The lads who have comprised this side have come from Public Schools, Secondary Schools, and village clubs, and their enthusiasm for each other's success has made the experiment well worth while.'

POST-WAR COUNTY CRICKET

On the nature of County cricket after this war many persons have maintained, sometimes with no little heat, their various opinions. Meanwhile, the Marylebone Cricket Club, neither unduly depressed by criticism nor noticeably elated by praise, took the wise and natural step of calling, for December 8, 1942, a meeting of the Advisory County Cricket Committee. To this body, whatever the public and the critics may say, belongs the ripest knowledge of what kind of cricket is likely to prove convenient, entertaining, and at the same time, cricket.

In effect, the members of this committee were asked to go back to their several homes and there to discuss various plans for the resumption of the County Championship after the war, and to bring again to Lord's, in the spring of 1943, those plans in the shape of specific resolutions. Haste, so ardently urged from some quarters, was not necessary or helpful. Plans, reasonably sifted and debated, were called for, and they will fall for consideration at the meeting of the M.C.C. and Advisory Committees in July.

All the first-class counties with the exception of Derbyshire were represented. Those present were:—

M.C.C.: S. Christopherson (President), Lt.-Col. Sir Stanley Jackson, Lord Cobham, W. Findlay, Sir Pelham Warner, Col. R. S. Rait Kerr.

Essex: A. J. Spelling; Glamorgan: F. D. Pipe; Gloucestershire: Lt.-Col. H. A. Henson, F. O. Wills; Hampshire: Col. W. K. Pearce, W. H. Sprankling, W. R. Ponting; Kent: Lord Cornwallis, J. R. Mason; Lancashire: T. A. Higson, Major R. Howard; Leicestershire: Sir Julian Cahn; Middlesex: R. H. Twining, Major G. O. Allen; Northamptonshire: Lt.-Col. T. E. Manning; Nottinghamshire: Sir Douglas McCraith; Somerset: Brigadier E. H. Lancaster; Surrey: B. A. Glanvill, H. D. G. Leveson-Gower, A. F. Davey; Sussex: Sir Home Gordon, W. L. Knoles; Warwickshire: Dr H. Thwaite; Worcestershire: Lord Cobham; Yorkshire: E. F. Holdsworth; Minor Counties: C. B. L. Prior.

In short, what will almost certainly happen is that the first season of County cricket after the war will be given over to experiments, without any set championship; a not unpleasing prospect; for then the public may be able to watch an old-fashioned 3-day match, an 'improved-model' 2-day match, an 'all-in' 1-day match, a hit-your-six-and-go time-limit match, and even, perhaps, a sharp bout of tip-and-run; and all, perhaps, within some ten days. The Festival Circus of Imperial Rome went little better than this.

There may be rain, under whose tyranny the most ingenious planners and the most insatiable cricketers are just so much frustrated matter. And that, to borrow the sparing expression of an illustrious golfer who hit five balls out of bounds at one hole would be 'a little disappointing.'

While I think it likely that the majority of County votes would probably even now, and even more probably later on, be cast for 3-day County matches, my own hope, for what it is worth, still inclines towards the 'new-model' 2-day match, two matches to be played in each seven days; for I believe that this system, properly handled, would satisfy the discerning public, would divert and extend the players, and, avoiding travesty, would encourage and maintain the true standard of cricket.

Of these 2-day matches, 'one lot could be played on a Saturday and Monday, the other on a Wednesday and Thursday, the two latter days including the trade half-holidays in nearly all parts of England.' I quote from my own contribution to *Wisden* of 1942. Sussex have added some interesting suggestions: 'Normal hours of play, with declarations permissible at any time provided the side next batting has a full hour before stumps are drawn. Four points for a win on first innings, ten for a win outright, with six apiece in the event of a tie. Follow-on optional at 100 runs. In the event of rain preventing play on the first day, the rules of one-day matches to be adopted for the second. All the first-class counties would be able to meet each other.'

Here is a basis for good cricket, good watching, with enough of leisure surely to satisfy officials, umpires, scorers and ground staff, and to give the County teams the chance of reasonable travel and of playing local sides, with the enjoyment of those social pleasures without which any game is only half a game.

PROFESSIONALS AND AMATEURS

This is a question that calls for plain speaking and honest thinking. Its treatment demands realism, which you will rarely find either on a soap-box in Hyde Park or in a deep armchair of the Carlton Club.

I think that any man who has had the happiness of playing, even occasionally, in what is called first-class cricket will extend that somewhat arid adjective far beyond the confines of batting, bowling, and fielding. For in no other cricket, however rich in the strife, humour and benevolence of Nature, will you find such good company among players of all ages and all walks of life, or make and, if you will, keep such effortless and enduring friendships. But I also think that the hour is ripe, indeed over-ripe, for the sweeping away of anachronisms and the exploding of humbug.

Under the word 'Professional' in the *Concise Oxford Dictionary* you will find the words 'playing for money'; under 'Amateur' you will find 'one who is fond of' and 'one who cultivates a thing as a pastime.' You will also find, but not in the Dictionary, that, as regards modern cricket, these respective definitions are to a remarkable degree interchangeable; for, all professionals whom I have known are fond of cricket and regard it as a pastime as well as a living, and many amateurs, besides being fond of cricket, play it for the equivalent of money, namely for the publicity which attracts clients to themselves or to the business for which they may be working. The only difference here is that the professional's pay is direct, and the amateur's indirect. To both, cricket is in fact, whatever it may be in law, their source, partly or entirely, of livelihood. To distinguish between these two sorts of cricketer, on any commercial consideration, is surely humbug.

In the season of 1939 there still existed in County Cricket a few, a very few, amateurs who earned no money, directly or indirectly, from the playing of their game. They received only their travelling and hotel expenses, and, in some cases, not even these. Long may cricket encourage and be encouraged by such men. Their unbiassed leadership and natural generosity have served cricket honourably and long, and they have given to the game, from half-legendary times, many illustrious players, many great captains, many prudent legislators. But they are survivors of an almost lost society, of an age that is nearly gone.

For these reasons, with whatever feelings of regret or pleasure they may be regarded, and for many other reasons, some too obvious, others too intimate to be mentioned, I would welcome the total deletion of all distinction between professionals and amateurs in first-class cricket. To me at least such questions as the position of a cricketer's initials and the precise gate from which he is to enter the field have long seemed vastly absurd. Once on the field, a bowler is as good as a batsman, and a wicketkeeper probably better than either. But, how much County cricketers of the future are going to be paid, and whence the money is to come, are questions that I do not mean to discuss—yet.

Once again, at the end of these Notes, I should like to thank Mr. Hubert Preston, and Mr. Norman Preston and their colleagues of Pardon's Cricket Reporting Agency for their kind help and wise suggestions.

January, 1943

THE BEST FAST BOWLER [1944]

Account of 'W. G.' beard incident

BY SIR STANLEY JACKSON

In an Interview

The accession in 1944 of Hubert Preston (1868–1960) to the post of editor marked a return to the era of the Pardons, for Preston had first contributed to the compilation of the Almanack as far back as 1895, and had therefore served an apprenticeship for editorial command lasting exactly fifty years.

He was a gentle man whose hearing was so defective that in his early years in the Press box he wielded a formidable ear trumpet which later gave way to more sophisticated aids. He had first worked in journalism as a young man on 'The Manchester Guardian', but from 1893 to 1895 tried a career as a farmer in Canada. It was on his return from the mixed pleasures of agricultural life that he joined Wisden and witnessed a great many agricultural innings. He remains the only journalist ever to do the hat-trick at Lord's, in the annual match between Press and Authors, and the only known Englishman to propagate the cause in which he believed so passionately, that all pedestrians should walk on the right-hand side. An Honorary Freeman of the City of London, he was described by Neville Cardus as 'the most courteous and best-mannered man ever to be seen in a Press Box on a cricket ground'. His first edition was marked by the introduction of a new contributor, Sir Stanley Jackson, or, to give him his full typographical honours, Colonel The Honourable Sir Francis Stanley Jackson, P.C., G.C.I. (1870–1947), who had captained Harrow, Cambridge, England and the Conservative Party—he was Chairman of the Party at the time of the deplorable episode of the Zinoviev Letter. He later became Chairman of the England selectors and Governor of Bengal, in that order of precedence, and is famous as the only Test captain who ever finished a rubber top of the batting and bowling averages and also won all five tosses.

OPINIONS *differ considerably on the question, 'Who was the best fast bowler?' The passing of Ernest Jones, the noted Australian bowler who came to England with the* 1896, 1899 and 1902 *teams has raised again this absorbing topic. One of the few cricketers of long experience who can speak on the subject as an authority is the old Cambridge and England captain and Yorkshire player, Sir Stanley Jackson. He readily accepted an invitation to a chat, and has been good enough to agree to his opinion being set down in* Wisden.

Of all the fast bowlers the Australians have sent to this country, I think Jones was the best in my time. I have very good reasons for remembering him, as I took part in the first match he played in this country against Lord Sheffield's XI at Sheffield Park, Sussex, in 1896. He was one of the most powerful men I ever met. I believe he was a miner, and in his early days of the tour was very wild in his delivery. This was probably because the Australians came practically straight off the ship to the match and were short of practice. Jones gave me the impression that his main effort was to show his immense pace. The wicket was dry and he bowled short, bumpy stuff.

I went in first with W. G. Grace and we had to dance about a bit. One ball from Jones hit W. G. under the arm, and later in the innings another one went head-high past him and over Kelly's head to the boundary. This was the ball about which the 'Beard Story' originated. I can see W. G. now. He threw his head back, which caused his beard to stick out. Down the pitch went W. G., stroking his beard, to Harry Trott and said: 'Here, what is all this?' And Trott said: 'Steady, Jonah.' To which Jones made that famous remark: 'Sorry, Doctor, she slipped.' I do not think the ball actually touched W. G.'s beard. That story was told afterwards, and I believe I was responsible. When I was out and returned to the Pavilion, I said: 'Did you see that one go through W. G.'s beard?' The ball was bouncing, and only Ranji appeared to like it. The pace that Jones was bowling impressed me because in the second innings, when I had made about 10, I had the misfortune to stop one with my ribs, but with the assistance of W. A. J. West, the umpire, who rubbed me, I was able to continue my innings.

(*F. S. Jackson was not out 95 when the match was left drawn.*—EDITOR.)

When I went to London I had a good deal of pain, and my father sent for the doctor, who said, 'It's cracked horizontally.' He strapped me up, and I did not play for three weeks. Within a month of Sheffield Park I faced Jones at Lord's in the M.C.C. match, and he came up to me and said, 'I am terribly sorry,' and he clasped my hand in a vice-like grip that left me wondering which was the more painful—my hand or broken ribs.

Following those early incidents, Harry Trott took Jones in charge and changed him into a very fine bowler. He made him shorten his run and taught him the value of length and control. Jones developed a beautiful action. I believe it has been suggested that he threw, but this I personally regard as absolutely absurd. At that time, the action of some bowlers was not fair, and Sydney Pardon, by his campaign in *Wisden,* did valuable work towards stamping out the trouble.

I think it is often forgotten that bowlers, well supported by the field, are the match-winners. You can generally find plenty of batsmen, but genuine bowlers are scarce.

Although I never played against him, I would say that Larwood appeared to me the best fast bowler I saw. I have a great admiration for him, with his beautiful rhythmic run and a perfect action which gave him complete control over pace, direction and length. It was these qualities that made him such a fine bowler. I think that he achieved this because at the moment he delivered the ball he was poised high in the air with his left shoulder well up and pointing towards the wicket. It was then that he was complete master of himself, and the control at the end of his run gave him time to deliver the ball the way he wanted. Jones was similar.

Tom Richardson and Lockwood were great bowlers. Lockwood appeared to me the more difficult of the two owing to his ability to change his pace imperceptibly. He had more kinds of deliveries, and his variety, with an occasional very fast ball, made him great. I think Cotter for a few overs was a bit faster than Jones. Kortright was generally regarded as the fastest bowler of his time in this country. Not only was he a very fast bowler, but also a very good one.

While on this subject of bowlers I am very sorry that, besides Jones, another old Australian friend, Charles Turner, has passed away. I always regarded Turner as the best medium-paced bowler I ever played against. He had a graceful run and lovely action, with clever change of pace. I recall my first Test match (1893) at Lord's; I had made 91 when, late cutting one from Turner that kept lower than I expected, I was splendidly caught by Blackham. It was a a grand catch. His gloves must have been almost under my bat, and he remarked 'Bad luck, youngster. It is one of the biggest flukes I ever had.' In that innings England scored 334, and Turner's analysis was: 36 overs, 16 maidens, 67 runs, 6 wickets.

F. S. Jackson, then captain of Cambridge, got his runs out of 137, *added with Shrewsbury for the third wicket.*—EDITOR.

We are now thinking of cricket after the war and the best way to improve it. One of the most vital things is the preparation of wickets, and here Jones comes into the story again. The practice of artificial preparation was started by Apted at the Oval in 1899, and he had every excuse. There is very little soil there; within three inches, I believe, you come to gravel. It was the final Test Match, and Hayward (137) and I (118) each made a hundred. We scored 185 for the first wicket in two hours fifty minutes. During our stand Jones, who altogether bowled 53 overs and took four wickets for 164 runs, came to me and tossing the ball up in the air, let it light on the pitch. Instead of bouncing a bit, it stopped dead, and Jones said: 'This is going to ruin cricket.'

So, you see, as far back as then we had our problems. Unfortunately one cannot lay down a set rule for making pitches because nearly every ground requires different treatment, but we must try to prepare pitches so as to provide a more even struggle between the bowler and batsman without making the conditions dangerous.

In Yorkshire we never put on anything artificial following the end of March. After that, merely roll and water. We used to get real sticky wickets. I remember the time at Sheffield when a side that made 70 against us on a sticky wicket did well because we had such bowlers as Schofield Haigh, Wainwright, Peel, Hirst, Rhodes and myself. Yes, I used to bowl, and I enjoyed it more than batting.

In 1902 *at Leeds, F. S. Jackson and Hirst dismissed the Australians in the second innings for* 23, *each taking* 5 *wickets. Jackson's analysis was* 7–1–12–5. *The last four wickets fell to him in five balls. Hirst's five wickets cost nine runs. Each took four wickets in the first innings, Jackson's costing* 30 *and Hirst's* 35. *The two bowlers were mainly responsible for Yorkshire winning by five wickets. The Australians' only other defeat that season was in the Test Match at the Oval when England won by one wicket.*—EDITOR.

VIEWS AND VALUES [1945]

BY R. C. ROBERTSON-GLASGOW

By the time the 1945 Wisden appeared in the bookshops, it was obvious to all that the war in Europe was drawing to its close. Naturally, all minds turned to the prospects for a resumption of peacetime cricket, among them the two commentators invited by Hubert Preston to suggest what they thought might be the makeup of the England and Australia sides in the first post-war series. Of the two reviewers, Robertson-Glasgow for England, A. G. Moyes for Australia, it was the Englishman who came closest to the truth, although it is interesting that both men made the same mistake of predicting that the two captains in the last peacetime contests between the two countries, Hammond and Bradman, would be out of the running. Robertson-Glasgow was perfectly correct in his assumption that Hammond was long past his best, but he could hardly have been expected to anticipate the calamitous decision by the selectors to ignore the passing of time and appoint Hammond after all. The reader, armed with that weapon of deadly irony, hindsight, can also afford to smile over the claim that perhaps G. O. Allen was a shade too mature for the job. In fact it was Allen who, at the age of 45, succeeded Hammond as England captain on the West Indies tour of 1947–48.

As for Alban George Moyes, M.C. (1893–1963), his predictions turned out to be wildly off-course, for apart from doubting if Bradman would ever play Test cricket again—in fact Bradman was to score seven post-war Test centuries—and doubting the pedigree of Keith Miller, Mr. Moyes, judging from his essay, had no knowledge of Ray Lindwall. The joint effect of these two pieces of prognostication was to suggest that when England-Australia Tests resumed, the contests would be evenly balanced. Other ironies include the defection to Somerset of Bill Alley and the total disappearance from the first-class game of the gifted Cecil Pepper, who much preferred the backwaters of the Leagues.

WHILE the fate of the world was being determined, English cricket was the scene of an interesting little battle, which ended in the rout of the 'hustlers' and the triumph of conservatism over the heresy that progress and speed are synonymous. The defeat of the *soi-disant* progressives, with their programme of one-day and time-limited matches for first-class cricket, was a certainty so long as the issue of debate rested with the majority opinion of practising cricketers. In truth, it was an easy victory, as their opponents for the most part consisted of a few honest, if deluded, zealots, a few showmen, always ready for any change that might bring them into the light of publicity, and a few columnists, who instinctively hammer tradition.

Cricket reform has always attracted the attention of the eccentric. Golfers rest content with an unfinished argument about the weight and size of the ball. Rugby football sometimes regurgitates an ancient question concerning the points-value of a dropped goal. Association has flirted with the notion of one referee for each half of the field. But neither code has so far proposed that a match should consist of fifteen minutes play each way.

The cricket reformers should be more honest about their aims. They talk much about improving cricket, in the same way that some talk about improving the breed of race-horses. But what they are really talking about is money. They are not considering the art and technique of the game. They speak as financiers, not craftsmen. To them 'faster, faster' means 'richer, richer.' They believe that one-day cricket would mean more spectators. I believe it would empty the grounds as surely as the rain. A whole season of it, and there would be a clamour compared with which the sound of the reformer would be as a piccolo among a thousand cymbals.

Note that these crude plans for so many runs in an hour and so many hours for an innings are concerned entirely with the batsman. They are framed on the postulate of standard pitches, standard weather, and standard bowling. Note, too, that they attribute slow scoring to the batsman's ineptitude, never to the bowler's excellence. The 'brighter cricketers,' for their one-day carnivals, cannot allow for an hour in which survival with twenty runs is a far finer performance than five wickets gone for sixty. They have, literally, no time for the artistry of defence. To them a drawn match is a wasted match, no matter what skill, resource, endurance, have gone to its achieving.

The three-day match is a thing of hope. It gives time for recovery and surprise; as in that game at Edgbaston in June of 1922, when Hampshire, after being bowled out by Howell and F. S. G. Calthorpe for 15 (Mead 6 not out!), scored 521 in the follow-on and won by 155 runs. Besides, if cricket were to be reduced and levelled to a thing of one day only, it would lose those pleasures of old acquaintance and social entertainment that raise it above all other games which, so often, are just ninety minutes of mud and energy, a boiled face over a tea-cup or beer-mug, and a hurry for the station. Three days mean three evenings; and, as I look back, if I may, to Somerset scenes, I reflect that, without the three-evening match, I should never have seen Yorkshire's Arthur Dolphin, with his rufous face set off by a whitish apron, selling fried flat-fish in the twilight, at a whacking profit, to the citizens of Taunton; I might never have listened to Sam Woods's nightly conversation on cricket and the world, compared with which all books that have ever been written on sport are like cocoa and hot water; I should never have asked Jack Hobbs how he felt on the Monday morning after sitting out the week-end with six runs wanted to equal W. G. Grace's 126 centuries, and he would never have answered by hooking my third ball that morning to the boundary.

* * * * *

And now to wander in the paths of speculation. Suppose that we were to play Australia in 1946, who might be picked for England? After the last war it took five years to find an England team, as opposed to eleven people playing for England. After this war it may take as long again. Of the England team that overwhelmed Australia at the Oval in August of 1938, two have been killed in their country's service, Hedley Verity and Kenneth Farnes. These are the others, with their age as in June, 1946, appended: L. Hutton (30), W. J. Edrich (30), M. Leyland (45), W. R. Hammond (captain) (43), E. Paynter (44), D. C. S. Compton (28), J. Hardstaff (34), A. Wood (47), W. E. Bowes (37). Of these, Hutton, Edrich, Compton and Hardstaff would form a nucleus of batting. Hammond must be a doubtful candidate, as, in spite of a wonderful war-time season in 1944, he has been battling against fibrositis. Then there is L. E. G. Ames, verging on forty, but still the best wicket-keeper-batsman in the country.

There should be no lack of batsmen, established or on the eve of performance. There are C. J. Barnett (35), J. D. Robertson (29), N. Oldfield (35), H. E. Dollery (31), A. V. Avery (31), A. Fagg (31), H. Gimblett (31), D. Brookes (30), L. B. Fishlock (39), G. Cox (34), J. F. Crapp (33), B. H. Valentine (38), J. Arnold (38), H. T. Bartlett (31), C. Washbrook (31), C. B. Harris (37), J. G. W. Davies (34), N. W. D. Yardley (31), A. Nutter (33), the incalculable L. J. Todd (39), and the most promising R. T. Simpson, of Nottinghamshire. Where ages are given, they refer to date June 1946. I have doubtless left some partisan chewing on an omission, but these names cover most of the batsmen who are in or near the English class. Enough to cheer the gloomiest sector.

No such optimism can surround the bowling. Of those who overthrew Australia at the Oval in 1938 we have lost, as above mentioned, both Kenneth Farnes and Hedley Verity, respectively the best fast right-hand and slowish left-hand bowler that we had; and whence can they be replaced? William Bowes, who, at the time of writing, is still a prisoner of war, may show us for a few more seasons the art of control and pace from the pitch. Of fast-medium bowlers there should also be W. H. Copson, the brothers A. V. and G. H. Pope, R. T. D. Perks, R. Smith, T. F. Smailes, J. W. A. Stephenson, P. F. Judge, and, some years younger than any of these, C. J. Scott, who, at the age of twenty, took 121 wickets in 1939. Among the known leg-breakers, only D. V. P. Wright and R. W. V. Robins are of true England class, and the latter will be forty in June 1946. Of slow left-handers, I can think of none of the highest standard. Of slow right-handers, there are T. W. Goddard and E. P. Robinson. But there must be a limit to the former's defiance of the years. Memory goes back to the Oval Test of 1939, when England took the field against West Indies without Farnes, Verity and Bowes, and our bowlers were scattered like chaff. But perhaps the hour will once more bring the man. Let no one forget the story of Maurice Tate. One season he was first change for Sussex, the next he was the first bowler of his time. *Exoriare aliquis!*

The standard of wicket-keeping is high. There is something about the art that keeps men young. Arthur Wood, of Yorkshire, who celebrated the approach of his fortieth birthday by driving down England in a taxi-cab to play against Australia in 1938, headed the wicket-keeping list in 1939 with 83 dismissals. Fred Price, of Middlesex, at 37, came second with 81; Lancashire's W. Farrimond, at 36, third with 72; W. T. Luckes, at 38, fifth with 66; and Harry Elliot, of Derbyshire, who can give them all three years, sixth with 63. Ames did not keep wicket at all in 1939. Of those who have been able to play intermittently during the war, W. H. V. Levett, T. G. Evans and S. C. Griffith are all in the first rank, Evans being a discovery only by those who had not seen his earlier performances for Kent Second Eleven. In the first rank, too, is G. Dawkes, who began for Leicestershire in 1938 at the age of seventeen.

To suggest at this time a captain for England is an adventure. If the office were to be filled now, in the presumed absence of Walter Hammond, the choice might fall on A. B. Sellers, Yorkshire, or E. R. T. Holmes, Surrey, allowing that G. O. Allen, at 42, can no longer sustain his fast bowling. B. H. Valentine, in practice and form, would be a strong candidate. But with all these the years begin to argue. The name of S. C. Griffith comes to mind. He has the character and the position for captaincy. Nor must J. G. W. Davies be forgotten. Business may spike his cricket. But, could he consolidate his natural gifts as a batsman, he has much that goes to make the leader—acute intelligence, geniality, courage and decision, and his fielding is an inspiration.

But these are mere wanderings in the maze of possibility. Cricket-lovers will hope that the incomparable Hammond will be restored to lead England, if only once more, against the best that our old friend and enemy Australia can produce.

AUSTRALIAN SURVEY

Bradman—Past, Present and Future

BY LIEUT. COL. A. G. MOYES

WAR-TIME cricket in Australia has of necessity lacked the character which first-class matches alone can give to a season, but the State Associations, seized with the idea of providing amusement for Service-men and for maintaining public morale, have done an excellent job by continuing inter-club fixtures under difficulties. Very wisely, rules have been sufficiently elastic in character to enable Club officials to cater for the Serviceman on leave, and so, despite short supplies of finance and material, the game has been nursed along so that when peace comes to expansion to normal conditions will be relatively easy.

The New South Wales C.A. experimented for a time with one afternoon games. This naturally, suited the Serviceman on a fleeting visit, and the more audacious tactics of the batsmen seeking runs quickly pleased the onlookers who sought relief from their burdens and craved excitement as a counter to worry and anxiety. The matches attracted splendid crowds, but it would be foolish to say that they did—or could—produce or develop real cricketers. Actually there was a suspicion that a game of skill was being converted into a vaudeville exhibition, and though cricket must be entertaining, it can achieve that without sacrificing the dignity of craftsmanship to the hurly-burly of crude utilitarianism. Still, as a war-time measure the move was justified, but now that the Government has vetoed 'Daylight Saving,' two Saturday games are again the vogue.

In Sydney there has been no upsurge of talent. It could not be expected with so many engaged in warlike pursuits, but maybe, when we return to the piping times of peace, there may arise some whose good fortune enabled them to get cricket in other lands, and so develop their skill. W. Alley is undoubtedly the most promising discovery in Sydney, and he may easily win a high place in the game. Certainly he is older than is usual for budding Australian stars, but at 25 he is still young enough to climb the ladder of success. A left-handed batsman, he loves aggression, but is by no means reckless, despite ability and willingness to score fast. Last season, for Petersham, he batted 24 times and scored 1,413 runs, with a highest innings of 230. This was a real achievement, and that it was no flash in the pan, he showed recently when he scored 122 in better than even time against St. George, hitting O'Reilly freely and using discretion as well as power. He is also a grand field and a fair right-hand bowler. Alley seems a sure State star in post-war years, and a most probable Test match opening batsman. Experience in first-class cricket and a tour of England would mould him into a very fine player. For N.S.W versus the Services last season, he scored 60 and 54 not out.

Of others in this State, Barnes has developed his skill. He has undoubted class, and could be the star of post-war years. Against the Services he scored a brilliant 104 not out. O'Reilly remains the best bowler in the land, despite increasing years, and in 1943–44 season he took 147 wickets at 8.2 runs apiece. Morris, in his early twenties, made a notable entry into the first-class field before the war with a century in each innings, but he is in The Army, and we have seen very little of him. That he has skill and temperament is, however, undoubted. He is a left-handed batsman with something of the Bardsley touch; if he and Alley make good, they will prove a source of strength to Australian Test teams. Both Gulliver and McCool have done well in Sydney cricket as batsmen and slow bowlers.

Pepper you have seen in England. He is regarded as a Test possibility, and the opportunity to develop his powers on English wickets should be of real benefit. There is nothing like cricket in a strange land to bring to the surface any latent talent. Sismey and Cheetham you also know, and young Cristofani has accomplished startling performances in England. He may make the grade.

Keith Miller, the Victorian, always looked a fine player, but somehow did not deliver the goods in the quantities expected. The batting is there, and no doubt the buds of promise will open out one of these days into rich blooms of achievement, as they have shown signs of doing in England. Hassett, another you know and appreciate, has played big innings in Cairo during the war: Englishmen will remember his many fine efforts in 1938, especially at Leeds where, at a critical stage, he smote Farnes and Company and won the game in the nick of time. Victorians think highly of R. Harvey, who, at 18 years of age, is building up a batting reputation. In fact, several of the younger brigade give excellent promise for the future. I have heard good reports of Dempster, a left-handed batsman with some bowling skill, Tribe, a left-hander of the Fleetwood-Smith type, and Watters, a solid batsman, but they have yet to be tested in the fires of first-class cricket. Ron Hamence, of South Australia, now in the R.A.A.F., when playing with success in Melbourne, showed undoubted skill which seemed certain to take him into the Test side. Hitherto he failed to make the grade, probably through impetuosity, but there is yet time.

In Adelaide, cricket has been quiet with no stars appearing. Grimmett still takes dozens of wickets and seems to have the secret of eternal youth. Quite recently he toured battle stations with a team that contained McCabe, O'Reilly, Barnes, Alley, and Saggers, and did wonderfully well.

Queensland, like other States, has kept its competition in being, but has lacked the drawcards. Little has been seen of W. A. Brown, but, at the same time, enough to show that he has lost none of his skill. He scored two centuries in club games early this season (1944–45).

W. Tallon and R. Rogers, a burly left-hander, who made 41 and 39 for the Services against New South Wales, have done well, but J. Ellis, who was the best of the fastish bowlers, has not played much cricket.

Thus the present gives us little indication as to the future, except that there is every probability that batting gaps will be filled adequately —apart, of course, from Bradman. Wicket-keeping will be better than in 1938, with Saggers (N.S.W.), D. Tallon (Queensland), Livingstone (N.S.W.) and S. Sismey all first class, whilst the first three are fine batsmen; but the bowling is still resting on W. J. O'Reilly who cannot indefinitely retain his skill and hostility. Good reports are heard of Barras, a West Australian, while Carmody, unfortunately now a prisoner of war, must have improved by his English experiences. Of the 1938 side, I have mentioned Brown, Hassett, O'Reilly and Barnes.

Bradman has not played cricket for a few years, and is not, I think, a prospect for the next tour. His back trouble, which caused his discharge from the Army, was symptomatic of a general breakdown in health, the result no doubt of extraordinary cricketing efforts, which so strained his nervous system and depleted his physical resources that his medical adviser forbade him to take part in strenuous activities, ordering complete rest.

At the same time, it can now be disclosed that he would not have toured England again as captain had there been no war. He told me during our trip home in 1938, and no argument could move him. Even then, he was feeling the strain of making both centuries and speeches, and he was most definite that he would not be capable again of representing his country in such a capacity, either to his own satisfaction or in the manner expected of him.

Thus we must face the position that the greatest run-getter and amazing box-office attraction probably has made his last appearance on the Test Match stage. Cricket did much for Bradman, but he did much for cricket, and his going leaves a gap that will not easily be filled.

Whether he will again play for his club or State is a matter which cannot be determined now. Bradman himself does not feel that it is a time to talk of his cricketing future while the nation is fighting a 'life and death' war. He is, however, generally better in health though occasional setbacks are a worry. Evidently when he talked in 1938 of the future, he felt doubts about his health; doubts which would appear justified by events.

My mind goes back to 1926, when the Selection Committee, of which I was a member, brought him to Sydney for a trial. He came to my office. I opened the door and a lad said: 'Are you Mr. Moyes? I'm Don Bradman!' Twelve years later I listened to this country lad make speeches in England that were surely among the finest ever made by a cricketer. I saw him lead Australia; make centuries by the dozen, but the picture that remains is that of the lad who said so quietly: 'I'm Don Bradman.'

To me he has never changed. I believe that no one received more of his confidence in matters of cricket, and he was always the sportsman. Bradman was subjected to criticisms; that is inevitable with anyone who is great, but for the most part they were conceived in jealousy and nurtured in ignorance. Donald George Bradman was in the highest degree a 'cricketer.'

S. J. McCabe is another whose Test match career seems to have finished all too soon. He makes very rare appearances these days, owing to foot trouble, and unless a miracle happens he could not stand a first-class game. So we lose one whose every gesture with the bat was poetry; a man who was the artist painting a picture, as he did on that memorable day in 1938 at Trent Bridge. There are many in first-class, and even Test cricket, who are of solid mettle, no doubt, but they provide merely settings for the gems, among whom was McCabe.

J. H. Fingleton and A. G. Chipperfield have drifted out of the game, while E. L. McCormick, that humorist whom Worcester will never forget, had done likewise. M. G. Waite joined the Services, and is not, I think, a possibility for the next tour, F. Ward went overseas with the A.I.F. and is not any younger, while E. S. White, who did fine work in the

Middle East, retired from cricket before the war, in order to attend to his business. C. L. Badcock, suffering from lumbago, went back to Tasmania; apparently his health improved and he made runs in club games, but repeated failures in the 'big' events may mar his chances even if thoroughly fit. L. O'B. Fleetwood-Smith is out of the game, and, alas, that charming comrade Ben Barnett was taken prisoner in the tragedy of Malaya. And so it would appear that of the 1938 side, only O'Reilly, Hassett, Brown and Barnes are left as a basis on which to build a Test Team.

After World War One, the A.I.F. side gave us Gregory and Oldfield, while Collins, Pellew and Taylor developed their powers as members of that team. Perhaps World War Two likewise will produce something out of the ordinary, though the Gregorys of the game come but seldom. Still, we are not devoid of talent even if the bowling position is obscure, and, when the fight for 'The Ashes' is resumed, we may hope to find an Australian side ready to do battle with Hammond, Hutton, Compton, Edrich and Co., though my memories of 1938 suggest that on our wickets those young men from Yorkshire and Middlesex will give our bowlers many a headache.

EDWARD PAYNTER [1946]

BY R. C. ROBERTSON-GLASGOW

In 1946 came the last of the truncated wartime editions of Wisden, and its editor, perhaps sensing a gradual loosening of the ties of war, included in a 462 page Almanack three essays worth rescuing from the files. In the first of these Robertson-Glasgow, preoccupied as always by the quiddities of temperament of various cricketers, composed a sketch of the Lancashire left-handed batsman Edward Paynter, who had been in and out of the England side ever since his début in 1931. His exclusion from G. O. Allen's Australian touring side of 1936–37 seems in retrospect to have been particularly remiss. By the time the war ended Paynter was in his mid-forties, and resisted invitations to resume his career with Lancashire. In 1947 he weakened, appeared in two festival matches at Harrogate and made one of the most successful exits from the game in history, with scores of 154,73, and 127. He died in 1979, aged 77.

THE Society of Acrobats lost the chance of a promising member when Edward Paynter, left-hand batsman of Lancashire and England, decided on the profession of cricket and directed to it a resilient endurance which few players since Squire Osbaldeston can have exceeded and none, in our time, has quite equalled.

A picture returns; of the Lancashire team, after a hot day in the field, waiting in a railway station. Even George Duckworth is revolving dark thoughts on the purpose of Crewe, the significance of Bletchley, or the reason for umpires who disagree. But there, at two o'clock in the morning, is a smallish fellow, astonishing a sleepy Inspector and the rules of deportment with hand-springs up and down the platform. This short sequence from the life of Edward Paynter may explain and epitomize the agile smotherer of deadly breaks, the swift tireless runner and thrower, and what Dr. Watson would have termed The Adventure of the Sick Man of Brisbane.

Paynter is not what is called particular. There is more Truth than Beauty in his batting style. He has been known to hit the best bowlers for four with both his feet off the ground at once. He throws with either hand. All fielding is all the same to him; anywhere from the Bank Holiday bottles behind deep long-leg to the fancy places within easy glare or chat of the batsman, any time from sunrise to sunset. When permitted, or inclined, to bowl, he has up to now favoured the right hand, at least on public occasions; and, using it, he topped the average in D. R. Jardine's 1932–33 tour of Australia, with five wickets at 14.20 each. Later, in reference to this feat, he was heard to say that Lancashire captains have no real memory for figures.

Paynter might not rank on the short list of England all-rounders; not, that is, in the pure, and dull, sense; but in his prime—if he ever bothers to own up to so fragile a thing as a prime—he would have been any wise captain's early pick, by virtue of the composite gift of heart and nerve and skill. His very presence in a team was an instalment against timidity; a stay to the doubting, a comfort to the young newcomer, a silent joy to the tried companion.

He was born on November 5, 1901, at Oswaldtwistle; a date that suggests an earlier and less complete artist, a place that recalls the first fame of another humorist, and cricketer, Mr. Sydney Howard. When a schoolboy, Paynter, at any rate in his hours or play, was liable to no risk of excessive tuition, for there was no cricket ground. So he read all that he could find about the game, played through matches in books, and dreamt of centuries by Paynter at Old Trafford, with R. H. Spooner batting at the other crease and A. C. MacLaren almost approving from the committee room window.

Dr. W. G. Grace, at the age of sixteen, had already knocked centuries off some of the principal bowlers in the south and, including his own relations, the West of England. He was also training that beard in the way it should one day grow. At sixteen, Paynter was received into the Enfield Second Eleven, of which his father was then the captain; not, we may be sure, without some wagging of old heads at this rank example of nepotism. This was in the middle of the first World War, which carried off his elder brother, Arundel, a fast left-arm bowler of much promise.

In 1920 Paynter was introduced to the notice of the Lancashire Cricket Club, which passed him on for the interest and care of their professional coach, J. T. Tyldesley. Tyldesley, as wise in instruction as he had been brilliant in execution, knew that he had found something. But the Lancashire team was as hard to storm as any wary old bachelor's heart, and it was not till the season of 1926, in the County's twentieth match, that Paynter (E.), in the absence of Tyldesley (E.), appeared on the score-card, batting at number six. In the first innings he made eight; in the second, like many another good man, he was bowled for 0 by J. C. White. But he had the compensatory pleasure of seeing that nonpareil of last-ditchers, Somerset's C.C.C. Case, play a ball delivered by Richard Tyldesley while lying prone and forwards, with his bat in front of his forehead. In 1931, in his thirtieth year, Paynter became a regular player for Lancashire, and scored his first century, 100 against Warwickshire at Old Trafford. He also made 102 off the New Zealand bowlers at Liverpool, and played for England against New Zealand at Old Trafford.

But it was his first innings in a Lancashire versus Yorkshire match, cricket's Jarndyce v. Jarndyce, that fixed his fame and, according to the wags, nearly cost him his place in the Lancashire Eleven. It happened at Bradford in May of 1932. Opening the match with the calm-browed Frank Watson, he scored 152 at the rate of nearly 50 an hour. He hit five sixes and a most indecent number of fours. Indeed, such a performance on such an occasion was more than impropriety. It almost smacked of lunacy. Habitual celebrants at the Northern biennial rites were torn between pity and astonishment. It was as if someone had sung comic songs at a funeral, or deliberately dropped a tin of sweets during a lecture on the uses of Algebra. The news reached London, and Paynter was earmarked for Australia.

Even Paynter may have been a little startled by some of the goings-on during the M.C.C. tour of Australia in 1932–33, and he is said to have referred to the Third Test, at Adelaide, as a nice to-do. In that match, probably the noisiest on record, he was preferred to Pataudi. His 77 in the first innings was one of the hinges of the door that opened to victory. England made a shocking start, losing the wickets of Sutcliffe, Jardine, Hammond and Ames for 30 runs. Then Leyland and Wyatt added 156, briskly, as Test match timing is reckoned. But the first day's score, 236 for 7, Paynter and Allen not out, was not such as to send early morning listeners in England whistling from Radio to work. On the second day, after Allen had fallen to Grimmett's top-spinner, Paynter and Hedley Verity put on 96 for the eighth wicket, and the total reached 341. Then came Larwood. On the sixth day England won the match, the gallant Woodfull won the applause of the moment and of history by carrying his bat for the second time through a Test match innings.

For the fourth and, as it proved, deciding Test in the turkish-bath of Brisbane, Paynter gave a sort of repeat of his Adelaide performance. Again his chief assistant was Verity; again they put on over 90 together. But, this time, Paynter jumped hospital to play. His 83, spread over four hours on two days, varied from almost tottering survival to an heroic assumption of dominance. Nearly half his runs came from boundaries. On the sixth day of this deadly creeping struggle, Paynter, fittingly enough, was at the wicket to make the hit—a six to leg—that won the Rubber. Soon after his return to England he was the honoured guest at a social gathering of fellow Lancastrians. Speeches, and better things still, flowed warmly. Then the hero rose and, using a short but popular phrase, disclaimed, in a purely Paynterian sense, the suggested significance of his achievement.

Fame caught and depicted him as a rescuer, as the turner of the critical cause. But such a likeness would be only the snap-shot of a mood, not a portrait for posterity. A few timeless Tests were not to be enough to convert the boy who meant to be a hitter. The Massacre of Bradford was truer Paynter than the solemnities of Adelaide and Brisbane. Paynter is an answer-back, not a sitter-down. Nature made him fervid, which you could know from the attitude and exercise of his fielding. Necessity laid on him some measure of conformity. Few who live by cricket dare make long noses at those twin dictators, Average and Record.

So, in the years that followed his return from Australia, Paynter, judged by numbers, would appear to rise to a zenith. In summer 1937 he scored nearly 3,000 runs, with innings of 322 against Sussex at Hove and 266 against Essex at Old Trafford. In summer 1938 he made 216 not out for England against Australia at Trent Bridge, and in six Test innings he averaged 101.75. In the following winter, for England against South Africa, he scored 117 and 100 at Johannesburg, 243 at Durban. But, for all the outward splendour of these achievements, I regard them as a consolidation of worldly wisdom rather than a heightening of technical skill. He knew the fashion and followed it. Herein is no belittlement of worth, for no praise can flatter him who so combines expediency with pleasure, who is workman and artist indivisibly blended.

In 1939 Paynter captained the Players against the Gentlemen at Lord's and his team won by 160 runs. It comes back to memory like a match from another world. The ball behaved very oddly. It had an extra stitch in the seam, and it took a primitive delight in rapping the batsmen on knuckles and body. But the victims refused to attribute their injuries to the nature of the ball. It was of Australian manufacture.

Our cricketers may soon be introduced to this ebullient globe again, on its home ground. May they meet it with the middle of the bat; like Edward Paynter, fourteen years ago.

CRICKET UNDER THE JAPS [1946]

BY MAJOR E. W. SWANTON, R.A.

Immediately following on from details of Paynter's career, with its 43 centuries and nearly 20,000 runs, there appeared the Wisden début of E. W. Swanton, who had spent the last three and a half years of the war in a Japanese prisoner-of-war camp. His account of cricket played during this period is among the best-remembered to appear in Wisden, but there was one revealing detail which he omitted from his essay, no doubt considering it tactful not to extol the very publication for which he was composing his essay. In his autobiography, 'Sort of a Cricket Person', Swanton describes how he was able to muster a library of books consisting of 10,000 volumes, simply by organising the rescue from houses in Singapore of the one commodity which neither the Japanese nor the locals felt inclined to steal. After mentioning the most popular volumes in this library, by Priestley, Galsworthy, Evelyn Waugh and H. V. Morton, he describes the most popular of all:

> When the books began to disintegrate tattered remnants of gas-cape strengthened the original covers, and rice makes a good paste. My chief contribution was a 1939 Wisden, which, lovingly rebound several times by skilled men, and having been duly de-bugged and disinfected, is with me still. Marked with the Jap stamp (i.e: not subversive!), and, with the letters AD in pencil before 1939, it claims to be the most-read copy of Wisden ever published.

It is strange, perhaps, but true, how many of us agreed on this: That we were never so thankful for having been cricketers as we were when we were guests of the Japanese. There were periods when we could play 'cricket' if our antics do not desecrate the word. There were occasions when we could lecture, and be lectured to, about it. It was a subject that filled countless hours in pitch-dark huts between sundown and the moment that continued to be euphemistically known as lights-out. And it inspired many a day-dream, contrived often in the most gruesome setting, whereby one combated the present by living either in the future or the past.

In the days that followed shortly on the fall of Singapore, before work for prisoners had become widely organized, there was a certain amount of play on the padangs of Changi camp that really deserved the name of cricket. It is true that one never seemed able to hit the ball very far, a fact probably attributable about equally to the sudden change to a particularly sparse diet of rice, and the conscientious labours of generations of corporals in charge of sports gear, for whom a daily oiling of the bats had clearly been a solemn, unvarying rite. These Changi bats must have reached saturation point in the early thirties, and I never found one that came up lighter than W. H. Ponsford's three pounder. However, the pitches were true—matting over concrete—and there were even such refinements as pads and gloves. After most of us had been moved to Singapore City on the first stage of the journey up to Thailand, Lieut.-Colonel A. A. Johnson, of the Suffolk Regiment, promoted some excellent matches with the Australians, whose captain was none other than B. A. Barnett; I cannot write of these from first-hand knowledge, but this was, so to speak, Cricket de Luxe, and our jungle cricket bore little outward relation to it.

This first of the camps on the Thai-Burma railway in which we played cricket was Wampo. Christmas Day, 1942, was our first holiday, I think, since our arrival in October, and it was perhaps the fact of our so occupying the afternoon that caused our guards to receive subsequent requests to play cricket with suspicion, as having some religious significance and being therefore good for morale. (It was always the policy to keep prisoners' morale at the lowest level compatible with their being considered able to undertake whatever work was on hand. It was no doubt on this principle that, later on, the Allied chaplains were solemnly and sternly forbidden to pray for victory!)

This particular game was notable, I remember, for what is probably the fastest hundred of all time. It was scored in about five overs by a very promising young Eurasian cricketer called Thoy, who, with graceful ease, kept hitting the tennis ball clear over the huts! Nothing, of course, could have been more popular than the victory of the Other Ranks over the Officers, but the broad lesson of the match was that the merit of any contest depends on the preservation of the balance between attack and defence. (One could not help wondering, earlier in the war, when bombs were raining down on the Oval, whether the Surrey Committee were taking the hint.) For jungle cricket our bat, surreptitiously made by the carpenter, was obviously too big.

Our cricket for the next twelve months was confined to theory and reminiscence, but lower down the line, at the base camps of Tarsao and Chungkai, various forms of play were improvised, while still later, at Nakom Patom, the hospital camp, the technique was exploited in front of large and happy crowds of men anxious to forget the tiresomeness of dysentery, beri-beri, and malaria.

Cricket at Nakom Patom reached its climax on New Year's Day, 1945, when a fresh, and certainly hitherto unrecorded, page was written in the saga of England v. Australia. The scene is not easy to put before you, but I must try. The playing area is small, perhaps sixty yards by thirty, and the batman's crease is right up against the spectators, with the pitch longways on. There are no runs behind the wicket, where many men squat in the shade of tall trees. The sides are flanked by long huts, with parallel ditches—one into the ditch, two over the hut. In fact all runs by boundaries, 1, 2, 4 or 6. An additional hazard is washing hung on bamboo 'lines.' Over the bowler's head are more trees, squaring the thing off, and in the distance a thick, high, mud wall—the camp bund—on which stands a bored and sulky Korean sentry. (Over the bund no runs and out, for balls are precious.) In effect, the spectators are the boundaries, many hundreds of them taking every inch of room. The dress is fairly uniform, wooden clogs, and a scanty triangular piece of loin-cloth known (why?) as a 'Jap-Happy.' Only the swells wear patched and tattered shorts. The mound at long-on is an Australian preserve, their 'Hill.' The sun beats down, as tropical suns do, on the flat beaten earth which is the wicket. At the bowler's end is a single bamboo stump, at the other five—yes, five—high ones. There is the hum of anticipation that you get on the first morning at Old Trafford or Trent Bridge, though there are no score cards, and no 'Three penn'orth of comfort' to be bought from our old friend 'Cushions.'

The story of the match is very much the story of that fantastic occasion at the Oval in August 1938. Flt.-Lieut. John Cocks, well known to the cricketers of Ashtead, is our Hutton; Lieut. Norman Smith, from Halifax, an even squarer, even squatter Leyland. With the regulation bat—it is two and a half inches wide and a foot shorter than normal—they play beautifully down the line of the ball, forcing the length ball past cover, squeezing the leg one square off their toes. There seems little room on the field with the eight Australian fielders poised there, but a tennis ball goes quickly off wood, the gaps are found, and there are delays while it is rescued from the swill basket, or fished out from under the hut. As the runs mount up the barracking gains in volume, and in wit at the expense of the fielders. When at last the English captain declares, the score is acknowledged to be a Thailand record.

With the Australian innings comes sensation. Captain 'Fizzer' Pearson, of Sedbergh and Lincolnshire, the English fast bowler, is wearing BOOTS! No other cricketer has anything on his feet at all, the hot earth, the occasional flint being accepted as part of the game. The moral effect of these boots is tremendous. Captain Pearson bowls with shattering speed and ferocity, and as each fresh lamb arrives for the slaughter the stumps seem more vast, the bat even punier. One last defiant cheer from 'the Hill' when their captain, Lieut.-Colonel E. E. Dunlop, comes in, another and bigger one from the English when his stumps go flying.

While these exciting things proceed one of the fielders anxiously asks himself whether they will brew trouble. 'Should fast bowlers wear boots? Pearson's ruse condemned—where did he get those boots? . . . boots bought from camp funds: Official denial . . . Board of Control's strong note . . .' headlines seem to grow in size. Then he remembers gratefully that here is no Press box full of slick columnists and Test captains, no microphones for the players to run to—in fact, no papers and no broadcasting. The field clears at last. As he hurries off to roll-call he thinks of a New Year's Day six years before when the bund was Table Mountain, the field was the green of Newlands, and he decides that even the South Africans who jostled their way cheerfully back into Cape Town that evening had not enjoyed their outing more than the spectators of this grotesque 'Cricket Match.'

There was much more 'cricket' at Nakom Patom of similar sort, and not a few who came to jeer stayed on to cheer. One was reminded how hitting a moving ball demands the observance of certain principles, whatever the circumstances, while, as for bowling, I defy anyone who does not obey the cardinal rules to pitch six running to a length with a tennis ball.

Talks on Cricket were given at many camps, and there were cricket 'Quizzes' too, wherein a few so-called experts were showered with questions from all sides. These occasions were never lacking in humour, and there were generally enough Australians among the audience to give, as one might say, a bite to the thing. Sometimes the game was presented from a particular angle. Thus Len Muncer, of Middlesex, a sergeant in the Sherwood Foresters, described the life of a cricket professional, while Lieut.-Colonel D. V. Hill, of Worcestershire, showed the game from the point of view of a County captain. Admittedly in a prison camp there was not much in the way of alternative diversion. None the less the interest was wide enough and genuine enough to emphasize what a tremendously strong hold cricket has in England; a hold that among Australians is even stronger.

A few days after the Japanese surrender our camp at Kanburi began to assemble frequently for news bulletins. Emissaries, we heard, were flying hither and thither, instructions and encouragement were being relayed from Governments to P.O.W.'s; the air was heavy with the most momentous happenings. Moreover, many of those present had had no news of the outside world for months, or longer; yet, no item commanded so much attention as the Test match at Manchester.

I had, by then, already taken my first walk for three and a half years as a free man. We found ourselves in a Thai village on the edge of the jungle. In the little café our hosts politely turned on the English programme. Yes, we were at Old Trafford, and a gentleman called Cristofani was getting a hundred. . . .

HUNDRED YEARS OF SURREY CRICKET [1946]

BY H. D. G. LEVESON-GOWER

The return to the pages of Wisden of H. D. G. Leveson-Gower was brought about by the centenary of the Surrey Club. Inevitably, much of the writer's remarks were to do with the condition and future of the Oval ground, and the fact that the sum required to modernise it was £100,000 will strike as quaintly appealing to those readers who know of the desperate hunt for nearly £5,000,000 a generation later. Leveson-Gower's account of the Surrey club's fortunes is what might charitably be defined as somewhat partial, for in reviewing the great players who had presented the county over the years, he makes only passing mention of one of the greatest, Jack Crawford. There is no reference at all to the unusual nature of Crawford's association with the county, which stretched from 1906 to 1921, with a hiatus in mid-career running from 1909 to 1919, during which period Crawford lived in Australia. The Crawford débâcle, one of those internal scandals whose truth never seems to emerge for at least two generations, was almost entirely the fault of Leveson-Gower, captain of the Surrey Club at the time. It was his maladroit handling of a simple dispute, and his laborious ascent onto his high horse, which cost the club the services of one of the most brilliant all-rounders of the age.

Something else worthy of comment in Leveson-Gower's essay is its unconscious derisory humour. The Patron of the Surrey Club was the King, and the writer seems genuinely honoured that the reigning monarch should have sent to an organisation in desperate need of funds the breathtaking sum of £100. What would seem like comical parsimony to some apparently struck Leveson-Gower as reckless profligacy on the King's part.

To those who started the Surrey County Cricket Club and to those who obtained the Oval for cricket a very great debt of gratitude is due. It would be as difficult to imagine county cricket without the Oval, Test Matches without the Oval, as it would be to imagine the Oval without the Gasworks. The Editor of *Wisden* has paid me the compliment of asking me to contribute an article in connection with the Centenary of the Club. The invitation I readily accept, for it so happens, apart from the great interest I have always had and still have in Surrey cricket, it was in 1895—just fifty years ago—that I played in my first county match for Surrey at the historic Oval ground. August 22, 1945, will be remembered as one of the most important milestones in the history of the Club, for on this day the Club claimed the distinction of having existed a hundred years.

THE OVAL IN 1845

Let us now imagine that we are entering the Oval in the year 1845. In the spring of that year an interesting ceremony was performed: the first sod of turf was laid on the present ground; 10,000 turves came from Tooting Common. Only a year before the same ground was nothing more or less than a market garden. In the early months of this year the members of the famous Montpelier Club had to vacate their ground adjoining the Bee Hive Tavern, Walworth, required for building purposes. It was due to the personal influence of their treasurer, Mr. W. Baker, a fine all-round cricketer, that a lease of 31 years was secured from the Otter family, who held the ground on a 99 years lease, granted to them by the Duchy of Cornwall in 1835.

The autumn of 1844 may be said to have marked the foundation of the Surrey County Cricket Club, and the first game connected with the Surrey Club took place on August 21, 22, 1845—Gentlemen of Surrey against Players of Surrey. Following this match a dinner was held at The Horns, Kennington, when, strangely enough but appropriately, the chair was taken by Mr. William Ward—a splendid cricketer and influential friend of cricket. Previously Mr. Ward made himself responsible for the lease of 'Lord's.' The formal inauguration was deferred till later in the year, when another dinner at the same historic inn was held. The President on that occasion was the Hon. F. Ponsonby, afterwards Earl of Bessborough, and to him more than anyone we owe the continuance of cricket upon the Oval. The Surrey County Cricket Club was born, ever after increasingly to flourish, except for a few early vicissitudes. The question has been asked—and is worth answering—Was the Oval ever in danger of being built upon? Yes; about the year 1851; this was prevented by the Prince Consort when acting for Edward, Prince of Wales, and Duke of Cornwall, afterwards King Edward VII.

In the late Sir Jeremiah Colman's beautifully illustrated book, *The Noble Game of Cricket*, there is a reproduction of a picture of the Oval painted two years after the inauguration of the Surrey Club. A label attached to the back of the canvas bears the following inscription, 'Kennington Oval with the market garden dwelling turned into a Club House'; date about 1847, before any pavilion stand was erected. Another reproduction from an oil painting shows the first members' pavilion erected in 1855. From a market garden to what was destined to become one of the finest cricket grounds in the country may truly be described as a wonderful transformation, and it is difficult to realise that here was the spot devoted to the cultivation of the cabbage and the cauliflower.

It is not easy to assess accurately the standard of first-class cricket at that time as compared with the standard of cricket to-day, but it may be said that Surrey, amongst the other counties, provided her full share of the leading cricketers. For close on fifteen years the star of Surrey was unmistakably in the ascendant, thanks in no small measure to the able management of John Burrup and his brother William; the former occupied the post of hon. secretary from 1848 to 1855, and during the reign of his brother, who succeeded him, the Oval commenced a lengthy career of prosperity. Surrey were fortunate in having F. P. Miller as captain; he may be said to have been the first real captain to be elected and he played regularly from 1851 to 1866. He had a very strong eleven. Amongst the famous players, too numerous to mention, were Sherman, who in later days was to be met at Mitcham Green, the birthplace of many a Surrey cricketer of repute; W. Caffyn, the first professional coach that went to Australia, and doubtless it is in great part owing to this Surrey cricketer that Australia has been able to hold 'her own' on the cricket field in this country. Caffyn spent his last years at Reigate as a hairdresser, cutting, it is said, with the same precision with the scissors as he did with the bat. H. H. Stephenson, who captained the first team to Australia in 1861; Julius Caesar, Tom Lockyer, one of the most celebrated wicket-keepers; Felix; G. Brockwell and W. Martingell, the first two professionals engaged by the Club; both names survive in W. Brockwell, who played for Surrey 1886–1902, and A. R. Martingell, now a Surrey Colt. All the nine matches played in 1857 were won, but it was in 1861 that F. P. Miller's captaincy gained full reward, for in that year it may be said his powerful side reached its zenith when the county in their match against England gained a victory by 56 runs. This match was one of several between Surrey and England played from 1848 to 1895; the last of this fixture, after a break of 29 years, was in 1895, the Jubilee year of the Surrey County Cricket Club, and it was a fitting opportunity that this game should be renewed as a testimonial match to W. W. Read.

JOHN SHUTER REVIVES SURREY

Like so many other counties, Surrey have had their 'ups and downs,' and for several years after their triumphs in 1861 came a lean time; but even during this somewhat disastrous period Surrey possessed such players as Jupp, Humphreys, Southerton, Pooley, and, a little later, Barratt, who took all ten Australian wickets for the Players in 1878 at the Oval. The revival of the fortunes of Surrey cricket may be said to have begun with the appearance of John Shuter, and truthfully asserted that the steady restoration of the county to the high position it occupied half a century back was due to his personal influence and force of his example of unflagging enthusiasm. I had the honour of being at the same public school as he was, Winchester; and in Wykehamist language it was a 'Winchester notion' that Shuter, who was captain of the eleven in 1873, was the best captain the College ever had: to be a 'second Shuter' was the aim of every succeeding captain. From 1881–1890 the county were becoming stronger every year, and in the seasons 1887 to 1899 Surrey carried off the Championship no fewer than nine times. In a conversation with W. E. Roller, a splendid all-round cricketer who played with Shuter, he told me that the following Surrey side in his opinion was the most powerful during this period: J. Shuter, W. W. Read, K. J. Key, W. E. Roller, R. Abel, G. Lohmann, W. Lockwood, J. M. Read, W. Brockwell, H. Wood and J.

Sharpe—truly a great eleven, and also playing then were Tom Hayward and Tom Richardson. It is nice to think that W. E. Roller is still with us and on February 1st celebrated his 88th birthday. One cannot possibly mention all those who were associated with Surrey cricket during the 'golden age,' but George Lohmann must always occupy the position of the finest all-round cricketer Surrey, and even England, ever had. His early death deprived the country of a cricketer that could ill be spared.

FIRST OVAL TEST

Meanwhile, just prior to Shuter's reign, another very important landmark occurred in the history of the Club, for in 1878 the first Empire team to play at the Oval were the Australians. The arranging of this fixture was due entirely to the then Secretary of the Club, C. W. Alcock, who for so many years afterwards was instrumental in getting the Australians to the Surrey ground. Two years later came the commencement of Test matches in England, and the first was played at the Oval: England met Australia there on September 6, 7, 8, 1880. From that time up to the last Australian visit in 1938 the final Test Match in each season has taken place at the Oval, no matter who the visitors, and West Indies were there in 1939. Of all the great Test matches that have been played at the Oval the most sensational was the defeat of England in 1882 by seven runs—when wanting only 85 to win. Australia's victory made it clear that the supremacy of cricket in England was being challenged. In the 1884 Test Match every member of the England team had a bowl, and, to the surprise of every Surrey member and their supporters, their champion batsman, W. W. Read, was 'number 10.' He did not fail, but actually made 117. The 'Jessop' Test Match of 1902, England winning by one wicket, provided a great occasion—the superb batting of Hobbs and Sutcliffe that gave England the victory in 1926 after many years of disappointment—the delightful incident of the Australian team's farewell to Hobbs on the cricket field in 1930—and the mammoth score, 364, of Hutton in 1938. These are memories indeed, ever to be looked back upon with pleasure, with Kennington Oval as the scene.

Besides these Test matches there have been many extraneous games at the Oval, but most important of these were the long series of Gentlemen and Players which commenced in 1857 and continued well into the present century. The large programme of county matches and touring teams made it difficult for some little time before this contest was given up to get representative sides. One interesting fact in connection with this match: I was selecting the Gentlemen and Players sides at the Oval in 1906 and asked W. G. Grace to play; he was 58. He refused at first, but I told him I particularly wanted him to take part in the match, first because everyone would be delighted to see him at the Oval and, secondly, the days on which the match was being played included his birthday. To this 'W. G.' replied, 'My birthday is on the third day and it may be finished in two days.' 'Not if you play,' I said. He consented and made 74; his first appearance in this match at the Oval had been 41 years previously.

To return now to Surrey cricket. John Shuter, to the regret of everyone, resigned the captaincy in 1894, and K. J. Key was the natural successor. In 1895 I began my association with Surrey cricket, so that he was the first captain I played under—and a very good one too! Of those who played with Shuter, Maurice Read, Lohmann and Sharpe had practically finished, but Walter Read, Lockwood, Brockwell, Abel, Richardson and Wood were still available—Tom Hayward was fast becoming one of the best professional bats in the country.

Tom Richardson that season took 237 wickets in 25 matches—a great share in winning the championship—and this directly after touring Australia with A. E. Stoddart's team. In 1899 Surrey again won the Championship; only twice that year was the county defeated. Batting strength was very pronounced, and all-round cricketers, such as Lockwood, D. L. A. Jephson and Hayes, made the team formidable.

At the close of that season K. J. Key resigned the captaincy—a captaincy marked with judgment and success; and all who played under him—I was one of them—had every confidence in his leadership. A splendid batsman at a crisis, he over and over again stepped successfully into the breach.

GREAT FAST BOWLERS

In dealing with Surrey cricket from 1900 up to the First Great War it is somewhat difficult to decide whether the county sides were stronger than from 1887 to 1900. Although the decline of Richardson and Lockwood—surely there were never a finer pair of fast bowlers—had begun, there was distinct compensation in the rise of Hayward to his zenith, the arrival of Hobbs and J. N. Crawford.

It has been claimed that Lockwood at his best was the finest bowler of all time and Richardson the most consistent. This is probably the best summing-up of their respective merits. 'Day in' and 'day out,' Richardson has had no superior; Lockwood, on his day, with that slow ball of his, was the most difficult.

D. L. A. Jephson was a very fine all-round cricketer; free bat, clever lob bowler—known as 'the lobster'—and always alive in the field; but for a leader rather too sensitive and took too much to heart personal failures. Hayward, by general consent, was the best professional batsman of his era, or perhaps of any era to fast bowling. A fine, upstanding player, with the straightest of bats and a very sound knowledge of defence. One of his greatest innings when I was a member of the side was at Canterbury, facing W. M. Bradley, bowling down the slope, which gave never-failing aid to his off-break. Yes, I can see the great Hayward now, with his rubicund face and the brown cap pushed back from his forehead—a dangerous signal which opposing bowlers got to know and respect. The highest aggregate in a season, 3,518, still stands to the credit of Hayward in 1906.

Hayes, a fine slip and a winner of many matches when the turf was false, kept the batting strong. V. F. S. Crawford, a very powerful off-driver, often won matches, and his brother, J. N., ranked with the very best young all-round cricketers, while N. A. Knox, who for a short period was one of the fastest of our amateur bowlers—only a whit slower than the fastest of them all, C. J. Kortright—also did well.

Surrey, unlike Yorkshire and Kent, never commanded the services of left-hand bowlers of class, but during this period E. C. Kirk, though owing to business unable to play regularly, was the best left-hand Surrey bowler for a great many years; about the same pace as Voce, with a very loose and easy action, and he could make the ball turn on good wickets. Ducat, a fine, upstanding bat with strong on-side strokes and an untiring fieldsman in any position, also stood out. To Surrey cricket, after suffering for a few years from want of a regular captain, there came a distinct revival with Lord Dalmeny, now Earl of Rosebery, in charge. Lees, a splendid bowler of pace, was at his best; and there rose Hitch, a great personality. Why? The answer is: You must have these three—batting, bowling, wicket-keeping—for a first-class side; but there is a fourth of equal importance—fielding. I doubt whether there ever has been, at short leg or silly mid-on, a more brilliant exponent of catching or fielding than Hitch. If he had never bowled a ball or made a run, he would have been an asset to any eleven, and he was a very fast bowler for one of his few inches—a splendid cricketer to have on the side. Rushby, if the wicket helped him, was a high-class right-hand bowler, and W. C. Smith, rather slow, in my opinion had no superior on his day. Unfortunately, 'Razor' was not blessed with good health, so his triumphs were limited.

M. C. Bird, a very attractive batsman with a fine reputation from Harrow, found the responsibility of captaincy weighed on him too much. Alan Marshal, who came to the Oval on the recommendation of 'W. G.,' when batting seemed to display the utmost contempt for all bowlers; a fine field and a bowler, like so many Australians, deceptive in flight. About six feet three inches tall, he was very simple in character. I had to tell him on one occasion that he was overdrawn at his bank. He smiled and replied: 'That can't be right. I was looking at my cheque-book this morning–I have three cheques left!'

Surrey, with a powerful eleven, won the Championship in 1914 for the first time since 1899. Hobbs—the batsman of the year—and a wealth of run-getting talent, with C. T. A. Wilkinson, a very able captain, who studied the game closely, paved the way for this triumph.

Between the two wars Surrey, under the astute captaincy of P. G. H. Fender, followed by the dogged leadership of D. R. Jardine, and the magnetic personality of E. R. T. Holmes, was fortunate in her captains. Amongst the stars was Hobbs. Great player previously, he became even greater from 1919 to the year of his retirement. Strudwick, too, right up to the end of his cricketing career, never failed to give of his best, which gained for him the leading position among Surrey wicket-keepers—and Surrey always possessed wicket-keepers of prominence.

THE HOBBS GATE

To put on paper all that Hobbs achieved on the cricket field would be impossible. There is no necessity for this; all who have cricket at heart and followed cricket are well aware of his wonderful record. Amongst his many great seasons, 1925 may be termed 'Hobbs's Year.' He headed the batting figures with over 3,000 runs and an average of 70, while in August he surpassed W. G., Grace's record of 126 centuries by playing two three-figure innings at Taunton. Probably never has this ground held so many spectators, and never has such an enthusiastic crowd given such a welcome to such a popular cricketer.

Hobbs reached his 197th century before he laid aside his bat in first-class cricket. No wonder that there came a spontaneous response when it was decided to erect a Hobbs Gate at the entrance of the Oval. No more fitting tribute for those entering and leaving the historic ground than to read, 'In honour of a great Surrey and England cricketer.' I had the proud distinction, as President of the Club in 1934, of declaring the gates open on the first day of the match of that season. As one of Surrey's captains I know what Hobbs had done for the game in the county and what his influence has been. It is because of men like Hobbs and Strudwick that the professional cricketer of to-day is held in such high esteem. Their books are closed as far as active cricket is concerned, but the pages are still open, and on those pages will for all time be inscribed the happy memories of the pleasure they have given to so many people.

The bowling about this time did not reach the standard of the batting. Sandham, a beautiful fielder in the deep, was for some little time on the fringe of the England XI; he opened the innings for Surrey with Hobbs in 63 three-figure partnerships. Jardine, Ducat and Shepherd generally could be relied on for runs. D. J. Knight showed himself a potential England batsman in 1919. D. R. Jardine was a great asset to the batting strength, comparable with Hayward in defence; no one proved so often the saviour of the side, no one at a crisis was so dependable—an Oxford University Blue, captain of the County and captain of England was his record. F. R. Brown was a splendid forcing bat and clever slow bowler, and H. M. Garland-Wells came as the last captain before the long break in first-class cricket. Never short of run-getters, Surrey possessed other fine batsmen in Fishlock, Gregory and Barling; also a fast bowler in Gover. Despite his rather laboured action and his long run before delivering the ball, Gover did splendid work, and, like Richardson in 1897 and W. C. Smith in 1910, he took over 200 wickets in a season. He, with Barling, share benefit matches in 1946 and 1947; they both deserve large gates and good financial results.

RENOWNED OFFICIALS

Surrey enjoyed the guidance of many eminent people. The names of the Earl of Bessborough, Viscount Oxenbridge, Lord Alverstone readily come to mind; nor can one forget the great services rendered by Sir Frederick Marshall, Mr. Wildman Cattley, Treasurer from 1881 to 1902, Sir Jeremiah Colman, Earl of Midleton, Mr. G. H. Longman, and the President from 1940 Mr. B. A. Glanvill. Lord Alverstone, elected President in 1895, at what might be called a critical period, brought to bear the inestimable advantage of his advice and personal interests in strengthening the Club and making the Oval as we knew it up to the cessation of county cricket in 1939. Nor has Surrey been less fortunate in her secretaries, of whom C. W. Alcock came on the scene in 1872, and till 1907 his untiring energy and foresight gave to his county and to cricket generally powers of administrative assets that cannot be over-estimated. W. Findlay, who followed, at once proved himself a valuable successor; M.C.C. also could claim that they had in him the real definition of ability and tact which Surrey enjoyed for over twelve years. R. C. N. Palairet filled the position with infinite credit to himself and the Club; and the present Secretary, A. F. Davey, surmounting all the difficulties attending six years of war, has given his best with special success.

The Oval, with its reputation for 'famous' wickets, can boast of famous groundsmen. There were in the past George Street, John Newton, and Over, all experts; while to the present generation the names of Sam Apted and 'Bosser' Martin are associated with the splendid condition of the ground. 'Far too easy the wickets at the Oval—they spoil the game,' has been the verdict so often given. This is not the occasion to discuss this very debatable point; sufficient to say a county cricket club appoints the best man available for the position, and the man himself is determined to produce the best. The groundsmen mentioned certainly did this for Surrey.

Many personalities apart from the players on the field cannot be dissociated from the Oval, and one figure I would not like to forget—'The Surrey Poet,' A. Craig. Without any official connection with the Surrey Club, he earned the name of 'Surrey Poet' because he was most often found at the Oval. For many years his figure stood out as familiar to the spectators as that of the greatest cricketer. On the wettest days he would put the crowd in good humour. 'Captain of the spectators' he loved to call himself, and the spectators, he said, were his constituents. His skill in repartee was always pointed, and it was an unhappy moment for anyone who chaffed him. 'Oh, take these things away!' snapped a spectator once at the Oval. 'I beg your pardon, sir,' replied Craig, with the greatest politeness; 'these are not for you, these are only for people who can read.' But he was happiest when conciliatory; and he checked a heated argument about the correctness of the title 'Gentlemen v. Players' with these words, 'All the Players are Gentlemen and all the Gentlemen Players.'

Hardly had England and West Indies finished the Test Match at the Oval on August 22, 1939, when the ground was requisitioned, and, famous in peace, the Oval played its part during the war, to which many battle scars bore testimony. First used as a searchlight site, it then became a prisoner-of-war camp for possible parachutists, and, although fortunately no prisoners arrived, everything was ready for their reception. Hit by seven high explosives and countless incendiaries, the Oval was de-requisitioned in November 1945, and the work of reconstruction began: 40,000 turves were brought from Gravesend and laid by the ground staff in less than three months.

LASTING MEMORIES

The date, August 22, upon which Surrey completed 100 years existence they launched an appeal for £100,000 to carry out a big plan of reconstruction at Kennington Oval. Quite apart from 'war damage' repairs, it is proposed to improve seating, stands and other facilities, to provide, especially for spectators, increased comfort. The aim is to make the Oval one of the finest cricket grounds in the country. The Duchy of Cornwall, Surrey's landlords, have agreed in principle to a new lease which will extend the term of the present lease from the date of its expiry on January 1, 1953, for a further period of 31 years.

The King and the Surrey County Cricket Club, of which he is Patron, exchanged messages on August 21, and His Majesty through the Duchy of Cornwall, has given £100 to the Centenary, Appeal.

And so The Surrey County Cricket Club with its 'Kennington Oval' has reached and passed one hundred years of cricket history—rich in memories, rich in tradition. I have shared for fifty years these memories; I have been brought up to revere these traditions. Ever happy to me will be the recollections to have met, to have played with, and to have watched such famous cricketers that have represented the County of Surrey. Their names are legion—are they not written in the 'Books of Wisden'? They have handed down legacies of skill and the spirit of the game which present and future cricketers of Surrey will hold in safe keeping, and in their turn bequeath to those who follow.

Just a few lines more: I have very vividly before me many a scene at the close of play—the finish of many a great match. Time has been called, the umpires have doffed their white apparel. But the spectators are loth to go—they linger on—they crowd in front of the pavilion, and I hear their voices—to Abel, 'Bravo, Bobbie!' to Richardson, 'Good Old Tom!' to Hobbs, 'Jack's the Boy!' to Strudwick, 'You can't tire Struddy!' These are to me but examples for fifty years, from time to time, of the keenness and affection for Surrey players by those who have followed Surrey cricket down Kennington way. I picture to myself the scoreboard; I glance at it; it reads, Surrey Cricket Club 100 not out.

NOTES BY THE EDITOR [1946]

The period ended with Hubert Preston's editorial comments for 1946, looking back to the last wartime cricket occasions, the big international matches marking the victory of the Allies, and looking forward to the unknown pleasures awaiting the world of cricket in peacetime. Preston's commentary is necessarily optimistic, and it was perhaps just as well that he could have had no inkling of the crises to come. He was to survive as editor for a total of eight editions until his death in 1951, when he was succeeded by his son Norman who was to maintain the continuity for nearly thirty years and establish a Preston dynasty as longstanding as that of the Pardons. It was to Hubert that belonged the record of becoming the first editor of Wisden to produce an annual edition consisting of more than 1,000 pages. His final Wisden, in 1951, ran to 1,019 pages, the first of which advertised Gunn and Moore's hand-made bats, and the last of which proclaimed a truth becoming more self-evident by the year:
'WISDEN, the Most Famous Name in Cricket'.

EMPIRE TEAMS TAKE THE FIELD

AFTER five seasons of what may be called impromptu cricket the sudden end of the European war came just in time to permit a partial resumption of the first-class game last summer. To celebrate Victory, three days were allotted to the Whitsuntide match with the Australian Services at Lord's; then the M.C.C. and the Combined Services Committee further extended this start into five Victory matches of three days each between England and Australia. The remarkable success that attended this spontaneous gesture of renewing the happy accord associated with contests of this nature emphatically proved the enormous value of keeping the game going during the uphill years of strife. The R.A.A.F. players of 1944, augmented by the A.I.F., soon ripened into a capable all-round side that underwent little alteration in this rubber series of 1945. England, on the other hand, seemed to experience difficulty in finding the best of the available players. This was more noticeable at Lord's than at either Sheffield or Manchester. Some of the chosen men, coming almost straight from battlefields to the headquarters of cricket, must have regarded the first encounter primarily as a reunion with many old friends, so that a thoroughly serious view of the game, such as the Australians clearly held, was too much to expect. In the first match the onus of attack for the final stage was borne by two fast bowlers of mature age, A. R. Gover and Colonel J. W. A. Stephenson, both tired from their exertions on the previous day; and C.G. Pepper made the winning hit just at seven o'clock in the last over of this very much enjoyed contest. For the third match—

the second at Lord's—the choice of three youngsters without any experience of representative cricket afforded the strongest contrast; and again England lost. The work of George Pope, Pollard and Phillipson—kept out by injury until the final match at Old Trafford, which England won comfortably—showed that good bowlers of pace were available. This result, which divided the honours, came as a happy conclusion, and everyone could feel contented, especially as the last expressed wish of Mr. John Curtin, Prime Minister of Australia, for an immediate resumption of Test cricket, became practically an accomplished fact during the summer, even before his death in July.

Directly after the end of the season Dr. H. V. Evatt, Australian Minister for External Affairs, appealed to the M.C.C. to send a side to Australia as soon as possible, with the natural outcome of the acceptance of a definite invitation from the Australian Cricket Board of Control for England to visit Australia in the 1946–47 season. On the same occasion Dr. Evatt stressed that the tour of the Australian Services team which sailed in October last to India was official. So, with the Dominions, West Indies and New Zealand putting teams in the field, the whole British Commonwealth of Nations became identified actively with cricket almost before the joyous shouts for peace, raised on the collapse of Japan, ceased to echo. And now a very powerful side from India, under the leadership of the Nawab of Pataudi, further accentuates the happy relations which cricket brings to all competing countries.

BIG HITTING

Of the eleven matches, each of three days, played last summer which the M.C.C. ranked as first-class, that between England and Dominions at Lord's rivalled as an attraction those in which Australia took part, and we saw in M. P. Donnelly, the left-handed New Zealander, who toured England in 1937, a batsman ready to join company with the best exponents of the game now that he will have regular first-class experience while at Oxford University. His fine stroke play, notably to the off, provided some of the best cricket seen last season, and for arousing spectators to enthusiasm was exceeded only by gigantic hitting in which C. G. Pepper and Keith Miller emulated the giants of the past—not in the rate of scoring but in the carry of their big drives. In that same Dominions match at Lord's, Miller on-drove a ball to the roof of the broad-casting box over the England dressing-room at a height said to exceed that of the record hit by Albert Trott which cleared the pavilion. That was one of seven 6's by Miller in a score of 185. Pepper hit six 6's while making 168 in two hours and a half at Scarborough against H. D. G. Leveson Gower's eleven. He revelled in straight drives, one of which off Hollies cleared the four-storied houses and landed the ball in Trafalgar Square. In this he rivalled the historic efforts of C. I. Thornton in 1886, when A. G. Steel was the bowler and Thornton's 107 included eight 6's. While these tremendous drives remain chronicled because earning six runs, one may doubt if the length of carry and height of any of them equalled that by G. J. Bonnor in the first England and Australia match at the Oval in 1880. Always associated with the superb catch which G. F. Grace made, this hit was described to me quite recently by Mr. S. F. Charlton, an Old Cranleighan, who saw all the match. He wrote that Shaw, the bowler from the Vauxhall end, signalled with a gesture of his hand for G. F. Grace to look out, and the next ball with this guile in it brought about the catch near the sight screen—most certainly an amazing piece of cricket. The youngest of the three Graces playing for England just waited while the batsmen twice ran up and down the pitch before the ball fell into his safe hands. Hitherto my efforts to discover in what position G. F. Grace was fielding always failed.

LAWS OF THE GAMES

Until the M.C.C. publish the Laws of Cricket as re-drafted, mainly under the direction of Colonel Rait Kerr, the provisional decision for a declaration on the first day of a match when 300 runs have been scored, and the optional use of a new ball after 55 overs, must help towards definite decisions, and will be acceptable in all grades of cricket. The necessity for a closer observance of the laws became apparent when G. O. Allen, playing for South of England against the Australians at Lord's on June 30, was given out by Umpire Fowler 'handled the ball' on an appeal by A. W. Roper, the bowler. No matter what Roper thought or intended, he may be congratulated on bringing about the dismissal of a former England captain for an obvious infringement of Law 29 at the headquarters of cricket. 'The rigour of the game' cannot be too strongly impressed on all young players; and I may feel some personal satisfaction in having described in my notes last year what I saw at Weston-Super-Mare, where a batsman picked up the ball, tossed it to the bowler, and took his guard as if this was a regular procedure—a sad reflection on strict match play. Close followers of the game will remember previous cases of 'handled the ball,' some of which may be mentioned. A. D. Nourse, the South African left-hander, paid the penalty at Hove in 1907, when he stopped the ball that might have rolled on to the stumps. Then in February 1930, at Auckland, E. J. Benson, of the M.C.C. Australian touring team, was given out when he 'stopped as if to pick up the ball,' though the wicket-keeper said that 'Benson did not touch the ball'—a still stronger warning for a batsman always to leave the ball to the fieldsman.

An equal or even greater offence by a batsman is kicking at a ball wide of the stumps. Very rightly 'leg-byes may not be scored' in this way, but surely to kick at the ball is 'obstructing the field'; and merely pushing out the pad comes under the same category when no attempt is made to use the bat for a stroke. The wicket-keeper is prevented from taking the ball and so is obstructed. I will cite Keith Miller, the Australian, as being guilty of this ugly gesture—a strange weakness for so fine a batsman—and he was admonished for it by the umpire at Lord's.

So long ago as 1888, at the General Meeting of the Marylebone Club at Lord's, it was recommended by the Committee 'that the practice of deliberately defending the wicket with the person instead of the bat is contrary to the spirit of the game and inconsistent with strict fairness, and the M.C.C. will discountenance and prevent this practice by every means in their power.' Yet batsmen have been guilty of doing this on several occasions to my own knowledge, and once Frank Chester sent back a batsman who ran after kicking the ball through the slips.

TROUBLESOME LAST OVER

More finishes on time caused 'the last over' to remain a 'bone of contention,' and I was taken to task by R. E. S. Wyatt for my remarks about play ceasing at Coventry in 1944 when a wicket fell to the second ball of the over with ten runs wanted for victory by the side having four more men to bat. Mr. Wyatt thought that I condemned him for allowing the umpire to pull up stumps instead of letting another batsman come in. He explained that neither he nor the captain had power to over-rule the umpire. My intention was far from criticising Wyatt, the captain, or the umpire, but to call attention to difficulties bound to arise in such circumstances, and to strengthen my plea for a clear ruling that the last over should be finished in order that either the fielding or batting side could have the opportunity to snatch a victory and so bring about a definite result—always desirable in every contest. The difficulties of deciding the precise time for calling 'last over' and allowing another batsman to hasten to the wicket are obvious. Umpires' watches or outside clocks may differ from those inside the pavilion, and if that 'last over' were played out there would not be any hopeless discussions or heart-burnings. Another point: Who decides that it is to be the last over? Notes on Law 13 state that 'an over should always be begun if "time" has not been reached.' This applies to lunch and tea intervals and the close of play each day without any specific reference to the last over of the match—and that is what matters most.

ENTERTAINMENT TAX

While we have Australia emphasising the value of cricket in cementing the brotherhood of all countries in the British Empire and the imperative desire to maintain the happy gestures always apparent when England and Australia take the field in the keenest of Test matches, the Government cannot see that entertainment tax charged on gate receipts, not on profits, of a match is a heavy drag on county cricket, besides handicapping the organisations responsible for the international fixtures which mean so much for the general welfare of Great Britain and our various Commonwealth visitors—Australia, South Africa, New Zealand, West Indies and India. This continuous drain on revenue becomes all the more serious now when all the counties face the heavy cost of renovating their grounds, re-building blitzed pavilions and stands, with improved accommodation necessary to meet the requirements of the large crowds which are certain to assemble. True, the Chancellor of the Exchequer has reduced the tax on some outdoor sports, a concession partly turned by cricket clubs to the benefit of the paying public. We may hope that more may be done in this direction, so helping the clubs which foster cricket as a game for recreative amusement and not for financial gain.

War-time experiences showed, not only that good cricket maintained its hold on the affection of old lovers of the game, but also could be said to have given enjoyment to many people hitherto lacking clear knowledge of a pastime full of intricacies and yet easy to understand in its fundamentals. Their fancy for cricket must be fostered. Some Committees prefer to canvas for a much larger membership roll, but county clubs generally have raised their subscriptions and increased the price of admission at the turnstiles. This emphasises my remarks in last year's *Wisden* that membership gives splendid value besides comfort in all circumstances, and the privilege of introducing a friend to the pavilion. Various efforts for bringing in new members afford convincing evidence that officials all over the country will leave no stone unturned in the campaign to keep their clubs solvent, no matter how heavy the expenditure that must be met in the interests of making cricket a self-supporting entertainment for the general public, as well as a highly enjoyable and health-giving recreation for all concerned.

Mr. Stanley Christopherson, President of M.C.C. from 1939 throughout the war years surpassed the record established by Lord Hawke during 1914–18 war. Kindly answering an inquiry from me he wrote that he was the only survivor of the ten sons who, captained by their father, played as an eleven for several seasons from 1877 on Blackheath. The youngest brother, the Rev. Derman Christopherson, received his colours at Rugby from Sir Pelham Warner.

When finishing these notes during the marvellous spell of summer weather that marked the start of spring, a visit to Lord's revealed everything in preparation for a resumption of first-class cricket under the best possible conditions. The turf looked superb—a real green carpet without a blemish, in as good order as ever could be wished—encircled by the stands receiving a new coat of white paint, with 'Old Father Time' in position once more—a resplendent golden figure looking down with benign expectancy.